The Globalization of Pentecostalism:

A Religion Made to Travel

The Globalization of Pentecostalism:

A Religion Made to Travel

Editors:

Murray W. Dempster
Byron D. Klaus
Douglas Petersen

regnum

First published 1999 by Regnum Books International
in association with
Paternoster Publishing, P.O. Box 300, Carlisle, CA3 0QS, UK

Regnum Books International
P.O. Box 70, Oxford, OX2 6HB, UK
17951 Cowan, Irvine, California, USA
P.O. Box 676, Akropong-Akuapem, Ghana
Jose Marmol 1734, 1602 Florida, Buenos Aires, Argentina
Post Bag number 21, Vasant Kinj, New Delhi 110057, India

03 02 01 00 99   7 6 5 4 3 2 1

British Library Cataloguing in Publication Data
A catalogue record for this book is available from the British Library.

ISBN 1-870345-29-0

Typeset by Reesprint, Radley, Oxfordshire, OX14 3AJ,
and printed and bound in the USA by
R.R. Donnelley & Sons

Contents

Foreword   vii

List of Contributors   ix

General Introduction   xiii

Section I

Changing Paradigms in Pentecostal Scholarly Reflection

Changing Paradigms: An Introductory Overview   3
Douglas Petersen

1. The Struggle for Global Witness:
   Shifting Paradigms in Pentecostal Theology   8
   Frank D. Macchia

2. 'Try To Get People Saved'
   Revisiting the Paradigm of an Urgent Pentecostal Missiology   30
   L. Grant McClung, Jr.

3. Biblical Studies in the Pentecostal Tradition:
   Yesterday, Today, and Tomorrow   52
   Wonsuk Ma

4. Yielding to the Spirit: The Dynamics of a Pentecostal Model of Praxis   70
   Jackie David Johns

5. They Crossed the Red Sea, Didn't They?
   Critical History and Pentecostal Beginnings   85
   Everett A. Wilson

Changing Paradigms: A Response   116
José Míguez Bonino

Section II

Pentecostalism as a Global Culture

Pentecostalism as a Global Culture: An Introductory Overview   127
Byron D. Klaus

6. Latin American Pentecostalism   131
   Edward L. Cleary, O.P.

7. Unity or Division:
   A Case Study of the Apostolic Faith Mission of South Africa   151
   Japie LaPoorta

8. Globalization of Pentecostalism or Globalization of Individualism?
   A European Perspective   170
   Jean-Daniel Plüss

9. Pentecostal Challenges in East and South-East Asia   183
   Jungja Ma

10. Contextual Perspectives on Pentecostalism as a Global Culture:
    A South Asian View   203
    Ivan M. Satyavrata

11. 'Everybody Bids You Welcome'
    A Multicultural Approach to North American Pentecostalism   222
    David D. Daniels

    Pentecostalism as a Global Culture: A Response   253
    Vinay Samuel

Section III
Issues Facing Pentecostalism in a Postmodern World

Issues Facing Pentecostalism in a Postmodern World:
An Introductory Overview   261
Murray W. Dempster

12. Listening to the Margins:
    Re-historicizing Pentecostal Experiences and Identities   268
    Ronald N. Bueno

13. Pentecostals, Globalization, and Postmodern Hermeneutics:
    Implications for the Politics of Scriptural Interpretation   289
    Gerald T. Sheppard

14. 'Your Daughters Shall Prophesy'
    Pentecostal Hermeneutics and the Empowerment of Women   313
    Janet Everts Powers

15. Pentecostals and Ecumenism in a Pluralistic World   338
    Cecil M. Robeck, Jr.

16. The 'Toronto Blessing' in Postmodern Society:
    Manifestations, Metaphor and Myth   363
    Margaret M. Poloma

    'Pentecostalism and Global Market Culture'
    A Response to Issues Facing Pentecostalism in a
    Postmodern World   386
    Harvey Cox

    Index   397

Foreword

Pentecostals, for the most part, don't know their own strength. In the last five percent of Christian history, they have become a major global force in Christendom – second only to the billion Roman Catholics in the world (and numbering about half of the world's Catholics). Yet the most recent gathering of the World Pentecostal Fellowship (September 1998 in Seoul, Korea) drew delegates counted only in the hundreds.

Interestingly enough, those among them who are first discovering the immensity and astonishing diversity of the Pentecostal movement – and of its offspring, the charismatic movement – are the scholars. And this in a tradition uneasy with the academic enterprise.

This volume preserves the outcomes of a conference held in San José, Costa Rica, in 1996, where perhaps for the first time knowledgeable Pentecostal teachers probed the dawning globalism of the Pentecostalisms that circle the world all too often unaware of each other. The book unfolds with an instructive symmetry, looking in turn at changes in the academic disciplines, features of the geographic regions, and nuances of the cultural issues related all to global Pentecostalism, to what might be termed the New Catholicism (to restore the primitive meaning of 'catholic'). Readers will find an unparalleled garden of analyses, scholarly to be sure but not without a few irrepressible and characteristic breakthroughs of Pentecostal piety here and there. The tradition survives, even in the hands of its serious scholars.

So the book marks a milestone in the emergence of Pentecostal scholarship. More, it underscores the sturdy place as one of the centres of firm Pentecostal scholarship held by Vanguard University of Southern California (the former Southern California College, in Costa Mesa, which began life in the 1920s as a small Bible Institute). I am honoured to count all three editors among my former students, who anew have given their greying teacher the Elder's delight (3 John 4). All who read this work will better understand a fourth of the world's Christians.

Russell P. Spittler
Provost and Professor of New Testament
Fuller Theological Seminary
Pasadena, California 91182

List of Contributors

EDITORS

Murray W. Dempster (Ph.D., University of Southern California) is Vice-President for Academic Affairs and Professor of Social Ethics at Vanguard University of Southern California in Costa Mesa and editor of *PNEUMA: The Journal of the Society for Pentecostal Studies.*

Byron D. Klaus (D.Min., Fuller Theological Seminary) is Vice-President of Latin America ChildCare and Professor of Church Leadership at Vanguard University of Southern California in Costa Mesa.

Douglas Petersen (Ph.D., The Oxford Centre for Mission Studies, Oxford, UK) is the President of Latin America ChildCare and Director of the Bryan S. Smith Institute for the Study of World Christianity at Vanguard University of Southern California.

RESPONDENTS

José Míguez Bonino is Professor Emeritus of Systematic Theology at the Instituto Superior Evangélico de Estudios Teológicos in Buenos Aires, Argentina, and is a member of the Presidium of the World Council of Churches.

Harvey G. Cox is Victor S. Thomas Professor of Divinity at the Harvey Divinity School in Cambridge, Massachusetts.

Vinay Samuel is the Executive Director of the International Fellowship of Evangelical Mission Theologians and the Oxford Centre for Mission Studies. He is a Canon of St. Paul's Cathedral Embu in Kenya and is currently based in Oxford, UK.

CONTRIBUTORS

Frank D. Macchia (D.Theol., University of Basel) is Associate Professor of Theology at Southeastern College of the Assemblies of God in Lakeland, Florida.

L. Grant McClung, Jr. (D.Miss., Fuller Theological Seminary) is Coordinator of Education for Church of God World Missions and Associate Professor of Missions and Church Growth at the Church of God School of Theology in Cleveland, Tennessee.

Wonsuk Ma (Ph.D., Fuller Theological Seminary) is Academic Dean and Professor of Old Testament at Asia Pacific Theological Seminary in Baguio City, Philippines.

Jackie David Johns (Ed.D., Southern Baptist Theological Seminary) is Senior Pastor at the Covenant Church of God and serves on the Faculty at the Church of God School of Theology in Cleveland, Tennessee.

Everett A. Wilson (Ph.D., Stanford University) is the President of Bethany College, Scotts Valley, California and former Director of CINCEL (Centro de Investigaciones Culturales y Estudios Lingüísticos) in San José, Costa Rica.

Edward L. Cleary, O.P. (Ph.D., University of Chicago) is Professor of Latin American Studies at Providence College in Providence, Rhode Island.

Japie Lapoorta (Ph.D., University of Western Cape) is National Youth Director of the Apostolic Faith Mission (AFM) of South Africa and Deputy Director of the Executive AFM Welfare Council.

Jean-Daniel Plüss (Ph.D., Catholic University of Louvian) is Chairman of the European Pentecostal and Charismatic Research Association in Zurich, Switzerland.

Jungja Ma (Ph.D., Fuller Theological Seminary) is Professor of Intercultural Communications at Asia Pacific Theological Seminary in Baguio City, Philippines.

Ivan M. Satyavarta (Ph.D. cand., The Oxford Centre for Mission Studies, Oxford, UK) is the Principal at Southern Asia Bible College in Bangalore, India.

David D. Daniels (Ph.D., Union Theological Seminary, New York) is Assistant Professor of Church History at McCormick Theological

Seminary in Chicago, Illinois.

Ronald N. Bueno (Ph.D. cand., American University, Washington, D.C.) is Co-Founder and Director of Research Development of ENLACE in San Salvador, El Salvador.

Gerald T. Sheppard (Ph.D., Yale University) is Professor of Old Testament Literature and Exegesis at Emmanuel College at the University of Toronto in Toronto, Ontario, Canada.

Janet Everts Powers (Ph.D., Duke University) is Professor of Religion at Hope College in Holland, Michigan.

Cecil M. Robeck, Jr. (Ph.D., Fuller Theological Seminary) is Professor of Church History and Ecumenics at Fuller Theological Seminary in Pasadena, California.

Margaret M. Poloma (Ph.D., Case Western Reserve University) is Professor Emerita of Sociology at the University of Akron in Akron, Ohio and Visiting Professor of Graduate Religion and Sociology at Vanguard University of Southern California in Costa Mesa, California.

General Introduction

Over the past nine decades, the Pentecostal community has evolved from a small band of Christian believers to a world-wide movement with an estimated 450 million adherents.[1] Although the participants in the movement at the time of its inception at the turn of this century were on the margins of society, the expansion of charismatic experience has now pervaded all parts of world Christianity. Rippling like waves into the various sectors of mainstream Protestant, Roman Catholic and Orthodox faith confessions, the Pentecostal experience of the Spirit has prompted the birth of a neo-Pentecostal movement, a Charismatic Renewal movement, and a Third Wave movement, forming what Karla Poewe has identified as 'a global culture'.[2] In the words of Harvey Cox, as noted in our sub-title, pentecostalism was 'a religion made to travel'.[3]

Simultaneous with the globalization of the Pentecostal movement, 'a critical tradition' of Pentecostal scholars has also emerged.[4] The rise of these scholars within the movement has fortuitously developed at the very time that it is becoming 'self-evident that the future of world Protestantism belongs more to Pentecostalism than to the old "mainline" ' denominations.[5] It is now possible for Pentecostal scholars with sturdy academic preparation to study the movement from within while engaging with dialogical partners from outside the movement. Topics in need of research abound. For example, Dana L. Robert notes that 'the story of how Pentecostalism has affected missionary activity and emerging indigenous Christianity is just beginning to be told'.[6] In fact, the story of the movement as a whole in its various developments is just beginning to be investigated.

This convergence of the globalization of the movement and the rise of a critical mass of scholars within the movement provided an opportunity to make a contribution to the study of Pentecostalism through the voices of those inside the tradition who knew its texture, and in discussion with selected dialogical partners who could extend the conversation into the broader Christian church. In order to make this contribution, we organized a conference on 'The Globalization of Pentecostalism' for the explicit purpose of gathering Pentecostal/charismatic scholars from various academic fields of study and geographical regions to share research papers on the cutting edge issues facing the movement as it moved toward its century mark of existence. Three dialogical partners who had studied the movement from an outside perspective graciously consented to join in the proceedings of the conference to provide critical feedback and observations on the three main areas selected for scholarly investigation and open discussion: 1) changing paradigms in Pentecostal scholarly reflection, chaired and moderated by Douglas Petersen with José Míguez Bonino as the dialogical partner; 2) Pentecostalism as a global culture, chaired and moderated by Byron Klaus with Vinay Samuel as the dialogical partner; and 3) issues facing Pentecostalism in a post-modern world, chaired and moderated by Murray Dempster with Harvey Cox as the dialogical partner. From the time we conceived of the conference, we intended to publish the proceedings of the consultation in this volume in order to engage a larger audience in the dialogue generated by the research papers and responses of the participants.

The conference was held on June 10–14, 1996 in San José, Costa Rica at the Costa Rica Study Centre of Vanguard University. The date and location allowed for undergraduate and graduate students, including veteran missionaries from various countries in Latin America, who were enrolled for academic work in the centre's summer programme to attend the sessions of the conference as a basis to spark, inform and/or direct their own research interests and to engage in the discussion generated by the papers and responses of the dialogue partners. As a consequence, the research shared at the conference was significantly extended by the research of the students at the study centre. Also attending and participating in the discussions were missionaries enroute to or from a country in Latin America who were enrolled at CINCEL (Centro de Investigaciones Culturales y Estudios Lingüísticos), to start acquisition of, or to increase proficiency in, the Spanish language. Participants also included member scholars from the Latin American Theological Fraternity, as well as Costa Rican national church leaders and executives.

In offering this textbook to the academy – universities, colleges and seminaries – to the church, and to the public, we pay tribute to the many contributors who made the conference and this subsequent volume possible. First, we are grateful to the authors of the individual chapters for their original and groundbreaking contributions and to the dialogical partners for their provocative responses. They worked together so joyfully and seamlessly in accomplishing the overall objective of the conference and the book. It was so fulfilling for us on the personal level to work with such a stellar group of participants in the academic sessions, the observation trips to Pentecostal churches and the Latin America ChildCare school in Linda Vista, the table talks at mealtimes, and the festive dinner gathering with mariachi entertainment Tico style. We hope this textbook, when used in class or read by individuals with interest in the topic, will stimulate the same kind of animated discussions and internal dialogues that we experienced in Costa Rica.

Words are not adequate to express the appreciation we feel toward the multiple sponsors of the conference which made the consultation happen and this textbook a reality. A word of thanks is due to CINCEL (Centro de Investigaciones Culturales y Estudios Lingüísticos), directed by Dr. Everett A. Wilson, and to PIEDAD (Programa Integral de Educación de Las Asambleas de Dios), directed by Reverend Rodolfo Sáenz, known as Latin America ChildCare in the English speaking world. These indigenous sponsors gave the proceedings a multicultural dimension that was invaluable to a consultation dealing with the topic of globalization. A special word of gratitude is owing to Vanguard University of Southern California, which helped sponsor the conference through three of its centres/institutes: the Costa Rica Study Centre, the Lewis Wilson Institute for Pentecostal Studies, and the Bryan S. Smith Institute for the Study of World Christianity. The Smith Institute played a major role in financially sponsoring the conference by providing airfares, meals and accommodations at the Hotel Le Bergerac for all of the participants. The friendliness and warmth of the personnel at the Costa Rica Study Centre in hosting the conference made all of us feel so at home during our four days together. We are grateful for the commitment of the university, especially the support of President Wayne Kraiss, in sponsoring events and projects that assist in promoting a better understanding of Pentecostalism within the movement itself and the wider church world. Finally, the sponsorship of Regnum Books International meant that we were able to contract with the participants for the publication of their research papers and dialogical responses as part of the planning and organizing work of the conference. Without this commitment by Regnum, this manuscript would have been available for public consumption much later than the publication date.

Kudos is also due to Craig Hastie for designing the programme brochure for the conference, to Mary Mahon who functioned as the On-site Coordinator of the consultation, and to George Paul Wood and Christie Petersen Hastie for copy editing and producing the manuscript for Regnum Books International. We also express our thanks to Anthea Cousins, Jeremy Mudditt and Robin Rees for their editorial supervision of the publication of this volume. Their final editorial strokes improved the volume in ways that only we can truly appreciate. This anthology would not have been possible without the support of the leadership of the Oxford Centre for Mission Studies in the United Kingdom, especially Vinay Samuel and Christopher Sugden, whose encouragement finally translated the proceedings of the conference into the volume you hold in your hand.

Finally, a heartfelt thanks to our spouses – Coralie, Lois, and Myrna – who support wholeheartedly our academic pursuits by participating personally and intellectually in conferences such as this one, but who at the same time – with good humour – remind us that it is an important priority for the three of us 'to get a life'.

Murray W. Dempster
Byron D. Klaus
Douglas Petersen

Vanguard University of Southern California
Costa Mesa, California
Formerly Southern California College
Founded in 1920

Notes

1   David B. Barrett and Todd M. Johnson, 'Annual Statistical Table on Global Mission: 1999', *International Bulletin of Missionary Research* 23 (January 1999), p. 24. The estimation of the growth of the Pentecostal movement on a global scale is reported by Barrett and Johnson in every January issue of *IBMR*. Walter J. Hollenweger, the acknowledged Dean of Pentecostal studies, in his recent book *Pentecostalism: Origins and Developments Worldwide* (Peabody, MA: Hendrickson Publishers, 1997), expresses his belief that the movement's growth rate is unprecedented in the historical development of Christianity: '. . . the stupendous growth of Pentecostalism/ Charismatism/Independentism from zero to almost 500 million in less than a century, a growth which is unique in church history not excluding the early centuries of the church' (1).

2   Karla Poewe, *The Charismatic Movement as a Global Culture* (Columbia, SC: University of South Carolina Press, 1994).

3   Harvey Cox, *Fire from Heaven: The Rise of Pentecostal Spirituality and the Reshaping of Religion in the Twenty-first Century* (Reading, MA: Addison-Wesley Publishing Company, 1995), p. 102.

4   Walter Hollenweger, 'The Critical Tradition of Pentecostalism', *Journal of Pentecostal Theology* 1 (October 1992), pp. 7–17.

5   Dana L. Robert, 'From Mission to Mission to Beyond Missions: The Historiography of American Protestant Foreign Missions Since World War II', *International Bulletin of Missionary Research* 18 (October 1994), p. 152.

6   Robert, Ibid.

Section I

Changing Paradigms in
Pentecostal Scholarly Reflection

Changing Paradigms:
An Introductory Overview

Douglas Petersen

Pentecostal scholars have demonstrated through their writings that they are capable of looking critically at their own movement. Unlike some of their fundamentalist colleagues who feared various forms of criticism, Pentecostal academics have been open to apply the most recent advances in scholarship within their faith traditions. The five chapters in this section are designed to address recent paradigm shifts within various fields of academic inquiry. These chapters will, then, look at Pentecostalism through the various lenses of these academic disciplines. Pentecostal educators, like Christian scholars everywhere, face the challenge of keeping head and heart together, of being intellectually honest and spiritually alive, of staying abreast of the changing paradigms in their academic field, and being true to their Pentecostal character of mission.

Frank Macchia, the first contributor to this volume, is representative of a cadre of bona fide trained Pentecostal theologians and systematicians who demonstrate a keen awareness that one's scholarship must be placed in the service of the church. In the keynote chapter, Macchia is prepared to understand and give a critical account to others of the meaning of what Pentecostals are doing in practice. From its inception, emphasis upon supernatural empowerment for ministry, observes Macchia, rather than academic formation was the motivational force behind the ever-expanding pastoral and missionary activity of the movement. Characterized by the active participation of its members as 'doers' of the word, assessment of Pentecostalism, by themselves or others, according to Macchia, usually focused upon their enthusiasm, emotional expressions, or exponential growth. Pentecostal scholarly theological reflection was seldom recognized or appreciated and rarely encouraged. In contrast Macchia engages fundamental theological questions posed by contextual realities with an awareness and belief that active participation in ministry is an appropriate and necessary element in doing effective theology. This Pentecostal theologian articulately asserts that critical theological inquiry can flourish best when the scholar appropriates the 'creative or critical impulses' inherent within the distinctive Pentecostal experiences of divine healing and spirit baptism. These spiritual encounter moments serve as a corrective antidote for these distinctive theological beliefs which are traditionally embodied within the uncritical constructs and limits of doctrinal guides. When supernatural experiences are integrally linked together with the person of Christ, Macchia argues, they offer potential for Pentecostals to move beyond a personal experience of self-gratification toward becoming part of a prophetic movement for both spiritual and social liberation. This modification in paradigm, proposed by Macchia, can undoubtedly be critiqued and revised. Such future modifications should not imply weakness because a foundation has been laid with signposts to inform and direct future global and multicultural theologies of Pentecostalism.

'Mission as the mother' of all theology which is the life-purpose of the church, provides the theme for Grant McClung's chapter on missiological paradigms. McClung, who for more than two decades has been at the vanguard of missiological reflection within Pentecostalism, summons his fellow participants to establish unifying and interdependent partnerships with all 'Great Commission' Christians. In order to meet this challenge, McClung proposes a provocative paradigm for future mission which holds intact the essence of historic Pentecostal missiology with commitment to the integrity of creation and justice for the human community. His model, while emphasizing the four basic elements of ecumenism, evangelism, eschatology, and holism fuses together in dynamic tension and balance, the indispensable components of exegesis and experience. McClung argues that a missiology that is integrated, focused, and balanced will reflect authentic biblical revelation, remain true to the heritage of Azusa Street, and propel the Pentecostal movement into a unified, interdependent global mission for the twenty-first century. The quintessential question of mission – the often neglected *raison d'être* of the church in its purpose to the world – inherent within the Pentecostal community, must inform and nurture the Pentecostal scholar and practitioner in their various academic fields or arenas of labour.

Wonsuk Ma, in the next chapter, analyses past contributions and contemporary scholarly works by Pentecostals within the discipline of biblical studies. Acknowledging the fact that Pentecostals have been people of the 'Book' and their reading of Scripture has been traditionally seen through a lens of literal interpretation, Ma chronicles an emerging critical approach to biblical scholarship which is becoming a predominant exegetical and hermeneutical model of interpretation within the movement. Even granted the movement's unique features and short history, Ma describes significant events, publications, and the development of learned journals to illustrate what he considers to be a new level of sophistication reached within the discipline. As Pentecostals have studied at some of the world's most prestigious universities and seminaries, they have honed critical methods of inquiry, and are anxious and able to present their own interpretations of the meaning of biblical texts. In a word of caution, Ma predicts that the future of biblical studies in the post-modern era will present certain risks and opportunities for Christian scholars everywhere, including Pentecostals. Ma alerts Pentecostals to be careful to maintain a commitment to the 'immediacy of God's Word' without becoming trapped in the open-ended subjectivity of postmodernity. For better or worse, the South Korean Old Testament scholar suggests that the increasing numbers of non-western Pentecostals entering doctoral programmes from a variety of social contexts and cultures will surely have an impact upon biblical scholarship. Wonsuk Ma's chapter offers the hopeful expectation that the Pentecostal scholarly agenda within the field of biblical studies may well be set in the future by non-western Pentecostal biblical interpreters from within the very cultural contexts where the movement is flourishing.

There is an awareness among all the Pentecostal scholars who have made contributions to this volume that an adequate theological interpretation of global church mission must focus on an empowering gospel as good news for the poor, marginal, and the powerless. Jackie Johns engages this participatory task by deepening and enlarging from within the Pentecostal community an emphasis on theological praxis. Johns, in recognizing the phenomenon of global Pentecostal growth, especially found among the world's poor, appeals to Pentecostals to come to grips with the prophetic and corporate nature of redemption, an emphasis which engenders social transformation. Pentecostals need to recognize the importance of their social relationships as well as their potential influence on local political processes and seats of power in order to accomplish their redemptive task. It is imperative, therefore, that Pentecostals understand and contexualize their terms of social and political engagement. In response, Johns proposes a Christian praxis which utilizes a pedagogical method in which the participant 'engages, labels, and alters the social realities of his or her existence'. Within this participatory model, a believer may appropriate an experiential knowledge of God, brought alive by the dynamic of the Holy Spirit that leads to a process of social transformation within one's own historical reality. Thus, Johns encourages participants to integrate consistently Pentecostal experience into their pastoral theology, educational processes, and social ethical actions.

In the concluding chapter, Everett Wilson provides a historiographical overview of several historical interpretations of Pentecostalism. While acknowledging their rigorous and scholarly contributions, he suggests that the assembling of a more comprehensive demographic profile of early Pentecostalism may lead to a significant revision of what is taken for granted today about the movement. Wilson contends that when histories focus upon a pristine or Pentecostal 'Camelot' of sorts, or even when they present a representative-prototype of what they may consider to be representative, they overlook one of Pentecostalism's most compelling features: its diversity and grassroots nature.

Wilson notes that Pentecostalism has certainly spawned visionaries and highly motivated types, and it has also produced fascinating extremists characterized by their excesses, colourfulness, tangents and passion. Likewise, however, the historical spectrum of Pentecostalism, according to Wilson, must include the unrecognized and ordinary people of the pew. Wilson's substantial contribution to historical interpretation is made precisely in this area. In a splendid and convincing manner Wilson positions the usually ignored, stable, committed, and somewhat unemotional adherents as the backbone of Pentecostal congregations. Though generally left out of most historical accounts, this invisible mass of people was easily as crucial to the life and growth of the Pentecostal movement as any of their more acclaimed and charismatic leaders. The task for the historian, concludes Wilson, should not focus solely on the principal players but also on the cross-section of people and personalities who also shaped the character of the movement; none being more important than the unassuming but able men and women who made up the rank and file of almost every Pentecostal congregation.

The dialogical partner to this introductory section, José Míguez Bonino, often referred to as the Dean of Protestant Theology of Latin America, asks Pentecostal scholars if there may be a theological 'pattern' which could unite the various elements of Christological and pneumatalogical beliefs expressed so powerfully within the Pentecostal movement. Míguez suggests that Pentecostals may find this theological pattern within a classical trinitarian framework. Such an approach, reasons Míguez, recognizes that the entirety of God's actions – whether they be in nature, in history, in the church, in mission, or in our hearts – are inseparable. Within the trinitarian matrix of Father, Son, and Holy Spirit, Pentecostals could enjoy an even greater freedom in reflecting upon and practising their most distinctive elements – divine healing and Spirit baptism – as indispensable and integral acts of God who calls them to participate with equal dedication and expectation in creation, redemption, and sanctification.

Chapter One

The Struggle for Global Witness:
Shifting Paradigms in Pentecostal Theology

Frank D. Macchia

The entire question of 'paradigm shifts' in Pentecostal theology is difficult to explore. The difficulty involves the well-known fact that a fully developed Pentecostal 'theology' has not yet been written. Pentecostals have generally felt that Bible study and proclamation were sufficient to guide the church in its fellowship and mission. Any critical reflection on the meaning of the scriptural witness for the life and mission of the people of God from various contemporary contexts was an enterprise that few Pentecostals believed was essential enough to pursue.

THE PARADIGM OF THEOLOGY AS 'BIBLE DOCTRINES'

There are complex reasons for this lack of critical theological reflection among Pentecostals. The Pentecostal movement in its early decades was driven by a fervent eschatological expectation of the soon-coming kingdom of God. The basic tasks of biblical interpretation and proclamation gained the forefront of a vigorous effort to evangelize the world before the arrival of Christ in judgment and salvation. As Russell Spittler has stated so insightfully, 'Pentecostals have been better missionaries than theologians'.[1] When Pentecostal denominations began to establish Bible institutes and colleges in the 1920s and succeeding decades, the 'emphasis was placed on the mastering of doctrinal positions and the memorization of Scripture rather than critical thought or scholarly research'.[2] The push for accreditation and the addition of liberal arts to the curriculum that began in the 1950s encouraged the hiring of faculty with advanced seminary and university degrees. Pentecostal denominations in the United States also opened graduate schools of theological education, such as Southern California College Graduate School in Costa Mesa, California, the Assemblies of God Theological Seminary in Springfield, Missouri, the Church of God School of Theology in Cleveland, Tennessee, and the Charles H. Mason Theological Seminary located in Atlanta, Georgia. The latter seminary is distinguished by its ecumenical involvement in the six-school consortium of African American seminaries known as the Interdenominational Theological Center. At present all of these seminaries are striving to include theology in the curriculum and to encourage the production by faculty of critical and contextual theological reflection. With few exceptions, however, the major purpose of Pentecostal denominational schools has rarely been to produce a body of critical theological scholarship but to train ministers for evangelism and pastoring within the limited confines of denominational priorities and values. Very little effort has been made until recently to open students to the demands of intercontextual theological reflection among the whole people of God.

As Pentecostals gradually emerged from cultural isolation beginning in the 1930s, they increasingly sought acceptance from their fundamentalist antagonists. Aligned philosophically with the fundamentalist quest for scientific objectivity removed from the influence of historically and culturally conditioned biases, Pentecostals began to produce encyclopedic guides to 'Bible doctrines'.[3] These guides consisted of brief definitions of theological terms supported by clusters of proof texts. As guides to doctrine, they were written to define the essential beliefs of the Pentecostal churches. They were not theologies in the sense of being critically reflective on the church's belief and praxis in the light of the Scriptures and various contextual challenges. Spittler has thus characterized theology for Pentecostals accurately:

For classical Pentecostals, 'systematic theology' is an elegant name for doctrine. And doctrine consists of a concise statement of biblical truth presented in a logical order and marked by gathered scriptural support.

Spittler admits that '[w]hat theology on this level does not do is to address social issues or cultural situations'.[4]

Though these manuals of doctrine were not dialogical or contextual, Pentecostals found them attractive because they could be memorized and taught by pastors and laypersons who lacked theological training. Understanding theological thinking as a pedagogic tool in communicating sound denominational doctrine fitted well with the Pentecostal tendency to favour ministry over intellectual reflection. More recent guides to Pentecostal doctrine, though more scholarly and reflective than their predecessors, still harness the theological task to the summarization of doctrine for use in the pedagogic arm of the denominations.[5] The creative and critical impulses so essential to the flourishing of theology as a legitimate gift to the Pentecostal churches still need to be encouraged and supported by denominational leaders, thereby activating theological creativity and its critical prophetic voice.

Though the abstract and lifeless doctrinal guides were attractive to Pentecostals for various reasons, they were very different from Pentecostal preaching, which, though often lacking in theological substance, tended to be imaginative, contextual, and narrative in orientation. But this difference did not matter to the Pentecostals. These manuals of doctrine, in contrast to the creative nature of Pentecostal proclamation, functioned as distilled summaries of the theological grammar established to govern the kinds of language and themes that should emerge in the far more important tasks of preaching and evangelism. In other words, theology was catechism and, in a movement suspicious of formal training, was considered the 'least of the gifts'. Theology as a critical discipline was a tolerated necessity in a movement that wanted desperately to be true to its inherent, experiential nature without losing the acceptance of the fundamentalist 'orthodox'.

FROM IRREGULAR THEOLOGY TO THE RISE
OF CRITICAL THEOLOGY

The Bible doctrines textbooks, however, were not the only form of Pentecostal theology to come into existence during the life of the movement. Two Thirds World Pentecostals and minority Pentecostals in the

United States were not as doctrinaire or as thorough in their effort to mimic the fundamentalists as Anglo-American Pentecostals had been. In the context of Two-Thirds-World Pentecostals, theology rarely was initiated by doctrinal concepts. Rather, these groups emphasized experience as the vehicle to validate the authenticity of their doctrinal orientation.[6] In the context of minority Pentecostals in the United States, the unprecedented involvement of the Charles H. Mason Theological Seminary, from its inception in 1970 in an ecumenical consortium of theological schools, is symbolic of black Pentecostalism's reluctance to follow the dogmatic isolationism of fundamentalism. Furthermore, as Karl Barth informed us, next to the official theology of the churches and the academy there is the 'irregular' theology that appears in sermons, pamphlets, letters, and other non-official expressions of church life.[7] These 'irregular' forms of theology are not yet consciously methodical in their critical reflection, but they are much more in touch with the spirituality, proclamation, and praxis of the churches than official theologies sometimes tend to be. And so it was, to a degree, in Pentecostal literature. In general, Pentecostals achieved a critical edge and a degree of creativity in their irregular theological discourse, especially while defining their distinctives over against fundamentalist critics. One calls to mind Carl Brumback's *What Meaneth This?*, and *The Glossolalia Phenomenon* edited by Wade Horton.[8] Despite their limitations, these works do not pretend to be objective and dispassionate efforts at presenting encyclopedic definitions. They represent authentic efforts at elaborating a creative theological vision for the meaning and function of tongues in the worship and life of Pentecostal people. Without fundamentalist models to mimic, expositions on glossolalia had to chart new territory, accountable only to the text of Scripture and to the experience of the Spirit in the daily lives of those searching to be faithful to Jesus Christ. This accountability to Scripture in the context of Pentecostal worship and praxis opened the door to a theological creativity and freshness lacking in the manuals on doctrine.

Since the founding in the early 1970s of associations such as the Society for Pentecostal Studies (SPS) and the European Pentecostal/Charismatic Research Association (EPTA), Pentecostal scholarship has had a context within which to flourish independently of denominational supervision and censure. As was to be expected, historical research tended to dominate the work of these societies because of the importance attached to finding resources from the past for contemporary reflection and praxis. Recently, however, a number of papers and monographs have been published of a more theologically constructive nature. The *Journal of Pentecostal Theology* and its monograph series have joined with PNEUMA: *The Journal of the Society for Pentecostal Studies* and the EPTA *Bulletin* in publishing a number of such works. Notable beginnings in the area of Pentecostal theological reflection include Steve Land's *Pentecostal Spirituality: Passion for the Kingdom*, Eldin Villafañe's *The Liberating Spirit*, and Miroslav Volf's *Wir sind die Kirche*.[9] These works do theology from the vantage point of Pentecostal spirituality and praxis in the light of Pentecost and its fulfilment in the kingdom-to-come. I have sought to pursue directions similar to Land's and Villafañe's in my work on the Blumhardts and on glossolalia.[10]

True to their Pentecostal heritage, such recent critical theological efforts have a strong eschatological and pneumatological foundation, granting Pentecost and its fulfilment in the Parousia their rightful place along with the Exodus and the cross/resurrection of Jesus as focal points for contextual and critical theological reflection. Most of such Pentecostal works include, therefore, the pneumatic experiences – such as Spirit baptism, glossolalia, resistance to forces of darkness, and divine healing – that Emil Brunner noted have always been 'bugbears' for academic theologians who favour abstract issues more rationally defined and easily controlled.[11]

A number of recent Pentecostal scholars are attempting to interpret Scripture in the context of Pentecostal narratives and experiences of the Spirit. Late-modern and postmodern methods of biblical interpretation are explored unencumbered by the quest for dispassionate objectivity and absolute certainty that characterized both the modernism of the older liberals and the fundamentalists. Pentecostal and Holiness groups are discovering a heritage that is 'submodern' rather than modern in its hermeneutic. This submodern hermeneutic includes a vantage point from which these groups can confront the modernist struggle with the problem of history in ways that are not bound by the historical-grammatical method of fundamentalists and the historical-critical methods of liberals. The creative dialogue with evangelical siblings by many recent Pentecostal scholars is critical and based on the discovery of common interests. Such dialogue is open to discovering other relatives in the broader Christian family who offer definitions of orthodoxy that transcend the limitations of evangelicalism by emphasizing *orthopathos* (right affections) and *orthopraxis* (right living).[12]

Such developments will open Pentecostals to the ideological suspicion and criticism so vital for a contextual and liberating theology. If Pentecostal spirituality is to become identified with liberating praxis, an ongoing discernment of the forces of deception and their ideological defences utilized by corporate power to maintain the status quo will need to be utilized by Pentecostal communities of faith.[13] The Spirit of God is the Spirit of truth. Being filled with the Spirit will thrust one into a process of discernment that seeks to unmask the lies that support injustice and oppression. A prophetic spirituality and theology depends on such discernment. There is evidence of such a direction in recent Pentecostal theological reflection.[14]

CHRISTOLOGICAL CLARIFICATION OF SPIRIT BAPTISM

The Pentecostal movement is noted for its accent on what Hendrikus Berkhof termed the neglected 'third element' beyond the *duplex gratia* of justification and sanctification, namely, empowerment for witness in the world, such as is featured in Acts 2 at the Day of Pentecost.[15] The baptism in the Holy Spirit as a postconversion empowerment for gifted service in the world, especially as evidenced by unknown tongues, was at least the most controversial and, therefore, outstanding distinctive of classical Pentecostalism at the beginning of the movement. Pentecostals have traditionally made a sharp distinction between conversion to Christ and the baptism in the Spirit, the distinction being termed the doctrine of 'subsequence'. This distinction has provoked various charges of theological error, such as forsaking the all-sufficiency of Christ for spirituality and praxis or seeking a spirituality that abandons the needed criteriological function of the liberation story of Jesus. Some have noted in Pentecostalism a 'gnostic' spirituality that advocates levels of spirituality from basic faith to higher forms of enlightenment. Kilian McDonnell preferred the avoidance of the term 'Spirit baptism' among Catholic charismatics because of the Pentecostal usage of this term to quantify the Spirit as a 'less' and a 'more' with regard to a series of Spirit bestowals.[16] In the words of Simon Tugwell, 'more than fundamental Christianity can only be less than the gospel'.[17]

Pentecostal scholars have recently called into question older formulations of the doctrine of subsequence. Gordon Fee questioned its exegetical basis in the Book of Acts (though he respects its experiential value).[18] In a similar vein, Spittler called the doctrine of subsequence a 'non-issue', claiming that the early Pentecostals did not intend to establish a new *ordo salutis*. Rather, they were merely saying that tired Christians need to be renewed.[19] Pentecostal scholars Roger Stronstad and Robert Menzies have responded to criticisms of the Pentecostal doctrine of subsequence by shifting the focus away from the entire issue of whether or not there is still 'more' of the Spirit to be received after conversion to Christ or initiation into the Christian life. They have directed attention instead to the distinction between Paul and Luke with regard to the 'reception' of the Spirit. For Paul, the Spirit's reception is salvific and is identified with Christian initiation. For Luke, the reception of the Spirit is for prophetic service and is not salvific. The bestowal of the Spirit for Luke assumes initiation to salvation but is not an aspect of that initiation. Paul's understanding of the Spirit's reception is 'pre-faith' while Luke's understanding is 'post-faith'. Defining the precise relationship between these bestowals of the Spirit is the theological challenge facing Pentecostal scholars.[20]

It remains to be seen how the exegetical work of Stronstad and Menzies will be worked out theologically. How are we to negotiate theologically the continuities and creative tensions in the various understandings of the Spirit's reception shared by Luke and Paul and John as well? Many theologians from outside of the Pentecostal movement will wonder whether the Pentecostal understanding of the reception of the prophetic Spirit as a dramatically new event, distinct from Christian initiation, still does not contradict the identification of Spirit bestowal and gifting as an initiation event in continuity with the liberation story of Jesus. By distinguishing the Spirit of prophecy from the abiding Spirit granted at initiation and given to secure an enduring identity with Jesus, do Pentecostals run the risk of disturbing the continuity of Christian faith and service, thereby giving rise to discontinuous levels of Christian identity? This is the question that lay partly behind the hesitance of recent Pentecostal scholars to support a Pentecostal *ordo salutis* that separates Spirit baptism from conversion to Jesus. But whether we are addressing the need for tired Christians to be renewed (Spittler) or for a new engagement of the people of God in prophetic service (Stronstad, Menzies), a number of theological questions remain about how such events in the Christian life relate to initiation and the ongoing life of faith.

The distinction that Pentecostals have traditionally made between initiation and Spirit empowerment for gifted service must be viewed in the light of their radical eschatological orientation in which experiences of empowerment are not viewed as realizations of capacities already possessed – merely welling up from within – but as radically new possibilities called forth by the eschatological Spirit of God. This eschatological context is more helpful for understanding the distinction between conversion/initiation and Spirit baptismal experiences assumed by Pentecostals than the gnostic 'levels' of spirituality often used to interpret Pentecostal doctrine.

Pentecostals have never meant to sever the Spirit's empowerment of believers from the Spirit of conversion to Christ. After all, Pentecostals have always emphasized that Christ is the baptizer in the Spirit. But, admittedly, there has been some ambiguity in Pentecostal fellowships about the relationship between following Jesus and the empowerment of the Spirit. As we have noted with regard to the work of Stronstad and Menzies, many Pentecostals now stress the Spirit of prophecy as the continuation of the prophetic ministry of the charismatic Christ in order to grant greater christological clarification to pneumatic experience. This clarification is consistent with the strong Jesus piety of Pentecostalism, which Donald Dayton has shown involved devotion to Jesus as Saviour, Spirit Baptizer, Healer, and Coming King.[21]

How to relate Christ to the Spirit requires further reflection in Pentecostalism. Dialogue with the Oneness Pentecostal movement is crucial for trinitarian Pentecostal reflection since at stake, in part, is the need to clarify the work of the Spirit in relation to Christ. Allen Clayton has posed the provocative thesis that the Oneness Pentecostal movement fulfills the typically Reformed tendency of the non-Wesleyan wing of Pentecostalism to define pneumatology christologically. Clayton's view explains why Oneness Pentecostalism did not make many inroads into Wesleyan Holiness Pentecostalism, which tended to give a more fundamental role to the Spirit.[22] All trinitarian Pentecostals can accept a christological definition of pneumatology, but with the added insight that the work of the Spirit also defines Christology. One might argue that the redemptive work of the Spirit in all of creation comes to focus and finds decisive fulfilment in the person and work of Jesus. Rather than viewing the experience of the Spirit's empowerment as a journey 'beyond' the figure of Jesus, a consistent Pentecostal theology would stress a spiritual journey that gradually becomes more intensely involved through Spirit baptism in the charismatic or prophetic ministry of Jesus for all of creation. This mutual determination of Christology and pneumatology would be consistent with the Pentecostal understanding of the Spirit's empowerment of believers as bringing the Spirit's initiation of conversion to Jesus to greater 'fullness' in the lives of believers. If Pentecostals believe that messianic and prophetic service is the fulfilment of conversion, there is potential in Pentecostalism for helping to nudge the people of God from being a self-centred cult of personal gratification toward being a prophetic movement for both personal and social liberation.

FROM HOLINESS TO GLOBAL WITNESS:
THE SIGNIFICANCE OF TONGUES

Interestingly, Pentecostalism began as a paradigm shift from an exclusive focus on holiness to an outward thrust that involved a dynamic filling and an empowerment for global witness. Under the influence of the revivals that occurred in Keswick, England, Pentecostals viewed holiness not as an end in itself but as a preparation for empowered global witness. It was thought that in these latter days the Spirit would grant the people of God the apostolic capacity revealed in Acts 2:4 to proclaim the mighty deeds of God in the many languages of the world. Tongues were thought, therefore, to be the most striking evidence of a Spirit baptismal experience that urged one to bear witness of the gospel of Jesus Christ to the nations. Tongues were the primary evidence because Spirit baptism itself was viewed as an experience that thrust one into the challenges of a global witness that transcended established cultural boundaries.

The paradigm shift from holiness/righteousness to empowerment/tongues did not involve the abandonment of the former. The earliest Pentecostals wished to view holiness as a needed preparation for empowerment and tongues. Hence, a fierce controversy resulted from the entry of Reformed or 'baptistic' Pentecostals into the movement, who denied the existence of a dramatic holiness experience as a needed preparation for Spirit baptism. Though there is a way of negotiating the differences between Reformed and Wesleyan Holiness Pentecostals, the nature of the controversy itself reveals how seriously both groups responded to the challenges of holiness.[23] True holiness, understood as affections that are shaped by the righteousness of the kingdom-to-come, will be enhanced by the sense of dynamic filling and empowerment for global witness that tongues symbolize. Empowerment for service prevents holiness from becoming self-righteous moralism or merely an isolated sense of distinct Christian identity. On the other hand, tongues as a striking sign of the church's being empowered and sent for global witness will be misguided, even oppressive, if not guided by the righteousness of the kingdom-to-come foreshadowed by the messianic ministry of Jesus.

Pentecostals underwent another paradigm shift as they abandoned viewing tongues as the miraculous ability to 'jump-start' the global witness of the church. Originally, Pentecostals believed that tongues were given in the latter days to miraculously communicate the goodness of God to the people of all nations and tongues. *The Apostolic Faith* of September 1906, for example, claimed that the Lord had given the languages of the world to the unlearned in order to proclaim the gospel to all nations and peoples. Even a 'little orphaned colored girl' was given this commission.[24] Efforts at the beginning of the Pentecostal movement actually to communicate with people in foreign lands through tongues naturally failed from the start. Pentecostals were then inclined to look into the function of tongues as a sign of the Spirit's work in the depths of the individual and corporate life of prayer and obedience. Tongues remained as an enduring aspect of the charismatic life of the Pentecostal churches because Pentecostals abandoned a utilitarian view of tongues as simply a tool necessary to communicate miraculously to foreign people.[25] They came to discover what some have termed analogously a 'sacramental' understanding of tongues as a dynamic sign that is used by God to bring to realization the work of the Spirit in breaking through cultural boundaries and bringing people into solidarity with one another, particularly with those who suffer and are oppressed. Tongues as 'initial evidence' of Spirit baptism came to include the various theological understandings of tongues as symbolic of the depth of the divine mystery at the base of the gospel, the power in producing human liberation and reconciliation, and the struggle to express a prophetic word that reveals the will of God for the here-and-now.

However, though the mistaken notion of tongues as divinely given human languages as an evangelistic tool was abandoned, the vision of dynamic empowerment for the global witness of the people of God that originally cradled this notion remains fundamental to a Pentecostal understanding of tongues. The challenge is to broaden and deepen the theological understanding of how tongues symbolize an experience with God that continually urges the people of God to move beyond the confines of private piety or even church fellowship to the global issues of justice, peace, and the redemption of the world. After all, tongues in Acts 2 were given prophetic significance as a proclamation of God's mighty acts to Diaspora Jews who were aliens in their own land and had known only occupation by forces who wished to strip them of their unique calling and identity. Tongues also served to provide a visible link of solidarity of the hated Gentiles with the Jews who remained faithful to their calling by accepting God's decisive act of redemption and liberation in Jesus, the crucified and risen One (Acts 10:46). Thus, tongues symbolize the 'groans' too deep for words (Rom. 8:26) among the people of God, bringing them into solidarity with suffering humanity – even the entire suffering creation (Rom. 8) – in order to struggle toward their redemption and liberation. The early Pentecostals felt the urgency of the moment when they spoke in tongues as a miraculous sign of the gospel of Christ for all peoples. Contemporary Pentecostals must rediscover that sense of urgency, believing that tongues connect individual Christians and churches with the need for global justice, reconciliation, and redemption.

Tongues also symbolize the need for justice and reconciliation within the body of Christ. Tongues thus represent 'a broken speech for the broken body of Christ until perfection arrives'.[26] Tongues resist a complacent sectarianism that rests secure in its safe haven free from any accountability to the injustices and divisions within and outside the churches. Tongues also resist a complacent catholicism that rests secure in its possession of the fullness of catholicity, having therefore no responsibility to reach out in acts of justice and reconciliation to everyone, including the sectarians. Tongues allow the poor, uneducated, and illiterate among the people of God to have an equal voice with the educated and the literate. As Harvey Cox has noted, tongues protest the 'tyranny of words' in worship, allowing other forms of self-expression to have equal importance.[27] Tongues represent the 'cathedral of the poor', according to Walter Hollenweger, providing a sacred space for those who cannot afford to build expensive church buildings.[28] Such insights must be further developed if tongues are to guide a Pentecostal theology that is contextual and open to urgent social issues of global significance.

HEALING: FROM HYPER-FAITH TO THE RENEWAL
OF CREATION

Since tongues as the initial evidence of Spirit baptism was the most controversial theme of early Pentecostalism, Pentecostals have tended to focus attention on this aspect of worship. However, Spirit baptism and tongues were not the only distinctives of the Pentecostal movement. As David Martin noted of Latin American Pentecostalism, divine healing along with ecstatic speech, testimonies, and music served to create a distinctive atmosphere of lay participation in worship, in which the voiceless gained an important voice.[29] Similarly, Donald Dayton has shown that the Pentecostal message incorporated a distinctive approach to the fourfold gospel of Jesus Christ as Saviour, Spirit Baptizer, Healer, and Coming King. Dayton traces the nineteenth-century roots of each of these four themes in the American Holiness movement. What was unique about Pentecostalism in Dayton's argument was how these themes came together to form a gestalt of spirituality.[30] Recently, scholars of Pentecostalism have expanded their focus to include a broader gestalt of themes, such as the ones discussed by Martin and Dayton.

In this broader spectrum of themes, healing holds a prominent place. Clearly, the emphasis on healing in evangelical groups predates the rise of the Pentecostal movement. The belief in divine healing was so much a part of American revivalism in the late nineteenth century that by the 1870s the healing movement 'was a force to contend with in all major evangelical denominations'.[31] However, by the time Pentecostalism erupted in 1906 at the Azusa Street Revival, the belief in divine healing had waned considerably under the influence of intense controversy concerning the biblical justification for such miraculous signs of the Spirit in the modern world.[32] By making healing an important aspect of the church's mission, the Pentecostal movement became a haven for those who were dissatisfied with the decline of emphasis on healing in the mainstream evangelical churches.

Alexander Dowie, a major figure for mediating the central importance of divine healing to Pentecostalism, underscored healing as part of the 'signs and wonders' that accompany the work of the Spirit. Another, more christologically based, view of healing that influenced Pentecostalism was rooted in the victory of Christ in the atonement. Through the atonement, Christ, as *Christus Victor*, wrought redemption for both soul and body.[33]

Gustav Aulen has defined the classical theory of the atonement, which is most fundamental to the New Testament, the Church Fathers, and even Luther, as the victory of Christ over the forces of darkness that hold humanity captive to destruction and death. Aulen noted that the Middle Ages ushered in a preoccupation with wrath and penance, which inspired the substitution and satisfaction theories of atonement and eclipsed the classical theory.[34] Redemption as mere forgiveness replaced a more holistic understanding of redemption as deliverance from both sin and oppression.

The Blumhardts, father and son, were pivotal figures in the nineteenth century for the rediscovery of Jesus as victor over sickness and death and of healing as an essential aspect of the gospel.[35] The elder Blumhardt, Johann, played an important role in the divine healing movements that influenced directly or indirectly the rise of the Pentecostal movement. Karl Barth wrote insightfully of him:

> He saw the tension, the glaring contradiction between the magnitude of human need and the magnitude of the divine promise so intensely in such real terms, that he looked not only for a notional resolution of this opposition but for a real one, and looked for it from day to day.[36]

Johann's son Christoph took his father's holistic understanding of redemption and extended it to the implications of the gospel for social justice and reconciliation. He joined the Social Democratic Party and spent his life raising prophetic criticism against war, prejudice, and economic injustice. Even after he became disillusioned with party politics, he never ceased to cultivate a vision of the kingdom of God as a source for righteousness, justice, and social healing. He struggled to maintain a ministry of prophetic social criticism and transformation that avoided the temptation to identify the kingdom of God with human political agendas. In the words of Barth:

> The unique element, and I say it quite deliberately, the prophetic, in Blumhardt's message and mission consists in the way in which the hurrying and the waiting, the worldly and the divine, the present and the coming, again and again met, were united, supplemented one another, sought and found one another.[37]

From the thinking of Dowie, Aulen, and the Blumhardts, it is clear that the divine healing of the body, more than any other aspect of Pentecostal spirituality and belief, provides a potential corrective to a one-sided emphasis on inwardness and otherworldliness that tends to dominate Pentecostalism. The centrality of the healing doctrine for a Pentecostal understanding of the 'full' gospel implies that Spirit baptism and glossolalia cannot relate just to the 'souls' of persons. Moreover, from the younger Blumhardt, Pentecostals can learn that spiritual fullness and redemption must relate to the bodily or corporeal dimensions of human need and commitments as well. This integration of soul and body implies a broader holism of spiritual and social dimensions of existence and of the Spirit's work. In addition, one who thinks critically about sickness and healing will inevitably face issues of social injustice and poverty. The Christian Medical Commission (CMC) of the World Council of Churches noted that most of the world's health problems cannot be addressed adequately apart from social injustice and poverty. The CMC concluded that the causes of disease in the world are social, economic, political, and spiritual. Poverty, in particular, was recognized as the leading cause of disease in the world.[38] How can one talk about the healing work of the Spirit apart from social justice and healing?

The problem with much of the popular teaching of Pentecostal evangelists on healing is its implicit isolation of sickness from the broader plight of human injustice and suffering. Also involved in this emphasis is the isolation of healing from the work of the Spirit of God in all of creation to bring redemption and liberation.[39] As a consequence, this popular teaching on healing also tends to be isolated from the final eschatological redemption of the body and the renewal of creation that will occur when the kingdom of God comes in fulness. Only through a very narrow understanding of sickness and healing in isolation from such eschatological themes can the robust healing evangelist appear to offer guaranteed healing to all those who believe. Within such an individualistically narrow and isolated theological context, the robust faith and the strong body of the evangelist is all that is needed to convince a multitude of followers that healing has been accomplished and may be attained instantly by all who can lay claim to it. Those among the faithful who fall prey to bodily ailment can be dismissed for lack of faith.

Such an easy dismissal is not possible, however, once sickness and healing are placed in the context of Christian hope for the redemption and liberation of all of creation that is depicted, for example, in Romans 8. The struggle for healing in society and in all of creation lifts the believer out of the enclosed confines of private piety and an individualized living space and reveals both the need for courageous action in the face of such an enormous struggle for healing and the eschatological reservation involved in realizing the goal of this struggle. The Blumhardts characterized this tension as one of 'waiting and hurrying', *Warten und Eilen*, implying a patient action and an active waiting on God.[40] Believers struggle courageously for justice and healing but without illusions of realizing fully the promises this side of eternity. For would one wait patiently for the fulfilment of hope if such were already given (Rom. 8:24)?

How does one respond to the tension implied in this waiting and hurrying? The Blumhardts did not respond to this tension between waiting and action with theological answers but with 'groaning' and yearning in the Spirit in solidarity with the suffering creation for the redemption to come (Rom. 8:26).[41] This groaning in the Spirit, so important for the Blumhardts and for Pentecostals, holds implications for integrating the Pentecostal distinctives of healing and tongues. Both pain and ecstatic speech, therefore, reveal the inability of language to express the mystery of suffering humanity before God.[42]

In the context of the mystery of God in relation to human suffering, Dorothea Soelle maintains that suffering can produce two results. One is speechlessness. Suffering pushes those affected by it beyond the limits of language. Even the language of faith no longer seems adequate to express or to explain the reality of suffering. Secondly, suffering can cause one to withdraw into oneself and to become preoccupied with one's own condition and its improvement.[43] Though Soelle does not relate these two results, their relation is suggestive. Since language is a fundamental means of relating to others, the state of speechlessness and the withdrawal into the self in the midst of suffering appear related. Both cut at the root of self-expression and relationship to others that are essential to our humanity.

In the context of these insights from Soelle, the Blumhardtian groaning in solidarity with the suffering creation for the redemption-to-come seems particularly relevant. The groaning of the community of faith with those who suffer assumes the crisis of language in the midst of suffering but turns this crisis into a means of achieving deeper solidarity with the oppressed and the suffering creation as well as with the Spirit of redemption at work in healing. Instead of marginalizing those who suffer and confining them to their inner world of pain, groaning with them in ways too deep for words relates them ever more deeply to the world and to their true humanity. There are implications here for relating divine healing and speaking in tongues in a way that rescues both from self-centred illusions. Glossolalic piety could provide a valuable spiritual context for the struggle toward healing and wholeness in the midst of sickness and social oppression. Even in temporary defeat, glossolalic cries could proclaim a victory to come in God's final redemption. Pentecostalism's two most outstanding distinctives, healing and tongues, could be interrelated quite meaningfully in a liberating piety.

PASSION FOR THE KINGDOM: REVISIONING OF PENTECOSTAL ESCHATOLOGY

North American, particularly white, Pentecostalism has lost a degree of its eschatological fervour during its gradual move from the urban poor to the suburban middle class. Store-front and tent meetings that tended to function as eschatological 'colonies' of enthusiastic believers were replaced by megachurches and ministries that focused attention on success for middle-class Christians in the here-and-now. The potential for an identity crisis among these classical Pentecostals is obvious when one considers the formative role that eschatology played in the origin of Pentecostalism.

There is no doubt that Pentecostals need to rediscover the original eschatological fervour that allowed them in the early years of the movement to swim against the stream of the spirit of the age and to advocate female participation in the ministry and interracial fellowship at a time in American history in which such social relationships were considered demonic, insane, and criminal. Early Pentecostal eschatology was apocalyptic in the sense that the kingdom of God was understood as soon to break in and miraculously to transform the entire cosmos. This eschatological fervour may have hindered a vision among Pentecostals for long-term social transformation, but it did imply prophetic judgment upon the powers-that-be as temporal, relative, and even contrary to the will of God. The 'critical function' of apocalypticism inspired the early Pentecostal refusal to bow to the gods of sexism, racism, and wealth.[44] It also inspired such passionate social ministries as Teen Challenge. Coupled with the belief in divine healing, Pentecostal eschatology did not advocate an abstract salvation of the 'soul'. After all, if the healing of the body is the foretaste of the final resurrection of the body, why not consider the work of the Spirit in social transformation to be a foretaste of the kingdom of God to come?

The Pentecostals were not passive in their response to the early apocalyptic hope. As noted above, they believed that apostolic empowerment was granted to bear witness to all nations of the goodness of God before the end comes. This witness not only proclaimed the goodness of God but conveyed a foretaste of it in physical healing and renewed relationships. What was needed was the development of a full-blown social witness that would advocate a foretaste of the kingdom-to-come in the liberation of the oppressed, the embrace between communities at war with each other, and the renewal of creation. To accomplish this task, the apocalyptic hope of Pentecostals would have to be qualified by a broader prophetic vision of redemption in history and served by an ongoing criticism of oppressive powers and ideologies. The witness of early Pentecostalism begged for such a development.

Such a prophetic development was hindered by the effort of Pentecostals to adopt a dispensationalist eschatology that radically separated the Old Testament promises, the messianic ministry of Jesus, and the kingdom of God from the gospel and mission of the church. This eschatology directly contradicted the Pentecostal insistence that the fulness of the Spirit at Pentecost fulfilled the promises of the Old Testament (especially Joel 2:28ff.) and anticipated the coming of the kingdom of God. Yet, Pentecostals tried hard to graft a dispensationalist eschatology onto an incompatible theological tree, creating an 'uneasy relationship' with fundamentalist theology fraught with theological inconsistencies and problems.[45] A number of Pentecostal scholars have recently sought to move Pentecostal eschatology in the direction of a prophetic vision of the coming kingdom that brings the challenges of the Old Testament and the messianic ministry of Jesus directly to bear on the life and mission of the church.[46] Other Pentecostals, however, continue to link their apocalyptic hope with dualism and social passivity. In the context of these competing viewpoints, an apocalyptic hope that is rooted in God's transformative work in history and society is needed if Pentecostals are to rediscover and fulfil their original eschatological fervour.

FROM A SECTARIAN TO AN ECUMENICAL WITNESS

The holistic thematic approach utilized thus far in defining Pentecostalism is essential to the rise of a critical and contextual Pentecostal theology. Walter Hollenweger, however, believes that this *ideengeschichtliche* (idea-historical) approach is not adequate by itself. Fundamental for Hollenweger is the *realgeschichtliche* approach, which focuses on the actual spiritual life of the movement.[47] Hollenweger stated movingly,

> I am convinced that there is a theology hidden in this spirituality. A description of these theologies cannot start with their concepts. I have rather to choose another way and describe how they are conceived, carried, and might finally be born. I am not sure whether the moment of birth has come yet, but that something is growing, is in travail and will finally break forth with elemental strength is all too clear.[48]

At the root of Pentecostalism, Hollenweger finds a Catholic spirituality mediated through Wesleyanism being renewed by an African oral liturgy and expression of Christian identity involving story, vision, and prayers for bodily healing. The emphasis on bodily healing represents a potential resistance to the Western dualism between spirit and matter and opts instead for a holistic spirituality that proceeds from an integration of body and soul, nature and spirit, or society and person.[49] The unique harmonization of these theological strains may explain the potential ecumenical significance of the movement. Perhaps the greatest weakness of classical Pentecostalism has been its failure to realize its potential for ecumenical diversity.[50] In the words of Cecil M. Robeck Jr., Pentecostalism is ecumenical and multicultural, though much of the movement does not yet realize it.[51]

Pentecostalism is an extremely diverse movement, culturally and theologically. There is rich potential for a variety of Pentecostal theologies to erupt from different church struggles and cultural contexts. In addition to ecumenical discussion outside of the Pentecostal world, there is a needed intra-Pentecostal discussion on such issues as the Godhead (for example, between trinitarian and Oneness Pentecostals), sanctification, healing, tongues, and eschatology. Though the sectarian Pentecostal identity possesses potential for prophetic criticism of mainstream Christianity and society, there is something about a movement with the designation 'Pentecostal' that begs for an ecumenical vision of the kingdom of God yet to come. Does not Pentecost symbolize a fragmented people struggling through encounters with the Spirit of God to realize more and more of the ecumenical witness to which Christ has called them? Does not the book of Acts narrate the story of just such an ongoing struggle? Robeck has shown that the early Pentecostals viewed their movement as a witness to the work of the Spirit to create a unified witness to the gospel among the people of God.[52]

Perhaps the most significant paradigm shift for Pentecostal theology as Pentecostals approach the twenty-first century will be to realize concretely something of the implicit ecumenical and multicultural witness of Pentecostals for the kingdom of God in the world. Such a realization will be shaped as much by voices from among the people of God as by voices from the world that point to urgent issues of global significance.[53] The Spirit of God is not only the 'soul' of the church but is also the Spirit of creation and of the kingdom-to-come. The future ecumenical and multicultural theologies of Pentecostal communities must respond obediently to what the Spirit is saying in both the church and the world. Only from such obedience to the Spirit and the Word of God can Pentecostal theologies speak with integrity and relevance. All of Pentecostalism's shifting paradigms will be judged in the glaring light of this challenge.

Notes

1　　Russell P. Spittler, 'Suggested Areas for Further Research in Pentecostalism', *PNEUMA: The Journal of the Society for Pentecostal Studies* 5 (Fall 1983), p. 39.

2　　Lewis F. Wilson, 'Bible Institutes, Colleges, Universities', in *Dictionary of Pentecostal and Charismatic Movements*, ed. Stanley M. Burgess and Gary B. McGee (Grand Rapids, MI: Zondervan Publishing Company, 1988), p. 61.

3　　On the Pentecostal adoption of fundamentalist identity, see Gerald T. Sheppard, 'Word and Spirit: Scripture in the Pentecostal Tradition', Part 1 *Agora* (Spring 1978), pp. 4–5, 17–22; Sheppard, 'Word and Spirit: Scripture in the Pentecostal Tradition', Part 2 (Summer 1978), pp. 14–19; and D. W. Faupel, 'Presidential Address: Whither Pentecostalism?' *PNEUMA: The Journal of the Society for Pentecostal Studies* 15 (Spring 1993), pp. 9–27. On the rise of Bible doctrines, see Douglas Jacobson, 'Knowing the Doctrines of Pentecostals: The Scholastic Theology of the Assemblies of God, 1930–1955', paper presented at the Twenty-third Annual Meeting of the Society for Pentecostal Studies, 11–13 November 1993. Jacobson wishes to distinguish these Pentecostal Bible doctrines from fundamentalist doctrines, though his reasons for doing so are not given. Examples of Bible doctrines manuals include: P. C. Nelson, *Bible Doctrines* (Springfield, MO: Gospel Publishing House, 1934); Myer Pearlman, *Knowing the Doctrines of the Bible* (Springfield, MO: Gospel Publishing House, 1937); and E. S. Williams, *Systematic Theology*, 3 vols. (Springfield, MO: Gospel Publishing House, 1953).

4　　Russell P. Spittler, 'Theological Style among Pentecostals and Charismatics', in *Doing Theology in Today's World*, ed. John D. Woodbridge and Thomas Edward McComiskey (Grand Rapids, MI: Zondervan Publishing Company, 1991), p. 297.

5　　For example, Stanley M. Horton, ed., *Systematic Theology: A Pentecostal Perspective* (Springfield, MO: Logion Press, 1994), and French Arrington, *Christian Theology*, 3 vols. (Cleveland, TN: Pathway Press, 1992–94).

6　　See Douglas Petersen's discussion of a practical outworking of doctrinal confession among Two Thirds World Pentecostals in *Not By Might nor By Power: A Pentecostal Theology of Social Concern in Latin America* (Oxford, England

and Irvine, CA: Regnum Books International, 1996), pp. 81–111.

7   Karl Barth's remarks about Blumhardt are from his *Protestant Theology in the Nineteenth Century: Its Background and History* (Valley Forge, PA: Judson Press, 1963), p. 647.

8   Carl Brumback, *What Meaneth This?* (Springfield, MO: Gospel Publishing House, 1947); and Wade Horton, ed., *The Glossolalia Phenomenon* (Cleveland, TN: Pathway Press, 1966).

9   Steven J. Land, *Pentecostal Spirituality: A Passion for the Kingdom* (Sheffield: Sheffield Academic Press, 1993); Eldin Villafañe, *The Liberating Spirit* (Grand Rapids, MI: Wm. B. Eerdmans Publishing Co., 1994); Miroslav Volf, *Wir sind die Kirche* (Habilitationschrift, Tuebingen, 1992).

10   Note, for example, Frank D. Macchia, *Spirituality and Social Liberation: The Message of the Blumhardts in the Light of Wuerttemberg Pietism* (Metuchen, NJ: Scarecrow Press, 1993); Macchia, 'Sighs Too Deep for Words: Towards a Theology of Glossolalia', *Journal of Pentecostal Theology* 1 (October 1992), pp. 47–73; Macchia, 'Tongues as a Sign: Towards a Sacramental Understanding of Pentecostal Experience', *PNEUMA: The Journal of the Society for Pentecostal Studies* 15 (Spring 1993), pp. 61–76..

11   Emil Brunner, *Misverstaendnis der Kirche*, 3rd ed. (Zurich: Theologischer Verlag, 1988), chap. 5.

12   Note the special issue on hermeneutics in *PNEUMA: The Journal of the Society for Pentecostal Studies* 15 (Fall 1993), and G. T. Sheppard's response in, 'Biblical Interpretation after Gadamer', *PNEUMA: The Journal of the Society for Pentecostal Studies* 16 (Spring 1994), pp. 121–142. Note also G. T. Sheppard, 'How Do Neoorthodox and Post-Neoorthodox Approach the 'Doing of Theology' Today?' in *Doing Theology in Today's World*, ed. John D. Woodbridge and Thomas Edward McComiskey (Grand Rapids, MI: Zondervan Publishing House, 1991). The term *orthopathos* is taken from Steve Land, *Pentecostal Spirituality*.

13   I have gained insights here especially from Juan Luis Segundo's *The Liberation of Theology* (Maryknoll, NY: Orbis Books, 1976), p. 8ff.; Cornel West's 'The Crisis in Theological Education', in *Prophetic Fragments* (Grand Rapids, MI: Wm. B. Eerdmans Publishing Co., 1988), pp. 273–280; and José Míguez Bonino's 'Popular Piety in Latin America', in *The Mystical and Political Dimensions of the Christian Faith*, ed. J. Geffre and G. Gutiérrez (New York, NY: Herder & Herder, 1974), p. 156.

14   Note, Walter Hollenweger, 'The Critical Tradition of Pentecostalism', *Journal of Pentecostal Theology* 1 (October 1992), pp. 7–17.

15   Hendrikus Berkhof, *The Doctrine of the Holy Spirit* (Richmond, VA: John Knox Press, 1964), p. 90.

16   Kilian McDonnell, 'The Distinguishing Characteristics of the Charismatic-Pentecostal Spirituality', *One in Christ* 10 (1974), p. 123ff.

17   Simon Tugwell, 'Baptism in the Holy Spirit', *Heythrop Journal* 13 (July 1972), p. 268.

18   Gordon Fee, 'Baptism in the Spirit: The Issue of Separability and Subsequence', *PNEUMA: The Journal of the Society for Pentecostal Studies* 7 (Fall 1985), pp. 88–91.

19   Spittler, 'Further Research', p. 19.

20   Roger Stronstad, *The Charismatic Theology of St. Luke* (Peabody, MA:

Hendrickson Publishers, 1983); Robert P. Menzies, *Empowered for Witness: The Spirit in Luke-Acts* (Sheffield: Sheffield Academic Press, 1991).

21   Donald Dayton, *The Theological Roots of Pentecostalism* (Grand Rapids, MI: Zondervan Publishing House, 1987).

22   Allen Clayton, 'The Significance of William H. Durham for Pentecostal Historiography', *PNEUMA: The Journal of the Society for Pentecostal Studies* 1 (Fall 1979), pp. 27–42.

23   For a taxonomy of the various groupings within the classical Pentecostal and charismatic movements, including the Reformed, baptistic and Wesleyan Holiness Pentecostals, see Vinson Synan, *The Holiness-Pentecostal Movement in the United States* (Grand Rapids, MI: Wm. B. Eerdmans Publishing Co., 1971).

24   *The Apostolic Faith* (September 1906).

25   Jenny Everts, 'Missionary Tongues?' paper presented at the Twenty-third Annual Meeting of the Society for Pentecostal Studies, 11–13 November 1993.

26   Russell P. Spittler, 'Glossolalia', in *Dictionary of Pentecostal and Charismatic Movements*, ed. Stanley M. Burgess and Gary B. McGee (Grand Rapids, MI: Zondervan Publishing House, 1988), p. 341.

27   Harvey Cox, *Fire from Heaven: The Rise of Pentecostal Spirituality and the Reshaping of Religion in the Twenty-first Century* (New York, NY: Addison-Wesley Publishing Company, 1995), p. 93.

28   Walter Hollenweger, *Geist und Materia: Interkulterelle Theologie*, Bd. III (Munich: Chr. Kaiser Verlag, 1988), pp. 314–315.

29   David Martin, *Tongues of Fire: The Explosion of Protestantism in Latin America* (Oxford: Basil Blackwell, 1990), p. 163.

30   Dayton, *Theological Roots*.

31   R. Cunningham, 'From Holiness to Healing: The Faith Cure in America', *Church History* 43 (December 1974), p. 499.

32   Ibid.

33   Donald Dayton, 'The Rise of the Evangelical Healing Movement in Nineteenth Century America', *PNEUMA: The Journal of the Society for Pentecostal Studies* 4 (Spring 1982), p. 17.

34   Gustav Aulen, *Christus Victor: An Historical Study of the Three Main Types of the Idea of the Atonement* (New York, NY: Macmillan, 1950).

35   See Macchia, *Spirituality and Social Liberation*.

36   Barth, *Protestant Theology*, p. 647.

37   Karl Barth, 'Vergangenheit und Zukunft: Friedrich Naumann und Christoph Blumhardt', in *Anfaenge der dialektischen Theologie*, hrsg. Moltmann, Teil 1 (Munchen: Chr. Kaiser Verlag, 1977), p. 49.

38   David Hilton, 'Health and Healing', in *Dictionary of the Ecumenical Movement*, ed. N. Lossky et al. (Geneva: World Council of Churches, 1991), p. 450.

39   Walter Hollenweger, *Geist und Materia*, chap. 4.

40   See Macchia, *Spirituality and Social Liberation*, chap. 5.

41   Ibid.

42   Note what Cox says about tongues and the language of pain, *Fire from Heaven*, pp. 88–89.

43   Dorothea Soelle, *Leiden* (Stuttgart: Creuz Verlag, 1973), chap. 1.

44   On the critical function of apocalypticism, see, Wolfhart Pannenberg, 'Constructive and Critical Functions of Christian Eschatology', *Harvard Theological Review* 77 (April 1984).

45   Gerald T. Sheppard, 'Pentecostalism and the Hermeneutics of Dispensationalism: Anatomy of an Uneasy Relationship', *PNEUMA: The Journal of
the Society for Pentecostal Studies* 6 (Fall 1984), pp. 5–33.

46   Murray W. Dempster, 'Evangelism, Social Concern, and the Kingdom of
God', in *Called & Empowered: Global Mission in Pentecostal Perspective*,
ed. Murray W. Dempster, Byron D. Klaus, Douglas Petersen (Peabody, MA:
Hendrickson Publishers, 1991), pp. 22–43. Note also Macchia, *Spirituality
and Social Liberation*.

47   Walter Hollenweger, 'Priorities in Pentecostal Research: Historiography,
Missiology, Hermeneutics and Pneumatology', in *Experiences of the Spirit*,
ed. Jan A. B. Jongeneel (Bern: Peter Lang Verlag, 1989), p. 8ff.

48   Walter Hollenweger, 'Theology of the New World', *The Expository Times* 87
(May 1976): p. 229.

49   Hollenweger, 'Priorities in Pentecostal Research', p. 8ff.

50   Walter Hollenweger, 'After Twenty Years' Research on Pentecostalism', *Theology* 87 (November 1984), pp. 407–409.

51   Cecil M. Robeck Jr., 'Taking Stock of Pentecostalism: The Personal Reflections of a Retiring Editor', *PNEUMA: The Journal of the Society for Pentecostal
Studies* 15 (Spring 1993), p. 39ff.

52   Cecil M. Robeck Jr., 'A Pentecostal Looks at the World Council of Churches',
The Ecumenical Review 47 (1995), esp. pp. 60–62.

53   Note Yves Congar, 'Do the New Problems of Our Secular World Make Ecumenism Irrelevant?', in *Post-Ecumenical Christianity*, ed. Hans Küng (New
York, NY: Herder & Herder, 1970).

Chapter Two

'Try To Get People Saved'
Revisiting the Paradigm of
an Urgent Pentecostal Missiology

L. Grant McClung, Jr.

The first Pentecostal missiological formulation of the twentieth century may very well be in the pastoral admonition of William J. Seymour – 'Try to get people saved' – and in the first written report of the events surrounding the outpouring of the Holy Spirit at the Azusa Street revival in Los Angeles, California, where Seymour was the recognized leader from 1906 to 1909.

The first edition of the Azusa Street periodical, *The Apostolic Faith* (September 1906), was headlined: 'PENTECOST HAS COME'. The lead article, under the heading, 'Los Angeles Being Visited by a Revival of Bible Salvation and Pentecost as Recorded in the Book of Acts', provides a narrative insight into the early missiological worldview of those who came to be known as 'Pentecostals'. It read:

> The power of God now has this city agitated as never before. Pentecost has surely come and with it the Bible evidences are following, many

being converted and sanctified and filled with the Holy Ghost, speaking in tongues as they did on the day of Pentecost. The scenes that are daily enacted in the building on Azusa street and at missions and churches in other parts of the city are beyond description, and the real revival is only started, as God has been working with His children mostly, getting them through to Pentecost, and laying the foundation for a mighty wave of salvation among the unconverted.[1]

It is the purpose of this chapter to revisit the paradigm under which the early missiology of the Pentecostal movement was formed, to look for signs of shifts and adjustments in that paradigm during its first century, and to propose what the current paradigm of Pentecostal missiology has become and how that agenda will carry the Pentecostal/charismatic movement into a unified, interdependent global mission with all Christian families into the twenty-first century.

'PENTECOSTAL MISSIOLOGY'?

As a specific theory, body of knowledge, and field of academic discipline, 'missiology' has been defined by Alan R. Tippett as:

> ... the academic discipline or science which researches, records and applies data relating to the biblical origin, the history (including the use of documentary materials), the anthropological principles and techniques and the theological base of the Christian mission. The theory, methodology and data bank are particularly directed towards:
>
> 1. the processes by which the Christian message is communicated,
>
> 2. the encounters brought about by its proclamation to non-Christians,
>
> 3. the planting of the Church and organization of congregations, the incorporation of converts into those congregations, and the growth and relevance of their structures and fellowship, internally to maturity, externally in outreach as the Body of Christ in local situations and beyond, in a variety of culture patterns.[2]

Positioning this rather lengthy, technical definition of 'missiology' as a science alongside Seymour's basic missiological charge at Azusa Street – 'Try to get people saved' – and juxtaposing both with the still developing, embryonic field of more recent Pentecostal expositions on mission may appear at first to result in a contradiction of terms. Is there really such a thing as 'Pentecostal missiology'? 'Pentecostal' and 'missiology', however, actually turn out to be more synonymous than oxymoronic. Given the following observations of similarities between Pentecostalism and the field of missiology, it is quite natural to speak of 'Pentecostal' and 'missiology' in the same breath. At least five convergencies can be identified between Pentecostalism and missiology.

Pentecostalism by its very nature is intrinsically missiological.

David Hesselgrave has reflected on the 'deep-seated missionary motivation' of the Pentecostal movement, a motivation 'that has propelled it to its present role as perhaps the most missionary-minded segment of world Christianity'.[3] He asserts that:

> If anything is generally characteristic of Pentecostal churches world-wide, it is an ethos of growth. In a time of defeatism, stagnation, and retreat in many churches, a growth climate may prove to be one of the great bequests of Pentecostalism to the larger church of Christ.[4]

Even Frederick Bruner, often critical of Pentecostalism, admitted that 'Pentecostalism and mission are almost synonymous'. But before Pentecostals remove the 'almost' and rejoice over a 'back-handed compliment', they should remember that Bruner also typified Pentecostalism as 'heresy with vitality'.[5] Assemblies of God missions historian Gary B. McGee, an insider much more sympathetic to the cause, has accurately observed that 'The history of Pentecostalism cannot be properly understood apart from its missionary vision.'[6]

There is a simple straightforwardness to both Pentecostalism and missiology.

Tippett's short-hand version of his lengthier, more technical definition is basic, 'The simplest definition of missiology is "the study of individuals being brought to God in history". . .'[7] This sounds like something that could go down well in a Pentecostal testimony meeting or missions service.

Pentecostalism and missiology are in process, eclectic, and characterized by synthesis.

'Every branch of theology – including missiology – remains piece-work, fragile, and preliminary.' This was the claim of David J. Bosch, who also said that, 'There is no such thing as missiology, period. There is only missiology in draft.'[8] Bosch also drew from the poetic insights of Ivan Illich who pointed out:

> Missiology studies the growth of the Church into new peoples, the birth of the Church beyond its social boundaries; beyond the linguistic barriers within which she feels at home; beyond the poetic images in which

she taught her children.... Missiology therefore is the study of the Church as surprise.[9]

As a relatively younger movement, Pentecostalism is yet in historical process, and Pentecostal missiology as an interdisciplinary academic field is still very much in the formative stage, its results prone to exhibit surprise.

Both Pentecostalism and missiology, however, are distinctive, marked with unique characteristics.

Tippett has argued for the interdisciplinary interdependence of missiology with other disciplines, yet also asserts its unique distinctiveness:

> Immediately it will be apparent that such research requires some familiarity with the tools and techniques of anthropology, theology, and history. Yet even this is not all. The missiologist may call on the resources of, say, linguistics or psychology. Nevertheless, missiology is a discipline in its own right. It is not a mere borrower from other fields, for these dimensions are related to each other in a unique manner. They interact, influence and modify each other. Missiology is dynamic, not static.[10]

Both Pentecostalism and missiology are younger movements which have moved from marginalization to acceptance.

Whether one traces his or her modern Pentecostal heritage to a schoolhouse near Murphy, North Carolina (1896), a Bible college in Topeka, Kansas (1901), or to an inner city mission in Los Angeles, California (1906), there is only room today for a ninety- to one-hundred-year-old 'history' in modern Pentecostalism.[11]

Missiology also has a short-lived history. As Wilbert Shenk has noted, 'Missiology as a discipline was not supported by a professional association until the formation of the Association of Professors of Missions in 1952. Evangelicals did not become active in professional missiology until the 1950s.'[12] As I will demonstrate later in this chapter, Pentecostals, largely through the efforts of Melvin Hodges, were also just getting involved in formal missiological reflection in the early 1950s. Continued academic self-definitions of Pentecostal missiology did not fully flower, however, until the decade of the 1980s.

Missiology as a science is also quite young, and Wilbert Shenk has reminded us that the discipline of missiology as a field of scholarship 'has had an uncertain status in academia since its introduction in the nineteenth century. David Bosch, with others, has shown that under the impact of the Enlightenment, the discipline of theology was subdivided into two areas: theology as practical know-how necessary for clerical work (theology as practice) and theology as a technical and scholarly enterprise (theology as theory). From that subdivision, there was an evolution of what Edward Farley called the 'fourfold pattern': the disciplines of Bible (text), church history (history), systematic theology (truth), and practical theology (application). This pattern, says Bosch, became virtually universal for Protestant theological schools and seminaries in Europe and North America and was finally exported elsewhere. Through the influence of Schleiermacher, missiology was eventually appended to the area of practical theology. Subsequently, persons such as Charles Breckenridge were appointed to teach such areas as 'missionary instruction' at Princeton Theological Seminary in 1836 although he was, at the same time, professor of pastoral theology.

Ultimately, through much struggle against the bastions of theological tradition, missiology was taught as an independent subject in its own right, as was the case with the establishment of Alexander Duff's 'chair of evangelistic theology' at Edinburgh in 1867. The ultimate innovation, however, of the establishment of missiology as a *discipline in its own right*, came through the indefatigable efforts of Gustav Warneck, the so-called father of German missiology, who taught at the University of Halle from 1896 to 1910.[13] Bosch notes that Warneck's contribution elicited responses not only in Protestant but also in Catholic circles: 'The founding of the first chair of missiology at a Catholic institution – in 1910, at the University of Münster – ... was undoubtedly influenced by developments in Protestantism and, more specifically, by Warneck's contribution.'[14]

Interestingly, the period of Warneck's tenure at Halle (1896–1910) was also a formative era in the rise of the modern Pentecostal movement. Concurrently, by 1910, on the other side of the world, a new *Pentecostal* missionary force, neither Protestant nor Catholic, but 'The Third Force in Christendom'[15] was emerging from humble beginnings. In fact, by 1910, some 185 new Pentecostal missionaries had been marshaled over a four year period from the outset of the 1906–1909 Azusa Street revival.[16] The occupant of the Azusa Street 'chair' was not a trained theologian/missiologist but a humble black preacher named William J. Seymour. His setting was not a lecture hall in an academic department of a prestigious university, but a forty-by-sixty-foot tumble-down shack known as the Azusa Street Mission. His teaching was not from the lectern of a classroom, but from behind rough shoe boxes made into a simple makeshift pulpit.[17] From this pulpit and from the prayer benches in the altar, a new missiological paradigm would emerge for the twentieth century.

PENTECOSTAL EXPERIENCE AS A MISSIOLOGICAL PARADIGM

To this point, only the latter half of William Seymour's evangelistic injunction has been quoted: 'Try to get people saved.' There was no particular distinction or uniqueness in that challenge to fellow Pentecostals as compared to their contemporaries in other 'Bible-believing' churches and predecessors in the Holiness movement and in the broader Christian world. In fact, the exhortation was coming at the close of what most *Protestant* observers agree to be the 'Great Century'[18] of Christian missions (1792–1914) which was ushered in by such notable and noble renewal/missions movements as Pietism, Puritanism, Moravianism, the Evangelical revival in England and the related Wesleyan revival, and the Great Awakening in the American colonies.[19] The Protestant missionary movement of the nineteenth century, and for that matter, the prior missionary activities in Roman Catholic missionary orders, which had accomplished no small global achievements in their own respective understandings of what it meant to 'Try to get people saved'.

The uniqueness of Seymour's injunction is found in its preceding phrase combined with the one already quoted. In its entirety, Seymour's admonition was: '*Now, do not go from this meeting and talk about tongues, but try to get people saved.*'[20] For me, Seymour's charge could be the preamble for an emerging Pentecostal missiology dating to the earliest days of its growing global significance from Los Angeles. Seymour's reminder to his flock was the beginning of an informal Pentecostal missiology (remember Tippett's simple, short-hand definition of missiology cited above). Seymour's Pentecostal missiology, and the group experiences of the early Pentecostal communities, reflected an essential trialogue of factors: 'Now, do not go from this meeting and talk about tongues [*eschatology* and *experience*], but try to get people saved [*evangelism*]'.[21] In its first stage, the Pentecostal missiological paradigm could be diagrammed as follows:

Eschatology – Experience – Evangelism

FIGURE 1. Seymour's Pentacostal Missiology

At the heart of the early Pentecostals' missiology was their personal experience with the Holy Spirit found around an altar of prayer with fellow seekers. This profound experience was integrated with an eschatological urgency and a passion for souls (*eschatology/experience/evangelism*). Apparently, their earliest understandings of the experience that came to be known as the 'Baptism in The Holy Spirit' was that it produced a missiological fervour and ministry and it provided the empowerment for the same.

Basic to this understanding are the following incisive observations written in 1908 by J. Roswell Flower, initially the foreign editor and later the associate editor of a monthly magazine known as *The Pentecost*, published during the years 1908–1910 first from Indianapolis, Indiana, and then from Kansas City, Missouri. Later, Flower and his wife, Alice Reynolds Flower, would begin the *Pentecostal Evangel* (in 1913) which became, and remains today, the official publication of the Assemblies of God, USA. Remarkably, Flower had been converted just a year earlier on April 14, 1907, and was baptized in the Holy Spirit sometime in 1908 prior to writing the following editorial in August that same year.[22] Based upon the year of his birth in 1888, Flower could not have been more than twenty years old when he penned this remarkable missiological insight, and, from my observation, what could be one of the first written missiological statements on the relationship of the baptism in the Holy Spirit to world evangelization:

> The baptism of the Holy Ghost does not consist in simply speaking in tongues. No. It has a much more grand and deeper meaning than that. It fills our souls with the love of God for lost humanity, and makes us much more willing to leave home, friends, and all to work in His vineyard, even if it be far away among the heathen.... 'Go ye into all the world and preach the gospel to every creature.' This command of Jesus can only be properly fulfilled when we have obeyed that other command, 'Tarry ye in the city of Jerusalem till ye be endued with power from on high.' When we have tarried and received that power, then, and then only are we fit to carry the gospel. When the Holy Spirit comes into our hearts, the missionary spirit comes in with it; they are

inseparable, as the missionary spirit is but one of the fruits of the Holy Spirit. Carrying the gospel to hungry souls in this and other lands is but a natural result of receiving the baptism of the Holy Ghost.[23]

Flower's observation matched numerous testimonies such as that of pioneer preacher Aaron A. Wilson who said he 'felt the call to preach from a child, but when filled with the Spirit such a burden for lost souls came upon me'.[24] Indeed, early Pentecostal missiology was not only a missiology of the pulpit and pew, but, more importantly, a 'missiology of the altar' (of prayer and worship).

When supernatural phenomena burst on the scene at Azusa Street and other locations, Pentecostals were sure that they were living in and directly experiencing the end-time restoration of New Testament apostolic power. Signs and wonders were a portent of Christ's imminent return. Everything else was put aside for the urgent business of world evangelization as 'their hearts glowed with the expectation and conviction that this was destined to be the last revival before the coming of the Lord, and that, for them, all earthly history would soon be consummated by the "Rapture" '.[25]

In telling the story of the West Central Council of the Assemblies of God, Eugene H. Hastie took note of a number of missionaries who urgently left *before* the formation of a missions board. One group, the Crouch family, left in 1912 for Egypt on a one-way trip. 'The Crouch party', says Hastie, 'went mostly at their own expense, expecting to remain there until the rapture, which they believed was very near at hand.'[26] Such workers have been characterized by Vinson Synan as 'missionaries of the one-way ticket'.[27]

A look inside the Azusa Street paper, *The Apostolic Faith*, provides numerous revealing glimpses of the early Pentecostal eschatological paradigm. One of them says it all:

> There is no man at the head of this movement. God Himself is speaking in the earth. We are on the verge of the greatest miracle the world has ever seen, when the sons of God shall be manifested, the saints shall come singing from the dust (Isaiah 26:19) and the full overcomers shall be caught up to meet the Lord in the air. The political world realizes that some great crisis is at hand, the scientific world, the religious world all feel it. The coming of the Lord draweth nigh, it is near, even at the doors.[28]

PEOPLE OF 'THE BOOK'

A key linguistic indicator in the subheading of the first issue of *The Apostolic Faith* was the phrase 'as Recorded in the Book of Acts'.[29] Early Pentecostals were marked by their exactness in following a literal interpretation of Scripture. They saw their movement as a fulfilment of Joel 2:28–32 and related their experiences as normative from what they saw in the pages of the New Testament, primarily, the Book of Acts. They sought, said Pentecostal missiologist Paul Pomerville, to be 'people of "The Book." ':

> While some may question their *use* of The Book, their hermeneutics, nevertheless Pentecostals seek to be led by Scripture as by the Spirit in their missions efforts. Their textbook for missions strategy often boils down to the Book of Acts.[30]

Pomerville's 'Scripture-Spirit' expression is at the heart of the *eschatology/experience/evangelism* trialogue and was central to early Pentecostal preaching, which frequently cited Joel 2 and Acts 1–2. Note, for example, the 'trialogue' italicized in the following passages (NIV):

Joel 2:28–32

1. *Eschatology*
(2:28) And afterward, I will pour out my Spirit on all people
(2:29) I will pour out my Spirit in those days.
(2:30) I will show wonders . . .

2. *Experience*
(2:28) Your sons and daughters will prophesy, your old men dream dreams, your young men see visions.
(2:29) Even on my servants, both men and women, I will pour out my Spirit in those days.

3. *Evangelism*
(2:28) Your sons and daughters shall prophesy
(2:29) And everyone who calls on the name of the Lord will be saved . . .

Acts 1:7–8

1. *Eschatology*
(1:7)   It is not for you to know the times or dates . . .

2. *Experience*

(1:8)   But you will receive power when the Holy Spirit comes on you ... .

3. *Evangelism*

(1:8)   ... and you will be my witnesses . . .

Acts 2:1–41

Interestingly, the trialogue is reversed, with the experience coming first, and the 'eschatological explanation' coming second (*experience/eschatology /evangelism*).

1. *Experience*

(2:1–13)   Outpouring of the Holy Spirit, supernatural signs

2. *Eschatology*

(2:14–36)   The 'eschatological explanation'

3. *Evangelism*

(2:37–41)   The application, call to repentance

The Azusa Street focus on the Word of God and the fact that the early Pentecostals saw themselves as a prototype of the restored community prophesied about by Joel and fulfilled on the Day of Pentecost is highlighted in their use of a one-liner from Scripture, carefully positioned under the name of the paper, *The Apostolic Faith*. It is Jude 3, 'Earnestly contend for the faith once delivered unto the saints.' The second page of the paper's first issue lists an early, formative doctrinal statement for which Jude 3 is the preamble:

> *The Apostolic Faith Movement* – Stands for the restoration of the faith once delivered unto the saints – the old time religion, camp meetings, revivals, missions, street and prison work and Christian unity everywhere.[31]

Remembering 'Seymour's Pentecostal Missiology' including the trialogue of *eschatology/experience/evangelism* and the centrality of the 'Scripture-Spirit' approach to ministry and adding the dimension of the *Apostolic Faith* purpose statement just cited – especially the final words, 'and Christian unity everywhere' – early Pentecostal missiology at Azusa Street and into the formational years of the Pentecostal movement included five essential elements in dynamic relationship (see figure 2). These elements will be linked together by Pentecostal leaders in an evolving missiological trialogue.

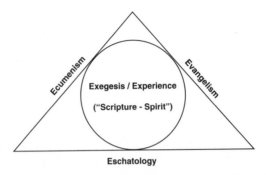

FIGURE 2. Foundational Pentecostal Missiology (Azusa Street)

Fundamental to this model are the indispensable central elements of the authority of the Scripture (*exegetical*) and personal experience (*experiential*) of the trinitarian God in the power of the Holy Spirit. These were interpreted and actualized for early Pentecostals out of the realization that they were a part of an eschatological process. The *eschatological/exegetical/experiential* movement then proceeded outward to mission in the world (*evangelism*) and inward to other members of the Body of Christ (*ecumenism*).

Early Pentecostal Ecumenism

Looking back from the midpoint of twentieth-century Pentecostalism, Donald Gee noted in 1949 that one of the central attractions of the movement was not a system of doctrine or church government but a 'powerful individual spiritual experience' producing a 'new, deep fundamental unity in spirit'.[32] Researcher John Thomas Nichol agreed that the early Pentecostals emphasized experience over issues of doctrine or church government. Thus, he observed in his oft-quoted *Pentecostalism*:

> Arminians and Calvinists, Holiness folk who believed in a 'second work of grace' and Baptists who adhered to the theory of 'the finished work at Calvary', Methodists, Brethren, and Anglicans – all of whom represented variant forms of church doctrine and polity – all met around the same altar to pray and expect the impartation of the Holy Spirit and his charismatic gifts.[33]

Gary McGee traces the ecumenical cooperation abroad on the part of early Pentecostal missionaries and the eventual increased cooperation in the United States which more fully developed after 1942. Some of the key developments in that decade were the formation of the National Association of Evangelicals (NAE, including Pentecostal denominations) in 1942; the founding of the NAE missions arm, Evangelical Foreign Missions Association (EFMA, also including Pentecostals), in 1945, now known as Evangelical Fellowship of Missions Agencies; the formation of the Pentecostal World Conference (PWC) in 1947; and the initiation of the Pentecostal Fellowship of North America (PFNA) in 1948.[34] With the affiliation of Pentecostals in the EFMA, for example, Pentecostal missions leaders were able to 'gain broader exposure to each other's missions programs and those of other evangelical agencies. Notwithstanding, a formal caucus of Pentecostal missions agencies has never developed.'[35]

From the Fringes to the Fraternity: Encouragement from the Outside

Had the Pentecostals been just another isolated sect emphasizing controversial doctrines and inward-looking practices, their existence could probably have been ignored. But by the middle of this century, the inconvenient reality for some was Pentecostalism's ever-pervasive expansion and presence around the globe. Many were asking the obvious missiological question, 'Why are they growing?' From a current standpoint, that is a fifty-year-old question that has been investigated thoroughly in the major missiological circles during the last half of the twentieth century. C. Peter Wagner has provided an exhaustive essay on 'Church Growth' in the *Dictionary of Pentecostal and Charismatic Movements* and concluded:

> While Pentecostal churches experienced good growth rates during the first half of the century, the total impact on world Christianity was minimal. It was mainly a period for building momentum, which would mushroom after World War II. The greatest growth for Pentecostals, joined by charismatics in 1960, has come in the latter half of the century.[36]

Wagner and his mentor, Donald A. McGavran, of the church growth school of thought, are to be credited for analysing and extensively popularizing the worldwide growth rates and dynamics of Pentecostals. This was beginning to be especially evident some thirty years ago with the formation of McGavran's Institute of Church Growth. But there were other pre-McGavran voices.

The Decade of the 1940s: Initial Recognition of Pentecostal Church Growth

J. Merle Davis studied the leadership styles, message, training methods, and lower class audience of Brazilian Pentecostals and published his observations in *How the Church Grows in Brazil*, a 1943 World Missionary Council study. He concluded that Pentecostals were 'suited to the task of evangelizing the masses of Brazil'.[37] Presbyterian researcher William R. Read, one of the team of Read, Monterroso, and Johnson who produced the landmark interdenominational study, *Latin American Church Growth* (Eerdmans, 1969), claimed that Davis was 'one of our first missionary statesmen to see the dynamic factors involved in the Pentecostal movement, and he called attention particularly to the rapid growth of the Pentecostal churches'.[38] Twenty years later, in his *Church Growth in Mexico*, McGavran credited the church growth conclusions of Davis and also incorporated the groundbreaking work of Eugene Nida on Pentecostals.[39]

In 1952, L.F.W. Woodford, then the missionary secretary to the British Assemblies of God, was able to report to the triennial Pentecostal World Conference:

> Informative articles and references to pentecostal missionary work are now appearing from time to time in responsible missionary journals and magazines, including the *International Review of Missions* and *World Dominion*, the values and extent of the pentecostal contribution to world missions is thus receiving acknowledgment from these authoritative quarters.[40]

The Decade of the 1950s: Formal Pentecostal Missiological Reflection

While noting comments of outside observers, one must pause here to insert the first formal attempt at missiological theory from an insider. Assemblies of God missionary/missiologist Melvin L. Hodges, whose name became synonymous with indigenous church principles, gave a series of lectures at a missionary conference in 1950 and later expanded them for publication by the Gospel Publishing House in 1953 under the title, *The Indigenous Church*. Moody Press reprinted it the following year. McGee states that this was the first book on missiology published by a Pentecostal (both within and beyond his denomination)[41] and also asserts that, 'The application of Hodges' teachings have played a major role in the spectacular spread of Pentecostalism overseas, particularly in Latin America.'[42]

The following year, Bishop Lesslie Newbigin of the United Church of South India may have startled many when he suggested in his *The Household of God* (Friendship Press, 1954) that Pentecostals be seen as 'The Community of the Holy Spirit' (Chapter 4). Just four years later, Henry P. Van Dusen was calling the Pentecostals 'The Third Force in Christendom'.[43]

The Decade of the 1960s: Thinking Strategically about Church Growth

What happened to Donald A. McGavran in the 1960s, and its resulting effect on Pentecostal missiology, was actually a longer progress related to what was happening to him in the 1930s. Commonly regarded as the 'Father of the Church Growth Movement', McGavran was deeply influenced by the writings of a Methodist bishop, J. Wascom Pickett. In 1936, McGavran and Pickett, both missionaries in India at that time, teamed with A. L. Warnshuis and G. H. Singh to produce *Church Growth and Group Conversion* (later revised by William Carey Library, 1973). By the time of his *Bridges of God* in 1955 – the book which technically set the church growth movement in motion – McGavran was firmly convinced of the 'people movement' approach to missions as opposed to the traditional 'missions station' approach.

It is not the purpose of this overview to document when McGavran first studied, much less knew about, the Pentecostal movement. It is evident, however, that when referring to his article, 'What Makes Pentecostal Churches Grow?' (*Church Growth Bulletin*, January 1977) he reflected, 'The question underlined above has animated my mind since the early sixties.'[44]

McGavran included Pentecostals in the first class of the original Institute of Church Growth in Eugene, Oregon, in 1961. He traced various case studies of Pentecostal church growth from the inception of the *Church Growth Bulletin* in 1964 (later changed to *Global Church Growth*) and featured Robert T. McGlasson, a foreign missions executive of the Assemblies of God, USA, in a new series of articles on 'Notable Missions Leaders on Church Growth', initiated in March 1965.[45]

The Decade of the 1970s: Evangelicals and Pentecostals Joining Hands on Church Growth Research

McGavran had introduced a Pentecostal missions leader in the early stages of his *Church Growth Bulletin* (McGlasson in 1965). By the time of the January 1977 issue he devoted the entire issue to Pentecostals with his own lead article, 'What Makes Pentecostal Churches Grow?'

A large part of McGavran's genius in forming the church growth movement was his ability to attract to himself persons of high calibre who joined him in research and writing. One of the most notable of his colleagues who took an exceptional interest in Pentecostals was C. Peter Wagner, a former missionary to Latin America. Wagner's study of Latin American Pentecostalism, *Look Out! The Pentecostals Are Coming* (Creation House, 1973), was read extensively as a textbook in seminaries and Bible colleges and by church leaders. Later it was revised as *What Are We Missing?* and more recently as *Spiritual Power and Church Growth* (Creation House, 1986). From the 1970s onward, the Fuller Theological Seminary School of World Mission and the church growth movement became the breeding ground for numerous studies of Pentecostal church growth by outside observers and Pentecostal insiders.[46]

The 1970s also brought additional insights on mission theology and strategy from among the Pentecostal ranks. One of them was David A. Womack's *Breaking The Stained-Glass Barrier* (Harper & Row, 1973). Melvin Hodges continued his publishing ministry, which had been encouraged in literary forums with Donald McGavran. In 1977 he wrote *A Theology of The Church and Its Mission: A Pentecostal Perspective* (Gospel Publishing House).

The Decade of the 1980s: Pentecostal Missiologists
Speak for Themselves

Vinson Synan believes that 1980 was 'a watershed year in the history of Christianity, and particularly of the charismatic movement'.[47] He says in that year David Barrett finished his basic research for the monumental *World Christian Encyclopedia* (Oxford Press, 1982) which was to appear in print two years later. Two significant developments were documented by Barrett and his research team. By 1980:

• The number of non-white Christians surpassed the number of white Christians for the first time in history.
• The Pentecostals surpassed all other groups of Protestants to become the largest Protestant family in the world.[48]

In 1982 Wagner observed, 'If the Lord tarries, Pentecostalism will undoubtedly go down in future history as the most significant religious phenomenon of the twentieth century.'[49]

The 1980s were significant in that Barrett's data began to draw even more attention to Pentecostal growth. In addition, in the 1980s there was a growing number of missiological 'self-definitions' from Pentecostals. Probably the most significant Pentecostal missiology to appear in recent years is *The Third Force in Missions* (1985) by Paul A. Pomerville.

In 1986 there were additional works by Pentecostal missions historians, missiologists, and missionaries including *This Gospel Shall Be Preached: A History and Theology of Assemblies of God Foreign Missions*, Volume 1 (Gospel Publishing House) by Gary B. McGee (Volume 2 was published in 1989), *Azusa Street and Beyond: Pentecostal Missions and Church Growth in The Twentieth Century* (Bridge Publishing) edited by L. Grant McClung Jr., and *The Apostolic Nature of The Church* by Delmer R. and Eleanor R. Guynes (Kuala Lumpur, Malaysia: Calvary Church Press). 1986 was also the year for two special issues (January and April) of the *International Review of Mission* on Pentecostals and charismatics, and the release of John Wimber's *Power Evangelism* (Harper & Row).[50]

The Decade of the 1990s: An Expanding Missiological Paradigm

Two of the early bridges from the 1980s to the 1990s and from *Pentecostal* to *Pentecostal/charismatic* missiology were provided by David Shibley's *A Force in the Earth: The Charismatic Renewal and World Evangelism* (Creation House, 1989) and by Edward K. Pousson's *Spreading the Flame: Charismatic Churches and Missions Today* (Zondervan, 1992). Certainly one of the most far-reaching contributions to date is a collection of essays edited by Murray W. Dempster, Byron D. Klaus, and Douglas Petersen, *Called and Empowered: Global Mission in Pentecostal Perspective* (Hendrickson, 1991). One of the most instructional emphases of *Called and Empowered* is upon the emergent Pentecostal interface with issues of culture, and the church's social responsibility. This holistic approach provides a final component for what I would see as an emerging paradigm for Pentecostal missiology into the twenty-first century.

Into the Twenty-first Century: From Trialogue to Quadralogue

Figure 3, 'A Pentecostal Missiological Paradigm' illustrates four basic components held in balance by the two indispensable components of exegesis and experience. It provides a dynamic tension which both revisits Azusa Street and the early church (Luke-Acts) and, at the

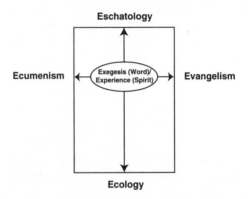

FIGURE 3. A Pentecostal Missiological Paradigm

same time, projects an engagement with the realities of the twenty-first century, already upon us.

The integrated balanced agenda presented in Figure 3 is urgently needed in light of what seem to be out-of-control global changes such as an ominous technological revolution, environmental decay, the arms race in a new ethnic tribalism, international indebtedness, urban deterioration, plagues and viruses, drugs, and the decline of the traditional family. These are reminiscent of the prophetic lines from 'The Second Coming', an insightful poem written in the early part of this century by William Butler Yeats:

> Turning and turning in the widening gyre
> The falcon cannot hear the falconer;
> Things fall apart; the centre cannot hold;
> Mere anarchy is loosed upon the world,
> The blood-dimmed tide is loosed, and everywhere
> The ceremony of innocence is drowned;
> The best lack all conviction, while the worst
> Are full of passionate intensity.
>
> Surely some revelation is at hand;
> Surely the Second Coming is at hand.
> The Second Coming! Hardly are those words out
> When a vast image of the Spiritus Mundi
> Troubles my sight: somewhere in sands of the desert,
> A shape with lion body and the head of a man,
> A gaze blank and pitiless as the sun,
> Is moving its slow thighs, while all about it

Reel shadows of the indignant desert birds.
The darkness drops again; but now I know
That twenty centuries of stony sleep
Were vexed to nightmare by a rocking cradle,
And what rough beast, its hour come round at last,
slouches toward Bethlehem to be born?[51]

If indeed we have moved into a global era in which 'things fall apart' and 'the centre cannot hold', then more than ever global Pentecostalism needs to be held together by a focused, integrated, and balanced missiology that remains true not only to the heritage of Azusa Street, but beyond that to the very foundation of biblical revelation and experience from all of Scripture and salvation history.

Pentecostal Missiology: An Integrated Balanced Globalization

Central and integral to the paradigm of Figure 3 is a continued focus in Pentecostalism upon the Word (*exegesis*) and the Spirit (*experience*). This internal soul of Pentecostalism then reaches *outward* in continual prioritized evangelism, and *across* in ecumenical cooperation with those who are the true Body of Christ within every Christian communion. It reaches *up* in a constant eschatological expectation of Christ's return while at the same time reaching *down* in prophetic social activism and change, and in the responsible care of earth's resources until the day of the new heavens and a new earth (Isaiah 65:17).

I suspect that with the reality of David Barrett's description of worldwide Pentecostalism, there is more integrated balance than what the casual critics of the Pentecostal/charismatic movement would suppose. The *explosion* of worldwide Pentecostal growth – now at more than 500 million, growing by 19 million per year and 54,000 new adherents every day – should not overshadow the intrinsic *ethos* of this global family:

- More urban than rural (active in 80 percent of the world's 3,300 largest cities)
- More female than male
- More Two-Thirds world (70 percent) than Western (30 percent)
- More impoverished (87 percent) than affluent (13 percent)
- More family oriented than individualistic
- On the average, younger than eighteen.[52]

If the global Pentecostal family can remain focused with an equal balance of all the biblical elements of the Pentecostal missiological paradigm of Figure 3, and not become exclusively entrenched in any of its separate elements, then I believe that God can use the Pentecostal movement as his instrument to reverse what seems to be the fulfilment of Yeats' dismal projection: 'Things fall apart; the centre cannot hold'.

It is the Christocentric confession of Pentecostal missiology that the 'centre' is Christ and that he holds all things together – that Jesus Christ is Saviour, Sanctifier, Spirit Baptizer, Healer, and Coming King. Peter's confession in the first Pentecostal sermon on the Day of Pentecost was that Jesus Christ was, 'Exalted to the right hand of God', and that 'he [Jesus Christ] has received from the Father the promised Holy Spirit and has poured out what you now see and hear' (Acts 2:33). What we now see and hear in the globalization of Pentecostalism is so eloquently stated by Croatian Pentecostal leader Peter Kuzmic:

> When we speak about the Great Commission, we speak about the *Divinely ordained* globalization because the gospel of Jesus Christ is a universally valid, globally relevant message of hope and salvation. We as Pentecostals know that through the power of the Holy Spirit this Word is not only preached but it is being confirmed by signs and wonders and by millions of changed lives who have found the true, internal liberation in Christ and who have been drinking at the well of the living water and who are the avant garde of the new creation.[53]

Should the Lord of Creation, Lord of the Universe, Lord of the Church, Lord of the Harvest delay his imminent return and allow us to extend his work into the next century, global Pentecostalism will be extended far beyond its borders in an interdependent partnership with all 'Great Commission' Christians. My prayer is that it will be characterized then as it has been for its first 100 years by the description of *The Apostolic Faith's* lead article in 1906:

> . . . the real revival is only started, as God has been working with His children mostly getting them through to Pentecost, and laying the foundation for a mighty wave of salvation among the unconverted.[54]

Our missiology will continue to define our meaning and if our focus remains consistent with the first Pentecostal missiological formulation of this century – 'Try to get people saved' – we will continue to be truly global and truly Pentecostal.

Notes

1   *The Apostolic Faith* (September 1906), p. 1.
2   Alan R. Tippett, *Introduction to Missiology* (Pasadena, CA: William Carey Library, 1987), p. xiii.
3   David J. Hesselgrave, *Today's Choices for Tomorrow's Mission: An Evangelical Perspective on Trends and Issues in Missions* (Grand Rapids, MI: Zondervan Publishing House, 1988), p. 118.
4   Ibid., p. 126.
5   Frederick Dale Bruner's 'The Doctrine and Experience of the Holy Spirit in the Pentecostal movement and Correspondingly in the New Testament' (Th.D. diss., University of Hamburg, 1963, 667 pages), was strongly critical of Pentecostals. It was later published as *A Theology of the Holy Spirit: The Pentecostal Experience and the New Testament Witness*, (Grand Rapids, MI: Wm. B. Eerdmans Publishing Co., 1970) and cut almost in half to 390 pages.
6   Gary B. McGee, 'Early Pentecostal Missionaries – They Went Everywhere Preaching the Gospel', in *Azusa Street and Beyond: Pentecostal Missions and Church Growth in The Twentieth Century*, ed. L. Grant McClung Jr. (South Plainfield, NJ: Bridge, 1986), p. 33.
7   Tippett, *Introduction to Missiology*, p. xiii.
8   David J. Bosch, *Transforming Mission: Paradigm Shifts in Theology of Mission* (Maryknoll, NY: Orbis, 1991), p. 498.
9   Ivan Illich, *Mission and Midwifery: Essays on Missionary Formation* (Gwelo, Gweru: Mambo Press, 1974), pp. 6–7.
10 Tippett, *Introduction to Missiology*, p. xiv.
11 Personally, notwithstanding the admitted subjectivity of my own denominational membership, I agree with those who can speak of 'A Century of Holy Spirit Revival 1896–1996' (the current centennial observance of Pentecostal blessing in the Church of God, Cleveland, Tennessee). Supposedly, those who mark the 'beginning' of the American Pentecostal movement on the basis of one person (Agnes Ozman) who spoke in tongues on January 1, 1901 in Topeka, Kansas, would also want to be historically honest in acknowledging a whole room full of people who spoke in tongues at the Shearer Schoolhouse Revival near Murphy, North Carolina, five years prior in 1896. I agree, however, with most observers who see the Azusa Street revival in Los Angeles, California (1906–1909) as the 'Jerusalem' (missiologically, the 'Antioch') of twentieth-century *global* Pentecostalism. For this reason, for my own study of the missions and church growth dynamics of Pentecostalism, I took the title, *Azusa Street and Beyond* (see footnote 6).
12 Wilbert R. Shenk, 'North American Evangelical Missions Since 1945', in *Earthen Vessels: American Evangelicals and Foreign Missions, 1880–1980*, ed. Joel A. Carpenter and Wilbert R. Shenk (Grand Rapids, MI: Wm. B. Eerdmans Publishing Co., 1990), p. 319.
13 Bosch, *Transforming Mission*, p. 491.
14 Ibid.
15 Henry P. Van Dusen, 'The Third Force in Christendom', *Life*, 9 June 1958.
16 Gary B. McGee, 'Missions, Overseas (North American)', in *Dictionary of Pentecostal and Charismatic Movements*, ed. Stanley M. Burgess and Gary B.

McGee (Grand Rapids, MI: Zondervan Publishing House, 1988), p. 612. (Hereafter *DPCM*.)

17   H. Vinson Synan, 'Seymour, William Joseph', in *DPCM*, p. 781.

18   The phrase, and the designated time period, are attributed to Kenneth Scott Latourette, *A History of Christianity*, vol. 2 (New York, NY: Harper & Row Publishers, 1953), pp. 1013–1035.

19   Edward K. Pousson, 'A 'Great Century' of Pentecostal/Charismatic Renewal and Missions', *PNEUMA: The Journal of The Society for Pentecostal Studies* 16 (Spring 1994), p. 81ff.

20   Quoted in Stanley H. Frodsham, *With Signs Following: The Story of the Latter-Day Pentecostal Revival* (Springfield, MO: Gospel Publishing House, 1946), p. 38.

21   Ibid., emphasis added.

22   Gary B. McGee, 'Flower, Joseph James Roswell (1888–1970) and Alice Reynolds (1890–)', in *DPCM*, p. 311.

23   J. Roswell Flower, Editorial *The Pentecost* (August 1908), p. 4; quoted in Gary B. McGee, *This Gospel Shall Be Preached*, vol. 1 (Springfield, MO: Gospel Publishing House, 1986), pp. 45–46.

24   Quoted in McClung, *Azusa Street and Beyond*, p. 8.

25   Donald Gee, *The Pentecostal Movement* (London, England: Elim, 1949), p. 30.

26   Ibid.

27   Vinson Synan, *The Spirit Said 'Grow'* (Monrovia, CA: MARC Publications, 1992), p. 39.

28   *The Apostolic Faith* 1, no. 11 (October–January 1907–08), p. 1.

29   *The Apostolic Faith* 1, no. 1 (September 1906), p. 1.

30   Paul A. Pomerville, 'Pentecostalism and Missions: Distortion or Correction?' (Ph.D. diss., Fuller Theological Seminary School of World Mission, 1982), 352; published as *The Third Force in Missions* (Peabody, MA: Hendrickson Publishers, 1986).

31   *The Apostolic Faith*, p. 2.

32   Donald Gee, Ibid.

33   John Thomas Nichol, *Pentecostalism* (New York, NY: Harper & Row Publishers, 1966), p. 55.

34   McGee, 'Missions, Overseas (North American)', p. 617.

35   Ibid.

36   Ibid., p. 181.

37   J. Merle Davis, *How The Church Grows in Brazil* (New York, NY: World Missionary Council, 1943), p. 68.

38   William R. Read, *New Patterns of Church Growth in Brazil* (Grand Rapids, MI: Wm. B. Eerdmans Publishing Co., 1965), p. 123.

39   Donald A. McGavran, *Church Growth in Mexico*.

40   Quoted in H. W. Greenway, ed., *World Pentecostal Conference – 1952* (London: The British Pentecostal Fellowship, 1952), p. 50.

41   McGee, 'Hodges, Melvin Lyle (1909–88)', in *DPCM*, p. 404.

42   McGee, 'Missions, Overseas (North American)', p. 621.

43   Van Dusen, 'Third Force'.

44   Donald A. McGavran, James H. Montgomery, and C. Peter Wagner, *Church Growth Bulletin*, 3 (Santa Clara, CA: Global Church Growth, 1982), p. 97.

45 A complete overview of the relationship between 'Pentecostals and the Church Growth Movement' is found in Part Four of my *Azusa Street and Beyond* (pp. 109–118) and as 'From Bridges (McGavran 1955) to Waves (Wagner 1983)' in PNEUMA: *The Journal of the Society for Pentecostal Studies* 7, (Spring 1985), pp. 5–18.

46 Ibid.

47 Synan, *The Spirit Said 'Grow'*, p. 5.

48 Ibid.

49 McClung, *Azusa Street*, p. 114.

50 For a more extensive list of publications through the 1980s and early 1990s see the following by L. Grant McClung Jr.: 'Mission in The 1990s' *International Bulletin of Missionary Research* 14, no. 4 (October 1990), pp. 152–157; 'The Pentecostal/Charismatic Contribution To World Evangelization', in *Mission in the 1990s*, ed. Gerald H. Anderson, James M. Phillips, Robert T. Coote (Grand Rapids, MI: Wm. B. Eerdmans Publishing Co., 1991); 'Forecasting The Future of Pentecostal/Charismatic Church Growth', *Global Church Growth* (October–December 1991): pp. 4–6; 'Pentecostal/Charismatic Perspectives on a Missiology for the Twenty-First Century', PNEUMA: *The Journal of the Society for Pentecostal Studies* 16 (Spring 1994), pp. 11–21; and 'Interdependence in Global Pentecostalism', *World Pentecost* 28 (Spring 1991), pp. 18–20.

51 Quoted in Laurent A. Parks Daloz, 'Slouching Toward Bethlehem', *Journal of Adult Training* 3, no. 2, (Spring 1990), p. 17.

52 David B. Barrett, 'The Twentieth-Century Pentecostal/Charismatic Renewal in The Holy Spirit, With Its Goal of World Evangelization', *International Bulletin of Missionary Research* 12, no. 3 (1988), pp. 119–129.

53 Peter Kuzmic, 'Globalism and The Post-Communist World', paper presented at the ICI World Missions Congress, October 1992.

54 *The Apostolic Faith*, p. 1.

Chapter Three

Biblical Studies in the Pentecostal Tradition: Yesterday, Today, and Tomorrow

Wonsuk Ma

In its relatively short history, Pentecostalism, has undergone a change in emphases. The first scholarly interest among Pentecostals tracked this change by treating historical questions. Early thinkers pondered questions such as the place and significance of the Pentecostal move-ment in the larger social and Christian history.[1] There is little doubt that historians also had the intention to preserve the historical informa-tion about the movement. Further, historical study had other crucial aims which were self-reflecting and apologetic. The apologetic nature of these historical inquiries was reflected in its quest to probe the early evidences of the Spirit phenomena.[2] This investigation continues and will continue for at least four reasons. 1) There is still a wealth of material in church history that Pentecostal scholars can utilize to illus-trate that the Holy Spirit has been working throughout all of the church's existence. 2) Modern Pentecostal history is replete with events and documents that merit analysis.[3] As the movement develops, more 'specialized' histories will be written.[4] 3) As Pentecostalism matures there will be a new set of historical questions coming into prominence.[5] 4) Pentecostal scholars from the Two Thirds World will write their Pentecostal histories from their own unique cultural, social, and historical contexts.[6] This interest in historical investigation of Pentecostalism continues with new models of the interpretation of the movement.[7]

In addition to these Pentecostal historians, a second group of scholars surfaced who diligently scrutinize the scripture. Since this is the topic of my chapter, detailed observation is reserved for below. The third interest of study may be provided by an emerging cadre of Two Thirds World scholars who theologize upon their own experiences within their respective contents. This task can be accomplished by the incorporation of Pentecostal theology into standard systematic theological categories or by context-sensitive local theologies. For the former category, several works have been available for some time.[8] For the latter category, Pentecostal scholars in the Two Thirds World should be encouraged to interpret their message within a given specific context.[9] Such reflection will provide a positive and relevant Pentecostal theology appropriate to immediate local settings. For example, the more naturalistic approach and orientation of Two-Thirds World people, especially these from animistic background, are uniquely equipped to understand the Supernatural world enunciated in Scripture within their social context.[10] Prospective theologians from Asia, Africa, and Latin America have enrolled in higher educational institutions and promise to produce theological insights which will enrich the Pentecostal tradition.[11]

This chapter, as the title suggests, examines interpretive approaches to Pentecostal biblical studies in three chronological periods: past, present and the future. The first era spans from the beginning of the movement to the emergence of critical scholarly works among Pentecostals in the late 1970s. The second overlaps, beginning with the early 1970s and continues to the present point. The third era will be the changing future environment in which the task of Pentecostal biblical scholarship will encounter fresh challenges.[12]

THE FIRST ERA: PENTECOSTAL BIBLICAL STUDIES THROUGH THE LATE 1970S

The Pentecostal movement has long treasured Scripture. These 'people of the Book' never questioned the authority of the written word.[13] In fact, the very beginning of the movement was justified by an appeal to diligent study of the Bible. Hence, the Pentecostals in a sense follow the Reformist's cry, *Sola Scriptura*. Their literalistic and simplistic understanding of the Scripture helped early Pentecostals make sense of their movement. However, Pentecostals in this early stage seldom engaged in serious and reflective biblical study. The pattern of Bible reading among Pentecostals in the past can be characterized in several ways.

LITERALISTIC APPROACH

The very birth of the movement was connected to a bold literalistic reading of Acts 2. Charles F. Parham, called by some the originator of the Pentecostal 'pragmatic' hermeneutic,[14] argued that the experience of Spirit baptism should be identical with what is found in Acts 2.[15] When Parham examined the findings of his students on the meaning of the Book of Acts, they unanimously agreed '. . . that the indisputable proof on each occasion (of the Spirit baptism) (is) that they spoke with other tongues'.[16] The subsequent outpouring of the Spirit, particularly at Azusa Street in Los Angeles, provided an unshakable endorsement of this approach.[17]

A literalistic reading of Scripture could also be a counter-movement against the rising influence of biblical criticism. As with other Fundamentalist groups, the Pentecostals felt responsible to 'guard' the sanctity of Scripture.[18] This protective attitude was often expressed by the prevailing anti-intellectualism among Pentecostals. Many suspected intellectualism to be an enemy of spirituality.

Even though critical approaches produced suspicion, a simple literalist reading caused great interest in Bible study especially among lay people. The Bible was emancipated from the exclusive claim of the clergy. The leader did not have to be a 'professional' Bible expert. Any 'enlightened' lay person could lead a study session. The laity-led Bible study which emerged during this early period continues even today. For instance, in Korea, the lay leaders, often women, lead the cell group Bible studies that have fuelled the unprecedented growth of Yoido Full Gospel Church.[19]

This literalistic approach had at least two effects in the ensuing Pentecostal movement. First, the centrality of Scripture was always stressed. The popular expression of the 'biblical pattern' reflected this focus. Secondly, the gap between clergy and laity was narrowed and prepared a way for the active participation of the lay people in ministry. Even terminology was altered by the closing of this gap. 'Brother' and 'sister' were commonly used instead of 'reverend' or 'minister'.

NON-CRITICAL DEVOTIONAL READING

Much study of the Bible by early Pentecostals existed in the form of sermons, Sunday school materials, and devotional readings. When issues arose such as the initial evidence of tongues, and the Oneness of God, treatments were more affirmative and declarative than reflective of other critical options.[20]

Pentecostals focused on the meaning of Scripture for the present. The Bible was read existentially where God's immanence was greatly emphasized. The word of God initially given to the ancient community of faith was appropriated just as if it was given to present-day Christians.[21] The Bible was read as a record of God's interaction with, and revelation to, his people.[22] Pentecostals readily accepted not only the validity of the supernatural events described in the Bible, but also God's ability to do similar miracles in their midst.

STRESS ON LUKE-ACTS NARRATIVES

The Book of Acts was a favourite book for Pentecostals.[23] Through Bible studies, sermons, and devotional works, the early Pentecostals recognized the importance of the Lukan narratives of Acts for providing not only a strong motivation to seek the empowerment of the Spirit, but also supplied a biblical pattern for contemporary believers.

Without probing the question of their doctrinal utility, early Pentecostals used narratives for their theological foundations. The validity of the narrative material for theological work was 'intuitively assumed rather than intelligently argued'.[24] Similarly, the Old Testament narratives from the ancient world were applied directly to the contemporary context.

APOLOGETIC USE OF SCRIPTURE

The Pentecostal movement has received much attention from both the Christian community and the secular world. The initial reaction of 'the outsider' was similar to the response of the crowd in Acts 2, 'What meaneth this?' Such responses prompted Pentecostals to develop a biblically-based apologetic. However, because the movement consisted of people from diverse backgrounds, their apologetics varied.

McGee demonstrates that some 'serious attempts' at developing a biblical apologetic for Pentecost appeared as early as the 1930s (Donald Gee, *Pentecost* {1932}).[25] He lists substantial Pentecostal works expounding the biblical foundations for the Pentecostal experience, especially the baptism of the Holy Spirit with speaking in tongues as its initial evidence. They include: Paul H. Walker, *the Baptism with the Holy Ghost and the Evidence* (ca. 1935); Robert Chandler Dalton, *Tongues Like as Fire* (1945); Carl Brumback, *What Meaneth This* (1947); Ralph M. Riggs, *The Spirit Himself* (1949); Harold Horton, *The Spirit Baptism in the Holy Spirit* (1956); Milton A. Tomlinson, *Basic Bible Beliefs* (ca. 1961); L. Thomas Holdcroft, *The Holy Spirit* (1962); William G. MacDonald, *Glossolalia in the New Testament* (1966), Wade H. Horton, ed., *The Glossolalia Phenomenon* (1966); Howard M. Ervin, *These Are Not Drunken, As Ye Suppose* (1988) and its 1987 revision with a new title, *Spirit Baptism: A Biblical Investigation*); Anthony D. Palma, *The Spirit – God in Action* (1974); Stanley M. Horton, *What the Bible Says About the Holy Spirit* (1976).[26] This first generation of biblists produced timely, although varied, pieces to clarify and strengthen the Pentecostal apologetic tradition.

ESCHATOLOGICAL/MISSION ORIENTATION

The earliest Pentecostals chronicled the eschatological significance of the Spirit's outpouring. The Spirit baptism was viewed as empowerment for the last day before Jesus' immanent return. Parham and '...Pentecostals before 1908' believed that tongues were existing known languages to be used for missionary purposes.[27] Reflecting this notion of missionary tongues, Parham wrote in his publication the *Apostolic Faith*:

> Glassy [sic!] now in Jerusalem, received the African dialect in one night. . . . She received the gift while in the Spirit in 1885, but could read and write, translate and sing the language while out of the trance or in a normal condition, and can until now.[28]

Although Parham's account of this event was later called into question and the earlier identification of tongues with xenolalia is no longer tenable, the missiological significance of tongues was never lost.

The relationship between missions and tongues is aptly demonstrated in *The Missionary Manual* (1931) of the Foreign Mission Department of the Assemblies of God. In this document, the Pentecostal Movement itself was identified as a mission movement. It identifies the period prior to the outpouring of the Spirit as the 'Dark Age' when the work of the Spirit was rejected and 'the Lord's missionary movement halted'.[29] It was only by the outpouring of the Spirit and the acceptance of it by Pentecostals that 'The Lord's Pentecostal missionary movement was resumed'.[30] The Pentecostal mission movement and popular writings frequently published in denominational publications such as the Pentecostal Evangel reflect this prevailing assumption. Often biblical references are quoted to reaffirm the notion.

THE SECOND ERA: THE EARLY 1970S TO THE PRESENT

Whether in the pulpit or the pew, popular readings of the Bible continued to prevail within Pentecostalism. However, in the late 1970s and early 1980s, there was a clear mark which signaled the appearance of a newly trained breed of Pentecostal scholars. Their works have appeared in a number of forums,[31] including journals, books, theses and dissertations.

PENTECOSTAL BIBLICAL STUDIES

Journals

The immense interest in printed material is almost a Pentecostal tradition. Publishing was an effective means of disseminating new doctrinal teachings. Understandably, most early periodicals emphasized proclamation and often lacked serious critical argument.[32]

Paraclete was published by the Assemblies of God beginning in 1967 for a more 'sophisticated' readership. The journal enjoyed longevity through the 1970s and 1980s until its demise in 1993, and cultivated wide acceptance. In fact, for some time, *Paraclete* was only an 'academic periodical' representing Pentecostal scholarship. Even though the majority of the contributions in biblical studies seldom moved beyond a devotional level, *Paraclete* regularly published many expository essays by Pentecostal scholars and ministers.

Another journal, *Agora*, which first appeared in 1977, tackled contemporary issues. Contributors and editors represented a select group of Pentecostal scholars. *Agora*'s offerings openly addressed issues questioning various aspects of denominational life which *Paraclete*, because of its denominational editorship, would not have published. However, in its five years existence (1977–1981) with at least sixteen issues, biblical study was not consistently emphasized. Considering the fine biblical scholars among the editors and contributors, articles selected for publication most probably reflected the prophetic purpose of the magazine.

The forum for Pentecostal scholarship changed drastically with the organization of the Society for Pentecostal Studies (SPS) in 1970, and the subsequent publication of its journal, *PNEUMA*. From its inaugural issue in 1979, substantial biblical studies regularly appeared. More notably, in the first two years five biblical studies were published out of a total of seventeen articles. Between 1986 and 1994, however, no single biblical study was included out of a total of eighty-six articles. There were active discussions during these years on hermeneutics, often viewed as part of biblical studies. Other discussions were centred around history and ecumenical issues.[33] Recent changes in the journal since 1992 seem to reflect the editorial direction of a new editor assuming the job. Lately, each issue has dealt with a more defined topic or two, such as Pentecostal Missiology or Pentecostal Hermeneutics. In addition, one should consider that papers presented in SPS annual meetings include many biblical studies, not all of which are subsequently published in *PNEUMA*. The role of SPS, its journal, and *SPS Newsletters* can hardly be ignored.

The emergence of other interdenominational Pentecostal/charismatic learned journals reflected the rapidly growing volume of scholarly work.

In 1977, *Spirit: A Journal of Issues Incident to Black Pentecostalism*, appeared. *Renewal Theology*, a collaborate effort among Orthodox, Catholic and Baptist Charismatic/Renewal groups, was published in Australia. The European Pentecostal/charismatic community initiated two learned societies. The European Pentecostal & Charismatic Research Association (EPCRA) holds occasional conferences and presented papers are published in its journal, *European Pentecostal Theological Association Bulletin (EPTAB)* as well as in Peter Lang series. The European Pentecostal Theological Association (EPTA) also hosts annual conferences. The Association publishes its journal, *EPTA Bulletin*. An increasing number of Pentecostal-related articles written by Pentecostal/charismatic scholars appear in a variety of academic journals. Some of these journals include the *Journal of Empirical Theology, International Bulletin of Missionary Research*,

One World, Ecumenical Review, Ecumenical Trends, Evangelical Review of Theology, Journal of Contemporary Religion, Evangelical Missions Quarterly, Missiology, International Journal of Frontier Missions, Journal of Hispanic/Latin Theology. Additionally, regional periodicals are emerging and conferences are being held on a regular basis outside North America and Europe.[34]

The recently inaugurated *Journal of Pentecostal Theology* (1992) seems to endeavour to fill the vacuum , especially in the areas of theological and biblical reflections, which editors perceived that *PNUEMA* did not adequately address. It is too early to judge its direction, especially in the area of biblical studies. So far, much emphasis has been given to the disciples of theology, biblical studies,[35] and hermeneutics.

A more technologically advanced electronic journal, *Cyberjournal for Pentecostal-Charismatic Research*, has been launched by a joint effort between Harold Hunter and Regent University Divinity School.[36] The Regent University web site is hot linked to the index of articles published in *PNUEMA*: *The Journal of the Society for Pentecostal Studies*, and in *The Journal of Pentecostal Theology.*

In the 1980s, the publications of biblical studies by Pentecostals proliferated. Some of these works included Harold D. Hunter, *Spirit Baptism: A Pentecostal Alternative* (University Press of America, 1983); David Fleming, *Spiritual Exercises: A Literal Translation and Contemporary Reading* (St. Louis: Institute of Jesuit Sources, St. Louis University, 1975). The emergence of the Hendrickson Publishers further increased Pentecostal/charismatic scholarly works in the published forms.[37] In 1984, Roger Stronstad's book, *The Charismatic Theology of St. Luke* and Howard M. Ervin's, *Conversion-Initiation and the Baptism in the Holy Spirit* appeared, followed by a collection of essays, Paul Elbert, ed., *Essays on Apostolic Themes: Studies in Honor of Howard M. Ervin* (1985). More monographs and *Festschriften* followed: Siegfried Schatzmann's *A Pauline theology of Charismata* (Hendrickson, 1987); Gordon D. Fee, *The First Epistle to the Corinthians* (Eerdmans, 1987); Gary M. Burge, *The Anointed Community: The Holy Spirit in the Johannine Tradition* (Eerdmans, 1987); *Faces of Renewal: Studies in Honor of Stanley M. Horton Presented on his 70th Birthday* (Hendrickson, 1988); Roger Stronstad and Laurance M. van Kleek, *The Holy Spirit in the Scripture and the Church: Essays Presented to Leslie Thomas Holdcroft on His 65th Birthday* (Western Pentecostal Bible College, 1988). Also informative are articles contained in *Dictionary of Pentecostal and*

Charismatic Movement, edited by S. M. Burgess, G. B. McGee, and P. H. Alexander (Zondervan, 1988). In addition to these works, important bibliographical works should be mentioned by Watson E. Mills: *Speaking in Tongues: A Guide to Research on Glossolalia* (Eerdmans, 1986) as well as his two earlier works, *Glossolalia: A Bibliography* (Edwin Mellen, 1985) and *A Theological/Exegetical Approach to Glossolalia* (University Press of America, 1985).

In the 1990s, more biblical studies were published. Some of them are: James B. Shelton, *Mighty in Word and Deed: The Role of the Holy Spirit in Luke-Acts* (Hendrickson, 1991); David Lim, *Spiritual Gifts: A Fresh Look* (Springfield: Gospel Publishing House, 1991); Robert P. Menzies, *The Development of Early Christian Pneumatology* (Sheffield: Sheffield Academic Press, 1991); *Festschrift in Honor of Dr. Walter J. Hollenweger: Pentecost, Mission and Ecumenism*, edited by Jan A. B. Jongeneel (Frankfurt: Peter Lang, 1992); Gordon D. Fee, *God's Empowering Presence: The Holy Spirit in the Letters of Paul* (Hendrickson, 1994); Wilf Hildebrandt, *An Old Testament Theology of the Spirit of God* (Hendrickson, 1995). JPT Supplement Series of Sheffield Academic Press holds the promise of a place to find Pentecostal theological and biblical studies. Already several biblical studies have appeared: Robert P. Menzies, *Empowered for Witness: The Spirit in Luke-Acts* (a revised edition of his earlier work from the same publisher); Max Turner, *Power from on High: The Spirit of Prophecy in Luke-Acts* (1995). Its 1996 Spring catalogue includes John Christopher Thomas, *Footwashing in John 13 and the Johannine Community*. Also collected essays proved to be a wealthy resource for biblical studies: Gary B. McGee, ed., *Initial Evidence: Historical and Biblical Perspectives on the Pentecostal Doctrine of Spirit Baptism* (Hendrickson, 1991). Gordon D. Fee, *Issues in New Testament Hermeneutics* (Hendrickson, 1991). Mark W. Wilson, ed. *Spirit and Renewal: Essays in Honor of J. Rodman Williams* (Sheffield, 1994); Harold D. Hunter and Peter D. Hocken, eds., *All Together in One Place: Theological Papers from the Brighton Conference on World Evangelization* (Sheffield, 1995). Non-Western publishers have also offered impressive possibilities. APTS Press, a publication division of Asia Pacific Theological Seminary in the Philippines, produced Roger Stronstad, *Spirit, Scripture and Theology: A Pentecostal Perspective* (Baguio, Philippines, 1995). More publications are expected from Africa, Latin America and Asia.

Theses and Dissertations

Theses and dissertations are an often untapped area of rich studies. Many significant works in the area of biblical studies have been produced, and some have appeared in published form. *SPS Newsletter* has taken the considered effort to include a list of updated dissertation/theses titles. Dissertations on biblical studies by Pentecostal scholars include Harold D. Hunter, 'Spirit-baptism: Evaluated Biblically, Historically, systematically' (Ph.D., Fuller Theological Seminary, 1979); Winfred Scott Hall, II, 'Paul As a Christian Prophet in His Interpretation of the Old Testament in Romans 9–11' (Ph.D., Lutheran Seminary, Chicago, 1982); William Edwin Richardson, 'Liturgical Order and Glossolalia: Corinthians 14:26–33a and Its Implications' (Ph.D., Andrew University, 1982); Robert P. Menzies, 'The Development of Early Christian Pneumatology with Special Reference to Luke-Acts' (Ph.D., University of Aberdeen, 1990); Deborah Menken Gill, 'The Female Prophets: Gender and Leadership in the Biblical Tradition' (Ph.D., Fuller Theological Seminary, 1991). Though the number of biblical studies dissertation is somewhat limited, this fertile, and yet hard-to-reach area should be actively explored.

CHARACTERISTICS

Unquestionably Pentecostal biblical scholarship has produced impressive works. Scholars have also shown academic maturity in engaging in scholarly dialogues with other Evangelical thinkers. Although a decade or so is rather a short period for any balanced evaluation, nonetheless, Pentecostal scholarship seems to display the following three.

Employment of Critical Scholarship

It is a pleasant surprise that the rise of Pentecostal critical scholarship and the employment of critical methods have not raised significant suspicion among ecclesial leadership. The attitude of Pentecostal leadership is a drastic contrast to what Evangelical critical scholars have experienced in gaining the acceptance of their use of critical methods by Evangelical church leadership. Cautious acceptance by Pentecostal ecclesiastical leadership does not imply that church leaders readily accept critical methods nor critical works. A certain suspicion of higher education is still prevalent. However, when critical works initially appeared, leaders and churches were more concerned about the impact on the vitality of the church and its mission than they were about the critical methodology they employed.[38]

Some have associated the employment of critical tools of scholarship with the 'evangelicalization' of Pentecostal biblical scholarship.[39] Pentecostal scholars, like their evangelical cousins, employed critical methods with a commitment to the authority of Scripture. Pentecostal biblical exegete Timothy Cargal, however, warns that this methodological 'evangelicalization' may result in the domestication of the Pentecostal message, ultimately losing its own uniqueness. Although Cargal's concern may be genuine, the domestication of the Pentecostal message is not contingent upon the utilization of the critical tool one uses. After all, the use of critical methods in and of itself will not determine the meaning and significance of the biblical text. The theological presuppositions of the exegete is often a determining factor in the process of biblical interpretation. Further, pre-critical reading of the biblical text by Pentecostals, though invaluable for personal edification, does not set an ideal paradigm for scholarly biblical reflection. The Pentecostal tradition of participatory reading of Scripture does not have to be entirely reader-oriented. A properly guided historico-literary reading will not only serve as guidance but will also set parameters for 'affective' reading.[40] Pentecostal critical biblical scholarship should be credited with providing an informed and reflective theology in order to serve the church in the mutual cultivation of our rich Pentecostal tradition.[41]

Use of Narratives

Pentecostal use of biblical narratives is normative practice. This has often been criticized both from within[42] and from without.[43] The majority of Pentecostal beliefs and doctrines have their basis in the historical narratives of the Book of Acts. These doctrines include Spirit baptism, subsequence issues, and speaking in tongues as initial evidence. Pentecostal biblical scholars, such as Robert Menzies, Roger Stronstad, and others have convincingly emphasized the legitimacy of Luke-Acts for its Pentecostal theological basis. Though the use of narrative for constructive theological work and doctrinal formulation has been criticized from both within and without, narratives are still viewed by Pentecostals, not only as an effective, but also an authentic means of communicating traditions and truth.

MISSIONAL FOCUS

Due to the prevailing missional focus of the Pentecostal experience, an emphasis on missions has influenced, and will continue to influence, biblical studies done by Pentecostals. Naturally, the Book of Acts has been a favourite object of study. This intrinsic missional interest in a sense predetermines what kind of biblical material will be studied.

Biblical studies, reflecting a missional orientation, have grown increasingly more sophisticated. This advancement in Pentecostal scholarship is well demonstrated by several recent publications. For example, the various contributions found in *Called and Empowered: Global Mission in Pentecostal Perspective*, edited by Murray W. Dempster, Byron D. Klaus and Douglas Petersen (Hendrickson Publishers, 1991); Especially relevant to biblical studies in this volume is the chapter by Gordon D. Fee, 'The Kingdom of God and the Church's Global Mission'. Another example is the superb articles gathered by guest editor Byron Klaus in *PNEUMA* 16 (Fall 1994) which focused on Pentecostal Missiology.

THE THIRD ERA: INTO THE TWENTY-FIRST CENTURY

Significant changes in the religious environment and the social context will influence the reading of Scripture in the coming years. These changes will greatly impact hermeneutics and ultimately the formation of theology. Negotiating these changes positively represents a great challenge to the future of Pentecostalism.

'Postmodernism' has already started to impact the biblical and theological worlds. Several studies on 'Postmodernism' have been already published in Pentecostal journals, and a hot debate about its validity and significance is currently underway.[44] Postmodernism is particularly appealing to Pentecostals because it provides legitimacy for their intuitive reading of Scripture. The immediacy of God's word in Scripture has been a long held Pentecostal value, even before the term 'Postmodernism' came into popular usage.[45] Future Pentecostal biblists need to nurture this unique dimension of their heritage without falling into the trap of open-ended subjectivity.

The great interest in spirituality that paradoxically exists in a 'post-modern' world opens a vast opportunity to Pentecostals. Given their revivalist identities, Pentecostals believed they had a call to bring a spiritual dimension to the institutionalized church world.[46]

At the same time, the spiritual challenge also exists within the Pentecostal movement itself. Developing a spirituality rooted in God's word found in Scripture and nurtured by the Holy Spirit is greatly needed if Pentecostals are going to successfully negotiate effective ministry in a Post-modern world. Such biblically-based spirituality will empower Pentecostals to address the issues of the institution-alization of Pentecostalism,[47] the engagement of Pentecostal social concern,[48] the inclusion of women in Pentecostal ministry,[49] the con-tinued vibrancy of the church's global mission,[50] the necessity of racial reconciliation,[51] and the renewal of the vision held by early Pen-tecostal pioneers for a healthy ecumenical relationship with other Christians.[52]

May the Pentecostal movement prove to the world that it is more than a one-time revival event. For a healthy existence and continued development, Pentecostal biblical scholarship can make fundamental contributions by providing solid biblical foundations which preserve and revitalize Pentecostal uniqueness.[53]

Notes

1 Cecil M. Robeck Jr.'s informative survey of 'the most important literature' in recent decades (1961–1987) consists of historical studies with the highest number and doctrinal issues, 'The Decade (1973–82) in Pentecostal-Charismatic Literature: A Bibliographic Essay', *Theology, News, and Notes* (March 1983, Fuller Theological Seminary), pp. 24–29, 34. Early historical works include Klaude Kendrick, *The Promise Fulfilled: A History of the Mod-ern Pentecostal Movement* (Springfield, MO: Gospel Publishing House, 1961) and William W. Menzies, *Anointed to Serve: The Story of the Assemblies of God* (Springfield, MO: Gospel Publishing House, 1971).

2 Examples include the articles in Cecil M. Robeck Jr., ed., *Charismatic Experi-ences in History* (Peabody, MA: Hendrickson Publishers, 1985) and Robeck, *Prophecy in Carthage: Perpetua, Tertullian, and Cyprian* (Cleveland, OH: Pilgrim Press, 1992).

3 For instance, Vinson Synan, *The Holiness-Pentecostal Movement in the United States* (Grand Rapids, MI: Wm. B. Eerdmans Publishing Co., 1971) and James R. Goff Jr., *Fields While Unto Harvest: Charles F. Parham and the Missionary Origins of Pentecostalism* (Fayetteville, ARK: University of Arkansas Press, 1988).

4 E.g., Gary B. McGee, *This Gospel Shall Be Preached: A History and Theology of Assemblies of God Foreign Missions*, 2 vols. (Springfield, MO: Gospel Pub-lishing House, 1986–1989).

5 For instance, Pentecostal historians will be prompted to view the Toronto Blessings in light of larger Christian and smaller Pentecostal history.

6 For instance, Fred G. Abeysekera, *The History of the Assemblies of God in Sin-gapore, 1928–1992* (Singapore: Abundant Press, 1992); José N. Saracco, 'Ar-gentine Pentecostalism: Its History and Theology' (Ph.D. diss., University of Birmingham, 1989); and Elias Dantas Filho, 'O Movimento Pentecostal

Brasilleiro: Su Historia e Influencia Sobre las Denominacoes Tradicionais no Brasil' (MA thesis, Fuller Theological Seminary, 1988).

7   For example, Edith W. Blumhofer, *Restoring the Faith: The Assemblies of God, Pentecostalism, and American Culture* (Urbana, IL: University of Illinois Press, 1993).

8   Early works include Ernest S. Williams, *Systematic Theology*, 3 vols. (Springfield, MO: Gospel Publishing House, 1953) and later, J. Rodman Williams, *Renewal Theology*, 3 vols. (Grand Rapids, MI: Zondervan Publishing House, 1988–1992).

9   For example, see Simon Chan's book *Spiritual Theology* (Downers Grove, IL: Intervarsity Press, 1998) on Asian spirituality from the perspective of a Pentecostal believer.

10 Julie Ma, 'A Comparison of Two Worldviews: Kankana-ey and Pentecostal', in *Pentecostalism in Context: Essays Presented to William W. Menzies*, ed. Wonsuk Ma and Robert P. Menzies (Sheffield: Sheffield Academic Press, forthcoming).

11 In the forthcoming *Pentecostalism in Context: Essays Presented to William W. Menzies*, there are six Asian contributors along with ten from the Western world. It is also true that in the forthcoming Pentecostal commentary series from Sheffield Academic Press, Two Thirds World Pentecostal scholars are participating.

12 My investigation is based primarily on published English works by Pentecostals in the area of biblical studies, especially in Pentecostal-related topics, although attention will be given to scholarly works such as dissertations. I have gathered much of this information from the *SPS Newsletter*, first edited by Russell P. Spittler and subsequently by Peter Hocken. Publications in Pentecostal-related or interested topics by non-Pentecostal scholars are not included.

13 Cited in L. G. McClung Jr., 'Missiology', in *Dictionary of Pentecostal and Charismatic Movements*, ed. Stanley M. Burgess and Gary B. McGee (Grand Rapids, MI: Zondervan Publishing House, 1988), p. 607. Hereafter *DPCM*.

14 For example, Roger Stonstad, *Spirit, Scripture and Theology* (Baguio, Philippines: APTS Press, 1995), p. 11.

15 Mrs. Charles F. Parham, *The Life of Charles F. Parham Founder of the Apostolic Faith Movement* (Joplin, MO: Hunter Printing, 1930), p. 52.

16 Ibid.

17 For Parham's hermeneutics, see, James R. Goff Jr., 'Initial Tongues in the Theology of Charles Fox Parham', in *Initial Evidence: Historical and Biblical Perspectives on the Pentecostal Doctrine of Spirit Baptism*, ed. Gary B. McGee (Peabody, MA: Hendrickson Publishers, 1991), pp. 57–71. Hereafter *Initial Evidence*.

18 Gerald T. Sheppard, however, argues that the 1970 position paper on the authority of the Scripture is motivated by political reasons rather than doctrinal interests. See his 'Word and Spirit: Scripture in the Pentecostal Tradition, Part 1', *Agora* 1, no. 3 (Winter 1978), pp. 4–5, 17–22.

19 Paul Y. Cho, *Successful Home Cell Groups* (Plainfield, NJ: Logos Books International, 1981), pp. 13–20, 23–29.

20 Myer Pearlman, *Knowing the Doctrine of the Bible* (Springfield, MO: Gospel Publishing House, 1937). Gerald T. Sheppard also observes that even the

doctrinal use of the Scripture among the Pentecostals was a pre-critical 'literal' reading of the Bible. See his 'Word and Spirit: Scripture in the Pentecostal Tradition, Part Two', *Agora* 2, no. 1 (Summer 1978), p. 14.

21   For instance, Stanley M. Horton, ' "I Will Put My Spirit Within You" ', *Paraclete* 11, No. 2 (Fall 1977), 8 reflects this notion by beginning with the questions, 'Are the prophecies of Israel's restoration being fulfilled? Can *we* expect God to put a new heart and spirit within the *people of modern Israel*?' (Emphases mine).

22   Sheppard, 'Word and Spirit, Part Two' pp. 17–18 observes that the Pentecostal acceptance of the relevance of Scripture for modern Christians is different from that of the fundamentalists and modernists.

23   Parham, *Charles F. Parham*, p. 52 argues that the contemporary experience 'should tally exactly with the Bible . . . with the 2nd Chapter of Acts.'

24   William W. Menzies, conversation with the author, 5 April 1996, Seoul, Korea.

25   Gary B. McGee, 'Popular Expositions of Initial Evidence in Pentecostalism', in *Initial Evidence*, p. 119.

26   Ibid., pp. 119–120.

27   Goff, 'Initial Tongues', 58.

28   Ibid., 64, quoting *Apostolic Faith* 3 (May 1899), p. 5.

29   Quoted in McGee, 'Popular Expositions', pp. 120–122.

30   Ibid.

31   An excellent publication informing readers of recent scholarly works published is the *SPS Newsletter*. From its inaugural issue, the *Newsletter* has always allocated generous space and attention to recently published works either by Pentecostals, charismatics, or non-Pentecostals that deal with topics relevant to Pentecostalism. Presently the editor is D. William Faupel. Another useful newsletter comes from Harold Hunter. His *Pentecostal/Charismatic Theological Inquiry International (PCTII) Newsletter* includes substantial written works on Pentecostal/charismatic topics. The first five issues were printed, but subsequent issues will be available through his Hunter's website (http://members.gmi.com/archives/pctii.htm). This newsletter tries to inform its readers of conferences, seminars, and the like germaine to Pentecostals.

32   In addition to Warner, 'Publications' in *DPCM*, see Michael Taylor, ' 'Publish and Be Blessed': A Study of the Influence of Periodicals in Early Pentecostalism' (Ph.D. diss., Kings College, 1994).

33   By my count, the ratio of biblical studies articles to the total number of articles published is as follows: 3:9 in 1979; 3:8 in 1980; 1:9 in 81; 2:8 in 82; 1:8 in 83; 0:3 in 84; 3:9 in 85; 0:7 in 86; 0:9 in 87; 0:7 in 88; 4:8 in 89; 0:6 in 90; 0:6 in 91; 0:11 in 92; 0:8 in 93; 0:16 in 94; and 0:9 in 95.

34   In the *PCTII Newsletter*, editor Harold Hunter lists numerous conferences and periodicals initiated by Pentecostal/charismatic groups. In Asia, according to him, there are three such groups: the Pentecostal Society for Theological Studies (India), the Asia Pacific Theological Association (Philippines) and the Asia Charismatic Theological Association (Sri Lanka). There are also three in Africa: the Association of Evangelicals of Africa with its publication *Afroscope* (Kenya), the Society for Pentecostal Theology with *Pneumatikos* (South Africa), and the Relevant Pentecostals with *Azusa* (South Africa). In Latin America, there is the Comisión Evangélica Pentecostal Latinoamericana

with its publication of the conference papers, *Pentecostalismo y Liberacion: Una experiencia latinoamericana* (San José, Costa Rica, 1992). Also some notable recent conferences are 'Word, Kingdom, and Spirit' (Malaysia, March 1994) and the Association of Pentecostal and Charismatic Bible Colleges of Australia (PCBC) annual meeting.

35   Out of seven issues so far, there are at least nine articles in the area of biblical studies.

36   Its site URL is http://www.regent.edu/cpcr.html. The *PCTII Newsletter* 5 (1995), edited by Harold Hunter, is available to groups online such as the Christianity Online Forum on America Online and the Religion Forum on CompuServe.

37   The SPS *Newsletter* announces that the publisher will produce 'serious theological literature, including major pieces by Pentecostal and Charismatic scholars'.

38   Gordon Fee's position is case in point; see his chapter, 'Acts: The Problem of Historical Precedent', in *How to Read the Bible for All Its Worth: A Guide to Understanding the Bible*, Gordon Fee and Douglas Stuart, 2nd ed. (Grand Rapids, MI: Zondervan Publishing House, 1993). Regarding this, the Assemblies of God was more concerned about the historical precedence issue, which would have a direct bearing to the denominational position. Few questioned the validity of using critical methodology itself.

39   Timothy B. Cargal, 'Beyond the Fundamentalist-Modernist Controversy: Pentecostals and Hermeneutics in a Postmodern Age', *PNEUMA: The Journal of the Society for Pentecostal Studies* 15 (Fall 1993), pp. 163–187; see also French L. Arrington, 'The Use of the Bible by Pentecostals', *PNEUMA: The Journal of the Society for Pentecostal Studies* 16 (Spring 1994), pp. 101–107.

40   See Robert O. Baker, 'Pentecostal Bible Reading: Toward a Model of Reading for the Formation of Christian Affections', *Journal of Pentecostal Theology* 7 · (1995), pp. 34–48.

41   James D. G. Dunn, 'Baptism in the Spirit: A Response to Pentecostal Scholarship on Luke-Acts', *Journal of Pentecostal Theology* 3 (1993), pp. 3–27 started the dialogue. Pentecostal responses continue to appear: Robert P. Menzies, 'Luke and the Spirit: A Reply to James Dunn', *Journal of Pentecostal Theology* 4 (1994), pp. 115–138; James B. Shelton, 'A Reply to James D. G. Dunn's 'Baptism in the Spirit: A Response to Pentecostal Scholarship in Luke-Acts' ', *Journal of Pentecostal Theology* 4 (1994), pp. 139–143; William Atkinson, 'Pentecostal Responses to *Dunn's Baptism in the Holy Spirit*: Luke-Acts', *Journal of Pentecostal Theology* 6 (1995), pp. 87–131; Atkinson, 'Pentecostal Responses to Dunn's *Baptism in the Holy Spirit*: Pauline Literature', *Journal of Pentecostal Theology* 6 (1995), pp. 49–72.

42   See Gordon D. Fee, 'Hermeneutics and Historical Precedent – A Major Problem in Pentecostal Hermeneutics', in *Perspectives on the New Pentecostalism*, ed. Russell P. Spittler (Grand Rapids, MI: Baker Book House, 1976), pp. 118–132.

43   Clark H. Pinnock and Grant R. Osborne, 'A True Proposal for the Tongues Controversy', *Christianity Today* (8 October 1971), pp. 6–9, and more recently James D. G. Dunn, 'Baptism in the Spirit: A Response to Pentecostal Scholarship on Luke-Acts', *Journal of Pentecostal Theology* 3 (1993), pp. 3–27. Later, Pinnock seemed to have modified, if not changed, his opinion; see

his rather toned-down reflection, 'The New Pentecostalism: Reflections of an Evangelical Observer', in *Perspectives on the New Pentecostalism*, pp. 182–192, and his more enthusiastic words in his Preface to Roger Stronstad, *Charismatic Theology of St. Luke* (Peabody, MA: Hendrickson Publishers, 1984). Also, see Ray C. W. Roennfeldt, *Clark H. Pinnock on Biblical Authority: An Evolving Position* (Berrien Springs, MI: Andrews University Press, 1993).

44   Specific discussions of postmodernism focus on hermeneutics. See Cargal, 'Beyond the Fundamentalist-Modernist Controversy', pp. 163–187, and the following articles in *PNEUMA: The Journal of the Society for Pentecostal Studies* 16 (1994): French L. Arrington, 'The Use of the Bible by Pentecostals', pp. 101–107; Hannah K. Harrington and Rebecca Patten, 'Pentecostal Hermeneutics and Postmodern Literary Theory', pp. 109–114; Robert P. Menzies, 'Jumping Off the Postmodern Bandwagon', pp. 115–120; and Gerald T. Sheppard, 'Biblical Interpretation After Gadamer', pp. 121–141. Also, see Jackie David Johns, 'Pentecostalism and the Postmodern Worldview', *Journal of Pentecostal Theology* 7 (1995), pp. 73–96.

45   A unique Pentecostal approach to the Bible has been recognized by several scholars, e.g., Paul D. Hanson, 'Scripture, Community and Spirit: Biblical Theology's Contribution to a Contextualized Christian Theology', *Journal of Pentecostal Theology* 6 (1995), pp. 3–12 and Robert O. Baker, 'Pentecostal Bible Reading: Toward a Model of Reading for the formation of Christian Affections', *Journal of Pentecostal Theology* 7 (1995), pp. 34–48.

46   For instance, Daniel E. Albrecht, 'Pentecostal Spirituality: Looking through the Lens of Ritual', *PNEUMA: The Journal of the Society for Pentecostal Studies* 14 (Fall 1992), pp. 107–125. See also the sympathetic treatment of Pentecostalism by non-Pentecostal theologian Harvey Cox, *Fire From Heaven: The Rise of Pentecostal Spirituality and the Reshaping of Religion in the Twenty-first Century* (Reading, MA: Addison-Wesley Publishing Company, 1995).

47   Bong Rin Ro, 'The Korean Church: Growing or Declining?' *Evangelical Review of Theology* 19 (1995), pp. 336–353.

48   See, for instance, Murray W. Dempster, 'Christian Social Concern in Pentecostal Perspective: Reformulating Pentecostal Eschatology', *Journal of Pentecostal Theology* 2 (1993), pp. 51–64. At the practical level, a plan is under way to develop a family planning program, for the tribal people, Christians as well non-Christians, in the northern Philippines. In contrast to the previous government attempts which all failed, a new approach will add a philosophical dimension. A Christian group will produce biblical/theological material that will lay a philosophical foundation for the legitimacy of family planning. At the implementation level, local pastors and Christian medical professionals will work together. Although not distinctly Pentecostal, this developing plan serves as an example for the social involvement of the Pentecostal churches.

49   Barbara Caveness, 'God Calling: Women in Assemblies of God Missions', *PNEUMA; The Journal of the Society for Pentecostal Studies* 16 (Spring 1994), pp. 49–62 and especially 61–62 for her challenge to the Assemblies of God, especially in the United States. Also, see the following articles in *PNEUMA: The Journal of the Society for Pentecostal Studies* 17 (Fall 1995): Edith L. Blumhofer, 'Women in American Pentecostalism', pp. 19–20; David

Roebuck, 'Perfect Liberty to Preach the Gospel: Women Ministers in the Church of God', pp. 25–32;. Deborah M. Gill, 'The Contemporary State of Women in Ministry in the Assemblies of God', pp. 33–36.

50   For instance, the theme for Evangelical Missiological Society's 1996 regional meetings throughout the United States is 'The Holy Spirit and Missions'.

51   William W. Menzies, the first president of SPS, viewed the interracial dialogue between black and white Pentecostal academicians as a significant contribution of SPS. For an analysis of the recent Racial Reconciliation dialogue among Pentecostals, see *PNUEMA: The Journal of the Socirty for Pentecostal Studies* 18 (Spring 1996), pp. 113–140.

52   See the chapter by Cecil M. Robeck, Jr. on Pentecostalism and its ecumenical vision in this volume.

53   I cannot adequately express my thanks to Dr. William W. Menzies for his valuable comments. I also wish to acknowledge the kind help received through Kate McGinn, project archivist of David du Plessis Archive of Fuller Theological Seminary.

Chapter Four

Yielding to the Spirit:
The Dynamics of a Pentecostal Model of Praxis[1]

Jackie David Johns

Historically, Pentecostals have existed on the margins of their societies. Seldom have they been active participants in the acknowledged political systems of social transformation. In many parts of the world this social quietism is no longer the case. Pentecostals are growing in influence within Christianity and in the world. They are being sought out and enlisted to participate in the political processes of their communities. They are being placed in seats of power. With this trend it is imperative that they define the terms of their participation. Their commitment to the gospel demands that they be committed to full participation in all that God is redemptively doing in the world, including the liberation of oppressed persons. For many Pentecostals, however, their understandings of redemption and of the role of the church in the world has often restricted their involvement in social reform only to evangelism and its attending personal transformations. Others find their recent political influence fully compatible with their faith.

During the period in which Pentecostalism has arisen as a recognized social/religious force in the world, other social movements have emerged which call for reconstructing the social order through education. Epistemologies have been developed which challenge the exclusiveness of the scientific method. Of these, the most prominent is Paulo Freire's epistemology of *praxis*. The purpose of this paper is to explore the compatibility of Pentecostalism with the leading *praxis* models of education and social reform and thereby to construct a model for Pentecostal *praxis*.

The model which will be developed suggests that Pentecostals are inclined toward an epistemology and corresponding approach to social reform which is generally compatible with Freire's model of *praxis*, but which is better understood as a contemporary expression of the epistemology found in the Scriptures. This model requires that Pentecostals take care to preserve their historic self-understanding as a prophetic movement – the humble who speak with and for God. The structure of this inquiry is to address three questions: What is a *praxis* model of education and social transformation? What is the Pentecostal paradigm for knowledge and truth? How should Pentecostalism relate to the *praxis* model?

WHAT IS A *PRAXIS* MODEL OF EDUCATION AND SOCIAL TRANSFORMATION?

In recent years the term *praxis* has become a significant word within the jargons of several academic fields, including social ethics, education, and practical theology. In order for one to understand the term there must be a conscious move away from dichotomizing ideas and matter-in-motion and toward seeing them as dialectically united within the same activity.[2] The term expresses a form of knowledge in which reflection and action are joined as twin-moments. It is an epistemological concept in which theory and practice are dynamically linked as a singular movement.

Aristotle treated *praxis* as one of three principle ways of knowing, the other two being *theoria* and *poesis*. *Theoria* was a property of the intellect alone and was the highest form of knowledge. Only through *theoria* could an individual attain unto *sophia*, the highest level of wisdom. *Praxis* merged thought with doing, primarily in the sense of interaction with society. *Poesis* merged thought with making in the sense of shaping material objects, for example, the artisan's work.

Because it focused on interaction with society, *praxis* was beneficial for moral training, but could not bring an individual to *sophia*.

G.W.F. Hegel re-introduced the term *praxis* in modern times. He adapted the term to the Enlightenment's emphasis on critical reason. He saw *praxis* in relation to *Geist*, the all-powerful and encompassing Spirit which guided the universe toward the actualization of itself. For Hegel *praxis* was the *praxis of Geist*. This use of the term united theory and practice in an even stronger dialectic than had Aristotle. Human knowing was not realized by speculative theorizing apart from the world, but rather was attained through reflection on, and participation in, the *praxis of Geist* within history.

Thomas Groome has pointed out that Hegel's understanding of *praxis* left little room for self-initiated active/reflective engagement in the world. Knowledge comes instead by phenomenological observation of *Geist's* activity in the world. Thus, Hegel remained functionally caught in a Greek theory-centered manner of knowing.[3]

Karl Marx was influenced by Hegel's concept of *praxis*. He, however, put humankind in the place of *Geist,* calling for humans to influence and shape their own history. In this usage *praxis* is totally an endeavour within nature. It is void of any transcendent authority. Human critical reflection and action are considered sufficient for the ongoing reformation of social reality.

Paulo Freire[4] was a Brazilian, Roman Catholic, humanist, educator whose works have most influenced contemporary usage of the term *praxis*. He based much of his understanding of *praxis* upon Marx. For Freire the world is divided into economic categories. He calls for human participation in transforming these structures. People are to be active subjects in the historical process, not passive objects caught in a world in which they have no control. Thus *praxis*, as active participation in one's own history, is necessary for a person to be fully human. While Freire considered himself a Christian, his works leave most of the responsibility for *praxis* up to humanity. At best God is a subjective presence in the historical process. It is largely through Freire's influence that *praxis* has been integrated into present-day movements of social change, including educational systems of social reconstruction, liberation theologies, and the agendas of various political parties especially within the two-thirds world.

Current popular usage of *praxis* often seems to treat the word as a synonym for practice. Caught in a Greek/Enlightenment dichotomy between theory and action (matter in motion), many seem to infer from the word the mere existence of a conscious attempt by persons to tie their actions to a theoretical base. In such usage *praxis* is little more than human activity that has been motivated by prior critical thought. In this popular usage *praxis* is simply purposive action.

Scholarly use of the term *praxis* should reflect the more technical distinctions set forth by Aristotle, Marx, and Freire. While the philosophical base of each differed somewhat, collectively they provide a common distinctive usage for *praxis*. *Praxis* refers to a way of knowing in which the subject unites thinking and doing. Theory and action are held in dialectic tension as twin moments experienced as a single event within human history. Critical reflection is both an essential ancillary movement and an ingredient of *praxis*. The individual must see the self as distinct from the surrounding world and must choose to engage purposively those external realities. The subject must understand his or her self as an individual having power to influence the world in which he or she lives. However, contrary to the theory-to-practice paradigm, in *praxis* action and theory are dynamically intertwined in a manner that fosters ongoing *praxis*.

The central focus of *praxis* is social transformation through what Groome has termed *shared-praxis*.[5] In Freire's model of *praxis* humans must follow a moral imperative to honour all others as subjects in history. In this way the oppressed of society are empowered to become full partners in the ongoing transformation of their world. The supremacy given by Aristotle to theory is rejected as inherently oppressive. In true *praxis* the educated can not apply their realities to others without invoking the human objects in their *praxis* to enter their own *praxis* thereby becoming active and equal subjects in the processes of society. The professional educator must risk being an object of others in order to be engaged by the *praxis* of the very persons he or she is seeking to serve.

In summary, *praxis* may be understood as a pedagogical method, the essential method of a philosophy of education which espouses as its objective the full humanization of persons through the attainment of the skills necessary to 'read' the realities of their lives and thereby to become actors in their own histories. It may also be understood as the central method of those social reformers who seek a full democratization through the empowerment of the oppressed to confront and change the social realities of their world. *Praxis* is a type of knowledge in which the learner engages, labels, and alters the social realities of his or her existence. Through its processes it empowers the oppressed to read their own realities and it gives them voice to speak to those realities. *Praxis* results in the denunciation of dehumanizing systems and relationships. It is therefore a political process of democratization that challenges oppressive social structures. *Praxis* is therefore a prophetic movement, according to Freire and his followers, one that is infused with Marxist ideologies. It has been widely adopted by and associated with liberationist movements. This identification with revolutionary groups has led to conflicting responses by Pentecostals, especially in Latin America.

A few years ago during a ministerial class session in Guatemala I was asked by one student, 'Can I be faithful to God and the church and align myself with a *praxis* epistemology? Is it not Marxist?' Before I could answer, a classmate answered with his own question, 'Can I be faithful to God and the church and not align myself with a *praxis* epistemology, even if it is used by the Marxists?' In the lively discussion that followed, I suggested that the answer to both questions must be found in an analysis of the compatibility of *praxis* with the Pentecostal paradigm for knowledge and truth, which must itself be rooted in the Scriptures.

WHAT IS THE PENTECOSTAL PARADIGM
FOR KNOWLEDGE AND TRUTH?

In spite of the popularity of *praxis* in academic and revolutionary settings, in the modern world wisdom dictates that critical thought precedes action; look before you leap. Knowledge is best derived through the scientific method: make observations (gather data), formulate an hypothesis (develop a theory), test the hypothesis (experiment), and revise the hypothesis (discard or refine the theory). Pentecostal spirituality embraces a different type of knowledge, one that transcends theory to demand faithful response to that which is known. For Pentecostals all knowledge is grounded in God and God is known through encounter. This Pentecostal epistemology is congruous with the ancient Jewish approach to knowledge (described below), but is also compatible with a refined epistemology of *praxis*.

Pentecostals have an alternative epistemology because they have an alternative world-view.[6] At the heart of the Pentecostal world-view is transforming experience with God. God is known through relational encounter which finds its penultimate expression in the experience of being filled with the Holy Spirit. This experience becomes the normative epistemological framework and thus shifts the structures by which the individual interprets the world. Several characteristics of this framework are worth noting. However, it is not suggested that these are exclusively the characteristics of Pentecostals. It is their gestalt which identifies them as uniquely Pentecostal.

First, the Pentecostal world-view is experientially God-centred.[7] All things relate to God and God relates to all things. The phenomenological experience is fused with God but without collapsing God into his creation. The Spirit-filled believer has a predisposition to see the transcendent God at work in, with, through, above, and beyond all events. Therefore, all space is sacred space and all time is sacred time. Worship is primarily an event characterized by appropriate response to perceived manifestations of the Divine presence. It has been my experience and observation that this event may take place in any setting and is normative wherever the 'saints' are gathered together.

Second, the Pentecostal world-view is holistic and systemic.[8] For the Spirit-filled person God is not only present in all events, he holds all things together and causes all things to work together. Even evil, which is opposed to the sovereignty of God and wars against his children, is ultimately made to contribute to the good which God intends. Likewise, time is viewed as a whole. Historically, Pentecostals have subscribed to a dispensationalism that emphasizes a progressive unfolding of revelation and the interrelation of the ages.[9] All events, past, present, and future are related to a single master plan of God that will be consummated at the second coming of Christ.

Third, the Pentecostal world-view is transrational.[10] Knowledge is relational and is not limited to the realms of reason and sensory experience. The spectrum of knowledge includes the physical senses, cognitions, affections, emotions, behaviors, and spiritual discernment. Each of these is fused to the others with the affections serving as the integrating centre.[11]

Fourth, in conjunction with their holiness heritage, Pentecostals are concerned with truth, but not just propositional truth. Pentecostals were historically anti-creedal. They eschewed the 'dead doctrines of men'. Their concern was for a truth that gives life. As Steve Land has suggested, in their paradigm truth is known and expressed through *orthodoxy, orthopraxy, and orthopathy.*[12] Elsewhere, I have suggested that these form the purpose, function, and structure/essence of truth.[13] For Pentecostals Orthodoxy, both in the sense of giving glory to God and in the sense of correct belief,[14] is the *purpose* of knowledge. It is toward that end that the church must always be moving. Glory will be given to God most purely when we are finally transformed in entirety so that our being, behaviour, and beliefs conform fully to the truth intended for us.

Orthodoxy is also *purposive*; it is a qualifying facilitator of the two other forms of truth. Doctrinal constructs such as the creeds cannot serve as a primal source of the knowledge of God. As abstract propositions, they may by their very nature serve as a barrier to a transforming encounter with God. However, sound doctrine must always be a dynamic element in all quests for truth. Pentecostals thus express love for sound doctrine, both as an expression of their living faith and as a normative standard which informs the church in its deliberations and actions.

Orthopraxy is 'right reflection/action' and constitutes the *function* of truth. To encounter God is to know oneself as a subject and object in history.[15] It is to respond in faithful obedience and to join consciously in the ongoing mission of the Holy Spirit. Hence, in a world in which wisdom dictates that all action follow reason, Pentecostals are often perceived as emphasizing action over reflection. But reflection/action as a human activity cannot transcend the ontological barrier between subject and object; humans can not initiate knowledge of God. Without the integration of orthodoxy and orthopraxy all praxis will degenerate into sinful praxis.[16] Wholeness is achieved through an ongoing communion with the Spirit, the Word, the community of the Spirit and Word, and the world.

Orthopraxy refers to right affections which provides the *structure/ essence* for a Pentecostal paradigm of truth. It is through the grace of sanctification that the believer's character is transformed into the image and likeness of Christ. This transformation forms the integrating centre of the knowledge of God. It brings together the Spirit-led processes of orthopraxy and the Spirit-accomplished orthodoxy. This transformation is not a balancing of the three, but rather an integration, an affective understanding and behaviour which is essential to and flows out of the knowledge of God.

The transformation of the affections is three-dimensional.[17] First, it is grounded in repentance, literally a 'change of mind'. This is a transformation of attitudes and dispositions which takes place at the very core of an individual's world-view. The transformation originates in the grace of God as the Spirit calls the sinner to repentance. Often the drawing of the Spirit first strikes the affective chords of the uncon-scious mind. Godly sorrow worketh repentance. The individual responds to the Spirit's wooing with a volitional/rational act of faith and confesses Christ as Lord. This initial orthopraxy is a twin moment in which God knows the person as justified in Christ and the individual knows God as redeemer. The individual is regenerated and a new vision[18] is formed at the core of her or his world-view. A process of reconstruction begins, one in which the old core vision, which was a disposition toward the self, wars with the new core vision which is a disposition toward God and others. Sanctification has begun.

In sanctification Christ is known as the power of God unto salvation (orthodoxy) and the suffering servant (orthopathy). The love of God springs forth as a fountain of love and inclines the believer toward a life of responsible action (orthopraxy). However, a crisis event may be needed to break the power of the old, sinful core vision and remove it from the defining center of the believer's mind. Once broken, the tem-plate of the old core vision remains within the memory of the believer. Powerless, the old is known for what it is, a law which is unto death.

A second dimension of the transformation of the affections is their nature as being objective.

> To say that Christian affections are objective means that affections take an object. In this case the object is also the subject: God is the source and object of Christian affections. . . What God has said and done, is saying and doing, will say and do is the source and *telos* of the affections.[19]

The objectivity of the affections binds them to the dimension of reason and understanding. Thus the paradigm by which the believer lives must continually be shaped by godly affections.

The third dimension of the transformation of the affections is their relational character. Their transformation alters the manner in which the individual relates to God, the church and the world. The altered world-view shifts the focus of problems from selfish desire toward the needs of others. Thus, the model of godly affections is community, the koinonia of the saints, and orthopraxy is always shared-orthopraxy. The significant role of the affections within the Pentecostal paradigm suggests the need for a metaphor of shared narrative, perhaps 'story'.[20]

Fifth, the Pentecostal epistemology of encounter with God is closely aligned with the biblical understanding of how one comes to know. There is in the Old and New Testaments a relatively consistent understanding of how one comes 'to know'.[21] This understanding is rooted in Hebrew thought and may be contrasted with Greek approaches to knowledge. The Hebrew word for 'to know' is *yada*. In general, *yada* is knowledge that comes by experience. O.A. Piper has stated that this knowledge implies an awareness of the specific relationship in which the knower stands with the object being experienced so that 'full comprehension of the object manifests itself in action which corresponds to the relationship apprehended'.[22] Groome concluded *yada* is a knowing 'more by the heart than by the mind, and the knowing arises not by standing back from in order to look at, but by active and intentional engagement in lived experience'.[23]

This dynamic, experiential, relational knowledge stands in stark contrast to the Hellenistic approach to knowledge (*ginoskein*), which involved a standing back from something in order to objectively 'know it'. In comparing *ginoskein* to *yada* Bultmann states, 'the OT usage is much broader than the Greek, and the element of objective verification is less prominent than that of detecting or feeling or learning by experience'.[24] With this understanding, one is ignorant or a fool when he or she fails to do the will of God, not when they merely do not know the facts about God. Ignorance, then, implies guilt as Bultmann explains,

> Thus knowledge has an element of acknowledgment. But it also has an element of emotion, or better, of movement of will, so that ignorance means guilt as well as error...To know Him or His name is to confess or to acknowledge Him, to give Him honour and to obey His will.[25]

Accordingly, if a person knew God, he or she was encountered by One who lived in the midst of history and who initiated covenant relationship which called for a response of the total person. Knowledge of God, therefore, was not measured by the information one possessed, but by how one was living in response to God. Bultmann has further noted that knowledge in the Hebraic sense was 'possessed only in its exercise or actualization'.[26] It is significant that *yada* is used as a euphemism for lovemaking and that the past participle of *yada* is used for a good friend or confidant.

The New Testament, while employing Greek terms, continues the Hebraic understanding of *yada*. Knowing the Lord is still viewed as being in relationship with God and in submission to his will. Thus,

> the Christian view of knowledge is...largely determined by the Old Testament. An obedient and grateful acknowledgment of the deeds and demands of God is linked with knowledge of God and what He has done and demands...this Christian knowledge is not a fixed possession

but develops in the life of the Christian as lasting obedience and reflection.[27]

John's first epistle provides a rich illustration of the epistemological grounding of the New Testament. He seems intentionally to play against the Greek understanding of knowledge and attacks its implications for the Christian life, that is, that it is possible to know Jesus Christ without conforming to him. For John, knowledge of God is grounded in a loving relationship (I John 4:8, 16, 20) and this knowledge is manifest through obedience to the known will of God (2:3 ff.). God is known through his having entering into human history as flesh, and knowledge of him is inseparable from the manifestation of his lordship over life (5:6–12). Thus, we know that we know him if we obey his commands (2:3).

Finally, the Scriptures hold a special place and function within the Pentecostal world-view. Pentecostals differ from Evangelicals and Fundamentalists in approach to the Bible. For Pentecostals the Bible is a living book in which the Holy Spirit is always active. It is the Word of God, and therefore to encounter the Scriptures is to encounter God.[28] In my view the Scriptures serve at least three functions for Pentecostals.[29] First, they function as a primary reference point for communion with God. Pentecostals encounter God in the Scriptures. Second, the Scriptures function as a link to God's people and God's presence in the world throughout the ages. In this they facilitate the primitivistic and futuristic purposes of the people of God and thereby maintain their apocalyptic emphasis. Third, the Scriptures serve as the template for reading the world. It is in the light of Scripture that the patterns of life are recognized and woven into the divine-human narrative. Through the Scriptures human critical reflection is judged, negated, transformed and/or enhanced producing a new perception of reality.

In summary, a Pentecostal paradigm for knowledge and truth springs from an experiential knowledge of God which alters the believer's approach to reading and interpreting reality. For Pentecostals truth must be expressed as orthodoxy, orthopraxy, and orthopathy. Truth is known through conformity to the character, affections, and will of God. And to know God is to participate in his redemptive presence in the world.

HOW SHOULD PENTECOSTALISM RELATE
TO THE *PRAXIS* MODEL?

From the above discussions certain similarities and dissimilarities between Pentecostalism and *praxis* emerge. From a Pentecostal perspective there are problems and limitations with a *praxis* epistemology. Some of these arise from the roots of *praxis* in Hellenistic thought. In spite of all efforts to join theory and practice into a singular moment, there remains in *praxis* a fundamental dualism between matter and reason. Because of this dualism, *praxis* assumes an unbridgeable distance between the knower and the known. In spite of efforts to the contrary, the system elevates theory, in the form of the reasoning skills needed for critical reflection, above all other forms of knowledge. The objectification of others is an unavoidable aspect of this knowledge and the power of transformation is of necessity grounded in the spirit of the individual. Without an authority beyond the self that transcends and even negates reflection-action, we are left, in spite of worthy intentions for the transformation of society, with sinful, oppressive *praxis*. Consider the history of Marxist revolutions.

Realization of the inherent limitations of *praxis* has caused some liberationist theologians to speak of an 'epistemological break' which 'consists in the existential and historical following that yields a praxis knowing which is distinct from 'natural understanding' as well as contrary to it'.[30] Daniel Schipani has reformulated liberationist *praxis* in favour of an 'epistemology of obedience', which is characterized by discipleship as 'the dynamic, dialogical, and discerning following of Jesus'.[31] He asserts that the liberationist's view of *praxis* must be evaluated in light of the criteria derived from revelation and from biblical revelation especially 'lest doing the truth becomes equivalent to making the truth through historical *praxis,* rather than practicing the truth which is ultimately being revealed to us'.[32] A Pentecostal view of Scripture requires this same realignment.

Praxis in the Pentecostal context must further be qualified by the immanence of God. God is always present and active. He is always working for the believer's good even if he acts in a manner perceived to be against the believer in discipline or judgment. The Spirit-filled person never engages his or her environment alone. Because God is known as working in, with, and through all things, critical reflection/action is always with God. The Spirit who gives freedom both invites and compels the individual to join in God's *praxis*. With God we co-create and co-tend his creation. Critical reflection by the believer is a helpful but non-essential ingredient in this process. Love is essential so that the person must bring his or her full being to all situations. The critical element is the desire and willingness to be known by God and to know God. This *praxis* of the Spirit 'unveils reality in a manner which incorporates but supersedes human *praxis*'.[33]

Pentecostalism goes beyond *praxis* in the very area the proponents of *praxis* uplift as its strength, shared human fulfilment. With the Holy Spirit functioning as Paraclete the individual is empowered to know others for who they truly are, subjects in history. Through the Spirit individual dignity and integrity are actualized because the human is restored to wholeness which by design exists only through union with the God who created and sustains all that is. In the Spirit it is known that the individual's integrity, which is attained and maintained only through union with God, is being actualized in the context of corporate union with others in the body of Christ. Others are honoured as equal participants in making history not because of an external mandate, but rather from two internalized fountains. First, as the believer knows God he or she becomes a participant in God's affections. Second, in unity with the body of Christ persons are known for who they are, children of God created and empowered by him to make history. Thus, Pentecostal affections incline the individual and the church toward human liberation, which is understood to be ultimately attainable only through personal knowledge of God. It is only in the church as an expression of the kingdom of God that human fulfilment can be actualized and shared. Yet, the mission of the church dictates that it engage the world; remaining in but not of the world.

Finally, Pentecostal *praxis* differs from Freire's *praxis* in approach to social transformation. When *praxis* limits humanization to the *natural* dimensions of thinking and acting it becomes oppressive and dehumanizing.[34] Pentecostals must invite the person as a whole being to journey into the realm of all truth: orthodoxy, orthopraxy, and orthopathy. Affective conscientization through encounter with God brings true freedom to confront injustice, but it begins with the supernatural encounter with the injustice of the individual's own heart. This demands that Pentecostals offer to the world a truly prophetic and holistic *praxis*; one which first of all integrates godly affections into reflection/action; secondly, it is modelled in the life of the church; and thirdly, it is integrated into the missional presence of the church in the world. Under the leading of the Spirit the church may indeed enter into a shared *praxis* with persons and groups of the world. Such engagement with the oppressed will put to the test the church's existence as salt and light. If the proponents of *praxis* are saying, 'Let us know you as subjects and objects in our world', can the church respond in any other way than to say, 'Let us know you and you know us so that you might know the One who lives in us.'

In summary, secular models of *praxis* fail to recognize the affective dimensions of truth and thereby may be guilty of dehumanizing persons by restricting their world to reason and matter-in-motion. The Pentecostal paradigm for truth and knowledge integrates orthopraxis with orthodoxy and orthopathy. This integration provides a purpose (orthodoxy) and structure (orthopathy) for *praxis*. In the person of God, an objective/subjective reality which transcends the privatized self and its society engages the individual with a transforming knowledge of the self and others. Pentecostals need not shrink back from engaging in the *praxis* of the world, but they must take great care not to be co-opted into non-critical support of a *praxis* that denies the glory of God. Their *praxis* must truly be prophetic. They must read the realities of their world through a lens shaped by God.

Notes

1   This chapter draws heavily upon two earlier articles by the author: Jackie D. Johns, and Cheryl B. Johns, 'Yielding to the Spirit: A Pentecostal Approach to Group Bible Study', Journal of Pentecostal Theology 1 (1992), pp. 109–134; and Jackie D. Johns, 'Pentecostalism and the Postmodern World-view', Journal of Pentecostal Theology 7 (1995), pp. 73–96. Much of the material gleans from and dialogues with two works by other scholars: Steven J. Land, *Pentecostal Spirituality: A Passion for the Kingdom* (Sheffield: Sheffield Academic Press; Journal of Pentecostal Theology Supplement Series 1, 1993), p. 13; and Cheryl Bridges Johns, *Pentecostal Formation: A Pedagogy Among the Oppressed* (Sheffield: Sheffield Academic Press; Journal of Pentecostal Theology Supplement Series 2, 1993). The latter work is the most extensive treatment of the relationship between praxis and Pentecostalism.

2   The following history of the usages of the term *praxis* is primarily drawn from Thomas Groome, *Christian Religious Education* (New York, NY: Harper & Row Publishers, 1981), Chapter 7, 'In Search of a Way of Knowing'.

3   Ibid., p. 166.

4   Freire was a prolific writer, his best known work being *Pedagogy of the Oppressed* (New York, NY: Herder & Herder, 1970). For a Pentecostal critique of Freire see Cheryl Bridges Johns, *Pentecostal Formation*. This work is a revision of her doctoral dissertation, 'Affective Conscientization: A Pentecostal Response to Paulo Freire'.

5   Groome, *Christian Religious Education*, pp. 196–197.

6   I am using world-view as an epistemological term representing 'a disposition toward a perception of reality'. As such, 'it is that system of a priori assumptions with which an individual interacts with and interprets his or her universe'. Johns, 'Pentecostalism and the Postmodern World-view', p. 75. This usage is to be distinguished from an ideological usage in which world-view, or better, 'world view', represents a belief system.

7   J. Johns, 'Pentecostalism', p. 88.

8   Ibid., pp. 88–89.

9   French Arrington, 'Dispensationalism', *Dictionary of Pentecostal and Charismatic Movements* (Grand Rapids, MI: Zondervan Publishing House, 1988), pp. 247–248. Also, Land, pp. 79, 198.

10   J. Johns, 'Pentecostalism', p. 89.

11   Land, pp. 32–47.

12   Ibid.

13   J. Johns, 'Pentecostalism', pp. 92–95.

14   Orthodoxy takes its meaning from a time in church history when faith was equated with creed and confession of the creed was the purest form of worship. Hence, the literal meaning of 'right glory' is changed into 'right belief' as appropriate worship.

15   Cheryl Bridges Johns, *Pentecostal Formation*, p. 115.

16   Johns and Johns, 'Yielding to the Spirit', pp. 121–122.

17   Land, pp. 134–136.

18   I am here using vision as a near synonym for world-view. In both cases I am using the concept of sight metaphorically to represent all perceptions of reality. The windows of our world-view should be thought of as port-holes of engagement. A vision then is what we sense or feel before we have constructed any systemic reasoning that could be called a theory, much less deduced any specific consequences as hypotheses to be tested against evidence. A vision is our sense of how the world works. For example, a primitive person's sense of why leaves move may have been that some spirit moves them, and his or her sense of why tides rise or volcanoes erupt may run along similar lines. Newton had a different vision of how the world works and Einstein still another. For social phenomena, Rousseau had a different vision of human causation from that of Edmund Burke.

19   Land, p. 134.

20   I am using the term 'story' in the sense of 'myth' but only in the technical sense of a story, or any symbol, that embodies the a priori beliefs, affections, and values of a society. The observation that an object is a myth is not a statement about its historicity or verifiability.

21   Johns & Johns, 'Yielding', pp. 109–134.

22   O.A. Piper, 'Knowledge', *International Dictionary of the Bible*, Vol. 3, pp. 42–48.

23   Groome, *Christian Religious Education*, p. 141.

24   Rudolf Bultmann, ginosko, Theological Dictionary of the New Testament, Vol. 1, p. 687.

25   Ibid., p. 698.

26   Ibid.

27   Ibid., pp. 1, 707.

28   R. Hollis Gause, 'Our Heritage of Faith in the Verbal Inspiration of the Bible'

in Centennial Heritage Papers 1986: Presented at the 61st General Assembly of the Church of God (Cleveland, TN: Pathway Press, 1986), pp. 33–37.

29   J. Johns, 'Pentecostalism', p. 90.

30   J. Sobrino, *The True Church and the Poor*, trans. M.J. O'Connell (Maryknoll, NY: Orbis Books), p. 25. See also his *Jesus in Latin America*, trans. Robert R. Barr (Maryknoll, NY: Orbis Books, 1987), especially chapter five, 'Following Jesus as Discernment'. For the most comprehensive treatment to date on the epistemological grounding of liberation theology, see Clodovis Boff, *Theology and Praxis: Epistemological Foundations*, trans. Robert R. Barr (Maryknoll, NY: Orbis Books, 1987).

31   Daniel Schipani, *Religious Education Encounters Liberation Theology*, (Birmingham, Alabama: Religious Education Press, 1988), p. 125.

32   Ibid., p. 136.

33   Cheryl Johns, *Pentecostal Formation*, p. 62.

34   Ibid, pp. 38–41.

Chapter Five

They Crossed the Red Sea, Didn't They?
Critical History and Pentecostal Beginnings

Everett A. Wilson

A boy was responding to his father's probing about that morning's Sunday School lesson.

'Well, it was about when Moses and the Children of Israel were trying to get away from Pharaoh and came to the Red Sea. So Moses called in some air cover and landing craft and built some pontoon bridges to get the people across.'

'Was that really the way your teacher told the story?' questioned the father.

'No, Dad', confessed the boy, 'but if I told it the way she did, you'd never believe me!'

ABOUT PENTECOSTAL ORIGINS

Although the writing of critical Pentecostal history has been undertaken only in recent decades, interpreters have already begun to research the Pentecostal phenomenon with the same rigour that one would expect from the serious study of any social movement. Given this competence, reconstruction of the Pentecostal past should be fairly manageable – but is it?

WHAT MAKES A PENTECOSTAL?

The difficulties of researching Pentecostal history begin with something as simple as profiling the adherents of the early movement. The 'charter' members, who were recruited for the most part from other conservative Christian traditions with similar values and theology, were not always readily differentiated from their fundamentalist or Holiness 'cousins' when they were not taking part in a rousing meeting or speaking in tongues. Moreover, from available biographical information it appears that the recruitment of Pentecostals was a selective process. The movement often divided families whose members accepted or rejected these novel emphases in varying degrees between generations, siblings and even spouses. And while 'other worldly' Pentecostals were usually considered exclusive and extremist, in this respect they were not entirely unlike some other Christian groups, reform movements and social crusades that also made unreasonable demands on their adherents' attention, time and resources.

While much has also been made of the Pentecostals' undistinguished social standing, reflective of their often rural, ethnic or immigrant origins and their humble or precarious occupations, the vast majority of persons within these and similar social categories were never involved with Pentecostalism, raising questions about the specific motivations of those who were. Moreover, there were enough upwardly mobile or better-situated adherents among the Pentecostals to question deprivation or other social explanations as a primary reason for the members' inclusion. And the assumption that association with Pentecostals *ipso facto* points to an emotionally volatile or mystical personality type, for reasons discussed here, is also dubious. While obviously the Pentecostal experience appealed to some social sectors more than to others, these considerations raise doubts about whether even at the beginning there was a distinguishable Pentecostal type.

Accordingly, the researcher can plot the movement's approximate net growth, but cannot compile a distinct profile of the adherents and, more importantly, detail their reasons for becoming part of the group. This lack of precision in identifying the composition of the Pentecostal community at least suggests that drawing inferences about

Pentecostals may be more complicated than analyzsing the member-ship and motives of the adherents of most voluntary organizations. The historian's working hypothesis must be that elusive, intimate, per-sonal dispositions, not easily identifiable personality types or social variables, gave rise to intense spiritual experiences and lay behind the emergence of the movement.

Description of the Pentecostal membership, accordingly, requires some evidence of active participation. Perhaps the real Pentecostals were the ones who night after night were shouting themselves hoarse, talking in tongues or energetically dancing or rolling in the saw-dust—or did whatever else, stereotypically, was supposed to identify members. But were there some Pentecostals whose retiring personali-ties defied the stereotype or some staunch members who were not representative of typical or idealized behaviour? And were all Pente-costals equally demonstrative and habitual, and was someone on hand to distinguish between profound spiritual experiences and an emo-tional happening that had little consequence either for the participant or the local congregation?

What does become the recurrent theme, the motif, of Pentecost-alism is personal crisis. The use of tongues, as well as uninhibited emotional and physical displays, are best explained by disengagement from the prevailing rationality brought on by a need for existential confirmation.[1] Prayer, at least at these climactic moments, was hardly perfunctory; taking rather the form of a consuming sigh, a sincere plea for confidence, wholeness and enlightenment, an audacious pursuit of the divine. Where there was some other indicated route to spiritual assurance, the seeker probably would opt for something less excruci-ating. But when other avenues were closed, common men and women found that their fervent appeals opened the door to emotional resources they never knew were available.

Crisis, not persuasion, is what has brought men and women to their personal Pentecost, even if that crisis was more a sense of their own spiritual need than some personal or social desperation. Pentecostal experience began, accordingly, at the moment when a seeker, like the procurer of the New Testament 'pearl of great price', determined that what he or she wanted above all else was available only at the devas-tatingly high cost of relinquishing all consideration to one's own claims and merits. Despite the frequent temptation to lapse, to ignore the beatific vision, the futility of any other approach to God typically left recipients of such a rapturous experience spiritually dissatisfied and longing to advance further into the depths of realization, whatever the cost. At least on occasion these men and women may have felt an inexpressible joy, but whether or not exuberance was necessary in order to have a climactic spiritual experience, some kind of abandonment was.

What followed after such pivotal junctures in seekers' lives varied from person to person. Some Pentecostals responded regularly with unrestrained expressiveness, usually in stylized or predictable ejaculations. But the euphoria that followed the initial ecstasy or self-revealing moment was typically hard to recover or reproduce. However much the searing glory of a peak experience remained to orient one's existence, the glaring realities had to be faced. Rather than living in perpetual bliss, the Pentecostal practitioner struggled in the real world, returning frequently to the site of the initial rapture to restore confidence and inspiration. From that point many Pentecostals found deepening spiritual resources that provided them with previously absent initiative, daring vision and persistence. That many men and women who had enjoyed such an 'intoxication' did not further pursue this spiritual climax is understandable. The intensity and motivation of such an experience was not easy to maintain. It demanded an extreme focus, an ongoing willingness to forfeit the claims to one's being that were relinquished at the outset, to open the wounds of self-denial, repeatedly, again and again. And while early Pentecostals appreciated the indispensability of an atmosphere where such honest spiritual assessment could regularly occur, it is not clear that they considered demonstrations in public meetings to be the best indication of what spiritually was happening within these seekers. Why, for example, for decades did one hear the remark, 'I don't care how high they jump, just as long as they walk straight when they come down', if lack of restraint was an appropriate measure of Pentecostal behaviour?[2] Identifying the 'real' believers, eventually became such a problem that groups resorted to issuing letters of introduction or organizational membership cards to screen out the opportunistic and undesirable. While these questions about motivation probably at the time were answered to the satisfaction of most members, they further point up the complications of presumptuously circumscribing what should be included in a reconstruction of Pentecostal beginnings.

Based on what is known about social identity, being labelled a Pentecostal was not merely a matter either of confessing one's identification with the group or of affecting some representative behaviour. Like the proverbial duck, if a person looked like one, walked like one and talked like one – especially if one were supportive of the beliefs and practices that Pentecostals advanced – friends and neighbours could assume that he or she in fact belonged. At least the often-sung refrain 'I'm so glad that I can say I'm one of them' apparently gained favour not just to establish identity or to convince believers that they were with the right crowd, but because adherents gave assent to the Pentecostal way of looking at reality, something about which they may have felt deeply even when their convictions were not overtly displayed.[3] Pentecostals may have put on a show at their meetings, but the underlying sentiments that inspired the faithful were far more important in determining their commitment in time and resources – and were far more important for the ongoing effectiveness of the emerging movement.

WHAT ABOUT THE SUPERNATURAL?

After considering criteria for determining the participants, the historian needs to address a second area of concern, what was it that has given substance to the phenomenon? At least until rapid growth tended to silence criticism, Pentecostalism has usually carried a stigma based in large part on its admission of the mystical, the 'supernatural' and the allegedly miraculous, all of which carry with them considerable implication for one's world-view. Undeniably, the transcendental, mystical and ineffable have always been inherent in the Christian faith, but to avow that such practices are the spiritual legacy of all believers which should be routinely practised – and especially to give place to their spontaneous expression in public services – gravely tests orderliness, predictability and established institutional authority. It has to be admitted that Pentecostals from the beginning have often been a pain for the ecclesiastical establishment – including their own, and the movement is still suspect in some quarters where it has never entirely escaped suspicion of being nothing more than a modern recurrence of the ancient Montanist heresy.[4]

Uninhibited emotion and the extraordinary authority attributed to supernatural power – the thaumaturgical dimension – present problems for the historian. If one confines the account only to the empirical facts and social theory acceptable to the academy – a description stripped to an abstraction – the movement loses its particular, dynamic qualities. In such accounts the motivation and emotion that inspire

Pentecostals to extraordinary effort and expectation tend to be reduced to destructive exercises and wasted energy. This kind of analysis makes the congregation into little more than a support group, leaving the movement without a satisfying explanation of why and how it appeared and why it should continue to demonstrate rare vitality and extraordinarily broad appeal. On the other hand, if Pentecostalism is considered to be an ineffable phenomenon, if it is permitted 'to play by its own rules', as Professor Grant Wacker has stated the matter, what distinguishes it from any other religious cult, fantasy or gnosticism that refuses to admit to being part of shared, reproducible human experience?[5]

The scholar is faced with a dilemma: either suppress the transcendental aspects of Pentecostal origins and tell the story as though Pentecostalism is governed by the same principles observable in any other social movement, or abandon critical explanation and tell it the way many participant observers vow that it actually happened. Are aspects of Pentecostalism – ecstatic experiences, glossolalia, visions and prophecies, healings and other miracles and dramatically altered circumstances attributed to providential intervention – simply beyond the historian's capacity to assess? At least writers and their readers must be able to take for granted from the outset that Pentecostal historical interpretation – including making sense out of the movement's obscure beginnings and unusual claims – must be related in generally intelligible terms.

As much as the writer or reader may believe that providential intervention is responsible for a given occurrence, the historian is not free to interject any such conclusion except by inference.[6] He or she, however, may juxtaposition a given set of circumstances and expressed expectations or desires with what followed. The reader must be left to determine the probability – or improbability – of what ensued. Analogously, one may draw inferences from listening to only one side of a two-party telephone conversation: the information is admittedly partial and circumstantial, but the observable behaviour of the person engaged in conversation is objective and may be revealing about the motivational impact of the call. In reconstructing Pentecostalism, the results, not the claims, are what count.

Scholars who treat Pentecostalism, however, are put in an uncomfortable position in respect to historicity. Rather than escaping into mysticism, Pentecostals claim extraordinary power to endure or change actual conditions. Miracles for these practitioners typically are not, for example, the normal recovery of one's health or simply a desirable change of circumstances, no matter how much prayer has been offered, but rather these or similar developments that are sufficiently rapid or improbable to make them impressive and reassuring signs of divine intervention. Surviving to the age of 90 does not inspire 'hallelujahs', but the surgeon's inability to detect traces of a previously verified tumour does.

The fact is that while Pentecostalism started out without much to recommend it socially and ecclesiastically and still remains difficult to explain, it somehow made it across the 'Red Sea', surviving to become stronger and more influential than ever could have been imagined. If questions remain about what lies behind this energetic expression of Christianity, analysis of Pentecostal beginnings should go beyond the initial episodes of the movement. As interesting as one may find the colourful practices of these early meetings and the idiosyncrasies of some high-profile early figures, the real story lies not in the Pentecostals' claims or colourfulness, but in their recurring experiences and sustained energy.

IN OR OUT OF HISTORY?

A third complication for the interpreter of early Pentecostalism arises from the phenomenon's lack of a distinguishable founder or inaugural event that clearly identified its beginnings and places it within the flow of history. Since 'Pentecost', as early enthusiasts referred to their collective experience, had several beginnings, the problem is to decide which of the claimants should take title to the distinction.[7] But multiple subsequent 'outpourings' demonstrate that in any event, no claim can be made to exclusivity. There was no containing these diffused outbreaks of fervour or of demonstrating in respect to sequence and causality the relationship between them.[8] Ultimately, it must be conceded that had the enthusiasm not found a reception independently in community after community, if it had not recurrently cast its spell over tens of thousands of men and women, Pentecostalism would probably have remained only one of the many seldom remembered oddities in American religious history. The persistent repetition of Pentecostal phenomena, the movement's unexpected resilience and audacious buoyancy have made it viable, not its reliably persistent, easily traceable growth and development.

While an idyllic, classical era of Pentecostalism, as has been often described or implied, would perhaps be a fitting inauguration and foundation for what was to follow, what is known of Pentecostal origins does not substantiate anything so precise and identifiable. Composite portraits of the founding generation must include members who were tentative and uncertain, inconsistent and self-contradictory. It is easier to idealize them and their work than to document what is believed about them. And among the faithful there tends to be an anachronistic mixing of later developments and figures in descriptions of the 'early days', so that Smith Wigglesworth, Charles S. Price and Aimee Semple McPherson, among many others, are frequently referred to as though they were charter members, even though they make their contributions mainly in the third and fourth decades of the revival. Whatever success the historian has in identifying the succession of Pentecostal outpourings in the early century, the issue is not 'who begat whom', but who or what brought to life and enthusiasm those many different specimens of Pentecostalism in diverse settings and sequences. A pedigree can show the relationship of each ascending generation to its predecessor, but each new generation still has to be born in reproductive passion. Revivals last not because the movement had an impressive beginning, but rather because periodic renewal keeps the enthusiasm vibrant despite energy-sapping generational, organizational and circumstantial changes.

If the origins of the Pentecostal movement were tenuous, its course since has similarly failed to be marked by a steady, unerring ascent. Pragmatic, opportunistic and plagued by failures and defections, the enthusiasm has not spread steadily but has sprawled, digressed and lurched. The picture is confused by the large numbers of former members, sometimes adults with second thoughts or children of Pentecostals who have chosen not to pursue the religious route taken by their parents. Moreover, Pentecostal groups have sometimes changed directions unpredictably or defied their own once unalterable standards. The impressive feature of this muddled picture is that despite its contradictions the movement is far from dissipating into oblivion or following a sharply downward spiral. On the contrary, Pentecostalism has recurrently found new life and vigour.[9]

Given these convolutions, how is the contemporary historian to force all of the subsequent history of the movement back into the restrictive confines of a parochial, stylized account that seems as inadequate to contain what followed the initial events as the Holiness movement was to accommodate the Pentecostal emphases in the first place? Histories of a group's origins cannot predict or even imply subsequent developments, but they must leave room for growth and development. Is it possible in a recounting of Pentecostal beginnings to explain what it was about the movement in its initial phases that permitted, even facilitated, what has happened subsequently?

Beyond pointing out the early movement's main sequences and personalities and alluding to the sentiments and experiences that survive in descriptions and recollections of an era long since passed, is it possible to place real life adherents in a specific social setting and demonstrate specifically what happened in the process of the movement's ensuing development? Such an analysis might not be difficult in explaining the evolution of almost any voluntary association, but the kind of organizational development that seems normal in other movements is hard to trace in Pentecostalism.[10] Even where net growth can be clearly demonstrated, the changes in leadership, approaches and emphases make the process appear extremely dynamic and often bewildering.

WHAT ARE THE HISTORICAL FINDINGS AS INDICATED BY A REVIEW OF THE LITERATURE?

A useful aid to assessing the investigation carried out by scholars to date has been provided by Augustus Cerillo, Jr., a senior scholar whose many publications deal with urban and ethnic history, Professor Cerillo brings the breadth, rigour, sensitivity and experience necessary to evaluate the rapidly accumulating treatments of Pentecostalism.[11] Given the quality and coverage of his bibliographical essay, students of Pentecostalism may be well advised to begin with his assessment before proceeding further in their investigations.

Professor Cerillo recognizes that early Pentecostals attributed their movement essentially to divine impulses. He sums up the early period of self-interpretation as one of 'spontaneous, providentially generated, endtime religious revival, a movement fundamentally discontinuous with 1900 years of Christian history'. This 'ahistorical' or 'antihistorical' interpretation, while never completely lost, was largely replaced in the 1950s with explanations more in keeping with the concerns and critical method of academic historians. Cerillo refers to this second phase as the 'new' Pentecostal historiography to distinguish it from the earlier 'classical' interpretation. A feature of this 'new' historiography is concern for recognizing the continuities between the religious impulses of the Holiness and emergent Pentecostal movements and the larger social reform currents of the Populist and early twentieth-century Progressive traditions. Since Pentecostalism did not begin in a vacuum, the task of the trained historian is to view it in its historical setting with due regard for antecedent developments and shaping influences. America, for many people, was and still remains a great quasi-religious social experiment.[12]

Although in the 1950s Progressive history as a prevailing perspective gave way to more critical, less ingenuous analyses, the basic notion of reform still underlies most political debate and discussion of America's mission. Thus, even while early century Pentecostals may not have looked much like social reformers – Pentecostals were looking for the Second Coming rather than a better world order – their quest for realization nevertheless lends itself to their inclusion in the broad picture of the popular activist efforts to fulfill the promise of America. American society at the turn-of-the-century to this extent was vulnerable to – if not in some sense preparing for – the unveiling of the Pentecostal message.

When Professor Cerillo tells us that 'modern students of Pentecostalism want to know precisely where and why the revival emerged, and how a Pentecostal movement was put together, functioned and survived during its formative years', he is not unreasonably requesting that the account be given in language and concepts that relate to the reader's understanding of this main stream of national social development. Not only is he asking Pentecostal historians to write conventionally for the sake of their readers' understanding, but as a trained historian he recognizes – as do many of his non-evangelical colleagues – that Pentecostalism often did look a great deal like a reform or a protest movement. The obvious borrowing and common point of departure between Woodie Guthrie's labour ballads and any number of gospel songs is hard to miss.[13] Had the Pentecostals not been having their Saturday afternoon street meeting in a given community, a political or labour rally could just as well have occupied that same corner with a small group of zealots singing rousing choruses, delivering impassioned, impromptu testimonies and speeches and inviting emotionally moved individuals among the group of curious listeners to join up. Even if the task assigned to the historian of Pentecostalism is merely to demonstrate that what early Pentecostals were doing was something quite different from similar appearing popular crusades, for the sake of clarity the historian needs to pay attention to how the movement took form within this context of social reform.

Cerillo singles out the pioneering contributions of university trained scholars Klaude Kendrick, John Nichols and Vinson Synan, as well as the ongoing work of Donald Dayton, as examples of historians who responded to this need for greater rigour and analysis in telling the Pentecostals' story.[14] These sympathetic investigators all give ample room for the movement's antecedents, showing how changing times made many rural and recently urbanized Americans and foreign immigrants sensitive to new religious options. They especially note the movement's close relationship to the evolving Wesleyan tradition and its tendency to encourage in popular idiom the spiritually sensitive to find deeper, more heartfelt religious experience. These emphases, Dayton concludes, made Pentecostalism a natural product of the religious forces already in motion, part of the larger drive to realize the still unfulfilled potential of the Holiness movement. Pentecostalism was such a direct outgrowth of that preceding revival, Dayton determines, that only glossolalia remained to establish a 'hairsbreadth of difference' between the two groupings thereafter. Pentecostalism, in this light, does not appear 'suddenly from heaven', but rather quite naturally from well documented Wesleyan perfectionist precedents upon which it built.

While the careful research of these historians largely meets the need for showing the theological and ecclesiastical origins of Pentecostalism, Cerillo sees the task of placing the movement in its social context advanced significantly by Robert M. Anderson, *Vision of the Disinherited* (1979).[14] Taking Pentecostal origins as the topic of his Columbia University doctoral dissertation, Anderson asked the same questions and applied the same investigative techniques that would be used for studying any social movement. While Cerillo acknowledges that Anderson's naturalistic, somewhat demeaning treatment of the 'disinherited' men and women who resorted to psychic and social escape from reality is unflattering, he considers Anderson's book still the best portrait of Pentecostal origins. For him, Anderson's 'landmark study still stands alone for its conceptual boldness, comprehensiveness and breadth of research'.

Interpretation since Anderson's book, according to Cerillo, has splintered. Recognizing the considerable importance of subsequent contributions, he nevertheless concludes that these treatments tend to raise new questions about the complexity of the phenomenon. Several of these studies, which Cerillo terms 'neo-classical', generally contest the reductionist tendencies of historians like Anderson who dismiss consideration of the transcendental in human affairs. They purport to find the mystery of the movement in the depth of personal religious experience, something Anderson had tended to find as incidental or at best concomitant. Some writers go to the other extreme, blatantly appealing to the supernatural and inferring from the apparent spontaneity of the global eruption of Pentecostalism a divine cause and coordination of the phenomenon. Cerillo finds just such a treatment in Vinson Synan's view of unity and continuity in all of the twentieth-century spiritual awakenings, 'outpourings' that while taking different forms – 'classical' Pentecostalism, the Charismatic Movement and the Third Wave movement – are represented as essentially part of the same ongoing twentieth-century impulse among Christians to spiritual renewal.[15]

A second notable trend is the emphasis on the black origins of Pentecostalism, the view espoused early on by Walter Hollenweger and adopted in the 1980s by James Tinney, Leonard Lovett and two of Hollenweger's students, Douglas J. Nelson and Iain MacRobert. These authors emphasize the priority of William Seymour over Charles Parham in the emergence of the movement, as well as the importance of glossolalia as a symbol of the momentary eclipse of racism in the early movement – another indication of the relationship of Pentecostalism to larger reform agendas.[16]

A third kind of historical explanation, advanced by writers who adopt the less sanguine analysis that has replaced Progressive interpretation, concerns itself less with either social dynamics or spiritual explanations and treats the men and women who brought the movement into being, emphasizing especially what can be determined about their motives, perceptions and aspirations. Cerillo acknowledges that the recent contributions of Grant Wacker, James Goff and Edith Blumhofer have made a significant impact on the reconstruction of Pentecostal origins, although he is still reluctant to pronounce their works singly or collectively as definitive. Apparently this reluctance stems from the increasingly more complex portrait of early Pentecostalism provided by these incisive, well researched works. Cerillo concludes that 'no one has yet integrated all of the newer research and perspectives into a scholarly book that treats the entire early Pentecostal movement'.

According to Grant Wacker, Pentecostalism is best explained by recognizing the movement's inner tensions and anomalies.[17] He sees the movement flourishing 'not in spite of the fact that it was out of step with the times, but precisely because it was'. The movement's supernaturalism provided reassuring escape from historical contingency by substituting a realm of the adherents' own making. In addition, Wacker asserts, the movement's 'dark primitivism was a protest against conventions and social structures'. For Wacker, the best way to describe the movement is by recognition of its irrationality, on the one hand, and its pragmatism, on the other. These 'spiritual wanderers' he tells us, were also 'ambitious, practical, go-getter, hardheaded, fiercely independent, creative, persistent, brash, tough and willful'.

These traits, according to Professor Cerillo, are amply illustrated in the career of Charles F. Parham, whose place in Pentecostal historiography seems all but guaranteed by the recent publication of James Goff's doctoral dissertation.[18] The opportunism and manipulation alleged by Wacker and others find support in Goff's study. Parham also has importance for Edith Blumhofer, who sees him providing a good example of her restorationist interpretation of Pentecostal origins. For Blumhofer, Parham and other early Pentecostals were essentially motivated by a millennial anticipation and an aspiration to return to New Testament practices.[19] In contrast to Anderson, whose Pentecostals tend to burn out quickly after a brief, spectacular blaze of religious excitement, Blumhofer and Goff see the Pentecostal subculture as an appropriate agency for sustained religious action, a form of expression that focuses the frustrations and aspirations of many forgotten Americans and, accordingly, places the movement within – rather than as an aberration at the margins of – the popular reform tradition. Cerillo, in conclusion, finds in the work of these authors abundant reason to see in Pentecostalism an 'exciting, growing and intellectually maturing subfield within the discipline of history'.[21]

HOW ADEQUATE IS THE HISTORIAN'S LENS?

The strength of these treatments, several of them doctoral dissertations and all of them by authors whose scholarship is solid and even distinguished, lies in their rigorous yet sensitive handling of the subject in the tradition of critical history. It is not surprising that the works that Cerillo considers the strongest are those that best illustrate the accepted canons of historical writing. As a group, they precisely and objectively point out the conditions that gave rise to the movement, provide insight into the nature of its adherents, reveal the basis and dynamics of their association and indicate the character and achievements of the early leaders.

But these treatments lead to significantly different conclusions. While discussion of Pentecostalism as a social movement, for example, yields a useful map of its spread, documenting its composition and demonstrating the range and activities of its participants, it provides little insight into the subjective and personal experience that for most adherents appears to be the movement's essence. On the other hand, interpretations that emphasize the providential, which may seem to sympathetic scholars to be an appropriate and necessary corrective to behavioural explanations, invoked causal explanations that lie outside the realm of history.

While the theory of the black origins of Pentecostalism may be viewed as an unduly restrictive interpretation – the Sunderland Pentecostalism of the Anglican Alexander Body and T. B. Barratt's Scandinavian variety seem to have little to do with 'soul' – it may be far more useful than this incongruity suggests.[21] The strategic importance of this view may not be so much ethnic and cultural as it is spiritual. As numbers of historians of the black experience have asserted, the prolonged travail that shaped the African-American view of human redemption fostered a profound yearning for deliverance that was especially appropriate for Pentecostalism. In substantial numbers black Americans experienced the longing, the spirituality and the faith – the 'groans that words cannot express' referred to in the Pauline Epistle to the Romans and described with great passion and sensibility in James Baldwin's *Go Tell It On The Mountain*.[22] If other populations found similar solace and hope in the experience, they were individually no less prepared by an anomic world and spiritual sensitivity for selectively surrendering to the promises and appeals of Pentecostalism.

As the forgoing analysis suggests, the issue may not be which of the several explanations of the rise and extension of Pentecostalism is most adequate but, rather, in what ways the several views help to contribute to a better understanding of a complex historical process. In adopting a 'blind men and the elephant' stance that permits dealing simultaneously with the phenomenon's many phases and perspectives, one can work toward an inclusive synthesis. Pentecostals clearly cross the lines between the subjective on the one hand and the objective on the other. Their growth is not accounted for simply by historical trends, because immediate circumstances themselves do not seem to generate sufficient cause for the kinds of energy and the concerns that contributed to their frenetic effort and unlikely expectations. Yet, they were hardly mystics or world-denying cynics who escaped into unreality. Their genuine commitment to spreading the good tidings reflected their upbeat assurance of salvation, and their down-to-earth practicality and comfortable accommodation to any number of temporal blessings disqualify them as ascetics. Perhaps, after all, the personal crisis of most early Pentecostals was that recognized by David Martin as a quest for survival and fulfillment in a hostile world.[23]

Pentecostalism has demonstrated enormous capacity for growth, evolution and adaptation that are not simply a matter of later developments, but which are inherent in its nature, the reason for Pentecostal effectiveness from the beginning. Accordingly, scholarly treatment of the early movement must do more than reconstruct a conventionally defined chapter to round out American religious history. Without assuming that religious experience lies beyond scrutiny and taking care not to write the present anachronistically into the past, researchers must determine what about the movement from the outset gave it the appeal, the resilience and the potential for global growth that it has since enjoyed.

WILL THE REAL PENTECOSTALS PLEASE STAND UP?

Accordingly, what progress has been made toward assembling a comprehensive profile of the early Pentecostals? A fairly adequate picture has indeed emerged in the process of identifying ideal types and generalizing about the movement's emergence. But the notion persists that additional investigation may provide a more reliable portrait of the founders, one that will depict the prototypical Pentecostals in pristine form. Perhaps, but such a search for a 'Holy Grail' may be as perverse as it is futile. The inference is that when one finds the original, blessed charter members, one will understand the real nature of Pentecostalism. This is to assert that there must have been a Gold Age, a Pentecostal 'Camelot', an inference that is less historical than hagiographic. And is not the desire to find an ideal first generation more an idolatry than it is frank recognition that the Pentecostal movement is essentially God's working with finite, defective men and women whom he uses to demonstrate his purposes not because of some special merits but despite the absence of them?

The available sparse outlines, as well as what we know about religious revivals generally, suggest that the treatments of the movement too often overlook one of the most obvious features of the entire Pentecostal phenomenon, its excesses, its colourfulness, its passion, its tangents, its pendulum swings, its creativity. The feeling that some of these studies evokes is like a turn-of-the-century posed family portrait. Clearly, all the children are neatly scrubbed, slicked down, buttoned up, stuffed into their Sunday best, groomed and tidy. But the stiffness of their pose and their out-of-character solemnity suggest that as soon as the shutter has clicked they will be off and running, probably creating havoc and behaving little like the figures caught by the camera. The early Pentecostals, had they been filmed, would have produced something less like a well composed family portrait and more like unflattering 'caught-at-one's-embarrassingly-worst' snapshots. Historians necessarily need to stop action in order to analyse sequence and causality, but Pentecostalism lends itself rather to ethnological approaches that find cohesiveness in the functionality of the total system but with special delight in the particulars. Such a view permits infinite variety and is much more appropriate to Pentecostalism than sanitized, carefully drawn profiles that impose order on the early events that simply never existed. Forcing Pentecostals into a definitional, stereotypical straitjacket distorts the picture and obscures their most salient and effective traits.

In looking for a representative type, it is especially easy for writers to eliminate from consideration the people at the extremes of the performance charts. To the casual observer – or the historian – active members are not easily distinguished from marginal participants. Even at the beginning, some Pentecostal adherents were not especially enthusiastic, aggressive or persuaded. Many people came to meetings out of curiosity or for the excitement or for the fellowship, occupying the benches but not becoming part of the sacrificial effort that advanced the movement. Some of these people drifted from congregation to congregation or simply sat (or danced or clapped) in meetings, happy to find human warmth and acceptance. At the other extreme from the perfunctory adherents, however, were the visionary, the inspired, the highly motivated types. The performance of the people in both of these categories is easily left out of the historian's portrayal of what was typical or representative. But this process of describing ideal constructs probably omits some of the best specimens of Pentecostal experience, the minority that presumably carried most of the responsibility.

The formation and growth of any congregation almost certainly reflected efforts of the disproportionately dedicated few. The movement demonstrably produced some extremely motivated, visionary, vigorous individuals who beyond measure took responsibility for the life of their congregations and the development of the movement. But highly dedicated workers, many of them women and a large proportion of them young people, often appeared only in supportive, not high-profile leadership roles. Virtually all Pentecostal congregations depended on stable, resourceful, dedicated men and women who acted as patrons without their being pastors. These largely unrecognized elements were at least as important to the survival and growth of the movement as the often colourful or acclaimed Pentecostal pulpiteers. They were there to pay the light bill after the evangelist left town, to provide a steadying example to the congregation and encouragement to new believers. In addition, these convinced types often were themselves lay preachers and church founders, mobile, even transient, in their efforts to evangelize from community to community. They tended to seek out the unreached populations among the most needy or responsive, preaching in tents, brush arbours, store-front chapels, rescue missions and jails. The essential task was to start a new 'work' whenever possible. Historians of Pentecostalism should, accordingly, look beyond the total number of adherents to the minority that became productive, from the proportion of effective but usually faceless, unidentifiable lay persons who, often at great personal sacrifice, made up the cadres that became the indispensable backbone of the movement, giving it substance and continuity.

From its beginning Pentecostalism has tended to fascinate – or spawn – extremists. For almost a half century, while the movement did not draw impressive numbers of adherents, it was always an option for individuals who went beyond the conventional. It became home to some persons who believed that they had special but elsewhere unappreciated gifts. It also made room for individuals who found in the freedom of Pentecostal meetings the opportunity for self-expression or the assumption of leadership roles, not to mention personalities whose persecution complex made them enjoy being among the 'Lord's despised few'.[24] Probably only a small proportion of adherents were psychopathic, but the sectarian splintering, the sometimes mean-spirited legalism and vitriolic denunciation of everyone who did not agree with some leader's opinions demonstrated that a fair number were obsessive, self-absorbed types.[25]

So the spectrum includes not only the passive adherents at one extreme and the eccentric activists at the other, but also a range of activists, most of whom were not eccentrics, exhibitionists or megalomaniacs. The stability and growth of the movement points to the probability that there were proportionately many more men and women than has been recognized who were earnest, enlightened and committed and whose 'fanaticism' was manageable and channelled. The movement collectively would hardly have had the leadership, staying power and confidence necessary to stabilize and develop it had there not been a considerable number of these inspired and inspiring men and women. The self-sacrifice of generous, sincere local leaders stands out, perhaps simply because they were exceptional, but not without their having made an extraordinary collective impact on the emerging movement.

While not typically men and women of social standing, many of these constructive, convinced types were able and responsible. A large number of them were still in their late teens or early twenties when they first assumed spiritual leadership. Reviewing what can be known about their careers, one gets the impression that at least for some of these individuals, early Pentecostalism may have actually offered considerable personal fulfilment and career opportunity, the chance to get started on the ground floor of a religious growth industry. Even for believers who felt no compulsion to devote their full time to ministry, Pentecostal groups offered an inspiring, purposeful life's work, and as they grew, these congregations, movements and denominations tended to find within their ranks men and women capable of filling responsible administrative and leadership positions well beyond anything for which they had been formally prepared.

And if the effective minority of the Pentecostals, ministering lay persons and lay ministers, was likely to be an amalgam of the commonplace and the sublime, neither did the principal figures constitute a set of towering spiritual giants. Many leaders emerged primarily because they represented splintered factions, many of them failing to agree with their fellow Pentecostals on anything but the most basic issues. Many if not most of these personalities were frankly independent in their thinking, having previously abandoned holiness or fundamentalist associations in order to identify themselves as Pentecostals. Some leading figures lasted only briefly before they left the scene, others vacillated in their convictions at some point in the course of their careers. Some aspirants to leadership failed after a time to secure a following, while others, of little note at the beginning of their Pentecostal association, later emerged with considerable influence. Given the movement's ebb and flow, often torn by dissension and stigmatized by other fundamentalists, it was not clear until at least well into the 1920s whether the movement would survive and if so, in what form.[26] Under these circumstances, what criteria could possibly be used to establish the firm credentials of a supposed initial set of founding Pentecostals or to equate their beliefs, experiences and teachings with those of the entire emergent movement?

DID THE MEMBERS MAKE THE MOVEMENT OR THE MOVEMENT MAKE THE MEMBERS?

Vague depictions of early Pentecostals have often been used to exemplify 'real' or 'genuine' practitioners, as though the movement began in perfection and has since been in decline or as though by emulating early-century prototypes the Pentecostal revival can be sustained. Available biographical sources suggest rather the great diversity of Pentecostals and the difficulty of using as models a relatively few identifiable early figures. The 'founding fathers and mothers' of Pentecostalism may in some sense have initiated the movement, but they were never able during their own careers to preempt or direct it.

Since Pentecostalism appears to some observers to be more regimented and orderly now than it has ever been, why should we expect to find a homogeneous Pentecostal type at the beginning?[27] As long as Pentecostalism was a poorly understood, non-threatening, marginal, sectarian phenomenon, and when almost anyone who cared to identify with the religious 'lunatic fringe' found acceptance, the movement's parameters could more or less be taken for granted. Anyone willing to be identified as such by confessing the faith or by associating with a group could find a measure of acceptance. There was then no need to explain the movement's many internal dissimilarities, tensions and contradictions.

Now, however, such a neat definition of the movement is impossible without severely distorting its diversity and inconsistency. Instead of looking for the movement's prototypical, uniform behaviour, the researcher needs to investigate the range of Pentecostal activities, approaches and styles. Rather than looking for the original 'one hundred and twenty' who were in the upper room at the time of the early-twentieth-century outpouring, it may be more productive to ask how such a disparate and dissonant collection of early participants somehow managed to hang together long enough to make a subsequent impact. Rather than assuming that leaders of considerable competence succeeded in pulling behind them a young movement with fairly well defined features, it would be closer to what we know of early Pentecostalism to see a poorly defined set of beliefs, practices and expectations pulling into its irresistible charms men and women who were not at all certain where they were going.

WHAT MADE PENTECOSTALISM SO EFFECTIVE?

What was so soul-satisfying about Pentecostalism? Grant Wacker takes Robert Anderson to task for failing to recognize that religious or other aesthetic satisfaction for some people can be as rewarding as material and social compensations. Ultimately, adherents of the movement have always had to find their motivation in something deeper than the normal social rewards of being a church member or a solid citizen. Pentecostals derived their compulsive drive and brazen audacity from within their own personal, spiritual experiences. If Pentecostal fervour was vented in animated pyrotechnics in rousing meetings, at least some of it found its expression as coercive 'fire in the bones' of convinced, visionary believers. An adequate study of the phenomenon must recognize the Pentecostal expressiveness was only the visible display of something personally and organizationally far deeper and more extensive, an ongoing process of recruitment, attrition and retention, growth and development to which such intense personal motivation gave rise. These are the personal struggles that turned Pentecostalism from a curious happening to a deeply rooted, rapidly spreading movement. The issue is not the numbers of people who had some exposure to or limited experience of the Pentecostal emphases, but what happened to the receptive individuals who cherished it, since uncontainable, highly motivated men and women, extraordinary even in Pentecostal congregations, gave the movement its unusual vitality. Pentecostalism has demonstrated uncommon, not readily explainable energy and resilience, and the source of Pentecostal power must certainly be more profound than the simplistic answers like mass hysteria, psychological manipulation and the power of suggestion, on the one hand, or vague appeals to providence on the other.

Here comparisons of Pentecostalism with other religious and secular movements point out the former's resilience and versatility. The destiny of most religious revivals and reform movements is to die, and if not to die, to ossify, having accomplished their immediate objectives, having lost their reason for being or having lost their ability to inspire and mobilize the rank-and-file. Religious groups, especially, tend to atrophy, savouring their time of glory and looking fondly on the past. When a continuingly dynamic social movement does persist, it exhibits deeply rooted, broadly based concerns, a great deal of flexibility, a well defined but easily embraced belief system, effective leadership and capacity for renewal at critical stages of its development. The facts about Pentecostalism are that it continued over time to generate vitality in new generations, distant venues and quite different circumstances.

Is it not these inadequately explained features, extraordinary initiative, rather than emotional displays and curious doctrines, that makes the movement increasingly interesting to the religious – and to the scholarly – world? The movement generated little fascination while it was believed to be merely a curious holdover of the 'old time religion'.[28] Reading the books reviewed by Professor Cerillo, one wonders whether there would be much present interest in the Pentecostal movement if it had not shown such sustained growth, had not diffused so widely and emerged in so many different cultures.

IDENTIFYING ESSENTIAL PENTECOSTALISM

The task is less to find the principal players in the game than to recognize that Pentecostalism, whatever its merits and achievements, is fascinating because its achievement has occurred without the resources presumed necessary for its expansion. How did a movement without a 'visible means of support' – the force of a great leader, a captivating theology, a national or social class impatient for expression – succeed in mobilizing large numbers of people, form communities of millions, organize an extensive network of churches, acquire real assets and effective social programmes with only what David Martin calls its 'own autonomous native power?'[29] Appealing to economic, cultural and social motives alone, there is no adequate explanation of how the Pentecostal groups have advanced. If Pentecostalism did not simply die an unmourned death in humble meeting places in the Southern Highlands, the Midwest, Southern California and elsewhere, neither did it follow a rational growth trajectory that convincingly explains its effectiveness. Far from offering a perfect blueprint of apostolic faith and power, the movement stands as a monument not to the astuteness of its constituents, often dedicated but rather common figures in the unfolding account, but to what God can do with so little. By declaring the first (or any subsequent) generation of adherents a classical model of Pentecostalism, the historian distracts the reader from the real story of how a few believers with little apparent likelihood of achieving their goals somehow made it across the Sea of Improbability.

It is also futile to assume that the experience of the first set of Pentecostals provides a model for the future. In Pentecostalism every generation is the first generation. If this is not recognized, then the written record of the founding fathers tends to stand unimpeachable, like a preemptive definition of everything that follows. If this were the case, Pentecostalism would appear in its ideal form in the first decade of the twentieth century and, having made a classic statement, all the subsequent developments would be little more than inferior reproductions of this 'genuine' or 'authentic' revival. Historians who place the movement in its initial context and presume thereby to identify the classical model of the phenomenon tend to play into the hands of a very un-Pentecostal notion: that a given group of people or set of beliefs or an ecclesiastical tradition has prior claim to the message and experience. Many adherents (to say nothing of sectarian leaders who have a mandate to preserve the sanctity of the faith) have promoted the concept of an early pristine Pentecostalism, hoping thereby to emulate or recover the transcendence of initial personalities, events, attitudes and expectations, even while they may neglect other aspects of the timeless faith they profess.[30] The assumption that there existed a classical spirituality in the early Pentecostal movement plays into this dubious, ahistorical assumption, distorting rather then illuminating the movement's nature.

Even for religious revival movements, the essence of history is life over time. Change, crucial events, development and longitudinal processes are the stuff of historical explanations. Accordingly, no matter how faithful the treatments of Pentecostalism are to the initial events, without reference to later developments their explanations are partial and truncated. Rather than stopping action, freezing motion – in the biblical metaphor 'building three tabernacles on the mount of transfiguration' – the momentariness, the fragility, the dynamic of the early movement should be recognized. For instance, many of the early

Pentecostals were quite young when they entered the movement and if they remained still active among the ranks of the Pentecostals a score or more years later they had to find entirely new vision and incentive for the quite different challenges they confronted. Moreover, the movement grew and developed so markedly in the decades after World War I that it could not be said to have acquired its mature character during its first generation. Accordingly, why then attribute so much importance to the conditions and participants of the initial happenings, the tentative precedents set by the first men and women to appear on the scene?[31] And if Pentecostalism at the beginning was more a fluid, difficult-to-track fervour than could neatly be contained in a relatively few, easily analyzed events, its record for almost a century can be characterized by the same unpredictability.

While there is good reason to investigate the movement's initial contexts, energies and aspirations to learn what we can of its infancy, Pentecostalism must not be allowed to become the exclusive possession of a given era, a specific tradition or a sectarian style, a given privileged set of participants. Why should such a far-reaching, internally diverse, extraordinarily dynamic phenomenon have begun as the sole possession of a relatively few participants, the captive of a brief period of time and a given culture? At best, the early believers played a crucial role in the birth of a movement, but they were only mid-wives to something that they neither created nor fully understood.

While decentralized, pragmatic Pentecostalism has been too unpredictable and variable to be cited as a model of organizational effectiveness – it did not soon accomplish its goals or develop a distinct ideology or achieve institutional solidarity or build on the charisma of towering leaders – neither did it fade away or lose its reason-for-being. Instead, to a remarkable extent it maintained its original outlook in vastly different populations and social environments in unanticipated ways and in undreamed of proportions. Pentecostal beginnings were characteristically shaky and tentative, ambiguous and inconsistent. What the movement did display was unremitting tenacity, more than matching declines in some communities with revivals in others to ensure continuous net increases over almost a century.

Although the origins of Pentecostalism may be arbitrarily circumscribed by a time frame, a given religious subculture and a particular set of participants, the movement that has burgeoned cannot be so neatly delimited. Pentecostalism, it may be argued, has had many beginnings. It has broken out or has been rediscovered or been appropriated recurrently since the beginning of this century – if not before. Just as Pentecostalism finds roots in Wesleyan perfectionism, so the Charismatic movement can hardly be explained without reference to preceding Pentecostalism. But in much the same way the 'Classical' Pentecostal movement itself was a continuous process, a whole series of recurrent revivals and awakenings. It did not initially come into being as a fully developed belief system and set of practices and throughout its history it has demonstrated remarkable resilience and plasticity.

THE BOUNDARIES OF THE PENTECOSTAL MOVEMENT

Accordingly, the rigid definitions of what makes up the Pentecostal community should be suspect. From the beginning some adherents were more loyal to a nucleus of Pentecostal beliefs or a given congregation than they were to specific doctrines and practices. Some early Pentecostals in effect had dual denominational membership, attending religious services of their own communion on Sunday mornings and frequenting Pentecostal meetings in the afternoon or when the opportunity presented itself. Many early Pentecostals who came from one of the already established revival movements or one of the main line denominations returned to their churches or vacillated during their careers. High rates of attrition in Pentecostal congregations (or at least the failure of many persons to pursue some initial step toward affirming its doctrines and implications) certainly occurred at the beginning, as they have since. Even among early Pentecostal leaders one finds substantial proportions who faltered or were selective in their emphases. At no time, within the ranks, did adherents make up a discrete, readily identifiable group. Early Pentecostalism appeared to be coherent only because it was generally isolated, not because members made up a homogeneous community.

Treatment of the foundations and precedents of Pentecostalism are especially sensitive and strategic. The promise of the Holy Spirit, given 'to you and your children and to those who are afar off', cannot be adequately related if it is couched in hagiographic deference, on the one hand, or prejudiced insensitivity, on the other. The Pentecostal past which either needs no defence or is too transparent and vulnerable to benefit from enhancement tends nevertheless to be veiled in sanctimonious language and stereotypical conventionality. The dynamic, visionary movement deserves far more of its interpreters. The message has never been copyrighted or otherwise placed beyond any-one's – including scholars' – scrutiny. If fact, everything we know about the Jerusalem Pentecostals at the beginning of the Christian church is preserved for us in the account of a discriminating, conscientious historian. If modern Pentecostalism is what it claims to be, it can withstand the critical examination needed to test its tensile strength.

AMERICAN OR GLOBAL PENTECOSTALISM?

Emphasis on distinct, early Pentecostal origins also begs the issue of the leadership role of North Americans in the movement. Since the early 1950s, at least, there have been more Pentecostals outside North America than in Canada and the United States. Far from being dependent, these national churches are essentially autonomous, have sustained their own growth, and have evolved in their own manner, for the most part with little assistance from outside agencies. By almost any standard, Pentecostalism presently is not what Charles Fox Parham or any of his successors has pronounced it to be, but rather what contemporary Brazilians, Koreans and Africans demonstrate that it actually is. The future of the movement, that is, lies in the hands of people who because of their superior numbers, vitality and appreci-ation for its emphases will determine its course. Even in the United States and the United Kingdom, ethnic churches, black, Hispanic, Korean and Caribbean congregations, now demonstrate considerably greater energy than the largely white denominations which, to the extent that they are self-satisfied and do not need to rely on extraordi-nary spiritual resources, place themselves outside the main stream of the revival, even if their denominational credentials are impeccable. Accordingly, the study of Pentecostalism need not focus exclusively on U.S. precedents, since these non-Western groups have cultivated their own analogous, cognate forms (including their own founders, origins and subcultures), but in a variety of settings, in different ways and with their own spiritual achievements. If they exhibit similar if not identical Pentecostal features, it is notable that they have never had more than the most tenuous ties to the North American institutions.

Moreover, it is often overlooked that the European and Latin Amer-ican Pentecostal movements began in less than a decade after the earli-est reported U.S. incidents of the phenomenon – certainly before any substantial institutionalization occurred – and earlier than the formation of several of the larger U.S. denominations. If Pentecostalism has its origins outside the temporal order, why should the experience of one sectarian group speak definitively for all other groups? Given the multiplicity of its beginnings, can all the groups that have come into existence within different cultures and circumstances be considered the offspring of a single set of events? Whether given the transcendental nature of Pentecostalism one wing of the movement can claim paternity for another may be only a moot issue. Because of their chronological priority and large and rapidly growing memberships, should non-Western movements not be considered in assessing the formative years of the movement? Not only is a historical reconstruction of the revival incomplete without reference to other 'first generation' Pentecostal churches, but the diversity of their experiences makes them veritable laboratories for confirming the essential character of the ongoing Pentecostal revival.

A FAITH FOR THE FUTURE

The task of explaining Pentecostalism, admittedly, is not easy. The phenomenon now appears more complex and enigmatic than could ever have been imagined a half century ago. But Pentecostalism, the faith of apostolic signs and wonders, represents itself as a self-validating expression of primitive Christianity. It is supposed to make believers out of sceptics, not demand blind, unvindicated trust from the still growing number of men and women who respond to its soul-satisfying emphases. Intellectually rigorous observers, both believers and those who, without religious commitment, claim scholarly objectivity, would like to know what really did happen historically to give rise to this remarkable religious development and inspire its spread. By placing Pentecostalism in broader perspective and under more intense scrutiny, one is better able to appreciate what it is and how it relates to the larger Christian movement. As a religious development of interest for observers approaching the subject from many different perspectives, the major question of the study of Pentecostal origins is whether the historian can escape the dualistic dilemma of flesh and spirit and weave everything known about it, from its profound capacity for motivating Christian faith to its tangible results, into a single, satisfactory narrative. What remains certain is that Pentecostalism has never been preempted. It is by nature highly dynamic and intense and will not long remain tethered to any tradition.

It belongs to whoever wishes to accept its promise – and its accompanying exorbitant price.

Notes

1   Disassociational states as they relate to Pentecostal experience have been treated by Erika Bourguignon, ed., *Religion, Altered States of Consciousness and Social Change* (Columbus, OH: Ohio State University Press, 1973); Felicitas D. Goodman, *Speaking in Tongues: A Cross-Cultural Study of Glossolalia* (Chicago, IL: University of Chicago Press, 1972); and by several authors in a section of Irving I. Zaretsky and Mark P. Leone, *Religious Movements in Contemporary America* (Princeton, NJ: Princeton University Press, 1974), pp. 223–274. The literature on glossolalia is treated by Russell P. Spittler, *Dictionary of the Pentecostal and Charismatic Movements* (Grand Rapids, MI: Zondervan Publishing House, 1988), pp. 335–341 (hereafter cited *DPCM*).

2   This and other personal comments are based on the author's association with Pentecostals since the 1940s and indirectly from family members and parents' friends whose participation went back to the first decade of the century. A theological backdrop for the thinking in this chapter is found in a number of published works on Pentecostalism, including Randall Holm, 'Varieties of Pentecostal Experience: Pragmatism and the Doctrinal Development of Pentecostalism', a paper presented to the Society of Pentecostal Studies, 1994. Holm, in turn, followed the scholarship on Pentecostal hermeneutics presented in papers presented at earlier SPS sessions by Gordon Anderson, 'Pentecostal Hermenuetics', (1992), Brian Robinson, 'A Pentecostal Hermeneutic of Religious Experience' (1992), and Roger Stronstad, 'Pentecostalism, Experiential Presuppositions and Hermeneutics' (1990). A broad cultural view of Pentecostalism is presented in Walter J. Hollenweger, 'Theology of the New World: The Example of Latin American and African Pentecostal and African Independent Spirituality', *The Expository Times* 87 (May 1976): pp. 228–232. Published sources relating to the early Pentecostal subculture include Grant Wacker, 'Bibliography and Historiography of Pentecostalism', *DPCM*, pp. 65–76. These references, however, barely scratch the surface of the materials held in scattered libraries and personal collections.

3   Music as an idiom of Pentecostal expression is treated in Delton L. Alford, *Music in the Pentecostal Church* (Cleveland, TN: Pathway Press, 1967), *idem.*, 'Pentecostal and Charismatic Music', *DPCM*, pp. 688–695.

4   Montanism was a movement within the second-century church that emphasized prophetic fervour and spontaneity to counteract increasing formality and secularization. Devotees proclaimed the dispensation of the Holy Spirit and anticipated the immediate return of Christ by practicsing strenuous asceticism. Montanus was declared heretical by synods of the bishops of Asia Minor about 160 A.D., in part because of his movement's identification with the pagan ecstatic cult of Cybele in Phrygia, of which Montanus is believed to have been a priest prior to his conversion to Christianity. Although the movement died out by the fifth century, it found a champion in the church father Tertullian (c.

150–c.225) and its writings influenced the developing monastic tradition within the Roman Catholic Church.

5   Grant Wacker, 'Are the Golden Oldies Still Worth Playing', *PNEUMA: The Journal of the Society of Pentecostal Studies* 8 (Fall 1986), pp. 81–100.

6   The classical modern study of what is knowable in religious experience was produced by the brilliant American philosopher William James in *The Varieties of Religious Experience* (1902). James rejected the determinism of a universe known only through scientific inquiry and asserted the epistemological necessity of faith, the test of which was what followed. In recent years concerns about what is knowable in historical investigation has led to 'deconstructionism', the questioning of historical certitude and recognition of the difficulty of achieving an impartial account, tendencies that historians have long asserted could be minimized or overcome entirely.

7   Most of the standard works on Pentecostalism referred to in this treatment of early Pentecostalism recognize the problem of identifying its precise origins, given the appearance of charismatic phenomena a decade or more before the Topeka, Kansas events in 1901 and the often greater emphasis that has been given to the later Azusa Street, Los Angeles developments of 1906.

8   For an alternative view see Cecil M. Robeck, Jr., 'Pentecostal Origins from a Global Perspective', in *All Together in One Place: Theological Papers from the Brighton Conference on World Evangelization* ed. Harold D. Hunter and Peter D. Hocken (Sheffield: Sheffield Academic Press, 1993). The issue here, the author believes, is not one of cultural diffusion, but rather of establishing the experiential bases of the movement, something independent of cognitive awareness of Pentecostal emphases and practices. J. Rosewell Flower, an executive leader of the Assemblies of God, in assessing the movement's progress in 1945, pointed out that his denomination was not formed until 1914 when 'there were hundreds of independent Pentecostal and Apostolic and Full Gospel Assemblies which had nothing in common with the exception that they had received the teaching and were experiencing the same spiritual phenomena'. In recognition of its tenuous character, Flower went on to say that the movement had for forty-five years 'survived every attack from without and every weakness found within'. J. Roswell Flower, 'An Evalutation of the Pentecostal Movement', *Assemblies of God Heritage*, 15 (Fall 1995), pp. 4–8ff.

9   A dramatic contrast emerges in a comparison between the low expectations for the Pentecostal movement in the 1930s as represented in Elmer Davis, *The Small Cults in America* (1936) and the optimistic predictions of Pentecostal growth projected by David Barrett, 'Statistics, Global', *DPCM*, pp. 812–829. By way of further comparison, studies of Pentecostal (evangelical) decline have begun to appear, such as Jan Harris, 'When Latin Americans Evangelize . . .', *Christianity Today* (April 5, 1993), p. 73; and Jorge Gómez, *El crecimiento y la deserción en la iglesia evangélica costarricense* (San José, Costa Rica: Publicaciones IINDEF, 1996).

10   See William Bruce Cameron, *Modern Social Movements* (New York, NY: Random House, 1966) for a discussion of the growth of mass movements and voluntary associations.

11   Augustus Cerillo, Jr., 'Interpretive Approaches to the History of American Pentecostal Origins', *PNEUMA: The Journal of the Society of Pentecostal Studies* 19 (Spring 1997), pp. 29–52 and 'The Beginnings of American

Pentecostalism: An Historiographical Overview', paper presented at the Society of Pentecostals Studies, 11 November 1994.

12   See the analysis by Arthur Mann, 'The Progressive Tradition', in John Higham, ed., *The Reconstruction of American History* (New York, NY: Harper Row Publishers, 1962).

13   Klaude Kendrick, *The Promise Fulfilled: A History of the Modern Pentecostal Movement* (Springfield, MO: Gospel Publishing House, 1961); John T. Nichol, *The Pentecostals* (Plainfield, NJ: Logos Books International, 1971), a revision of Nichols, *Pentecostalism* (New York, NY: 1966); Vinson Synan, *The Holiness-Pentecostal Movement in the United States* (Grand Rapids, MI: Wm. B. Eerdmans Publishing Co., 1971); Donald Dayton, *The Theological Roots of Pentecostalism* (Metuchen, NJ: The Scarecrow Press, 1987; Dayton, *The Higher Christian Life: A Bibliographic Overview* (New York, NY: Garland Publishing Co., 1984–85).

14   Robert M. Anderson, *Vision of the Disinherited: The Making of American Pentecostalism* (New York, NY: Oxford University Press, 1979).

15   Vinson Synan, *In the Latter Days: The Outpouring of the Holy Spirit in the Twentieth Century* (Ann Arbor, MI: Servant Books, 1987).

16   Leonard Lovett, 'Black Origins of the Pentecostal Movement', ed. Vinson Synan, *Aspects of Pentecostal-Charismatic Origins* (Plainfield, NJ: Logos Books International, 1975), pp. 125–140; James S. Tinney, 'William J. Seymour: Father of Modern-Day Pentecostalism', *The Journal of the Interdenominational Theological Society*, 4 (Fall 1977), pp. 34–44; Douglas J. Nelson, 'For Such a Time as This: the Story of Bishop William J. Seymour and the Ausa Street Revival', (Ph.D. diss., University of Birmingham, 1981); Ian MacRobert, *The Black Roots and White Racism of Early Pentecostalism in the USA* (New York, NY: St. Martin's Press, 1988); Walter J. Hollenweger, 'After Twenty Years' Research on Pentecostalism', *International Review of Mission* 75 (January 1986), pp. 3–12.

17   Professor Wacker's contributions to Pentecostal historiography are too numerous to cite completely here. Some major articles and books chapters include: Grant Wacker, 'The Functions of Faith in Primitive Pentecostalism', *Harvard Theological Review* 77 (1984), pp. 353–375; 'Pentecostalism', *Encyclopedia of American Religious Experience*, vol. 2, ed. Charles S. Lippy and Peter W. Williams (New York, NY: Charles Scribner's Sons, 1988), 933–945; 'Searching for Eden with a Satellite Dish: Primitivism, Pragmatism, and the Pentecostal Character', in Richard T. Hughes, ed., *The Primitive Church in the Modern World* (Urbana, IL: University of Chicago Press, 1995), pp. 139–166. Additional works are found in his article 'Bibliography and Historiography', *DPCM*, pp. 65–76.

18   James R. Goff, Jr., *Fields White Unto Harvest: Charles F. Parham and the Missionary Origins of Pentecostalism* (Fayetteville, Arkansas: The University of Arkansas Press, 1988).

19   Edith L. Blumhofer, *The Assemblies of God; A Chapter in the Story of American Pentecostalism*, 2 vols. (Springfield, MO: Gospel Publishing House, 1989).

20   Cerillo makes six recommendations for the further study of Pentecostal origins. They include (1) the way in which the Gilded Age and the Progressive Era contributed to the formation of Pentecostalism; (2) the continuities

between the Holiness and the Pentecostal movements; (3) whether Pentecostalism should be treated as a whole or in terms of its parts? (4) the need for a better profile of the Pentecostals; (5) the process of community formation among early Pentecostals; (6) more comparison of Pentecostals with other movements. 'The Beginnings of American Pentecostalism', pp. 24–25.

21 Introduction to the work of Alexander Boddy is treated in Edith L. Blumhofer, 'Alexander Boddy and the Rise of Pentecostalism in Britain', *PNEUMA: The Journal of the Society for Pentecostal Studies* 8 (Spring 1986), pp. 31–40. Thomas Ball Barratt is treated in Nils Bloch-Hoell, *The Pentecostal Movement* (Oslo: Universitetsflorlaget, 1964).

22 James Baldwin, *Go Tell It On the Mountain* (1953) includes several depictions of profound spiritual encounters in African-American churches that, according to a *Time* magazine review, were 'so intense that God's presence seems to live on the page . . . so moving that any reader must listen with the compassion Baldwin evokes'.

23 David Martin, *Tongues of Fire: The Explosion of Pentecostalism in Latin America* (Oxford: Basil Blackwell, 1990), p. 280.

24 A line in the gospel song, 'I'm Going Through, Jesus, I'm Going Through'. See Alford, ibid.

25 Literature on the mental health of Pentecostals is fairly extensive, including contributions by Roger Lauer, Vivian Garrison and Nathan Adler in Zaretsky and Leone, *Religious Movements in Contemporary America* (Princeton, NJ: Princeton University Press, 1974). A bibliography is found in J. Milton Yinger, *The Scientific Study of Religion* (New York, NY: Macmillan, 1970), pp. 153, 154.

26 The struggle between Pentecostals and the fundamentalists came to an open breech in 1928 with the former' denunciation by the latter at the Chicago conference. The statement issued on that occasion is found in *DPCM*, p. 326.

27 Margaret Poloma, *The Assemblies of God at the Crossroads: Charisma and Institutional Dilemmas* (Knoxville, TN: The University of Tennessee Press, 1989).

28 Richard Carter, 'The Old Time Religion Comes Back', *Coronet* 43 (February 1958), pp. 125–130.

29 David Martin has developed the notion that Pentecostals have found security and opportunity by forming zones of 'free space' in which they are partially freed from the social disadvantages of the larger society and from which they can launch their own efforts to control their lives. David Martin, 280.

30 The spontaneous expansion of Pentecostalism, at least the movement's extraordinary energy and adaptability, is recognized in Luther P. Gerlach, 'Pentecostalism: Revolution or Counter-Revolution?' in Irving I. Zaretsky and Mark P. Leone, *Religious Movements in Contemporary America*, pp. 669–699.

31 The 'spiritual' dimension of Pentecostalism, understood in this study as deriving from its own energies and resources as opposed to dependence on external support and motivation, is illustrated in descriptions of the house church movement in mainland China. The emergent pattern is the rapid, unsupervised growth of congregations through the efforts of often young, relatively inexperienced evangelists who though supported modestly by their own parishioners and suffering repressive official policies feel that they are led by the Spirit in their efforts. See Jonathan Chao, 'China's Cross', *Christianity Today* 39

(November 13, 1995): 49; and David H. Adeney, *China: The Church's Long March* (Ventura, CA: Gospel Light Publications, 1985).

Changing Paradigms:
A Response

José Míguez Bonino

The essays presented in this section amount to an updating of Pentecostal thinking on a whole spectrum of theological disciplines: systematics, missiology, biblical studies, history, and praxis. There is such a wealth of information and reflection in each of the essays that it would be futile to try to discuss them in any detail. I simply will pick up some topics that seem important to me as fruitful points of departure for a theological conversation.[1]

Before doing that, however, I want to make an introductory comment about this volume as a whole. Reading chapter after chapter, one will be impressed by the amount of theological work that has been going on in Pentecostal circles during the last two decades. This surprise is a sad comment on the awareness of so-called 'scholarship' about what is going on in the religious field. Studies on Pentecostalism, which are usually quite bold in their own interpretations of what Pentecostalism is and does, seldom stop to listen to how Pentecostal scholars themselves interpret their own faith and experience. Undoubtedly, one of the contributions of this volume is to provide, in their notes and discussions, a very useful guide for overcoming the provinciality of non-Pentecostal scholars in regard to Pentecostalism.

This contribution becomes more significant when we see that these essays tackle some of the specific points that characterize the Pentecostal witness: healing, tongues, and the experience of the Spirit, as well as the more 'classical' theological topics in which Pentecostalism has a specific contribution, such as sanctification, the interpretation of Scripture, and eschatology. All of these topics are important foci for a theological and hermeneutical dialogue which can and must take place. That this dialogue is intended becomes clear in the style of the essays, which set the discussion in the framework of the contemporary 'ecumenical' theologies of Barth, Brunner, Berkhof, Bultmann, Bosch, and Cox, to mention only a few. Perhaps this exercise could be enriched further by including in the conversation the theological work emerging from Africa, Asia, and Latin America, and the growing production of Pentecostal theologians from these regions.

I do not mention these facts just as a compliment or merely to indicate the quality of this volume but in order to underline the clear intention that it reveals to develop theology in an open yet critical relation to contemporary theological, philosophical, and social thought. In the consideration of some specific issues we will have occasion to return to this question.

THE USE AND INTERPRETATION OF SCRIPTURE

That Pentecostalism is a Bible-centred faith hardly can be debated. What this Bible-centeredness means, however, is not self-evident. It can and is frequently interpreted in literalistic/fundamentalist terms. In fact, several of our authors point out to a literalistic stage in Pentecostal biblical interpretation or speak of a tendency 'to seek the acceptance of their fundamentalist antagonists'. To be sure, if one asked the people in a Pentecostal congregation whether they believe in the plenary inspiration or inerrancy of the Bible, their answer is likely to be affirmative. But when one looks at Pentecostals' use of the Bible in preaching, prayer, worship, and daily life, the question looks quite different. This difference is frequently underlined in this section's essays: the Bible is used to receive inspiration; the interpretation is 'imaginative, contextual, and narrative' (p.10); 'the Bible was read as a record of God's interaction with, and revelation to, his people today' (p. 55).

The common Pentecostal reading of the Bible may not be critical. In fact, it is not critical in the modern sense of the word. But it is not 'literal' in the fundamentalist sense either – at least in two ways. First, the Bible is not read primarily in order to build doctrine but in order 'to receive inspiration' and to answer everyday problems, that is, to receive guidance. Naturally, if the Bible was being assailed, Pentecostalism would be on the side of the defence. But Pentecostalism's reasons for defending the Bible are different than fundamentalism's. Fundamentalism is a response to the challenge of modernist biblical criticism that presupposes the same positivistic epistemology that modernism does. Pentecostalism, on the other hand, is a quest for a direct and personal encounter with Christ in the power of the Spirit and for a new life of holiness. The Bible is a 'locus' for that encounter. Perhaps for this reason, as several authors in this volume have noted, 'biblical criticism' does not elicit a spontaneous opposition from Pentecostals as long as it does not seem to question the inspirational and directive value of 'God's Word'.

Given this emphasis, one hopes that Pentecostal scholarship will not recapitulate the fruitless debate between modernists and fundamentalists but will challenge both and facilitate the development of a multilevel hermeneutic. I think we can explore such a possibility in two directions: the first is a 'canonical reading of Scripture'. A canonical reading does not mean the elimination of lower criticism, the study of the sources, or of redaction criticism. It means, though, that, when everything has been said, we have a 'text' in which God speaks to us his word and as such it has to be heard and obeyed.

Such a consideration leads us back to the hermeneutical question. It seems to me that a fruitful way to discuss this issue is to look back to the traditional medieval concept of the manifold – in fact, usually fourfold – 'senses' of Scripture. Medieval interpreters used to speak of a 'historical/literal' sense. To be sure, Luther interpreted 'literal' in christological terms. But Calvin's tradition placed on this level the grammatical and historical location of a text. This level is the place for critical work and for the use of all the historical and linguistic tools. Interpretation, to be sure, can begin there. The error of modern or liberal theology was, however, to end interpretation at this point and to start looking for 'general ideas'. Medieval hermeneutics suggested that the first question, 'What does this text say?' has to be followed with a second one, 'What does this text teach about God, Christ, the Spirit, the church?' The text, placed in the context of the history of salvation as it comes to us in the full message of the Bible, is a source of doctrine. But even doctrinal teaching does not exhaust the quest. There is a spiritual interpretation, for the Spirit 'enlightens' a text and places the reader in the presence of God. The Spirit opens the our hearts so that the living Christ enters our lives as persons and as a community and inspires a response of prayer and praise. This illumination and entering into, in turn, result in a witness, a form of behaviour. We ask a biblical text, 'What should I do?' As one of the writers put it: 'discernment is a work of the Spirit which transforms a text into the instrument to discover God's will'. Finally, a text tells us what we can hope for, what God's 'promise' hidden in the text is – its eschatological dimension.

We all know the abuses and distortions that led the Reformation and modern scholarship to criticize the use of the fourfold pattern. There is a need to preserve a certain 'distance', a respect for the freedom of the text as a reality that 'confronts' us. But this distance need not result in a purely one-dimensional, horizontal, and rationalistic hermeneutic in which the operation of the Holy Spirit in the interpretation of the Word of God is limited to a kind of 'rubber stamp', certifying the validity of the text but saying nothing about its contents. Pentecostal theologians, as they explore the place of Scripture in Pentecostal life, worship, and witness, are already contributing to the reopening of the theological conversation about interpretation, lifting it up from a purely linguistic or historical matter to a concern for a theological and pastoral hermeneutic.

'RECEIVING THE SPIRIT'

Modern Pentecostalism[2] has to be understood in the context of the powerful revivals of the eighteenth and nineteenth centuries in the Anglo-Saxon world, and perhaps even more specifically of the Second Awakening and the holiness movement of the last half of the nineteenth century. All these movements understood themselves as the work of the Holy Spirit. Their pneumatological orientation, however, did not result in an explicit or articulated 'theology' of the Spirit. It is therefore particularly important that recent Pentecostal biblical and theological studies are exploring this area of theology. I found at least three significant aspects of this pneumatological exploration in this section's essays.

1 – Frank Macchia, for instance, has emphasized the need for 'a christological classification of Spirit baptism' (p. 13). This classifica-

tion is related to the need to relate intrinsically the three 'moments' which classical Pentecostalism sees in the 'receiving' of the Spirit: conversion, sanctification, and empowerment. Macchia refers to the exegetical studies of Roger Stronstad and Robert Menzies and advances the idea of a Christological continuity in which 'a consistent Pentecostal theology would stress a spiritual journey that gradually becomes more intensely involved through Spirit baptism in the charismatic or prophetic ministry of Jesus' (p. 15).

If Pentecostal theology moves in this direction, it can help us to go beyond the sterile debate between an 'objective' and a 'subjective' understanding of salvation that has plagued Protestant, particularly Lutheran, theology. Concerned to keep in focus the absolute priority of God's action and wary of the possible 'vagaries' of an 'experience' that becomes absolute, an extrinsicist view has interpreted the classical *extra nos* in a way that seems to exclude, or at least deny, any soteriological significance to the transformations that take place in human life in the encounter of faith. The problem is complicated by a Kantian epistemology in which 'the thing in itself' – in this case, the 'objective work of Christ' – remains in absolute transcendence, ultimately unknowable, and therefore entrapping all experience in subjectivity. In his discussion of 'praxis' Jackie Johns rightly argues that the biblical understanding of 'knowledge' breaks this distance: 'God is known through entering into human history as flesh, and knowledge of him is inseparable from the manifestation of his lordship over life.'

It seems to me that this is a fruitful path. I am not convinced, however, that the direction the Johns' article suggests, pointing to a Bultmannian or a postmodern model in which the 'moment' of recognition becomes disconnected from the flow of time and lifted beyond the common history of human life, is a fruitful way of moving. Biblical knowledge is certainly participatory knowledge, but it is communitarian and not individualistic, holistic rather than spiritualistic, eschatological rather than ahistorical. I think such a perspective is closer to the Pentecostal experience. Perhaps a better way of pursing this direction would be in dialogue with the Orthodox understanding of 'theosis' or the way in which some recent Scandinavian, particularly Finnish, scholars are interpreting Luther's strong emphasis on our union with Christ.

2 – 'Tongues', 'healing', and 'empowerment for witness' have been interpreted in Pentecostalism as privileged 'signs' of the empowerment of the Spirit. At several points, our authors offer what seems to

me a very intriguing and fruitful interpretation of the meaning of these signs, particularly of the first two. On the one hand, 'tongues' were seen, at the start of the movement, as a gift related to mission. Tongues would enable the witness to move to other language areas and announce the gospel. Although 'xenolalia' did not prove to be an evangelistic instrument in this sense, Macchia is probably right when he speaks of 'a "sacramental" understanding of tongues as a dynamic sign that is used by God to bring to realization the work of the Spirit'. A recognition of the 'presence' of God that cannot be expressed in human words does not remain hidden away in the subjective consciousness of the convert but finds an audible, 'material' expression. Because it can be heard and recognized, such 'babbling' communicates to others. This same 'sacramental' character can be recognized in healing. The materiality of the human body and of human health is assumed because the body is a dwelling place of God's glory. Mission, tongues, and healing are concrete and localized occurrences in which, in the power of the Spirit, Christ the Saviour, the Healer, and the Sanctifier continues his earthly ministry today.

3 – Not all questions are solved in these interpretations. The question of the relation between the distance from and the assimilation to the text, the anticipation and the 'waiting' of the Parousia, the 'ephapax' of the Incarnation, and the 'Christ in us' cannot simply be ignored or written off as insignificant. It is not merely a 'theological aporia'. It has to do with worship, with ethics, and with mission. When the distance and the waiting are transformed into a tantalizing 'otherness' that is forever 'out of reach', or when we can only act, hope, and pray 'as if', then we are threatened by doubt and despair and easily fall prey to immobility and passivity – in service, in mission, and in prayer. But, on the other hand, when the God who is always 'before us' as Father and 'with us' as the Incarnate Christ (to use Juan Luis Segundo's expressions) is collapsed into the God who is 'in us', the temptations of 'spiritual pride', 'ecclesiolatry', and the idolatry of a culture, a nation, or an ideology are close at hand.

Interestingly enough, this question came to the floor at the Costa Rica colloquium in regard to Margaret Poloma's excellent presentation about the 'Toronto Blessing'. In simplified terms, the question is: Does an 'experience' of the Spirit legitimate itself as genuine by its 'happening'? If, in postmodern terms, there is no continuity and meaning of events in time (no 'metanarrative'); or if, to use existential terms, there is no *Historie* but only *Geschichte*; or if there is only the moment, the mystical encounter with the 'nameless' – what happens to the biblical faith, to Jesus Christ, to the community of faith, to the call to mission? Of course, nobody at the Costa Rica colloquium was ready to accept such a consequence. As I see it, Pentecostalism has at least three powerful defences against these threats. The first one is its biblical rootage. While its interpretation may be 'spiritual', still there is the reverence for a 'text' in which God speaks to us. If, in the direction that we suggested earlier, this 'submission' to the text includes a recognition of its canonicity as text, then experience receives a 'referent' which is never totally absorbed. A second defence is the communal nature of Pentecostalism, which conditions and directs the individual. Praying, singing, witnessing in and with the community establishes parameters, even 'formulae', that internalize a certain 'shape' of the faith 'event'. Finally, there is an 'eschatological spirituality',[3] an expectation that mobilizes for mission, but at the same time establishes a provisionality of the present time and therefore a distance that cannot be collapsed simply into experience.[4]

Is there a theological 'pattern' that can bring together all these elements? I have increasingly felt that this whole 'evangelical' tradition – at the same time Christological and pneumatological – that has found in Pentecostalism a powerful expression would gain in depth and breadth if it was placed within a trinitarian framework. I recognize that this proposal raises a doctrinal problem in relation to a sector of Pentecostalism that does not share the classical trinitarian formulations. But it seems to me that the primary question is not the acceptance of such formulae – which I consider valuable – but the biblical witness to the unity of that God who is always, at the same time, the Father, who from eternity to eternity creates, cares for, and recreates all that is; who in Jesus Christ has dwelt among us, died, and is risen and reigns at the right hand of the Father; and the Holy Spirit whose breath gives life to all (Ps. 104:27–30) and who 'sheds abroad God's love' in our hearts (Rom. 5:5).

A trinitarian approach means the recognition that the whole operation of that God – in nature, in history, in the church, in mission, and in our hearts – belongs together. Creation, redemption, and sanctification are not separated and 'in-communicated' operations but distinct, interrelated, and mutually inclusive acts of the one true God in which we are called to participate with equal dedication, love, and expectation. Even more, they are acts of God that assume, direct, and transform our own action in the direction of God's purpose of being 'all in all'.

Whether we deal with nature, the body, community, life in society, the proclamation of the gospel, or the call to faith, we are 'caught into' God's activity as Father, Son, and Holy Spirit. In this perspective, we could discuss with greater freedom the continuity and discontinuity between, for instance, 'divine healing' and 'medical healing', 'gifts as God-given human capacities and as special operations of the Spirit', and 'tongues' or 'prophecy' as part of the human history of religion and as a special dispensation in the Christian community. We would recognize the operation of God in all of these and at the same time the particularity of the special manifestations in and by the community of faith. I am not suggesting that there are not important issues, and probably significant differences, in the understanding of these relationships, continuities, and distinctions. But I do believe and I am convinced that, at the theological level, the trinitarian approach opens possibilities of a constructive dialogue; indeed, it can provide the basis for a common action in prayer, mission, and service.[5]

Notes

1   I will not be quoting the chapters in detail since they are available in this same publication. In some cases I will simply mention the names of the authors.

2   I speak of a 'modern' Pentecostal movement because it seems clear to me that what we find in the Pentecostal movement of the last ninety years reflects a persistent tradition attested throughout the history of Christianity. The Peruvian Pentecostal theologian Bernardo Campos has spoken of a 'pentecostality' (*pentecostalidad*) as a permanent dimension of the Christian faith, and of 'the Pentecostal movement' of our times as an expression of that 'pentecostality under the condition of modern culture and religious life'.

3   This concept is developed by Steve J. Land, *Pentecostal Spirituality: A Passion for the Kingdom* (Sheffield: Sheffield Academic Press, 1993).

4   In relation to these protections against a totally anomic experience, it would be valuable to follow these three areas — Scripture (memory), community (discernment), and eschatology (the foretaste and the fullness) — in the Pauline discussion in 1 Corinthians 11:17 – 14:40 and Romans 8:1–27.

5   I have tried to suggest an outline for an ecumenical conversation on this theme in the final two chapters of my book, *Faces of Latin American Protestantism* (Grand Rapids, MI: Wm. B. Eerdmans Publishing Co., 1996).

Section II

Pentecostalism as a Global Culture

Pentecostalism as a Global Culture
An Introductory Overview

Byron D. Klaus

Pentecostalism has been the quintessential indigenous religion, adapting readily to a variety of cultures. As a religious movement it has taken on the likeness of a particular culture of people. In one sense, Pentecostalism – with its autochthonous character – is a regionalized Christian movement, differing in identity from one part of the globe to the next. In another sense, it can be argued that while regional differences are real, Pentecostalism has generated a global culture which shares a common spirituality. The chapters in this section explore this dialectical relationship by looking at Pentecostalism within six regions through a double-sided window. On the one hand, the chapters will examine the character of the Pentecostal movement within that region. On the other hand, each author will look at the wider Pentecostal movement from the vantage point of that particular region.

To begin the section, Catholic scholar Edward Cleary provides the focus on Latin American Pentecostalism. Cleary demonstrates a breadth of research in his chapter on how Pentecostalism achieved its present religious status throughout Latin America. Cleary also addresses the inherent problems that have emerged due to rapid Pentecostal growth throughout the region and his analysis demonstrates the realities facing expectations for future Pentecostal influences in the region. Cleary notes how research in Latin American Pentecostalism is moving through a major shift in research paradigms. For Cleary this shift in scholarly research, towards a more phenomenological approach in the study of Latin American Pentecostalism, is largely due to a new insistence by scholars on listening more carefully to what Latin Americans themselves say about faith and religion. The emergence of careful studies of Pentecostalism done by Pentecostal scholars themselves have also increased significantly. Cleary concludes his chapter by affirming that his research shows a recognizable core spirituality characterizing Pentecostals, that clearly differentiates them both from Catholics and from other Protestants in the region. While acknowledging the uniqueness of 'Pentecostalism' in the region, he does suggest that Pentecostals seem to affirm an underlying unity based on core beliefs that cast them in the mould of a *contra mundum* religious community.

Japie LaPoorta provides the look at the African context, offering a case study of the Apostolic Faith Mission (AFM) of South Africa (SA). Using a narrative theological model, La Poorta addresses the historical origin of the AFM of SA and its recent move towards racial reconciliation within its own ranks as a Pentecostal denomination.

La Poorta posits that the nature of Pentecostal theology is inherently narrative in form and structure and that it values experience as more important than normally found in traditional, rational western theology. He further argues that Pentecostal narrative themes are a rhetorical power for liberating instruction in the lives of individuals and this theological model does not separate systematic theology from ethics. He concludes that narrative theology is necessary for doing Pentecostal theology in his context because it is a theology that is holistic, does not distinguish between sacred and secular spheres of life, and affirms human experiences through 'story' that identifies with specific human experiences and contexts. La Poorta concludes that the narrative theological process for Pentecostals in South Africa has and will expedite the process of unity between black and white and accelerate the establishment of a unified, non-racial and non-sexist AFM of SA.

Swiss theologian Jean Daniel Plüss provides the results of a survey he conducted with thirty Pentecostal/charismatic theologians throughout Europe. Plüss' query to the European Pentecostal/charismatic scholars provides an evaluation of several issues. Is there, in fact, the possibility that there exists a global Pentecostal/charismatic culture? Secondly, Plüss investigates the way in which the Pentecostal/charismatic culture has impacted the development of local churches in Europe. He concludes with an evaluation of whether or not there really is a global Pentecostal culture and what, if any, impact or benefit may be forthcoming to a Pentecostal spirituality and theology from such a global Pentecostal phenomenon.

Asia is a vast region where generalizations are necessary while utmost care must be exercised in fairness to the people groups represented in the area. Jungja (Julie) Ma deals with the region of Asia stretching from Mongolia and western China in the north to Indonesia in the South and from Japan in the east to Myanmar in the west.

Ma posits that the Pentecostal movement in this region has had a varying impact over the last few decades. In countries like Korea, Indonesia, Malaysia, Singapore, Philippines and Myanmar the Pentecostal influence has been significant. However, countries like Japan, Taiwan and Thailand have been fundamentally resistant to Christianity. Resistance exists for political and economic reasons in nations like Vietnam, Laos, Cambodia, Tibet, Nepal and China. Ma describes the critical issues facing Pentecostal mission in the region, analyses present changes posing a challenge to Pentecostal ministry in the region and concludes with an agenda that the Pentecostal church will face in the 21st century.

Ivan Satyavrata is the author of the chapter on Pentecostals from South Asia. He notes that in his region a movement that is less than a thousand years old is still in its adolescence. He continues that the Pentecostal movement in South Asia has limited resources with which to come to grips with the critical question of self-identity. Satyavrata suggests that there are five basic influences on the growth of Pentecostals in South Asia: 1) spontaneous emergence of new indigenous church movements arising from ongoing Pentecostal revival; 2) the advent of new overseas independent and denominational Pentecostal groups in South Asia; 3) the impact of the charismatic movement upon established churches; 4) the emergence of independent healing evangelists and Pentecostal parachurch agencies; 5) the consolidation and maturation of earlier Pentecostal movements through organization, leadership development and the emergence of educational, social and other holistic ministry agencies. Based on cited research, Satyavrata posits that western influences on South Asian Pentecostals have been present, but relatively insignificant. The unique appeal of the Pente-costal movement in the South Asia region has been its autochthonous, culturally adjustable character and is due in part to its identity as an expanding global movement. Satyavrata concludes that the Pentecos-tal movement does not exist for itself, it exists for the purpose of bring-ing renewal to the church and new energy to the impetus of its mission.

David Daniels' chapter concludes this section, in the spirit of H. Richard Niebuhr's *Social Sources* thesis, by exploring the role that race has played in the development of North American Pentecos-talism. Daniels forcefully posits a multi-cultural lens through which to rethink the emergence of Pentecostals in North America. While Pente-costals certainly advanced more along ethnic and racial lines in the region, Daniels argues that interracial impulses did exist inspiring Pentecostal leaders throughout the 20th century to cross racial divides. He believes that this inter-racial impulse had historical catalysts from such sources as interracial commitments of the black holiness move-ment and some white holiness networks and the pivotal role of black holiness congregations in the emergence of North American Pentecos-tals. While noting that racial differences in the theological preferences of white, African American or Hispanic Pentecostal are difficult to interpret, Daniels affirms that North American Pentecostals reflect the capacity present in nascent Pentecostalism to represent and reform the religious cultures they have engaged. Daniels suggests that any attempt to discuss the historical epicenter changes in Christianity must now acknowledge Pentecostal lenses through which to interpret Christian tradition. Pivotal to the discussion of Christianity's defining epicenters, Daniels argues that scholars must acknowledge North American Pentecostalism's role in birthing the global Pentecost movement that presently is one of the most vibrant expressions of Christianity worldwide.

The response to the contributions in this section is offered by Dr. Vinay Samuel. His missiological insight and keen analysis provides critical evaluation of Pentecostalism as a global culture. His critique, offered as a observer from the Two Thirds world, provides an insight-ful review from the perspective of a person who represents the part of the world where Pentecostalism is growing most rapidly.

Chapter Six

Latin American Pentecostalism

Edward L. Cleary, O.P.

If for this volume Latin American Pentecostalism is bathed in the light of recognition, it is only after decades of neglect and discrimination. When we now celebrate growth in numbers and prominence, we also recall men and women who set deep roots in Latin American soil despite unpromising circumstances.

Pentecostalism has quietly grown into the largest Christian movement of the twentieth century.[1] Some 400–500 million followers can be found in most areas of the world.[2] Their number is almost half that of the largest Christian denomination, Roman Catholicism. Pentecostalism's otherworldly style and growth rate, by conversion and by inherited status, is astonishing, given the predictions that modern times would be increasingly secular.

Harvey Cox's *Fire from Heaven: The Rise of Pentecostal Spirituality and the Reshaping of Religion in the Twenty-first Century*[3] opened to general readers in 1995 what was barely known even in theological schools.[4] Pentecostalism has grown in Latin America where it challenges Catholic, historical Protestant and Mormon churches, voudou, macumba, and Indian religions.

Pentecostalism has a prominent place in several Latin American countries. What this position is, how it achieved this status, and the problems it faces are the issues I address. I also reflect on changes in research paradigms and the question of cultural unity. Many Pentecostals celebrate large-scaled growth in numbers and in holiness. But careful observers see clearly issues facing Pentecostalism in a post-modern world.

The following observations are made on the basis of twelve years of reading and investigation of Latin American Protestantism. This became almost exclusively a study of Pentecostalism. I am also reporting the results of a four-year research and publishing project of twelve scholars on Latin American Pentecostalism.[5] I am also especially guided in these remarks by Everett Wilson.

WHY ONLY NOW?

Only very recently could such a volume as this be published. Four conditions lacking previously now exist for surveying and assessing Pentecostal life in Latin America. David Martin and David Stoll opened the eyes of general readers and many in the evangelical and Catholic communities with their groundbreaking studies.[6] But studies would have to be undertaken by Latin Americanists with wider experience in various countries. Secondly, studies of Pentecostalism or Catholicism tended to be one-sided. Martin and many others ignore the Catholic resurgence in Latin America. Or, by contrast, accounts of the church in Latin America meant studies of the Catholic church. Various aspects of religion need to be accounted for simultaneously.

Thirdly, social science views of Latin American religion have gone through a salutary evolution. A new insistence of scholars is to listen carefully to what Latin Americans say about their religion. Along with this is an attempt to describe what goes on interiorly: how Latin Americans describe their faith and religion.[7]

Lastly, for the first time we have a critical mass of careful studies of Pentecostalism. More importantly, Pentecostal scholars and students of religion, such as Everett Wilson, Douglas Petersen, and Kenneth Gill, have entered into active exchange in the interpretation of Latin American Pentecostalism. Latin American scholars include Juan Sepúlveda, Norberto Saracco, Manuel Gaxiola, and Luis Segreda.

GROWING FIELD OF RESEARCH

As a result of the changes noted above, at long last, the paradigms by which research on Pentecostals is carried on are changing. Earlier works include those most cited by Latin Americans, as those of Emilio Willems, Christian Lalive D'Epinay, Francisco C. Rolim, and Jean Pierre Bastian.[8] Willems's summary article[9] and later book, *Followers of the New Faith,*[10] became minor classics. His book, published in 1967,[11] opened a window to what *Time* in 1962 had called 'the fastest growing church in the Western Hemisphere'.[12]

Samuel Escobar, one of the most respected Latin American scholars, summarizes his view of these studies and of documents from Catholic bishops, ecumenical organizations, anthropological and sociological studies in academic publications, and popular reports in the mass media as 'an amazing inadequacy to deal with their subject'.[13] Harvey Cox recalls his feelings as a number of 'large holes' appeared in Lalive's and other explanations.[14]

For Escobar and others a new and impressive stage of scholarship begins in 1990.[15] The year marked the appearance of the first comprehensive works on Latin American Pentecostalism and politics. These were also the first to appeal to a wide readership: David Stoll's *Is Latin America Turning Protestant?: The Politics of Evangelical Growth* and David Martin's *Tongues of Fire: The Explosion of Protestantism in Latin America.*[16] Their publication opened the way for numerous commentaries, some of them opportunistic and erroneous.

A critical mass of new studies has been reported since the Stoll and Martin volumes. Elizabeth Brusco, Cecília Mariz, Leslie Gill, Paul Freston, Rowan Ireland, Manuel Marzal, John Burdick[17] and others have recently completed works of unusual merit, upon which one might build.

WHO ARE LATIN AMERICAN PENTECOSTALS?

History is an indispensable tool for describing accurately the identity of Pentecostals and the religious character of Pentecostalism in Latin America. Constructing history has been a difficult process. The process is not complete, but enough is known to make confident statements.[18] The resulting picture of Pentecostals in Latin America dispels numerous, thoughtlessly repeated stereotypes. Rather than enumerate and refute these, I shall proceed positively, to establish as clear picture as possible of Latin American Pentecostalism.

A series of sparks were struck in various parts of the world at approximately the same time. Extraordinary experiences, reported from Los Angeles, Armenia, Wales, and South Africa, were also experienced in Chile, Brazil, and Argentina (1910); Peru (1911); Nicaragua (1912); Mexico (1914); and Guatemala and Puerto Rico (1916).[19]

Foreign missionaries helped to spark, not create, a new religious tradition within Latin America. The impulse for new churches, membership, and the vast majority of leaders came from Latin America. Thus, a number of Chilean and other Pentecostals point to themselves as *criollo* Pentecostals. Some are now third-and fourth-generation Pentecostal church members.

A spirit of tolerance for other religions in Brazil, Guatemala, and Chile may have aided in this reception and growth. A sense of spiritual anemia also pervaded some regions, to the point that the highly influential Jesuit Alberto Hurtado questionned in a written article whether Chile was Catholic, generations ago.

Samuel Escobar and other trusted observers rate the general Protestant population in Latin America and the Caribbean at 40 million.[20] This is in a population of about 400 million. Of these, 75–90 per cent are Pentecostals. Of some 20 million Pentecostals, half are in Brazil.

The percentage of Pentecostals to the general population gives a better view. Here Puerto Rico and Guatemala stand out. Protestants, most of them Pentecostal, represent about 40 per cent of the population. Countries with lesser, but impressive percentages include Brazil, Chile, Haiti and all of Central America. Pentecostalism is not prominent in two-thirds of the other countries, with less than 10 per cent of the general population. In these countries, though percentages are low, observers at the grassroots report impressive, even explosive, growth rates.

CATHOLIC SOUL AND LOWER CLASS?
CULTURAL AND SOCIAL ASPECTS

I regret dealing with numbers because other considerations are more important. Pentecostalism, throughout its almost 90 years of history, expresses something of the soul of Latin America. This affirmation contrasts with statements by Catholic church leaders and political scientists who argue that Protestants are interlopers since Latin Americans have a Catholic soul.[21] It is truer to say that many Latin

Americans have a Christian soul, one of the expressions of which is Pentecostalism.

Pentecostal churches have been led by Latin Americans almost exclusively from the beginning. Latin Americans embrace Pentecostal experience with little cultural adjustment. Converts from historical Protestantism and Catholicism find a suitable way to live within modern Latin America.

The myth of hegemonic Catholic culture has no valid basis.[22] Chilean and Brazilian Pentecostals vote and act as fully franchised citizens. They are no longer pilgrims, but are at home in Chile, Brazil, and elsewhere.

Further, a unified Pentecostal culture cannot be assumed. Brazilian, Chilean, Guatemalan Pentecostals, reflecting differing levels of development and cultures, choose whether or not to emphasize educational systems for laity, academic biblical education, and professionalized rehabilitation services, to name a few of a hundred aspects. It is no surprise to encounter Juan Sepúlveda from Chile pursuing a doctorate at Birmingham, England, or Norberto Soracco from Argentina reflecting high-level academic training.

Neither is it useful to describe the great growth of Pentecostalism in various countries without also mentioning the resurgence of Catholicism. Could they not both be a part of a larger phenomenon? Some, perhaps many Pentecostal scholars, do not have a firm grasp of the contemporary developments that are enriching the Catholic church. Virginia Garrard-Burnett in a recent study of Guatemalan Protestants shows the advantages of a wider perspective.[23]

In my own studies, I found a general religious awakening taking place, for Catholics and Pentecostals alike. In Guatemala lay persons have shown greater church participation and leadership.[24] Some 50,000 lay Catholics have participated in Cursillos de Cristiandad, one of many lay movements. Seminaries could not contain all the seminarians, and new ones had to be built. In three countries where Pentecostal growth is most prominent, Catholic seminary students increased dramatically. From 1972 to 1991, there was an 874 per cent increase in Guatemala, 709 per cent in Chile, and 522 per cent in Brazil.[25] Also, in Brazil, sales of Bibles have exploded. In the last four years 4.5 million complete Bibles were sold, 36 per cent by Catholic publishers.[26]

Class has long been a major issue in viewing Pentecostals in Latin America. At first most members came from the lower classes. Many converts have continued to come from urban poblaciones and, to a lesser extent, from rural peasant communities. This perception allowed extravagant theories about Pentecostalism as the 'haven of the masses'. Many reasons were educed for its attraction for the poor. The uneducated could not understand reformed Catholicism or the rationality of historical Protestantism. Many poor people, it was alleged, did not want an openly social or political position in society. Then, it was affirmed that strong authoritative pastors reproduce their paternalistic, patron-client relations of traditional Latin American society.

Often overlooked were key Pentecostals active in society as shop-keepers, small entrepreneurs, and school teachers. Many key persons became upper-lower and lower-middle classes, a creative strata, whose aspirations helped to give leadership.[27] Many Pentecostals came from the suffering poor, but not all.

Through the passage of time, by saving money, and working hard, children of these converts have entered into the middle classes. Direct recruitment from middle-class Protestants and Catholics has also occurred.[28] So, now, in Chile 48 per cent belong to the middle class, with educational achievement to back up middle-level economic status. In countries, such as Guatemala, Brazil, and Venezuela, a substantial incursion into the middle class is evident.

A major element in the advancement to middle social status has been education. Pentecostals stay in school longer. They run educational systems at considerable expense to themselves. A rather small number of pastors have more advanced biblical and theological educational opportunities. But the general educational attainment of clergy seems to lag behind that of many lay members.

Decades of informal education preceded these advances. Reading and studying have been the backbone of Pentecostal discipline. More careful studies, such as those of Rowan Ireland, show us Severino first going to literacy classes, meeting Pentecostals there, and then spending a lifetime, 'reading, reading, reflecting, reflecting'.[29]

The association of Pentecostalism and poverty easily leads to faulty logic and poor methodology. Observers, instead of asking the reasons for the attraction of Pentecostalism, often substitute the question, 'why do poor people convert?' The latter question, in turn, leads to certain kinds of responses. One implication is that Pentecostalism has grown because the poor and uneducated do not understand the contemporary, particularly progressive, Catholic message.

The stabilization of family life and the escape from personal dysfunctional behaviour has been one of the commonly observed effects of living a Pentecostal life. Pentecostal churches actively seek the welfare of family members. Here we come to the heart of the matter. Pentecostalism has a high moral character. One could characterize it as a perfectionist religion. This is highly important since the perfectionist tone helps to explain why many turn away, and why Pentecostalism adds a moral dimension to Latin American life and culture. Holiness, humility, and a strict moral code stand out as characteristics of Pentecostalism throughout countries studied in Latin America.

Being taken over by God, *tomada del Espíritu*, has become a foundational experience. But this is just the beginning. The rest of the journey involves a moral reformation. The guide here is a strict moral code. Humility results as Latin American Pentecostals hope for progress, if not perfection.

The economic consequences of Pentecostalism have yet to be explored fully. We know of millions who do not drink alcohol, gamble, and try to do a day's work.[30] Many *crentes* in Brazil and elsewhere heard stories from their grandparents of employers who would not hire them. Now non-Pentecostals complain that employers are too selective, preferring only Pentecostals.

Part of the perfectionist ideal is sacrificial giving. The great lie about Protestants in Latin America is that they needed outside monies from Jerry Falwell or Jimmy Swaggert. Latin American Pentecostals thrive in large part from their own resources. If they live largely from their own funds, they maintain to a great extent their Brazilian or other preferences. The fundamental source of financial support for Pentecostal churches in Latin America is the generosity of individual members. Church attenders[31] give frequently, and they give from their substance, not their surplus. Contributing ten per cent of income is not uncommon and is held up frequently as a goal.

The results of this generosity is impressive. Petersen estimates that the Assemblies of God in Central America, Panamá, and Belize possess combined assets of $150 million in real estate and improvements.[32] Throughout Latin America sacrificial giving has produced billions of dollars of property, buildings, and other resources owned locally, and to a lesser extent, nationally.

Gender has become a more focused issue. Scholars are taking a new look at the implications of Pentecostal gender relations. Building on the work of Elizabeth Brusco[33] and others, Drogus suggests that although Pentecostals' traditional gender divisions are intended to reinforce male dominance, the combination of emphasis on religious equality, new roles open to women in the life of the church, and the equalization of work traditionally relegated to 'women's sphere' all serve to undermine hegemonic ideologies of *machismo* and *marianismo*.

Cecília Mariz' and María das Dores Campos Machado's study on women in Brazil[34] underscores the notion that Pentecostalism can dismantle traditional *machismo*; yet, the authors argue that Pentecostal women choose to adhere closely to traditional moral and social codes. The difference for Pentecostal women is not that they reject traditional values regarding family, sexual codes or gender roles. Rather, the believer sees herself as an individual responsible for her own liberation from the oppression of evil, defined as natural passions and instincts. It is the process of individuation, coupled with the assertion of a primary responsibility to God (rather than one's spouse or family), that transforms women into active, responsible agents in their own and their families' lives. These authors assert, then, that not only does Pentecostal conversion 'domesticate' male roles, but it also results in greater individuation and autonomy (if still 'traditional' in social values) for women.

Further research must explore more carefully the kinds of roles played by women, the religious justification for female participation in the gendered spheres of the church, the effects (if any) of female religious leadership on other women in Pentecostal groups,[35] and the potential for empowerment in traditional 'women's work' within churches.[36] Another issue that has been largely ignored is the role of single women in Pentecostal churches. What is the concept of women within Pentecostal circles beyond the categories of wife and mother?

PASTORS AND CONVERSION

Distinctive features of Latin American Pentecostalism, in contrast to other Christian bodies, have been clergy and conversion. Clergy are paramount to the life of the church. Non-Pentecostals began marvelling at the pragmatic and spiritual characteristics, manner of recruitment, training, and leadership of Pentecostal pastors. Peter Wagner's 1970s article was one of the first. The lengthy training and testing of persons for the clergy is impressive. We found in Chile that pastors were seldom less than forty years old at ordination, having spent twenty years in training at various levels of responsibility.

This on-the-job training produces pastors who live within the social sphere of their congregation, in contrast to the isolated training and unmarried lives of Catholic clergy.[37] The result has been until recently a very large body of clergy, relatively close to the culture of the people served. Taking Guatemala, a slightly extreme example, I would estimate that there are about five to six times as many Pentecostal pastors as Catholic priests. Further, the majority of Catholic priests are foreign-born, and the vast majority of Protestants and Pentecostals are Guatemalan.

The Pentecostal pastor, his training, and the fragmentation of community members who follow diverse pastors is a familiar story. The effects of these divisions have not been well explored. Another type of division is better known. In Chile with almost ninety years of Pentecostal church life and with growing economic prosperity, problems are occurring due to the limited academic training and 'popular-class' style of pastors.

Change in social composition of Pentecostals and passage of time have made evident serious weaknesses.[38] Willems noted thirty years ago: 'Proud as the Pentecostals leaders may be of their lack of formal theological training, they still live in a society where formal recognition of professional skill is highly valued.'[39] A recent study shows the high value contemporary Pentecostal Sunday-school teachers place on university education.[40]

Paul B. Hoff, president of the Pentecostal Bible Institute in Santiago, points to class background and lack of education as issues. He observes: 'Lay pastors are seldom able to provide biblical teaching. This problem is intensified because the pastor's knowledge of the Bible is limited to what they hear from the older men, who themselves have had no systematic teaching... The preacher utters whatever comes to mind.'[41]

Thus, says Hoff: 'While middle-class Chileans often admire the zeal, faith, and sincerity of the Pentecostals, they are repelled by lack of preparation of their preachers... Parents complain that their college-age children are bored with the sermons and leave the church.'[42]

Older approaches are not working well for some sectors. Hoff quotes the president of a Pentecostal group in Vitacura, an affluent Santiago sector, as saying that few persons are won by street preaching. Hoff observes: 'It is not uncommon to see Pentecostals preaching to empty street corners. Yet they continue to rely on this method and seem incapable of adapting to new circumstances.'[43] Galilea in her study of Pentecostal preachers notes both their insecurity about what methods to use with the middle classes and fear about the outcome of preaching to them.[44]

Many Pentecostals regard conversion as the single most important event of their lives. Conversion serves as the basis of living and of membership, stabilizes families, and impels those who have undergone it to reach out to others. Popular Pentecostalism mobilizes members for mission. Catholic bishop Roger Aubrey notes the contrast between the inhibited character of Catholics and their priests and Pentecostals who audaciously go from house to house.[45] This difference in understanding Christianity and culturally acceptable methods of attracting recruits serves as an irritant between many Catholics and Pentecostals. Cecil Robeck has recently written an illuminating examination of the issue.[46]

Recent research, especially in Brazil, points to differences in conversions. Rowan Ireland, John Burdick, Paul Freston, and Cecília Mariz have helped to clarify real differences in understanding what it means to be a Brazilian Pentecostal, based on differing conversions. Years of listening to Pentecostals in national assemblies or year after year in person-to-person conversations have convinced Ireland that there are basically three types of conversions, as found in Brazil and seem to exist elsewhere.

Among the first two types of conversion, both include once for all and complete conversions which involve self-exclusion from full social engagement, as found among the church *crentes* of Campo Alegre, and those once for all and complete conversions which involve that decidedly uncritical inclusion found among members of the Universal Church of the Kingdom of God described by Paul Freston. There is a third type, one of continuing conversion.

POLITICAL ASPECTS

The implications of these types of conversion show up clearly in views of society and of politics. A pairing of three types of conversion and three types of political citizenship can be found among Brazilian Pentecostals. The abdicated citizen Ireland found in the church *crentes* of Alegre Campo has become that kind of citizen as a consequence of living out the religious culture acquired at conversion as a complete guide to salvation within the haven of the church. The pragmatic political person of 'third wave' Pentecostalism has experienced a once for all and complete conversion that encourages him or her to become included in the upwardly mobile post-modern Brazil. The critical citizen of some recent studies of Brazilian Pentecostals is likely to live out the Pentecostal religious culture in a continuing conversion that turns to social engagement.

After years of apparent quiescence Pentecostals have come to prominence in politics within the last ten years. In 1986 *Newsweek* noted that Protestants, especially Pentecostal ones, were entering party politics in Latin America.[47] Pentecostals became active in the public arena in Guatemala, El Salvador, Venezuela, Colombia, Perú, and Brazil.

From Christian Lalive D'Epinay's time forward, Pentecostals, within their refuges of the masses, had been depicted as carriers of traditionally conservative and anti-democratic values. Recent studies show a more complex view of Pentecostal political orientations.[48] While a few Pentecostals are dogmatically anti-political and some see politics as corrupting, many other Pentecostals contribute, especially at the local level, to community service. This is not new in Chile where many Pentecostals entered into the rural development schemes of Eduardo Frei. But all the countries studied show a relatively high degree to which Pentecostals involve themselves in social service networks, both locally and nationally. Moreover, Anna Adams, has shown how this tendency has moved to the U. S. mainland from Puerto Rico. Hannah Stewart-Gambino and Everett Wilson have repeated the comment of Jeffrey Gros: 'Pentecostals do not have a social policy; they are a social policy.'[49]

These studies show that Pentecostals have voted in large numbers, voting for such candidates as Allende, contrary to sociologists' expectations. When they have gone further to establish their own parties, Pentecostals have entered on a learning curve about public politics. An evangelical party failed in Perú. Subsequent efforts to ride Alberto Fujimori's coattails to power backfired when Fujimori turned his back on these supporters.

CONTEMPORARY ISSUES

In Latin America I have noted how questions have arisen about the distance between educated laity and less educated pastors, non-attendance by a very large numbers of Pentecostals, strongly aggressive recruitment tactics, the taking of moral positions by lay persons independent of their pastors, and the different kinds of conversions and of Pentecostalisms. Other issues remain for discussion.[50]

We began with history and found fervour. We end with contemporary times, and we still find amazing vitality. But Pentecostalism is aging and showing signs one expects of a ninety-year old movement. Chile is one of the old foundations. There a reputable research organization conducted two studies which showed that more than half of Protestants (most of them Pentecostal) did not attend church weekly. Pastors believe that Pentecostals are by definition not only observant but also militant. Chilean Pentecostal pastors in Chile thus took this as a stunning revelation. They entered on a series of discussions. What had alienated the dropouts? Pentecostal pastors have asked if they are dealing with second- or later-generation Pentecostals who still consider themselves Pentecostal but whose professional advancement has increasingly alienated them from the church.[51] Or, do young persons feel that the churches do not grant them enough 'space' to live as young persons in Chilean society?

Is Pentecostalism like a great harvester that takes in many new converts, but also leaves a large residue of non-practising Pentecostals? Pentecostalism in Chile still has a high growth rate, of some 4 per cent yearly growth. What happens to ex-Pentecostals? We do not know much about them.

A word needs to be said, too, about Neo-Pentecostals. The Universal Church of God in Brazil, for one, has added some 3.5 million members in less than twenty years. Are these groups which emphasize health and wealth benefits as central to religion to be considered part of Pentecostalism?

CHANGING PARADIGMS

The prevalent theory of modernization has attempted to explain how bureaucratization, urbanization, industrialization, secularization, and other processes will produce a complex society. Secularization will affect religion, bringing about its demise or at least its being pushed to the margins of society.

What changed so much was not religion but the theory.[52] Gilles Kepel captures this well, as *La revanche de Dieu* (The Revenge of God).[53] Many similar analyses followed.[54] None of six salient books announcing the end to secularization treat the globalization of

Pentecostalism. This major movement, for them, remains in the shadows.[55]

What I see is not the decline of religion, but its restructuring. I see the effects of agrarian concentration, large-scale migration, improved transport, expanded literacy, and access to media combining to undermine long-standing ties between elites and masses. Popular sectors were then made available for new kinds of organization and experimentation. Massive social forces affect especially (but not only) lower classes among which both Pentecostalism and various forms of reformed Catholicism flourish.

Here Everett Wilson's depiction of Guatemalan Pentecostalism is especially fitting. We do not have a store of images to portray Latin American Pentecostalism. Towers, bells, cathedrals, street processions have little to do with Pentecostalism. Neither do those irritating images of 'holy rollers', old-time religion, or Swaggart-style televangelism fit the picture. Wilson shows Pentecostals occupying space in local and national society as Popular Pentecostals. This is a new, national infrastructure of churches that, while being made up largely of poor individuals, own their own buildings, have juridical personality, and have organized well within and beyond their own communities.

The paradigm shift would also include a view of the general exuberance of religion. Probably thirty million Brazilians practise Afro-based religions.[56] Practice of Afro-Brazilian religion tends to be veiled, making it less accessible for judging than established religions. Social scientists had to walk around and count *terreiros* in crowded neighborhoods or go to authorities and look at registers, probably missing some religious centres in the process. In Salvador, Bahía in the 1930s, 67 houses of worship were entered in the registry at the Union of Afro-Brazilian Sects. Estimates for 1989 run to more than 2,500 centres.[57]

CONCLUSION: SPIRITUAL CORE

Throughout the studies reviewed, a recognizable core of spirituality characterizes Pentecostals in various societies and cultures. Reflection on Pentecostals in Latin America shows central practices and beliefs which set Pentecostals there apart from most Catholics and from other Protestants. Pentecostals centre their lives on experience of the Holy Spirit. This is better described as individual rather than subjective or illusory experience, an event radiating throughout one's body and evident to others. It is a vividly felt contact with God. Pentecostals' experience of God is a primary and constant part of their religion. The structures of their worship are designed to enhance these experiences on a routine basis through expressive, intense, and performance-oriented liturgies. *La tomada del Espíritu* (the taking over by the Spirit), noted years ago by Willems, is typical of the kinds of experience which have been core to Pentecostal practice.[58]

Emphasizing the gifts of the Holy Spirit, Latin American Pentecostals are confident that these gifts are present within the church and can be relied on, in a way that Catholics and other Protestants do not emphasize. Wilson agrees: 'Stated theologically, Pentecostal groups carry the doctrine of immanence accepted by all Christian believers beyond the usually accepted boundaries, since the grace, gifts, and power attributed to the church are believed to be accessible, at least on occasion to every believer.'

Christian experience, according to the modern view, is not so much affective experience, but the personal integration of an affective experience. Thus experience is, first, making contact with God and, then, maintaining communion with God. Contemporary theologians have recognized the function of affectivity. Jean Mouroux believes that spiritual affectivity (taking pleasure in the Lord is the way many Pentecostals describe it) heals and transforms through joy.[59] Contemporary theologians also focus not on experiences which are mystical, in the sense of extraordinary, but ones which occur within the ordinary and unforced religious life experiences of average persons.

Theologically, being grounded in experience has important consequences. In a profound sense, neither institution nor any other person mediates in a Pentecostal person's conversion to God.[60] No formal rite (not even baptism) is required and the role of the pastor is reduced. The testimony and the fervour of the person shows the faith of the Pentecostal person. The Pentecostal movement does not require more than this testimony for one to be accepted as a convert and participant in services. Unlike many other denominations, neither a certain level of preparation nor knowledge of Scripture is required at this entry level. Thus Pentecostalism offers an open field for personal liberty.

As a result of intense religious experience, persons have as their aim the bringing of their lives into conformity with the norms expected of a person living in contact and communion with God. These persons typically have a heightened sense of hope. This description fits what

Wilson says of Latin American Pentecostals: 'At (Pentecostalism's) roots lies the assertion that Christian faith, biblically and historically understood, no matter how orthodox or pietistic, must be existential (based on experience).[61] Though typically buoyant and enthusiastic, Pentecostals are basically skeptical of human intentions, efforts, and institutions. However, their movement views human brokenness not with despair, but with hope.'[62]

Pentecostalism has proved itself immensely adaptive and pragmatic. In terms of the central issue of unity Pentecostals apparently sense an underlying unity, one built on core beliefs.

Using history and theology, one could focus on the long history of attempts at spiritual renewal within Christianity. Pentecostalism is deeply rooted in the Holiness and revival traditions. These grow out of a centuries long impulse among ordinary Christians toward a deeper spiritual life, beyond mere church attendance, to have contact with God. In European Protestantism, after the Reformation, this renewal impulse was often guided by Pietists. They accepted as foundations: seeking of personal experience of God, commencing with a new birth by the Holy Spirit; holding the conviction that experience leads to reforming lives; and living within a community, a community taking a stand against a corrupt world. Communities thus took on a *contra mundum* cast. To a remarkable degree, Latin American Pentecostals mirror these characteristics.

Notes

1   A number of scholars accept William Menzies's description: 'The Pentecostal movement is that group of sects within the Christian church which is characterized by the belief that the occurrence mentioned in Acts 2 on the day of Pentecost not only signalled the birth of the church, but described an experience available to believers in all ages'. *Anointed To Serve* (Springfield, Mo.: Gospel Publishing House, 1971, p. 90.)

2   David B. Barrett in his 11th statistical survey for *International Bulletin of Missionary Research* 19, 1 (Jan. 1995), pp. 24–25, combines Pentecostals/Charismatics and estimates their number as 463,741,000 in mid 1995.

3   Cox, *Fire from Heaven: The Rise of Pentecostal Spirituality and the Reshaping of Religion in the Twenty-first Century* (Reading, MA: Addison-Wesley Publishing Co., 1995).

4   In addition to Cox, especially useful views on Pentecostalism have been provided by Robert Mapes Anderson, *Vision of the Disinherited: The Making of American Pentecostalism* (New York, NY: Oxford University Press, 1979); Walter J. Hollenwager, *The Pentecostals: The Charismatic Movement in the Churches* (Minneapolis, MN: Augsburg Publishing House, 1972) works by

Grant Wacker, as, 'Pentecostalism', in *Encyclopedia of American Religious Experience: Studies of Traditions and Movements,* ed., Charles H. Lippy and Peter W. Williams (New York, NY: Scribners, 1988) v. 2, pp. 933–945; Stanley M. Burgess and Gary B. McGee, ed., *Dictionary of Pentecostal and Charismatic Movements* (Grand Rapids, Mich.: Zondervan Publishing House, 1988); and *Pneuma* and other publications of the Society for Pentecostal Studies. Pioneering views of Pentecostal theology are taken up by Donald W. Dayton, *Theological Roots of Pentecostalism* (Metuchen, NJ: Scarecrow Press, 1987) and Matthew S. Clark, Henry I. Lederle, *et al., What is Distinctive about Pentecostal Theology* (Pretoria: University of South Africa, 1983). A central phenomenon for many Pentecostals is speaking in tongues, taken up by Cyril G. Williams, *Tongues of the Spirit: A Study of Pentecostal Glossolalia and Related Phenomena* (Cardiff: University of Wales Press, 1981). For bibliography, see Charles Edwin Jones, *Guide to the Study of the Pentecostal Movement* 2 vols. (Metuchen, NJ: Scarecrow Press, 1983).

5   Edward L. Cleary and Hannah Stewart-Gambino, ed., *Power. Politics, and Pentecostals in Latin America* (Boulder, CO: Westview Press, 1996).

6   Martin, *Tongues of Fire: The Explosion of Protestantism in Latin America* (Cambridge, MA: Basil Blackwell, 1990) and Stoll, *Is Latin America Turning Protestant? The Politics of Evangelical Growth* (Berkeley, CA: University of California Press, 1990).

7   Notable in this regard are Daniel Levine's *Popular Voices in Latin American Catholicism* (Princeton, N.J.: Princeton University Press, 1992); Rowan Ireland, *Kingdoms Come: Religion and Politics in Brazil* (Pittsburgh, PA: University of Pittsburgh Press, 1991); and John Burdick, *Looking for God in Brazil: The Progressive Catholic Church in Urban Brazil's Religious Arena* (Berkeley: University of California Press, 1993).

8   For a Latin American survey see: Jorge Soneira, 'Los estudios sociológicos sobre el pentecostalismo en América Latina', *Sociedad y Religión* 8 (March 1991), pp. 60–67.

9   Willems, 'Protestantism and Cultural Change in Brazil and Chile', in William V. D'Antonio and Frederick B. Pike, ed., *Religion, Revolution, and Reform* (New York, NY: Praeger, 1964), pp. 93–108.

10   Subtitled: *Culture Change and the Rise of Protestantism in Brazil and Chile* (Nashville: Vanderbilt University Press, 1967).

11   The fieldwork was carried out in 1959–60, before the first Frei government in Chile and the military coup in Brazil.

12   *Time* 80, 56 (Nov. 2, 1962). *America*, the Jesuit weekly, described 'The Pentecostal Breakthrough', in its Jan 31, 1970 issue.

13   Escobar, 'The Promise and Precariousness of Latin American Protestantism', in Daniel R. Miller, ed., *Coming of Age: Protestanatism in Contemporary Latin America* (Lanham, MD: University Press of America, 1994), p. 11.

14   Cox, *Fire*, pp. 161–184.

15   Three studies published before 1990 should be exempt from Escobar's evaluation. Cornelia Butler Flora's *Pentecostalism in Colombia* (Rutherford, N.J.: Farleigh Dickinson University Press, 1976); Stephen D. Glazier and colleagues received insufficient attention for *Perspectives on Pentecostalism: Case Studies from the Caribbean and Latin America* (Washington, D.C.: University Press of America, 1980); and Eugene A. Nida's 'The Relationship of

Social Structure to the Problems of Evangelism in Latin America', *Practical Anthropology* 5 (1958), pp. 101–123.

16   (Berkeley, Calif.: University of California Press, 1990) and (Oxford: Basil Blackwell, 1990). See also more recent works: Daniel R. Miller, ed., *Coming of Age: Protestantism in Latin America* (Lanham, MD: University Press of America, 1994) and Virginia Garrard-Burnett and David Stoll, ed., *Rethinking Protestantism in Latin America* (Philadelphia, PA: Temple University Press, 1993). For a critical view of treating Pentecostalism as part of fundamentalism, see Daniel Levine, 'Protestants and Catholics in Latin America: Family Portrait', Fundamentalism Project, University of Chicago, Nov. 1991. For a differing view, see Russell P. Spittler, 'Are Pentecostals and Charismatics Fundamentalists?; A Review of American Uses of These Categories', in *Charismatic Christianity as a Global Culture,* Karla Poewe, ed., (Columbia, SC: University of South Carolina Press, 1994), pp. 103–116. For bibliographies, see Martin and Stoll (above) and Cecil M. Robeck, Jr., 'Select Bibliography on Latin American Pentecostalism', *PNEUMA, The Journal of the Society for Pentecostal Studies* 13, 1 (Spring 1991), pp. 193–197. The most comprehensive source for works in Spanish or Portuguese, but one which lags in publication dates, is *Bibliografía teológica comentada del area latinoamericana* (Buenos Aires: Instituto Superior Evangélico de Estudios Teológicos, periodically).

17   Among other works, see: Brusco, 'The Household Basis of Evangelical Religion and the Reformation of Machismo in Colombia', (Ph.D. diss., City University of New York, NY, 1986.; Mariz, *Coping with Poverty: Pentecostals and Christian Base Communities in Brazil* (Philadelphia, PA: Temple University Press, 1994; Gill, 'Religious Mobility and Many Words of God in La Paz, Bolivia', in *Rethinking*, Garrard-Burnett and Stoll, pp. 180–198; Freston, 'Brother Votes for Brother: The New Politics of Protestantism in Brazil', in *Rethinking*, Garrard-Burnett and Stoll, pp. 66–110; Ireland, *Kingdoms Come: Religion and Politics in Brazil* (Pittsburgh, PA: University of Pittsburgh Press, 1991); Marzal, *Caminos religiosos de los immigrantes en la Gran Lima: El caso de El Agostino* (Lima, Peru: Fondo Editorial, Pontificia Universidad Católica Peruana, 1986) and other works; and Burdick, *Looking for God in Brazil: The Progressive Catholic Church in Urban Brazil's Religious Arena* (Berkeley, CA: University of California Press, 1993).

18   See Cleary and Stewart-Gambino, *Power*.

19   These conventional dates are accepted by David B. Barrett, ed., *World Christian Encyclopedia* (New York, NY: Oxford University Press, 1982).

20   Interview with Escobar, Grand Rapids, Mich., 7 June 1993.

21   For a discussion of John Paul II and the bishops see Cleary, 'Report from Santo Domingo', *Commonweal* 20 Nov. 1992, pp. 7–8. For social science and philosophical views, see works by Howard Wiarda and Glen C. Dealy, esp. Dealy's *The Public Man: An Interpretation of Latin American and Other Catholic Countries* (Amherst, MA: University of Massachusetts Press, 1977).

22   Ibid. In addition see Franz Damen, 'Las sectas, avalancha o desafío?', *Quarto Intercambio* no. 3 (Cochabamba) (May 1987), pp. 44–65.

23   'Living in the New Jerusalem: A History of Protestants in Guatemala', Virginia Garrard-Burnett, unpublished manuscript.

24   See, for example, *La Hora*, 18 July 1990.

25   Source: *Statistical Yearbook of the Church 1991* and *Catholic Almanac 1975*.

26   *A Biblia no Brasil* 48, 173 (Jan.–March 1996), pp. 16–20.

27   Everett A. Wilson, 'Identity, Community, and Status: The Legacy of the Central American Pioneers', in *Earthen Vessels: American Evangelicals and Foreign Missions, 1880–1980*, Joel A. Carpenter and Wilbert R. Shenk, ed., (Grand Rapids, MI: Wm. B. Eerdmans Publishing Co., 1990), pp. 133–151.

28   Garrard-Burnett, 'Living', passim, esp. chs. 6, 25.

29   Ireland, 'Pentecostalism, Conversions, and Politics in Brazil', in Cleary and Stewart-Gambino, *Power*, pp. 123–138. (1996).

30   The era of unusual statements about Pentecostals is not over. Arturo Fontaine Talavera and Harald Beyer reported on two wide surveys of Chileans in 1990 and 1991 for the Chilean research institute, Centro de Estudios Públicos (CEP). They concluded that economic habits of male Pentecostals would lead to the 'domestication of the macho.' See *Estudios Públicos* 44 (Spring 1991), pp. 120–122.

31   Edward Cleary and Juan Sepúlveda, 'Chilean Pentecostalism: Coming of Age' in Cleary and Stewart-Gambino, *Power*, pp. 97–122, and Everett A. Wilson, 'The Dynamics of Latin American Pentecostalism', in Daniel R. Miller. ed., *Coming of Age*, p. 97.

32   Douglas Petersen, 'The Formation of Popular, National, Autonomous Pentecostal Churches in Central America' in *PNEUMA, The Journal of the Society for Pentecostal Studies*, 16:1 pp. 23–48.

33   Elizabeth Brusco, 'The Reformation of Machismo: Asceticism and Masculinity among Colombian Evangelicals', in *Rethinking*, Garrard-Burnett and Stoll, pp. 143–158.

34   'Pentecostalism and Women in Brazil', in Cleary and Stewart-Gambino, *Power*, pp. 41–54.

35   Although not about Pentecostals, Evelyn Brooks Higginbotham's book on women leaders in the Black Baptist Church offers possible parallels with women in Latin American Pentecostalism. See her *Righteous Discontent: The Women's Movement in the Black Baptist Church, 1880–1920* (Cambridge, MA: Harvard University Press, 1993).

36   Similar work has been done on women's participation in traditional Catholic organizations. The most obvious is the focus on the highly visible women of the Plaza de Mayo in Argentina. See Marguerite Guzmán Bouvard, *Revolutionizing Motherhood: The Mothers of the Plaza de Mayo* (Wilmington, Del.: Scholarly Resources, 1994); Marysa Navarro, 'The Personal Is Political: Las Madres de Plaza de Mayo', in Susan Eckstein, ed., *Power and Popular Protest: Latin American Social Movements* (Berkeley, CA: University of California Press, 1989), pp. 241–258.

37   See, for example, Luis Idígoras, S.J., *La religión fenómeno popular* (Lima, Peru: Ediciones Paulinas, 1991), p. 242.

38   Besides Hoff, 'Chile's Pentecostals Face Problems due to Isolation', *Evangelical Missions Quarterly* 27, 3 (July 1991), see also Johnstone's summary of issues in *Operation World* (Grand Rapids, MI: Zondervan Publishing House, 1993), p. 161.

39   Emilio Willems, 'Validation of Authority in Pentecostal Sects of Chile and Brazil', *Journal of Scientific Study of Religion* 6 (Fall 1967), p. 258.

40   Matthew S. Bothner, 'El soplo del Espíritu: Perspectivas sobre el movimiento

pentecostal en Chile', *Estudios Públicos* 55 (Winter 1994), Tables 19 and 20, p. 295.

41   Hoff, 'Chile's Pentecostals', p. 246.
42   Ibid.
43   Hoff, p. 248.
44   Galilea, *El predicador*, pp. 41–43.
45   Peter Aubrey, *La misión siguiendo a Jesús por los caminos de América Latina* (Buenos Aires, Argentina: Ediciones Guadalupe. 1990), passim.
46   Robeck, 'Mission and the Issue of Proselytism', *International Bulletin of Missionary Research* 20, 1 (Jan. 1996), pp. 2–8.
47   *Newsweek* 108 (1 Sept. 1986), pp. 63–64.
48   Cleary and Stewart-Gambino, *Power*.
49   Gros, 'Confessing the Apostolic Faith from the Perspective of the Pentecostal Churches', *Pneuma: Journal of the Society of Pentecostal Studies* 9 (Spring 1987), p. 12.
50   These include: research which neglects the larger religious situation, need for economic studies, effects of Pentecostal religion on family life, and gender issues.
51   Arturo Chacón comments in a similar vein in *La Nación* (Santiago), 15 March 1995.
52   See David Martin's later views on secularization in his 'Sociology, Religion, and Secularization: An Orientation', *Religion* 25, 4 (Oct. 1995), pp. 295–303.
53   (Paris: Editions du Sueil, 1991), English translation: *The Revenge of God* (Cambridge: Polity Press, 1994).
54   The best known through notices in the *New York Times* (9 July 1994) and elsewhere is: Douglas Johnston and Cynthia Sampson, eds., *Religion: The Missing Dimension of Statecraft* (New York, NY: Oxford University Press, 1994). Others include: José Casanova, *Public Religions in the Modern World* (Chicago: University of Chicago Press, 1994); Emile Sahliyeh, ed., *Religious Resurgence and Politics in the Contemporary World* (Albany, NY: SUNY Press, 1990) and Peter Beyer, *Religion and Globalization* (Thousand Oaks, CA: Sage Publications, 1994); and Lester Kurtz, *Gods in a Global Village* (Thousand Oaks, CA: Pine Forge Press, 1995).
55   A partial exception is Jeff Haynes, *Religion in Third World Politics* (Boulder, Colo.: Rienner, 1994) who devotes 8 pages to Latin American Pentecostalism.
56   See: María Isaura Pereira de Queiroz, 'Afro-Brazilian Cults and Religious Change in Brazil', in James A. Beckford and Thomas Luckmann, ed., *The Changing Face of Religion* (Newbury Park, CA: Sage, 1989), p. 95, see also: fn. 7.
57   Béhague, 'Regional and National Trends in Afro-Brazilian Religious Music: A Case of Cultural Pluralism', *Competing Gods: Religious Pluralism in Latin America* (Providence, RI: Occasional Paper No. 11, Watson Institute for International Studies, Brown University, 1992), p. 13.
58   Willems, *Followers*, passim.
59   Jean Mouroux, *The Christian Experience: An Introduction to a Theology* (New York, NY: Sheed and Ward, 1954), p. 272.
60   Galilea (*El pentecostal*, p. 86) notes: 'It is only the living, personal experience of the believer that determines that the believer can count on possessing the power of the gifts of the Holy Spirit, which sometimes can be expressed as

charismatic gifts.'
61   Emphasis and parenthesis are mine.
62   Wilson, 'The Dynamics of Latin American Pentecostalism', in *Coming of Age*, Miller, ed., p. 93.

Chapter Seven

Unity or Division:
A Case Study of the Apostolic
Faith Mission of South Africa

Japie LaPoorta

INTRODUCTION

In the following chapter I shall examine the importance of narrative theology in reshaping contemporary Systematic Theology and Ethics, and indicate how narrative theology is done within Pentecostalism. I shall use the narrative theological model to address historical origins of the Apostolic Faith Mission (AFM) in South Africa (SA) and issues related to the movement towards greater unity in the body of Christ and a final conclusion.

STORY, HISTORY AND SYSTEMATIC
THEOLOGICAL REFLECTION

Various theologians have emphasized the importance of narrative theology in shaping contemporary Systematic Theology and Ethics. The contributions of four theologians are of particular importance in understanding the construction of narrative theology used in this chapter. The first of these theologians is Gabriel Fackre, a well-known evangelical, who defines narrative theology as follows:

> Narrative theology is the discourse about God in the setting of story. Narrative becomes the decisive image for understanding and interpreting faith. Depiction of reality, ultimate and penultimate in terms of plot, coherence, movement, and climax is at the centre of all forms of this kind of talk about God.[1]

He highlights the fact that 'story' is a determinant for the understanding and interpretation of faith. Story is inextricably linked to the expression of reality in all forms of theology.

Johann Baptist Metz, the second theologian treated, and professor of fundamental theology at the University of Münster in Germany, has made a major contribution to the advancement of narrative theology. Metz has the following to say about story:

> The story is itself an event and has the quality of a sacred action... It is more than reflection – the sacred essence to which it bears witness continues to live in it. The wonder that is narrated becomes powerful once more... A rabbi, whose grandfather has been a pupil of Baal Shem Tov, was once asked to tell a story: 'A Story ought to be told', he said, 'so that it is itself a help', and his story was this. 'My grandfather was paralysed. Once he was asked to tell a story about his teacher and he told how the holy Baal Shem Tov used to jump and dance when he was praying. My grandfather stood up while he was telling the story, and the story carried him away so much that he jumped and danced to show how the master had done it. From that moment, he was healed. This is how stories ought to be told.'[2]

As Metz has shown us, narrative theology deals with stories that are recited over and over, from one generation to another with empowering and therapeutic effects. The telling of the story moves both narrator and audience. These stories, narrated from one generation to another, are based on experiences of either that of the storyteller or of the listeners which are used to depict the experiences of those who listen to the storyteller.

Renowned Swiss theologian, Professor Walter Hollenweger, the third contributor treated, highlights the significant role experience plays in narrative theology. In a book titled *Umgang mit Mythen: Interkulturelle Theologie,*[3] Hollenweger used the word myth not in a negative sense as a false story, but he used the word in a positive sense as an overarching story. The sub-title, *Intercultural Theology*, is used by Hollenweger in the same way as the black theologian, James Cone, in applying story to the doing theology within different cultures.[4]

During his years at the University of Birmingham in England, Hollenweger was involved with black Pentecostal-Charismatic people whose theological thinking did not correspond to the categories used by traditional western theologians. In the light of this exposure he appeals to western theologians to learn from this new way of doing theological reflection.[5] This experiential theology does not produce new dogmas, new myths, or overarching stories in which human beings feel comfortable.[6] Hollenweger maintains that behind the seemingly rational western theology are various kinds of myths or stories, which have been forgotten. Their dogmas, he holds, are also stories that are built on history in which certain important figures like Calvin and Luther played fundamental roles.[7] He says in the same manner, other traditions in Christianity participate by telling their own stories, in which other historical figures are featured as heroes.[8] In the meeting of various cultures within Christianity a bridge is potentially constructed which makes possible the listening to each others's stories possible.[9] Pentecostal-charismatic participants should have the courage to seize the opportunity to present their own myths in the form of narrative theology.[10]

Hollenweger categorizes his discussion on myths in the following three categories:
(1) 'Erinnerungen' (Remembrance)
(2) 'Erfahrungen' (Experiences)
(3) 'Erwartungen' (Expectations)[11]
The first category deals with past memories, the second concentrates on present experiences and the third category focuses on future expectations. Remembrance, describing Hollenweger's past memories, examines Dietrich Bonhoeffer's concept of the church for others, and Johannes Christian Hoekendijk's dissertation that critiques the rise of German Missiology in which ethnicity occupied a determining role.[12] Hollenweger highlights the importance of Bonhoeffer's faith and hope in the myth of one, universal, catholic church that formed the basis for Bonhoeffer's involvement in the resistance movement of the Confessing Church in Germany during Hitler's reign[13] Hollenweger continued by noting the significance of Bonhoeffer's myth as expressed in the concept of church for others.[14] Hollenweger unmasked the preoccupation of German Missiology with ethnicity, which is in direct

conflict with the dream of Bonhoeffer as concretized in the church for others. For this reason the church of Jesus Christ cannot be restricted within the limits of one culture, one language and one theology. The church of the risen Lord is the place where different theologies, political opinions, races and myths should exist side by side.[15] Hollenweger retrieves inspiration for his vision of an intercultural theology from the stories and memories as expressed by Bonhoeffer and Hoekendijk, especially in the notion of the church for others.

Hollenweger further develops his understanding of myths through the lens of present day experiences. He observes that myths never die. Using the myths of heroes in Switzerland and the élitist myth in England, referring specifically to the notion that we are on the Lord's side, Hollenweger explained the cohesiveness of myths in the light of identity, creating traditions, that revolve around certain historical figures and events.[16] Therefore, if one claims to be standing in a certain tradition, this person should be in a position to make an appeal to specific historical figures and events, rather than appealing to certain dogmas. The essence of myth exists in a bundling of archetypal beliefs and stories, which beg for interpretation and project certain expectations.[17] The powerfulness of these archetypal beliefs and stories is found in the dynamic that more than one person or tradition can relate to them.[18] This dynamic role of tradition may lead to some paradoxical implications. For instance, the story of Azusa Street can also be claimed by white, conservative, tongue speaking Pentecostals as their source of inspiration and motivation, while potentially retaining their racist and sexist tendencies. In this regard, the non-racial and non-sexist fundamentals of the Azusa Street paradigm are the clearly demarcated boundaries for those who claim to be standing in this tradition.

According to Hollenweger these stories not only revolve around certain historical events, but also focus on heroes. To illustrate, the Wilhelm Tell myth was constructed and used by the Swiss at a time in their history when they were in desperate need of unity.[19] This myth was used as a unifying cohesive force, providing the people of Switzerland with strength for the present and hope for the future. The Wilhelm Tell myth gave them a sense of belonging and identity. Further, a special day was set aside for the celebration of remembrance of this significant hero.[20] Hollenweger also highlights the English myth of 'We are on the Lord's side' to debunk the pretentions of the western nations who pretend that they do not have myths. According to Hollenweger there are myths behind all dogmas and celebrations of the west and they are only later embued with some type of rationality.[21]

Hollenweger concludes his understanding of myth with an emphasis on future expectations. He proposes that we should involve ourselves in other people's myths, because this will enhance contact and dialogue, which is of paramount importance.[22] He suggests doing theology by listening to the myths of others.[23] He further holds that if we are talking about the Holy Spirit, we are talking about experience. The theme of pneumatology, he maintains, is a complex issue because it has to do with different experiences.[24] He proposes a pneumatology that would not be overshadowed by Christology. Such a pneumatology opens up a new way of addressing the filioque debate with the Eastern Orthodox tradition.[25] Story, he claims, is part of being human, and that in essence is the task of theology.[26]

Narrative theology with its key concepts of identity and tradition has the potential to give a community a sense of belonging. The heart of this type of narrative theology is embedded in the myths of history that could be called memory. These memories inspire the community and give them hope and a sense of destiny. If a people know where they are coming from and how they came to where they are, they will have confidence in mapping out the way towards the future, without repeating the mistakes of the past. For this reason Pentecostal-charismatic people should always remember the Azusa Street Mission paradigm. The events of the Azusa Street Mission must be commemorated continually. Therein lies tremendous power.

The fourth contribution to my construction of narrative theology is made by James Cone whose name has become synonymous with Black Theology throughout the world. The systematic theologian of Union Theological Seminary concurs with Hollenweger and Metz on the link between story and experience. Cone maintains:

> There is no truth for and about black people that does not emerge from the context of their experience. This means there can be no Black Theology which does not take the black experience as a source for its starting point. Black Theology is the theology of and for black people, an examination of their stories, tales and sayings. It is an investigation of the mind into the raw materials of our pilgrimage, telling the story of 'how we got over'... Black Theology must uncover the structures and forms of the black experience, because the categories of interpretation must arise out of the thought forms of black experience itself.[27]

The stories of subjective experiences in narrative theology are recited continually. These narrations serve as a '... glue that binds together such diverse, literary enterprises as history, autobiography, biography, novels, folktales, and myths'.[28] At the heart of the Black experience, according to Cone, is the struggle against injustice. Cone asserts, '...the form of black religious thought is experience in the style of story and its context is liberation. Black theology then, is the story of black people's struggle for liberation in extreme situations of oppression.'[29]

In chronicling the story of Black liberation, narrative theology through the story is a powerful tool of communication, because it brings reality within the reach of the ordinary people who cannot read. Through the story they are empowered and identify with the meaning of the story. Through the story the past is made present, and kept alive. Cone contends:

> Story is the history of individuals coming together in the struggle to shape life according to common held values. The Jewish story is formed in the Hebrew Bible and Rabbinic tradition. The early Christian 'story' is told in the Old and New Testament, with the emphasis on the latter as the fulfilment of the former. The White American story is found in the history of European settlements struggling against dark forest and savage people to find a new nation. The Black American story is recorded in songs, tales and narratives of African slaves and their descendants, as they attempt to survive with dignity in a land inimical to their existence. Every people has a story to tell, something to say to themselves, their children, and to the world about how they think and live, as they determine and affirm their reason for being.[30]

The link between story and history is clear. This in turn links story, past, present and future existence together.

The crucial link between story and experience is not restricted only to Black and Pentecostal theologies, but it is also evident in the theologies from the non-western world. Dutch Theologian, Theo Witvliet, in his edited volume *Bevrijdingstheologie In De Derde Wêreld*[31] outlines the relationship between story and experience as it emerged in Latin America and African theologies.[32] Witvliet contends that these theologies do not just raise different themes, they introduce an alternative way of doing theology.

These representative ethno-theologies distance themselves from theological thinking that pretends to be universal and objective, while in fact being conditioned by cultural, traditional, historical experiences and social interests of the Western world.[33] These theologies, according to Witvliet, are narrative in structure, and can be depicted as the product of storytelling communities.[34] Sum Nam-dong, the Minjung theologian, in his essay, 'Theology as the telling of stories', asserts that God's revelation does not consist of letters but stories. Old and New Testament stories are recited. God's language, he maintains is the language of stories, of his deeds in history. The sayings of Jesus, Sum says, bristle with stories and the Spirit of God is expressed in body language rather than mind language.[35]

PERSONAL AFFIRMATIONS CONCERNING NARRATIVE THEOLOGY AS VALID FOR BLACK PENTECOSTALS IN SOUTH AFRICA

My first affirmation is that Pentecostal theology is narrative in form and structure. Our point of theological departure is not from a specific doctrine, but from a particular paradigmatic experience. This experiential approach is a legitimate and essential way of doing theology. This approach is shared with feminist theologians, other non-western theologians and black theologians in the United States of America. They tell stories of their experiences of suffering, hopes, dreams and what they think is the essential truth.

Secondly, in this theological process experience becomes more important than in traditional, rational western theology. Narrative theology has to do with experiences that are recited from one generation to another. The experiences are conveyed in the form of stories about archetypal events. The memory of these experiences give *identity*. This identity is both individual and corporately applicable. In these stories I retrieve my inspiration and affirm my identity. Pentecostals, both as individuals and as a group, look back into history and retrieve the stories of the archetypal Azusa Street Mission, that stimulated a non-racial, non-sexist, spirit-filled, tongue speaking, united movement. These stories revolved around historical events, where certain heroes played fundamental roles. Bishop William Joseph Seymour was such a hero. The stories, experiences and history of the Azusa Street Mission would be incomplete, lopsided and inconceivable without him.

Thirdly, the advantage of narrative theology is that it makes possible contact and dialogue between different people. Contact and dialogue are evident in both the contributions of Cone and Hollenweger. Dialogue offers the opportunity to share the stories of one's particular experiences with others, while one is simultaneously exposed to the stories of others. In this sense narrative theology is reciprocal, because both parties involved in the contact and dialogue are engaged in the telling of and listening to stories. For this reason, the Azusa Street Mission paradigm offers a basis and a beacon of hope for a united AFM church in South Africa.

Fourthly, narrative theology is a rhetorically powerful and liberative instrument in the lives of individuals and communities. Stories have the ability to inspire, motivate, move and persuade people. That Pentecostal theology has to do with power is evident in the speeches and stories told in the gathering of the saints. Narrative theology also has liberating effects for both the story teller and the listener. The liberating effect important for Pentecostals, because in the sharing of their stories they can liberated from prejudice, to such an extent that it is possible to listen to the stories of others.

Fifthly, narrative theology does not separate Systematic Theology and Ethics. For example, Cone and Metz maintain that theology must deal with concrete human situations, where the moral issues of social justice, sexual and medical ethics are of vital significance. Theology is not simply the focusing on doctrines in which abstract concepts are at stake, but it is the grappling with issues of life and death.

Sixthly, the question of truth is one of the most difficult issues to be addressed by Narrative Theology. When one is not working with doctrines but with stories, the possibility is always there that these stories could be misused. Different people can identify with different stories while they ignore the fundamentals of these same stories. The fundamentals of non-racialism and non-sexism however offer parameters that express the truth of the Azusa Street Mission paradigm.

In conclusion, I would like to summarize the reasons why I have opted for narrative theology as the genre to do Pentecostal theology in South Africa.

• It is non-western. Such theology adheres to a holistic world-view that does not distinguish between the sacred and secular spheres of life.

• It is based on arch-type stories. These stories take human experiences seriously.

• It gives identity to those who identify with specific human experiences.

• It is liberating. To tell stories and to listen to the stories of other people enable one to arrive at a better understanding of one another.

The question that will be addressed next is, how do we, as Pentecostals do narrative theology?

The actual place where this type of narrative theology is done, is undoubtedly the local assembly, in the celebration services, the cottage meetings, the various board meetings and the open air services. Pentecostalism has been doing theology from its inception in a fashion that falls within the ambit of these non-western theologies. The experiences of being 'born-again' and being 'baptized in the Spirit' with the initial evidence of speaking in tongues break down walls of discrimination between races, sexes and classes.[36] The stories of God's intervention in the lives of people and in history are shared in the form of stories. Here we make time to listen to each other's stories, and nobody is in a hurry because time is not really taken into account. This is the tradition in which I am standing and doing theology. In this way I am following in the footsteps of my predecessors, who told stories of their experiences and made time to listen to the stories of the other saints.

The theological question is whether we go about it in the correct way with the Christian story, or whether my particular story is addressed in the correct way. The hermeneutical question regarding the story is what happened in the beginning of the paradigm and how should we interpret it, where are the boundaries and what falls outside the boundaries of this story? This is crucial because I share this paradigmatic story with white, conservative, Pentecostals who for various reasons interpret the story differently. The heroes that emerged in my story are not necessarily the heroes that these fellow Pentecostals admire. They have heroes like Charles Parham, John G. Lake, Pieter Louis Le Roux, Hendrik Verwoerd and many others who are incompatible with the Azusa paradigm's fundamentals. The significance of story, experience, history and identity are of theological relevance because these issues are interrelated. The stories of the struggle of the black churches in the Apostolic Faith Mission (AFM) of South Africa (SA), underscore these mentioned issues.

Stories of the experiences in this study include the following:

> The experiences of individuals such as William Joseph Seymour, Lucy Farrow, Neely Terry and groups such as the black saints who were the foundational members of Pentecostalism, that gathered in cottage prayer meetings before they moved to the Azusa Street Mission, the Pentecostals at the Azusa Street Mission[37] and the first Pentecostals that met in Doornfontein, Johannesburg, South Africa.

All of these saints had a unique experience called the baptism of the Spirit with the initial evidence of speaking in tongues and witnessed to the fact that this experience was responsible for the breaking down of walls of separation and discrimination in the body of Christ. They experienced the harmony of a non-racial, non-sexist and spirit-filled body of Christ.

The experiences of segregation, pain, suffering, hurt and dishar-mony were endured after several power struggles erupted. Together with these experiences of suffering were linked the struggle for unity and the hope that God would hear their prayers and someday intervene in history as he did in the case of Israel while they were in Egyptian bondage. The stories of the struggle for unity became a 'dangerous and subversive memory'[38] as well as a 'liberative memory'.[39] It became a dangerous and subversive memory to those who were doing their best to maintain the status quo in the church. For those who strug-gled to transform the church it became a liberative memory of hope. The story and history in this book revolve around the essence and character of the church of Jesus Christ. These stories of the struggle as it emerged in the history of the Pentecostal movement in general, and in the Apostolic Faith Mission of South Africa in particular, were as a result of the crisis in the church concerning the fundamental structure and essence of the church.

With these introductory remarks in mind we shall embark on a jour-ney to discuss the unity struggle of the black AFM churches in South Africa. The historical events and data that we shall cover will be used in order to tell the stories of the struggle. I am interested in history as story, as an overarching myth in which the Pentecostal tradition can identify itself.

The sequence of the stories of the struggle for unity within the AFM in this study will be as follows:

THE STORIES OF UNITY, HARMONY AND EQUALITY THAT WERE LATER SHATTERED DUE TO A POWER STRUGGLE AT THE AZUSA STREET MISSION

The early Pentecostal stories of unity, harmony and equality were later shattered by the power struggle that erupted between black and white. These are the stories of the historical origins of the world-wide Pente-costal movement at the Azusa Street Mission in Los Angeles. As we look at the black origins of the movement, there are stories that are frequently ignored and in some instances openly denied, particularly by white Pentecostals in South Africa and abroad. Central to the debate is whether or not the Pentecostal Jerusalem is the 'Azusa Stable' in Los Angeles or the Topeka Bible School in Kansas. This debate is actually a debate between two heroes. If Azusa Street is the central story, then William Joseph Seymour is the leader and founder of the movement. If Topeka is the central story then Charles Fox Parham is the leader and the founder of the movement. If Seymour is the central hero, then the initial evidence of the Spirit's baptism is not only the speaking in tongues, but the breaking down of the walls of racism and sexism, and the acknowledgement of the priesthood of all believers. If Parham is the hero of choice then speaking in tongues only is the focal point, and the dismantling of the walls of discrimination are ignored.[40] I believe the historical facts are overwhelmingly in favour of Seymour and the black roots of the movement. This in turn highlights the spiritual fountain from which Seymour drank, namely the African-American experience, which is a combination of the African world-view and the American experience of slavery.[41] This leads naturally to the type of worship that was evident at the Azusa Street Mission. At Azusa they told stories about the grace of God in their lives in a particular fashion. They told the stories with compassion, that moved, inspired, motivated and persuaded the listeners.

Worship in the African-American tradition was the reason why the first of three schisms took place at Azusa. This initial split was initiated by none other than Parham.[42] He was unwilling to recognize the African-American type of worship as the legitimate Pentecostal way of worship. The second split came about as a result of Seymour's marriage to Jenny Moore, one of the first elders of the Azusa Street Mission. This split was initiated by two white women, namely Mrs. Lumm and Mrs. Crawford, who moved to Portland, Oregon with the mailing list of Apostolic Faith Magazine that had more than fifty thousand names on it.[43] This move curtailed the influence of Seymour throughout the world. The third split was also initiated by a white person, Mr Durham.[44] This split occurred while Seymour was out of town busy on an evangelistic campaign. The reason for this split was a doctrinal dispute. These three schisms that occurred at the Azusa Street Mission were initiated by whites. The underlying causes were undoubtedly power struggles that shattered Seymour's dream of a non-racial and non-sexist movement. The devastating consequences of these schisms spread throughout the world-wide movement. The Apostolic Faith

Mission (AFM) of South Africa (SA) with its racially divided churches is a case in point.

HISTORICAL ORIGINS OF THE AFM OF SA

Like its Azusa Street sibling, the Pentecostal movement in South Africa started in a black township in Doornfontein, Johannesburg as a non-racial movement. It is sad to say that not long after its non-racial origins, the whites of the AFM of SA devised plans for the division of the movement on the basis of racism.[45] The move from a non-racial church to four ethnic based churches followed. This is exactly where the AFM of SA deviated from the divine intention for Pentecostalism in South Africa. This separation on the basis of race occurred at the baptismal pool.[46] It is here that the AFM followed in the footsteps of the Dutch Reformed Church by misusing the symbols that were given to the church to express its unity. In the case of the Dutch Reformed Church it was at the Lord's Supper where the division in the church was allowed, and in the case of the AFM it was at the sacrament of Baptism. This move by the AFM was in line with their ideological thinking that later culminated in their unconditional support for the apartheid regime. Commitment to racial separation is evident in the three documents drawn up by their Commission of Doctrine, Ethics and Liturgy and approved by their Worker Council (Synod). These documents were on Race Relations, United Worship of Believers and the Mixed Marriages Act.

The AFM's support for the apartheid regime allowed them to practise what may be termed 'politics from above', which was actually politics of the apartheid status quo.[47] This in turn led to the emergence of politics from below, which was actually politics of resistance to apartheid.[48]

The irony of the whole matter is that while the white AFM was satisfied about the racial fragmentation in their midst, they diligently endeavoured to foster unity amongst white Pentecostals in South Africa. Theologically this move did not make sense but ideologically it indeed made sense, because it was in line with their political thinking. The churches with whom they were engaged in unity discussions were the Full Gospel Church of God and the Christian Assemblies. The unity between the latter was successfully achieved while the unity with the former dismally failed. In this chapter of AFM history we can clearly see how the white AFM shattered the Azusa Street paradigm almost in the same way as their American counterparts. Needless to say, this gave rise to the unity struggles of the black churches in the AFM of SA.

THE QUEST FOR UNITY WITHIN THE AFM

The stories of the struggles for unity by the black churches within the AFM of SA emerged in the history of the AFM of SA – first through the unity struggle of the 'Coloured' church. This struggle was waged separately for more than ten years, before the joint struggle emerged. The stories of the unity struggle by the 'Indian' church as the second to emerge and moved in the direction of a joint struggle together with the 'Coloured' church. This struggle was waged for approximately five years separately before the joint unity struggle of all three black churches appeared on the scene. The stories of the 'African' church was a struggle waged for eight years separately before the joint unity struggle commenced. The sadness of these separate struggles was that we were so effectively divided and ruled that we were quite unaware of what was transpiring in each other's churches. The joint struggle started in 1985, when the three black churches together confronted the white church on the issue of church unity. The late Henry Adolph was instrumental in bringing the core groups of the 'Coloured' and 'African' churches together. The significant role of the Youth Departments in the three black churches in the joint unity struggle is also crucial.[49] Through contact and dialogue they created opportunities for the young people from different backgrounds in these churches to be together, and to listen to each others stories.

After an initial failed attempt the four churches came together around the table and drew up the declaration of intent, in which apartheid as a principle in the church and the kingdom of God was rejected.[50] This process led to the finalisation of an Interim Constitution to govern the proposed new united church. This Interim Constitution was duly circularized by all four Workers' Councils, but it was accepted, unamended only by the three black churches.[51] The white church unilaterally amended the Interim Constitution to such an extent that in actuality, it represented the rejection of the document. This action by the white church delayed the process for a year and gave rise to the formation of the Composite church consisting of the three black churches. From that day onwards, the negotiations with the white church were conducted by a single unit, and no longer were the black churches three separate entities.[52] The main issues that dominated the agenda in the unity negotiations with the white church were the questions of racism and the power imbalance between the two churches.

ISSUES RELATING TO UNITY IN THE AFM OF SA

The stories of the unity struggle focus on the theological concept of unity. The origins and importance of this issue are addressed in both the Old and New Testament. The notions of the *Kehal Jahwe*,[53] the *Ecclesia, Soma Christi* and the High Priestly Prayer of Jesus Christ are discussed.[54] Black and white perspectives of unity vary significantly. While both perspectives acknowledge and accept the same biblical texts on the theoretical level, their hermeneutical points of departure and practical applications are worlds apart.[55]

The AFM of SA professes to be part of the world-wide Pentecostal movement that sprang forth from the Azusa Street Mission where the Holy Spirit played a tremendous role. The role of the Holy Spirit in the whole unity struggle is crucial, particularly the significance of the baptism of the Spirit and the gifts of the Spirit in the unification of the church. The gathering role of the Spirit, the enabling power in the Spirit's baptism and the impartation of gifts as well as the manifestations of these gifts, regardless of race, sex and class must be acknowledged. The issue of the prophetic relevancy of a united church undoubtedly alludes to the questions of the economic and social responsibility of the church in a racially segregated society.

UNITY AND SPIRITUAL LIBERATION

The stories of the liberation of Spirit examine the move towards a united AFM of SA which necessitates liberation. This liberation has to take place on three levels. These are the liberation of black Pentecostals, the liberation of white Pentecostals and the liberation of Pentecostalism itself.[56]

Black Pentecostals need to be liberated from (i) inferiority, (ii) complacency, (iii) White inauthentic values and norms, (iv) sexism and from the fear to be fully black, African and Pentecostal.

Whites need to be liberated from (i) racism, (ii) sexism, (iii) a denial of the black roots of the movement, and set free to be Pentecostal and to be proud of the black roots of the movement.

Pentecostalism needs to be liberated from (i) ideology, (ii) an oppressive cultural mould and set free to be what it was at Azusa before racism altered it.

MOVING TOWARDS GREATER UNITY IN THE BODY OF CHRIST.

Uniting the AFM of SA is not an end in itself but only a first step in the correct direction. The AFM of SA needs to move toward broader expressions of unity, including greater Pentecostal-charismatic unity, greater Evangelical Unity, greater Ecumenical unity and greater international unity. The Pentecostal-charismatic divide is focused on the AFM of SA's link with the Zionist Movement who left the AFM of SA because of its practice of apartheid.[57] The road to greater unity obviously leads through contact and dialogue with differing groups. The second group that is addressed in this area is the AFM's relationship with the classical Pentecostals, which include groups like the Full Gospel Church of God, Pentecostal Protestant Church, Assemblies of God and the Church of God. The third group that is addressed in this area are the Charismatic Churches in South Africa, which include the International Fellowship of Christian Churches, Christian Network Ministries and the Restoration Movement.

The supporting level of importance is the move towards greater evangelical unity. In this area there are two important organizations, namely the Concerned Evangelicals (they constitute the progressive wing in evangelicalism in South Africa and are predominantly black) and the Evangelical Fellowship of South Africa (they constitute the conservative wing of evangelicalism and are predominantly white).

The Ecumenical Movement in South Africa includes the South African Council of Churches (SACC) and the Roman Catholic Church.

The final area to be considered in the move towards greater unity is the AFM and international Church relations. Four levels are distinguished here and they are, the World Pentecostal Conference, the World Evangelical Fellowship, the World Council of Churches and the International Roman Catholic and Pentecostal dialogue. The biblical imperative of unity necessitates that the unity of the church be local, regional, national and international.

FINAL CONCLUSIONS

In the light of the foregoing excursion regarding the unity struggle of the black AFM churches, we can draw the following conclusions:

That the divine intention for the Pentecostal movement, as a whole, was expressed in the Azusa Street Revival, and again repeated in Doornfontein at the formation of the AFM of SA.

Racism in both Azusa and Doornfontein was responsible for the building up of the broken walls of separation. Racism was ideologically justified by the misuse of scripture. This misuse of scripture blurred the biblical imperatives, such as love for the neighbours, who happened to be black.

The black church's understanding of scripture urged them to engage in the struggle for unity. This understanding of scripture, included the retrieval of the Azusa Street Revival paradigm as a hermeneutical key. For them, God's intention, will, and purpose for Pentecostalism was revealed and manifested in the Azusa Street Revival.

The different points of departure in hermeneutics of black and white AFM members, are evident in the issues relating to the unity struggle. The blacks asserted that unity should necessarily start with the changing of structures and the promulgation of laws that will reverse the imbalances of the past and eradicate ethnicity. The whites on the other side asserted that unity should start in the hearts of people and only later effect the laws and structures. The emphasis of tongues as initial evidence, without a change of heart and attitude is unacceptable for blacks. They assert that when the Spirit's baptism takes place racism is removed. They further maintain that the Spirit's baptism has political and socio-economic implications, because it does not stand aloof from the biblical injunction of Gal. 3:28 'In Christ there is no male nor female, slave nor free, Jew nor Gentile, but all are one.'

Racism has caused serious physical damage to both black and white. Both groups are in dire need of liberation. The Blacks need to be liberated from inferiority, shame, complacency that the apartheid system has instilled in them. Whites on the other hand need to be liberated from a false sense of superiority. Both groups need to re-orientate their minds about blackness in particular. This will enable blacks to boldly affirm their human dignity. This will enable whites to acknowledge the black roots of the movement and accept black leadership in the movement. Finally, Pentecostalism needs to be liberated from the ideological baggage it carries. This will enable it to be relevant and prophetic. These experiences will expedite the process of unity between black and white. It will accelerate the establishment of a unitary, non-racial and non-sexist AFM of SA.

The whole examination of the unity struggle affirmed that the unity, as expressed both at Azusa and Doornfontein, is the will of God for Pentecostalism. The fragmentation of the Pentecostal movement on race in general and AFM of SA in particular, is a deviation from the divine intention. Therefore, the unity struggle in which the black churches were engaged, was a noble struggle. This struggle is in line with the biblical imperatives and the divine paradigm of Azusa.

The achievement of unity between black and white AFM churches should not be the ultimate goal of the struggle. This is because the prayer of the Lord is that the whole church in the whole world should be one. The united AFM therefore, should actively work toward greater unity of the church both nationally and internationally.

Notes

1   Gabriel Fackre, G. 'Narrative Theology' in *Religion in Life 37* (October 1983), p. 343. Quoted also by W. De Kock in *Geloof, Geloofsinhoud en Geloofontwikkeling: 'n Fowleriaanse Interpretasie van die verhaalontplooiing van 'n Kerk in Krisis* (D.Th. Diss. University of South Africa, 1990), p. 53.

2   Johann Baptist Metz, *Faith in History and Society: Towards a Practical Fundamental Theology* (London: Burns and Oates, 1980), pp. 207–208.

3   Walter Hollenweger, *Umgang mit Mythen: Interkulturelle Theologie*, (München: Kaiser-Tassenbücher, 1982). Hollenweger is considered as an authority in the field of Pentecostal studies. He was instrumental in the realization of the Selly Oak Centre for Black and White Studies and Partnerships in ministry. This Centre has made it possible for Black Pentecostals with little or no theological training to be empowered in theological reflection. As Professor at Birmingham he has guided several doctoral studens in Pentecostal-Charismatic research. Both Cees and Paul van der Laan, Rosworth Gerloff and Douglas Nelson to mention but a few, received their doctoral degrees under his capable guidance.

4   James H. Cone, *God of the Oppressed*, (New York, NY: Seabury Press, 1975) pp. 90–91.

5   Hollenweger, *Interkulturelle Theologie*, pp. 9–14.

6   Ibid.

7   Ibid.

8   Ibid., p. 76.

9   Ibid., p. 81.

10   Ibid., op. cit., pp. 98–99.

11   Ibid., pp. 5–6.

12   Ibid., pp. 15–16.

13   Ibid., p. 19.

14   Ibid., p. 30.

15   Ibid., pp. 46–47.

16   Ibid., pp. 66–67.
17   Ibid., p. 63.
18   Ibid.
19   Ibid., p. 211.
20   Ibid.
21   Ibid., pp. 78–79.
22   Ibid., p. 228.
23   Ibid.
24   Ibid.
25   Ibid.
26   Ibid.
27   James H. Cone, *God of the Oppressed*, (New York, NY: The Seabury Press, 1975), pp. 17–18.
28   Stanley Hauerwas, 'Story and Theology' in *Religion in Life* 95 (1975).
29   Cone, *God of the Oppressed*, p. 54.
30   Ibid, p. 102.
31   Theo Witvliet, *'Bevrijdingstheologie In De Derde Wêreld'* (Meinema: S-Gravenhage, 1990). He remarks that the claims to Narrativity in these theologies are not unique because in the last two decades narrative theology has emerged forcefully onto the theological debate
32   Ibid., pp. 5–6.
33   Ibid., p. 12.
34   Ibid.
35   Sum Nam-Dong, *'Theologie als het vertellen van verhalen: een tegen-theologie'* in Witfliet, *Derde Wêreld*, p. 123.
36   Cecil Robeck, 'William J. Seymour and the Biblical evidence' in *Initial Evidence: Historical and Biblical Perspectives on the Pentecostal Doctrine of Spirit Baptism*, ed., Gary B. McGee (Peabody, MA: Hendrickson Publishers, 1991), p. 81.
37   Douglas Nelson, *For Such A Time as This: The Story of Bishop J. Seymour and the Azusa Street Revival* (Ph.D. diss., University of Birmingham, 1981), p. 138.
38   Ibid, p. 202.
39   Ibid.
40   Walter J. Hollenweger, *Priorities in Pentecostal Research: Historiography, Missiology, Hermeneutics and Pneumatology*, paper delived at Conference on Pentecostal and Charismatic Research in Europe, Rijksuniversiteit, Utrecht, 1989, p. 13.
41   Ian MacRobert, *The Black Roots and White Racism of the Early Pentecostalism in the USA*, (New York, NY: St. Martin's Press, 1988), p. 9.
42   Ibid., p. 60.
43   Ibid.
44   Ibid.
45   Christian De Wet, *The Apostolic Faith Mission in Africa: 1908–1980: A Case Study in Church Growth in a Segregated Society* (Ph.D. diss., University of Cape Town, 1989, p. 423.
46   Isaak Burger, *Geskiedenis van die Apostoliese Geloof Sending: 1908–1958* (Braamfontein: Evangelie Uitgewers, 1988), p. 175.
47   Ibid., pp. 328–337.

48 Frank Chikane, *No Life of My Own* (Braamfontein: Skotaville Publishers, 1988), p. 80.
49 Organizing Youth Meeting Minutes, 27 December 1974.
50 Secretarial Report, Committee for Unity 1990.
51 Ibid.
52 Verslag van die Kommissie vir Eenheid soos voorgelê aan die Werkersraad op 26 September 1990, Kuilsrivier.
53 J.J.F. Durand, *Una Sancta Catholica in Sendingperspektief* (Amsterdam, Uitgewerej W. Ten Have, NV, 1961) pp. 18–20.
54 J. Du Rand, 'Johannes 17 Jesus se gebed om Eenheid en Solidariteit te midde van Krisis en Konflik', in C. Breytenbach *se Eenheid en Konflik* (Pretoria: NGKB, 1987).
55 Secretarial Report, Committee for Unity 1990.
56 Japie LaPoorta, *Black Theology: A Quest for a True Humanity in South Africa* (MA diss., University of Cape Town, 1988), p. 44.
57 Sundkler, B., *Zulu Zion and some Swazi Zionists*, (London: Oxford University Press, 1976), 51. See also Ian Anderson's, *Bazalwane: The African Pentecostals in South Africa* (Pretoria: University of South Africa, 1992).

Chapter Eight

Globalization of Pentecostalism or Globalization of Individualism? A European Perspective

Jean-Daniel Plüss

The phenomenal spread of the Pentecostal/charismatic movement, and especially of the many indigenous churches with a Pentecostal flavour in Asia, Africa and Latin America presents a challenge to Pentecostal Christians in Europe. European Pentecostals are faced with a series of questions including whether there are there common characteristics that transcend geographical borders. Could it be, that this global family needs help from their European brothers and sisters? Or, perhaps, could we learn something from them?[1] If God's Spirit has invigorated the believing community to live as witnesses to the freedom and grace that he has bestowed through Christ, could it also be that there is a shared spirituality?

Before exploring an analysis of Pentecostalism from a European perspective, I would like to relate a personal experience that illustrates the difficulty one faces when attempting to answer the above questions. We were eager freshmen students in a small Pentecostal Bible school in Europe. It was an attractive school, partly because of its international appeal. The student body of about eighty represented twenty-five nations and almost as many languages. Most teachers were North American and nobody thought anything of the fact that our textbooks had mostly come from the same publishing house. On one particular occasion the teacher, obviously well prepared, lectured on the 'initial evidence' supported with examples from the Book of Acts. At first, we were making copious notes on Spirit baptism and glossolalia. Suddenly an Asian student could not follow a conceptual point. His question sparked a remark from a German student. The German said that in his church they did not teach 'initial evidence'. Shortly, other students got involved offering perspectives that differed on the contents, timing and meaning of a 'second blessing'. The teacher was at a loss as to how to proceed in order to salvage the global harmony of interpretation that his Pentecostal textbook had taken for granted. The questions posed were challenging. Would not a common experience result in a common theology? What was common about a particular experience in the first place?

We did not lose our faith. On the contrary, we gained a wider understanding of God's grace. I am truly thankful for having been a student at that Bible school. The professors, perhaps at times unintentionally, taught us something about the relationship between unity and diversity. There may be Christian unity in the bond of love, but our cultural upbringings were so diverse, that it subsequently brought forth a mosaic of interpretations and appreciative respect for other traditions.

This enriching lesson in unity and diversity happened more than twenty years ago and continues to impact my research. In an attempt to assess the current situation on the hypothesis of Pentecostal charismatic Christianity[2] as a global culture I sent a questionnaire to about thirty Pentecostal/charismatic theologians in Europe. The aim was to address the following issues: a) the possibility of the existence of a global Pentecostal charismatic culture, b) the effects a Pentecostal charismatic culture may have had in the development of local churches, c) the questions relating to global culture as such, and d) the inquiries relating to spirituality and theology. After an attempt at a European assessment I will venture to question the claim of globalization as such. In my concluding remarks I would like to point to possible benefits that the discussion on globalization may have in store.

SUMMARY OF RESPONSES

GENERAL QUESTIONS

Most of the respondents classified themselves as Pentecostal, charismatic or independent. The first general question inquired as to the validity of a working presupposition that the Pentecostal experience of the Spirit was essential to the future of world Christianity? Although most answered in the affirmative, almost without exception they qualified their answers. These qualified responses included attempts at defining the essence of Pentecostal experience by putting the work of the Spirit in relation to other aspects of church life, or, as Roswith Gerloff suggested, a definition of the intentionality of the experience of the Spirit was necessary.[3]

Question two evaluated the idea that Pentecostalism and the charismatic movements had generated a uniform Pentecostal/charismatic faith community in Europe. The respondents responded definitely that the European culture was so strong (e.g. protestantism, catholicism, nationalism) that the Pentecostal/charismatic culture could not easily change paradigms. On the contrary, many considered the charismatic context to be open to adaptation and cultural pluriformity. In other words, the very reason why the Pentecostal experience had spread so quickly around the world was also the reason why it cannot be considered uniform or universally defined.[4]

A third general question probed the essence of differences related between regional/denominational identities and global similarities. The respondents also reviewed tensions between teutonic religiosity and more vibrant forms of spirituality,[5] between East and West, Europe and the USA, North and South, and perhaps more importantly on localized moral, political, ecological and social responsibility issues.[6]

RELATING TO THE MOVEMENT

Following the general questions, another block of questions addressed the apparent effects of charismatic experiences in the movement or church with which the respondents affiliate with. Some positive responses included the desire to recover a deeper and more historical spirituality,[7] a longing for a new move of God's Spirit,[8] an increasing awareness concerning the importance of discussing Pentecostal issues and teaching sound theology.[9]

Answers with negative aspects of recent developments in Pentecostal and charismatic circles were more elaborate. Especially emphasized was the phenomenon of the 'Toronto Blessing'. Though not denying that the 'Toronto Blessing' could generate positive effects on certain individuals, there was a considerable feeling of uneasiness. Would this phenomenon be interpreted as a new 'type' or norm.[10] Hans Harter, a Pentecostal minister in Germany, was concerned that any kind of new spiritual wave seems to be welcome in the Pentecostal/charismatic circles. Most respondents voiced a call for discernment.[11]

Many respondents indicated the apparent tendency of some charismatic groupings to overemphasize subjective experiences, personal satisfaction, and the sensational. A consumer mentality as found in our secularized societies, causes concern for Pentecostal leaders.[12]

In summary, respondents indicated that the church had grown numerically and spiritually due to the charismatic emphasis.[13] However, the more established churches experienced less noticeable growth. Similarly, it was argued that the most relevant benefit of charismatic worship was an opening of rigid structures.[14] The strongest consensus moreover, however, was that spiritual growth produced a new awareness of basic theological truths,[15] the need to find a balance between the Spirit and the Word, an orientation to basic Christian values characterized by dedication, honesty, faith, love, prayer, generosity and a willingness to persist in the completion of tasks. A commitment to basic Christianity would also lead to an appreciation of other Christian traditions.[16]

RELATING TO GLOBAL CULTURE

A third block of questions focused on the perceived influence of a global charismatic culture upon local congregations. The respondents noted commonalties in the shared use of familiar songs, comparable wholesome worship, agreement on basic doctrinal issues and proactive evangelism.

The majority of respondents emphasized, however, that similar expressions of music, worship and doctrine were absolute indicators of Christian unity. In fact, most agreed that because expressions of spirituality were culturally conditioned they did not provide a guarantor of Christian unity. One participant, Roswith Gerloff, clearly described the tension between common spirituality and cultural diversity in the context of Western Europe by noting, 'I have learned, by moving between Britain and Germany, that there is nowhere an easy and direct transfer of any experience: histories, systems, laws and "Weltanschauungen" are so different that God's Spirit must enter in quite different ways. But enter the Spirit must. I have found out, you know where the Spirit is and where the Spirit is not!'[17] In other words, while there is ideological respect for diverse experiences of divine grace evidenced across cultural boundaries, there is also a sense of cultural relativity which serves as a corrective critical agent check mating the move toward uniformity. Many could have agreed with Matthias Wenk's response that unity should not be confused with uniformity, and Pentecostal unity may be considered unity precisely because it affirms plurality.

A fourth set of questions centred upon the relationship between the rapidly progressing secularization of European societies and the development of a global spiritual culture. Many recognized a similar emphasis upon individualization in both secular society and charismatic churches. Other respondents retained a critical approach towards secularization and defined charismatic spirituality in contrast to it.[18] Given these divergent responses, one may wonder, if there could also be a synthetical approach towards a secular religiosity.

RELATING TO SPIRITUALITY

The final group of questions examined the possible contributions of a common global spirituality to the field of theology. On the one hand, some respondents indicated that if a Pentecostal/charismatic experience[19] could contribute to spiritual growth, the experience should relate more of God's love, establish faith, impart boldness, and serve to mobilize the laity. On the other hand, others answered in a corrective sense, arguing that it is a Christian experience that brings spiritual growth, not a particular Pentecostal/charismatic phenomenon or any other presently fashionable experience.[20]

In a related question in this final group, the respondents were asked if a Pentecostal/charismatic experience would help in understanding the belief systems of Christians from other spiritual traditions. From an ideological point of view it was reasoned, especially by the respondents living in a multi-cultural context, that charismatic experiences should produce intercultural awareness and greater openness, characterized by an appreciation of plurality and differences in ministry or function.[21] Others pointed to the unreflective nature of many church-goers who place an insistence upon a dogmatized-type experience, such as Baptism of the Holy Spirit evidenced by speaking in other tongues. Such a language defined experience inevitably leads to an understanding that other spiritualities produce a different type of 'language'.[22] Often a fundamental experience within another cultural context produces an attitude of spiritual openness. Unless one has another 'language' in one's cultural context, one will see neither the benefit nor the need for changing one's position. In this sense, the idea of a global spiritual culture might be a dream like the promotion of Esperanto after the First World War. I am not saying that it might not be worth while to maintain this dream, especially if we have the courage to make it come true.[23] One thing, however, is certain: the proliferation of the English language throughout Europe, the invitation of English speaking conference celebrities, and the singing of English language hymns and choruses do not automatically produce a global spiritual culture as did the extensive speaking of Latin during the Middle Ages in a time when Europe was still united by the same religious world-view.

The final question in this set inquired if a global spirituality could contribute to world Christianity in the fields of mission/evangelism, ethics/justice, ecumenism/theology, and worship. In the mission and evangelism category, a tension was perceived between the desirability of united witness in order to raise effectiveness and the danger of uncritically importing specific aspects of the evangelizer's culture to accomplish the task. Further, an undue influence of secularization upon mission and evangelism was also reported. The positive outcome of secularization was also noted. If secularization emphasizes individualism, then the call for personal conversion would be easier to accept.[24] Moreover, if charismatic spirituality was genuine, then the experience would open channels of dialogue and address the whole person with a mutual respect.[25]

In the field of ethics and justice it was reasoned that if theological teaching was deficient, spirituality would have little chance to promote adequately moral and social concerns.[26] There was agreement, however, among several respondents that a charismatic spirituality could provide a bridge between humanly-devised barriers: men and women, black and white, and poor and wealthy. A charismatic spirituality could affirm these differences as intrinsic to basic humanity.[27] According to one of the participants, Matthias Wenk, a global concern for the poor, the oppressed and the marginalized would make Christianity a force with which to be reckoned. He adds that a charismatic/Pentecostal pneumatology must become relevant for the pressing needs of our global society. To Wenk's assertions, I would add, if one can speak about global spirituality, then perhaps one should also envisage the possibility of an ethic of global concern or 'Welt Ethos'.

In the domain of ecumenism and theology some expressed the fear that experience becomes more important than theology. Experience and theology, however, seemed to belong together. Charismatic spirituality could foster ecumenical dialogue because its oral tradition encourages listening. Huib Zegwaart contended that if traditional churches spoke more about their experiences, Pentecostals might be inclined to evaluate and accept their stories more easily.

The respondents viewed as positive the active and personal involvement of the believers in worship. In worship, Pentecostal believers exhibited an openness to receive healing, as well as a willingness to apply elements of worship to an attitude of life style in daily activities. There seemed to be agreement that a global spirituality had common aspects: worship styles were particular regional 'hobby horses' and would be the last element to be globalized, and secular styles were reflected in praise songs, for example, utilizing elements of pop music. Respondents pointed out that though types of worship appeared as very innovative, it could also, at times, seem quite superficial. Here again, the ambivalence remained between common elements found across various cultures and the particularities of regional forms of worship.

IS A EUROPEAN ASSESSMENT OF GLOBALIZATION OF PENTECOSTALISM POSSIBLE?

It should be made clear that the word 'European' is just as difficult to use as the word 'global'. The term 'European' can denote only a geographical location. The word should not be [filled] with cultural and historical undertones, anymore than the word '[Pentecostal] globalization' should imply that aspects of similar spirituality commonly designated as Pentecostal or charismatic can be found in different parts of the globe. To illustrate, one may claim that butterflies can be found on all continents of the globe, but the statement says nothing about species, size, colour or quantity.

The questionnaire, although it cannot be called representative,[28] has shown that a significant ambivalence among the European respondents is apparent. While there was a basic openness toward experiences of the Spirit, even among the more critical respondents, there was also a cautiousness in placing an ideological significance on these experiences as well as understanding their cross-cultural impact.

It may be that this ambivalence points to a rapidly approaching crisis of Pentecostal identity in Europe which could extend to the charismatic wings of the established churches. This crisis of identity, perhaps emerges from the progressing secularization in the First World where societies insatiably demand ever 'new experiences', which erode a sense of firm identity.

Apparently, however, there is an awareness, at least among many theologians and clergy, that a Pentecostal/charismatic spirituality has an open-ended intentionality. In other words, experiences of the Spirit are acknowledged to be diverse and clearly cross geographical boundaries. There is an increasing acceptance that Christian spirituality in Europe might not only receive new impulses from North America, but perhaps more importantly from the East and South as well. Almost certainly these impulses toward a global Christian spirituality would not come from the materially satisfied and socially respectable, but rather from the poor and the marginalized who have discovered that they have an Advocate who can suffer with them and who moves and heals the hearts of all alike.

THE CLAIM OF GLOBALIZATION
FROM DIFFERENT VANTAGE POINTS

Many forces influence and describe the charismatic phenomena found in different parts of our globe. First, there is the reality of a secularization which proposes new values and provides a novel criteria for the mapping of one's life. Second, there is the question of a predominant method of communication and the language it uses: what is said, what is actually implied and how a message can be understood. Finally, there is the question of what a global culture means theologically.

SECULARIZATION AND GLOBAL CULTURE

By secularization we commonly mean the impact of modernity on religious institutions and human consciousness.[29] Whereas forty years ago secularization was mainly a western phenomenon, today its presence can be found in most developing countries as well. In the process of secularization, there is a progressive detachment of religious beliefs from societal life. At the end of the twentieth-century, people have become very selective as to what they want to appropriate from their religious sentiments into their view of the world. They distance themselves from traditions and hand pick the norms and values by which they decide to live. This practice has fostered an emphasis on both personal experience and on individual interpretation of experience.

In a sense, the Pentecostal/charismatic movement constitutes a possible response to the present status of the relationship between our societies and human consciousness. On one hand, there are traditional values that still seem worthwhile to maintain. On the other hand, there is freedom to make personal choices and to have personal affirmations of faith. For the Pentecostal/charismatic there exists a dialectic between what 'the Bible tells me' (i.e. tradition) and what 'the Spirit told me' (i.e. experience). The court which deliberates on this dialectic is the church comprised of the community of believers.[30] From this point of view, secularization holds a promise for the integration of tradition and experience in the life of the twenty-first century believer.

Furthermore, it can be argued that the process of globalization, witnessed in such terms as 'the global economy', 'the global citizen', or even 'the global community' constitutes a major site for the contemporary generation's concern with the sacred.[31] The world becomes in many aspects like a single space, both with regard to the interdependence of various spheres of activity as well as with respect to the consciousness pertaining to the global.[32] But it is of vital importance as to how this globalization is interpreted. If the claim of globalization is understood as an attempt to re-establish a world order in view of progressing secularization, pluralization and subjectivization, then logically this process would inevitably seek to reassert control by establishing a closed system, even if that system would encompass the entire world. This type of globalization would be anything but Pentecostal, for it would inevitably exclude all those who, for whatever reasons, could not associate themselves with that particular brand of 'spirituality'. Rather those setting it up, or those providing the definitions, would wield authority and the resultant global order would no longer embody the power of the gospel that sets people free. In contrast, if the concept of globalization fosters mutual respect and an awareness that all of humanity shares in God's creation and redemption, then the sacred comes back to a secularized world as a plausible point of reference.

COMMUNICATION AND GLOBAL CULTURE

One could argue philosophically that the language of a global culture would constitute a drawback. Along these lines, the phenomenologist Paul Ricoeur proposed that a universalization of values, norms, and imperatives would lead to a system of law that closed communication, and freedom would no longer know its origin.[33] The hermeneutical circle between subjects (the self, the other, the transcendent other) would be interrupted. As soon as one considers the other as either an unequal subject or object, there is inevitably a loss of respect. An antidote to this interruption of the interpretative circle would be the recognition that language and culture cannot be treated as neutral. The identification and practice of diverse forms of communication – not just the analytical and conceptual language of a mostly western elite, but also the language of the underprivileged, namely to speak in and listen to stories arising from their particular human condition – would make global coherence and pluralism more likely.[34]

Finally and in contrast, a linguistically and culturally closed global assessment of Pentecostal/charismatic spirituality would lose its dynamic foundation and multi-cultural expression. There would no longer be room for misery, metaphor and miracle. Orthodoxy would have a routine ortho-praxis devoid of an ortho-passion[35] so fundamental to human existence and to the Christian message.

THEOLOGY AND GLOBAL CULTURE

The concept of an open-ended global culture is also of theological significance. Such a futuristic perspective would necessitate a shift from a theology of victory to a theology of humility. This open-ended global culture would not be the product of theological correctness nor pragmatic strategies based on membership, maps and viewer quotas, but rather a humble recognition that God's Spirit is sovereign, working worldwide.

Furthermore, an openness within the European Christian to a variety of forms of spirituality or spiritual cultures within the global community would be an honest admission that God's Spirit is sovereign. As a consequence, those cultures which have enjoyed a rich Christian heritage, but have lost some of their momentum, may freely turn to more vibrant forms of spirituality.

Perhaps the most challenging consequence, because it runs against human nature, would be for the believers in Europe to stretch out 'the right hand of fellowship' to minorities and marginalized communities and together address global concerns with a vibrant message adequate to answer the pressing spiritual and moral needs of the world. For the western Christian, such reaproachment and unqualified acceptance of these marginalized communities would result in a theology of listening rather than a theology of telling.

By way of conclusion, I would say that a global spiritual culture could be beneficial, if it is a revival of an incipient Pentecostal spirituality acknowledging a common Christian attitude of respect and love towards the other because of the overriding awareness of God's active Spirit. Such a community could be called a culture in the sense that believers have been socialized to live a meaningful metaphor of Christ's life, death and resurrection, respecting the voices of all people and mutually experiencing God's Spirit moving through and with them. The Pentecostal/charismatic experience is a symbol not only 'giving rise to thought', but also a symbol giving rise to love, and therefore allowing for its continual re-definition for the sake of what was and for what is to come.

Notes

1   The succession of the questions is chosen deliberately to indicate that the western approach is far too often related to how we, in a position of power, could relate to others (subject/object), rather than by accepting the possibility that others are equal partners (subject/subject).

2   I use the adjective charismatic or Pentecostal interchangeably, unless the context makes a clear distinction desirable.

3   Roswith Gerloff suggests that the potential for a global spiritual culture has been betrayed, for instance because its historical roots have been abandoned, because many adopted an a-political or a-social approach to the Gospels, and because there was a split between the marginalized and disadvantaged on one side and those who favoured a Prosperity Religion on the other side.

4   Similarly, Michael Harper (England) argues that the potential for global culture is strongest, where there is a cultural vacuum.

5   Huib Zegwaart (the Netherlands).

6   Matthias Wenk (Germany).

7   Michael Harper.

8   Hans Harter (Germany). In this context it is interesting to note that the post-World War I Wesleyan 'Fellowship of the Kingdom' and the resulting Swanwick Conferences in the 1920s produced similar spiritual expectations in Great Britain like: 'hungry for the rich experience of Christ', 'a new form of

evangelical spirituality', and generally an 'expectation of fresh spiritual discoveries'. Cf. Ian Randall, 'Quest, Crusade and Fellowship: The Spiritual Formation of the Fellowship of the Kingdom', *The Fellowship of the Kingdom* (Horsham: Stuard A. Bell, 1995).

9   Keith Warrington and William Kay (England).

10   Michael Harper.

11   Jakob Zopfi, the General Superintendent of the Swiss Pentecostal Mission, wrote in an article on the 1995 World Pentecost Conference held in Jerusalem, that the 'Toronto Blessing' was cautiously discussed among the participants, but the Advisory Committee did not want to make an official statement, 'Weltpfingstkonferenzen: wozu?' in *Wort und Geist* 1,1996.

12   So for instance, Ian Randall, Nigel Walker, Keith Warrington, Matthias Wenk, Huib Zegwaart and Jakob Zopfi in 'Weltpfingstkonferenzen: wozu?'

13   Hans Harter, Huib Zegwaart, Nigel Walker and Ij-Jin Kim, a Korean missionary to Germany.

14   Roswith Gerloff.

15   The need for well trained ministers was mentioned several times. The emphasis on experience should not be lost, but one had to remain in constant dialogue with a theological reflection. Otherwise, one would lose touch with the Pentecostal/charismatic past and do things without knowing why. William Kay, Nigel Walker, Matthias Wenk and others.

16   Roswith Gerloff and Huib Zegwaart.

17   Quote is from Gerloff, questionnaire. Huib Zegwaart argued along the same lines in agreeing that there might be a similar basic experience or common faith, but pointing out that every denomination has its own 'culture' of doing and emphasizing things.

18   Because of the secularization and commercialization of human lives there is a contrast in upholding human dignity, faith as 'belonging' in spite of diversity (Roswith Gerloff). A global spirituality with an emphasis on community and care will be the only alternative to the fragmented society and individualization (Matthias Wenk). 'A secular society will be responded upon. Many believers/congregations will adopt a spirituality that will turn out to cope best with secularization, and will be able to move forward in spite of it'(Huib Zegwaart).

19   I did not define its criteria.

20   So for instance Michael Harper and Ian Randall.

21   Roswith Gerloff with her work with migrant communities in Germany and England, Nigel Walker ministering to Anglicans in bi-cultural Brussels, and Matthias Wenk, a Swiss, teaching a multi-cultural student body in Germany.

22   This critical note was voiced from Pentecostal as well as from charismatic Christians.

23   This paraphrase of a statement by Cardinal Suenens during the II Vatican Council would also ring true to Martin Luther King and probably to William J. Seymour.

24   Hans Harter

25   It seems clear that genuine charismatic spirituality can no longer be colonial, for theological as well as for secular reasons. In this respect see also W.J. Hollenweger, 'The Pentecostal Elites and the Pentecostal Poor', in *Charismatic Christianity as a Global Culture,* ed., Karla Poewe (Columbia, SC:

University of South Carolina Press, 1994), p. 200ff.

26 Michael Harper from the point of view of creation theology and Huib Zegwaart in relation to eschatology. They would probably agree that creation and eschatology are best understood and related theologically if considered together. A charismatic spirituality involved in practical moral action could be a paradigm between these two theological fields.

27 Jin -Ig Kim, Roswith Gerloff and Matthias Wenk

28 Men and women, whites and non-whites, West and East, North and South Europeans, Pentecostal, charismatic and independent Christians returned the survey, although not in a representative ratio.

29 We may use Peter L. Berger's definition of secularization. 'By secularization we mean the process by which sectors of society and culture are removed from the domination of religious institutions and symbols. When we speak of society and institutions in modern Western history, of course, secularization manifests itself in the evacuation by the Christian Churches... in the separation of Church and state... or in the emancipation of education from ecclesiastical authority. When we speak of culture and symbols, however, we imply that secularization is more than a social-structural process. It affects the totality of cultural life and of ideation, and may be observed in the decline of religious contents in the arts, in philosophy, in literature and...in the rise of science as an autonomous, thoroughly secular perspective on the world. Moreover, it is implied here that the process of secularization has a subjective side as well. As there is a secularization of society and culture, so is there a secularization of consciousness.' Peter L. Berger, *The Social Reality of Religion* (Baltimore, MD: Penguin Books, 1967), p. 113.

30 For an analysis of the situation of trial in secular speech and its impact on religious testimony see: J.D. Plüss, 'Therapeutic and Prophetic Narratives in Worship', *Studies in the Intercultural History of Christianity*, vol. 54 (Frankfurt, A.M. Lang, 1988), pp. 117–147, 161–186.

31 So argued by Roland Robertson, 'The Sacred and the World System' in *Sacred in a Secular Age*, ed. Ph. E. Hammond (Berkeley, CA: University of California Press, 1985) p. 347 ff.

32 R. Robertson, *The Sacred*, p. 348.

33 Paul Ricoeur, 'The Problem of the Foundation of Moral Philosophy', *Philosophy Today*, 22 3–4 (1978), p. 186.

34 W.J. Hollenweger, 'The Pentecostal Elites and the Pentecostal Poor' in *Charismatic Christianity as a Global Culture*, ed., Karla Poewe (Columbia, SC: University of South Carolina Press, 1994).

35 Matthias Wenk makes this point in the questionnaire answering why he believes the Pentecostal experience of the Spirit to be essential to the future of world Christianity.

Chapter Nine

Pentecostal Challenges in East and South-East Asia

Jungja Ma

Asia is a vast and diverse geographical region. Each country is unique in its social, cultural, political, economic, and religious experiences and orientations. In a chapter that deals with East and Southeast Asian countries and their people generalization is necessary, although utmost care will be exercised to be fair to the people groups in the region. For the purposes of this chapter, I will treat a region stretching from Mongolia and northern China in the north to Indonesia in the south, and from Japan in the east to Myanmar in the west.

Oppression and deprivation characterize the countries of East and Southeast Asia. Unequal distribution of resources causes the poor to become poorer and the rich to become richer. Rapid changes in various economic, political, and social sectors in many countries affects the social environment and the life pattern of the people. Advanced technology fuels economic growth, bringing affluence to some. As a result, people are increasingly influenced by materialistic and secular priorities. Sexual promiscuity, communication evolution, and urbanization are growing concerns in the region. These rapid changes create dissonance and stimulate a transformation in the world-view of people in the region. The mindset of the people is shifting from a group-orientation to an individualistic and task-orientation.

At the same time that many societies have opened to the outside world, a major portion of the population live in tribal environments. Often these tribal groups are deprived of their resources and territories. Social infrastructure such as roads, electricity, medical services, communication services, and educational facilities do not exist. Often, we hear news of the violation of human rights from this marginalized segment of the region.

The emerging Pentecostal movement in these countries has had a varying impact over the last few decades. In Korea, Indonesia, Malaysia, Singapore, Philippines, and Myanmar, the Pentecostal influence has been significant. The Pentecostal message of hope and power appealed to people in the low social strata. The success story of Yoido Full Gospel Church under the leadership of Rev. David Yonggi Cho is classic. His initial members were poor farmers, widows, and Shamans. Koreans who were desperate to find hope for their lives, especially at the end of the Korean War, responded to the powerful message of God as Healer and Blesser. Today, in Korea, the common message of Pentecostalism is often heard in churches across the denominational lines. While much information about Christianity in present day China is anecdotal, Pentecostals have reaped a great harvest in the years subsequent to the Communist takeover.

Not every nation has been receptive to the Pentecostal message. Countries like Japan, Taiwan and Thailand have been fundamentally resistant to the Christian message. Their dominant religious cultural dimensions are often blamed for this resistance to the gospel. Phenomenal growth among some Pentecostal churches in Japan, however, indicates that Pentecostals have potential to thrive even in a difficult environment.

Yet another group of nations in the region – Vietnam, Laos, Cambodia, Tibet, Nepal, Mongolia and China – are resistant to changes from the gospel primarily for political and economic reasons. Although some countries such as China had a strong Christian presence, prior to the socialist regime, decades of a controlled political system did not allow any western missionary presence and all religious activities were banned. As with most Christian groups, Pentecostals have re-established their presence in this repressive climate. North Korea remains a country which has not yet opened its doors to the outside world.

Throughout the region, the effect and impact of the Pentecostal movement differs markedly. Even in the countries where Pentecostal churches once experienced unprecedented dynamism, the rate of church growth has either plateaued or declined. Within this brief description of the Asian environment, this chapter will deal first with the critical issues that form the context for Pentecostal missions. Second, 'changes' in the region that pose a challenge to Pentecostal ministry will be analyzed. Finally, this chapter will examine the impact of Pentecostal churches to date, and suggest an agenda of issues that the Pentecostal church will face in the twenty-first century.

CRITICAL ISSUES THAT FORM THE CONTEXT
FOR PENTECOSTAL MISSION

OPPRESSION AND DEPRIVATION

For much of the twentieth century, the majority of the countries in the region were under colonial rule. The political system did not work for the interest of the people, but for those who held power. Even after liberation from oppressive foreign rule, many countries suffered under dictatorial military rule.

In such a political environment, force was often used to suppress any demands for political rights, human rights, and freedom of speech. Labourers and peasants became a suffering majority. Governments maintained absolute power to imprison, resulting in an increasing number of political prisoners. Prisoners were seldom given a fair trial. Others were even 'salvaged'.[1] The practices of injustice were overt, drawing media attention which was closely monitored by the authorities. Innocent people were often caught in the cross fire between the government troop and anti-government forces. Tragically, the innocents became double victims of injustices perpetrated by the opposing parties. For example, inhabitants in the mountain region of the Philippines were victimized both by the New People's Army (NPA) communist guerrillas, and by government military forces. Similarly, innocent inhabitants were caught in the middle between oppressive governments and the opposing forces in the East Timor conflict in Indonesia, the Moslem militant separatist group in Mindanao of the Philippines, and the independence movement in the mountain area of Myanmar. The ravages of war destroyed millions of lives in this region. Armed conflict has continued unabated. The Korean War and the Vietnam War cost millions of lives. Racial conflicts in Malaysia, the Sino-Communist struggle in Indonesia, and the Cambodian 'Killing Field' extracted a terrible toll on human resources.

In this oppressive political climate, women became double victims: marginalized by both the social system and by cultures influenced by male-dominant values. Women had neither an identity nor a voice in politics, economics, religion, and other aspects of cultural life. Although they were generally aware of the political situation in their countries, their participation and development were greatly stifled. Women in such societies were vulnerable both sexually and intellectually. In the rural areas especially, women were called upon to raise children, to function as home-makers, and to serve as the majority of the manual labour force. Historically, women in Asia have been the exploited victims of the societal structures of domination.

POVERTY

Economic progress in this region has been hailed by the entire world. Yet poverty remains a challenging reality. For instance, over 70% of the entire Filipino population lives below the poverty line. The Philippines is an example of a country with a colonial past, a present-day neo-colonial economy that is structurally and materially controlled and manipulated by the economic superpowers. Negative results include economic debt crisis, export-oriented production, unemployment, and migration of workers.

In most East Asian countries industrial production is controlled by the national elite and multi-national corporations. The resultant export economies, depending largely on foreign capital and technology, do not address the needs of the local population. Conversely, the elite in Asia's political and economic life have used the international banks and transitional corporations for their own purposes.

The rural districts have remained static. Inadequately developed, reform measures did not change disparate social realities in the rural area. Only the middle and upper-class landowners who could afford technology tended to benefit from reform processes. Large numbers of peasants were systematically removed from their subsistence farms in the rural areas resulting in the creation of slums in the region's cities. Though counterproductive in the long run, landowners often reinvested in crops for export or invested their profits in urban industries, thus preventing the growth of local food production. The countries then had to import food and encountered hunger and poverty for many years to come.[2]

Asian peoples in both rural and urban areas have been influenced by the sociopolitical powers which have promised them the right to secure their future. Today, significant movements of social renewal and political change that promote critical cultural action are being designed to destroy old myths and create new symbols in continuity with the cultural treasures of the past.

CHILD PROSTITUTION

The rapid emergence of child prostitution is a salient representative example of eroding traditional ethical values. According to some estimates in Metro-Manila, there are 60,000 street children involved in prostitution. Angeles City and Olongapo, near former U.S. bases are infamous for the proliferation of 'funhouses' and massage parlors. Similar phenomena are occurring in areas such as Bangkok's Patpong red-light district. Child prostitution is a tragic symptom of the destruction of traditional values, the materialistic desire of adults, and the pleasure-seeking impulses of corrupted minds.[3] Child prostitution has been rising rapidly over the past several years.

SEXUAL PROMISCUITY AND FAMILY VALUES

A cultural war rages in the Eastern Asia countries between sexual liberty and traditional values. People in China are more inquisitive about sex, sexual techniques, and sexual aids. China is undergoing a 'Great Sexual Leap Forward'. Government agencies openly dispense advice on problems that were previously strictly taboo.[4] Homosexuality, the principal of taboos is no longer a crime in China. However, anecdotal evidence suggests that homosexuals are still subject to criminal treatment.

Even in conservative Malaysia, traditional attitudes appear to be relinquishing ground, particularly in reference to premarital sex. Malaysian couples who engage in sex before marriage are no longer ostracized. In the past, parents were insistent that their son asked if his fiancee's virginity was intact. Such demands are no longer made.[5] Lifestyles of casual sex increasingly reflect the decline in traditional attitudes toward sexuality.

In Japan, observers point to the rising popularity of a new type of *manga* (comics) designed to attract women. Printed on cheap paper and drawn in the thin, quick style of other popular *manga*, they are more romantic than the erotic comics designed for men. More sophisticated is *Kirei*, a glossy monthly magazine filled with photographs of nude young men and sexual prose. The editors are women, and the magazine is produced for a female membership.[6] In a Tokyo sex shop for women, sales assistants show off notebooks containing messages from female customers describing their erotic experiences or solicitation of sexual partners. Male strip shows are fastly becoming mainstream entertainment.

The war between sexual freedom and family values is certain to continue. The drive to procreate, and the need for a nurturing family are fundamental human attributes. In reconciling the two, Asians still attempt to put family first. The family remains a central cultural value, remains in the life of the people. However, it is being eroded by influences such as the individual freedom so popular in the West.

TRIBAL GROUPS

The powerful influence of rapid urbanization and 'civilization', has not yet reached a substantial number of tribal groups still living in rather secluded areas and maintaining their traditional identities, lifestyles, and animistic orientation.[7] These regions lack basic infrastructure such as roads, electrical power, and communication system. Social services, including medical service and education, are minimal. Religious pagan practices often result in unbearable economic burdens. For instance, in burials among the Igorots of the northern Philippines, community expectation brings a hardship to the deceased family. The entire community expects to eat until the entire livestock of the family is butchered and 'offered' to the deceased loved one, so that proper respect can be shown to the formerly deceased ancestors. In effect, the family has to feed the entire village sometimes for two weeks. They are then forced to borrow money to buy more animals.

The tribal people have often been exploited for their property rights. They hold to the traditional notion of community land ownership. This notion permits their natural resources, such as minerals, lumber, and hydro energy to be developed by communities and governmental agencies for the consumption of urban people at the cost of relocation and environmental destruction of the tribal groups.

As countries are spending more time and money on preserving their cultural heritage, the tribal groups are increasingly 'showcased' and become a source of tourist attraction and profit-making. This destructive mixture of the novelty of tradition with modern materialistic interest further degenerates their morale and threatens their existence.

CHANGES THAT POSE A CHALLENGE
TO PENTECOSTAL MINISTRY

FREE MARKET ECONOMIES

Countries in this region have experienced tremendous economic achievement in recent decades. 'The Four Dragons', Korea, Taiwan, Hong Kong and Singapore, moved from under-developed to developed status, while other 'Tigers', such as Malaysia and Thailand are experiencing rapid economic expansion. China has emerged as a huge economic power, adopting a market economy system.

Korea represents this emerging successful group. South Korea suffered painful experiences during the Japanese occupation and the communist invasion from North Korea. These exploitive events left a ruined country. Since the end of the Korean War, South Korea has built its economy from the bottom line with meagre resources. The former president Park Jung Hee made a strong effort to rebuild the economy. Ironically, his military background, along with his tyrannical leadership, directed the country toward great economical improvement.[8]

However, more acute problems lie behind these economic success stories. The drive for economic growth has permanently altered the basic social structure, work ethic, and fundamental mindset of the people. The success-oriented work environment has impacted the relationship-oriented behaviour of these cultures. Whether successful or not, every country in this region is working hard toward industrialization. Countries are struggling to separate political ideologies from the new western-style economic system. China is trying to benefit from a free market economy without ideological change, while other countries such as North Korea are nervously watching that process. However, in many countries, the gap between the haves and have-nots is widening. The economic gap between urban and rural areas is also increasing. As industrialization continues, the society and family will feel the growing pressure to find alternative values rather than to maintain the old traditions.

CONFLICTS, ETHOS AND VALUES

INDIVIDUALISM VS. GROUP IDENTITY

Asians are group- or family-oriented. Maintaining 'dignity', 'respect', 'honour', and harmonious relationships are highly important. The most valued human qualities are those which help preserve group loyalties and which maintain congenial social relationships. Asians, in general, view the group, and not the individual, as the building block of the society. People do not see themselves as autonomous, but as members of the groups to which they belong.

As industrialization continues, people are becoming increasingly individualistic. Individualism particularly affects the family system, from the extended family to the nuclear family. The responsibility of children for their parents is declining.

TASK ORIENTATION VS. PERSON ORIENTATION

Asians are people-oriented. Their emphasis is on building a relationship with people. They find satisfaction in interaction with others. Their high priority is to establish and maintain personal relationships.

Such a relational orientation is being altered as free market economies emerge. In such a changing climate, people become task-oriented. They tend to develop a notion that self-worth comes from accomplishment and success. People seek greater competence and recognition in their workplace. People also desire to have an affluent life. This change toward a task orientation is seen particularly in Hong Kong, Singapore, Japan, and Korea as these countries rapidly industrialize.

This new and emerging work ethic has a profound impact on the social life of the people. Coupled with individualism, the spirit of competition is everywhere, including the churches. Everyone is viewed as a competitor rather than a co-worker. This changing environment was recently demonstrated when a huge department store in Seoul collapsed and killed numerous people. The owner made a statement which angered the entire nation. This statement basically said, 'You think you lost your loved ones. Look, I lost everything I accumulated in my lifetime.'

POLITICAL CONFLICTS

Truly significant is the change in the political systems of this region.

After World War II, the region was divided into two major blocks: democratic and Communist countries. This struggle left three countries divided into two parts: China, Korea and Vietnam. Korea and Vietnam had destructive wars among their own people. Conflicts, particularly racial conflicts are also present in this region. These include Malay-Chinese conflict in Malaysia, East Timor independence movement in Indonesia, Mindanao's Muslim separatist movement in the Philippines, and the Tibetan struggle against Chinese rule. There have been constant struggles against oppressive political systems. The Tienanmen Square massacre in China is just one example. The rebel activities of the New People's Army in the Philippines is due, in part, to the corrupt and oppressive rule of Marcos. The less known Kwangju revolt in Korea and the bloody suppression by the military government has left hundreds dead and missing.

RELIGIOSITY AND EXPANDING RELIGIOUS PLURALISM

Religions have played, and continue to play, a critical role in this region's cultures. People are deeply religious and many countries have their own state religions. Several world religions dominate Asian culture. Islam controls millions of lives in Indonesia, Malaysia, Brunei, part of the Philippines and China. Buddhism and its variations rule the populations of Tibet, Nepal, Thailand, Myanmar, and much of China. Hinduism is another major religion in this part of the world. Roman Catholicism and Mainline Protestantism have had an influential historical presence in the region. In addition to these 'high religions', many sects and folk religions including animism, have greatly impacted the region. Moreover, new religious expressions are emerging in the Asian context. The following are some examples of recent religious movements.

CULTIC MOVEMENTS IN JAPAN

The Japanese religious sentiment was derived from ancient Shintoism with its meta-cosmic orientation, attributing sacred power to natural objects or people so long as they share in the force (or in *kami*) that comes from above. The introduction of Buddhism in the sixth century AD altered this meta-cosmic conviction.[9]

The Japanese, however, are interested in exposure to varied religious practices. The majority of Japanese no longer seem attached to the traditional religion. The government tends to give special care to religious organizations with strong constitutional warrants of religious freedom. No cult has ever been dissolved, even though many have been accused of corruption.

The Aum Shinrikyo cult gained global notoriety on March 20, 1996. The *Aum* cultists attacked civilians with gas in a Tokyo subway. This attack killed twelve and left 5,000 injured. Police reported that an Osaka university trained astrophysicist designed the cult's complex chemical laboratory in Kamikuishiki village at the base of Mount Fuji.[10] A cult temple was discovered with the lab in an adjacent three-story building. The report said that in spite of such a chaotic situation, the cult members continued to undergo a daily routine of worship, chanting *sutras* and reading the works of their supreme leader, whose image, dressed in a purple tunic, is still prominently displayed on the walls.

It is certainly an unusual religious phenomenology which challenges these traditional religious people. Scientism is no longer the religion for the Japanese. Obviously the Japanese are getting a chance to be exposed to more religious diversity and more challenging religions are invading their lives.

INFLUENCE OF BUDDHISM IN CONTEMPORARY THAILAND

Buddhism has influenced the sociopolitical fabric of Thailand and its modernization. The government of Thailand has embraced the influence of Buddhism from the time of the great kings of the nineteenth-century (Mongkut and Chulalongkorn) through the numerous post-1932 constitutional military regimes, and up to the present. There has been a remarkable firmness and continuation of the political process, and an evenly marked absence of social upheaval or demonstration. For such reasons, the Thai governments have been said by many onlookers to have 'managed' modernization well.[11]

Most people in Thai society agree that Buddhism is a key in bringing stability and continuity to the political process during the present period of institutional changes. The traditional role of Thai Buddhism in Thai society is not just to perpetuate itself, but also to maintain the balance between the national religion and socio-political processes. Buddhism is regarded as a source of moral authority which may support a particular government, or series of governments in one national tradition. [12]

Thai Buddhism has contributed to the socio-political stability in the post 1932 period. It has stood publicly with all the post 1932 governments as legitimate custodians of Thai national symbols and traditions. Thai Buddhism has an authority to confer legitimacy upon specific governments because its leading practitioners, Buddhist monks, are highly respected. The ability of the national religion to grant legitimacy to governments, and thereby to contribute to the stability and continuity of political processes, has popularized the veneration of institutional Buddhism.

MINJUNG THEOLOGY IN KOREA

Minjung theology has a political connotation. This theological system emerged in the 1970s and has its own theological stance based on Deuteronomic and Covenant codes.[13] It advocates the rights of the poor people in the light of their socioeconomic historical background. Minjung theologians argue that the prophets are the spokesmen for the poor and the psalms are the joyful songs of the poor people.

Seminary professor, Ahn Byung Mu, has made an important contribution to *Minjung* theology, based on his study of the Gospel of Mark. Ahn discovered the historical context of Jesus' message in Jesus' relationship with the *ochlos* (*Minjung*). He used broad socioeconomic historical materials to interpret Jesus' message to the people (*Minjung*). It is one of his arguments that the writer of the Gospel of Mark protests against the Pauline kerygmatization of Jesus' message and recovers the historical message of Jesus to the *ochlos*.[14]

The most significant aspect of *Minjung* theology is liberation – liberation of people who struggle under oppression. *Minjung* theologians not only take the revolts and rebellions of the people seriously, but affirm the literary and artistic expressions of the Minjung's struggle and aspirations. The literary works of poet Kim Chi Ha and other writers are a prominent source of inspiration. '*Han of Minjung*' (righteous rage of the people under oppression) has emerged as one of the most important themes in the social life of the *Minjung*, as reflected in Korean theological circles.

Minjung theology thus attempts to apply the gospel message to the struggle and aspiration of Korean people in their current conditions. It stands on the side of the people and searches for freedom in real life, beyond philosophical and ideological frameworks.

PENTECOSTAL IMPACT IN EAST AND SOUTH-EAST ASIA

PAST IMPACT

Throughout the twentieth-century, the Pentecostal movement in East Asia has certainly contributed significantly to the Asian cultural, social, and religious pluralism with its unique message. This section will probe the various aspects of the Pentecostal movement and its establishment in the region of East and Southeast Asia.

In spite of the process of modernization and the advances in science and technology, Asians are relatively animistic and superstitious in comparison with westerners. They tend to regard natural phenomena, like storms and typhoons, as supernaturally caused. Asian people frequently regard spiritual powers as taking control over their environment. Thus, they give attention to spirits to keep themselves from being impaired or harmed. They believe that accidents, sudden death, and bad luck are caused by malevolent spirits. They view the spirit beings as inhabiting and having control over nature. The spirit beings also cause sickness, volcanic eruptions, success or failure. Often the spirits are vengeful and capricious. An appropriate means of soothing the spirits is offering animal sacrifice. Through the sacrificial ritual, the anger of the spirit is appeased. Their perception of deities is tied to their power to bless or curse.

Pentecostalism is most effective among the animistic people. As animistic religion is centred around the concept of power, the Pentecostal message not only provides a truthful proclamation, but also demonstrates God's supremacy over their deities through the demonstration of power. One tangible form of this supernatural demonstration is healing. Pentecostals have historically emphasized the power of physical healing and exorcism. This power is demonstrated particularly in an environment where medical service is not available. The early Pentecostal ministry of the Assemblies of God in the tribal areas of the northern Philippines is a good example.

God's power demonstrated among various sick people through healing ministry became a catalyst to bring the animistic people to Christ. The Kankana-ey tribal people to whom the Assemblies of God workers and missionaries have ministered are animistic and ancestral worshippers. Ministry members preached the gospel in open-air services in mountain areas during the early stages of the ministry. They boldly proclaimed the healing power of God based on Mark 16:15–18,

'They shall lay hands on the sick and they shall recover.' They saw the need of these people, and with simple faith in the Word of God, called on their ministry team members to pray for the sick.[15]

Many dramatic testimonies spread like a wild fire. A young boy, of fourteen, suffered from ulcers on his leg. When he was seven years old, he had fallen down and had broken his leg at the knee. The boy was treated by witch doctors, but he could not be cured. The next five years of his life were very difficult, since the bones grew together bent as the leg healed. His leg was stiff and he could not straighten it. He struggled to walk, hopping along with the help of a stick or by just crawling along on the ground. He certainly lived a miserable life.[16] The widow missionary Vanderbout laid her hand upon him and prayed, believing in Christ to heal. This boy threw away his stick, trusting in the healing power of God. From that time on he did not use his stick, and little by little his leg straightened out. The ulcers disappeared by God's power. Many souls were saved in response to such a healing experience through God's power manifested in the ministry of Vanderbout and her team members. Healings such as these brought parents to Christ as well as entire households normally consisting of three generations, ranging from between ten and thirty people. This 'power encounter' was the pattern of the Pentecostal evangelism in many rural parts of the region. As a result, Pentecostals penetrated well into rural areas, often avoiding urban centres.

SPIRITUAL DYNAMIC AND CHURCH GROWTH

Phenomenal church growth in some countries is often attributed to the vibrant form of Pentecostal worship adopted by many of the growing churches, whether Pentecostal or not, in the region. Church growth in Korea is an example. Korean churches have been growing so rapidly that Korea has a number of the largest churches in the world. In fact, of the 50 mega churches in the world today, 23 are in Korea. Ten local churches in Seoul alone have memberships of over 30,000 each. There are hundreds of other churches with a membership of between 500 and 1,000. The explosive church growth from 1980 to 1990 was so remarkable that in the capital city of Seoul there are more than 6,533 churches. In the 100 year history of the Korean church, four chief periods of very rapid church growth are marked: 1905–1910, 1919–1931, 1945–1960, and 1980–1990. There are over 12.2 million Protestant Christians, 36,832 churches, and 67,008 pastors and evangelists in

South Korea.

Bong Rin Ro in his recent article[17] lists several key contributing factors to church growth: 1) the dedication of pastors to ministry and their dynamic leadership; 2) the commitment to prayer especially in time of national crises; 3) the emphasis on evangelism and missions especially among lay people; 4) the cell group system which nurtures personal growth and provides time for intercessory prayer;[18] and, 5) the ample supply of highly trained workers from seminaries.[19] Pentecostal practices such as the baptism in the Holy Spirit, speaking in tongues, and prayer for healing are commonly held in most Evangelical churches, especially during revival meetings.

The Pentecostal impact is not limited to Korea. Indonesian church growth owes much to the Pentecostal movement. The growth of indigenous Pentecostal churches in Indonesia is particularly notable. In the Philippines, the sudden surge of independent Pentecostal/charismatic groups as well as traditional Pentecostal denominations receives much attention. For instance, a recent study of ten fast growing churches in Metro Manila revealed that eight of them were strong Pentecostal/Charismatic churches.[20]

The growth of Pentecostal/charismatic churches is especially significant in Singapore. Classical Pentecostals such as Assemblies of God, and Anglican and Baptist charismatic churches, as well as other independent churches are making a significant impact on the society. Malaysia has also seen a substantial growth among the Pentecostal churches. Even in Japan, several Pentecostal churches have recorded an unprecedented growth. Pentecostal contribution to church growth throughout the region, therefore, is unquestionable.

PENTECOSTAL INFLUENCES ON CHRISTIANITY IN THE REGION

Pentecostalism has been an object of suspicion in the Asian Christian community. Its emphasis on an experiential spirituality has drawn criticisms from mainline denominations. For instance, until recently, a major Korean Presbyterian group officially branded David Yonggi Cho as having a questionable doctrinal stand. However, typical Pentecostal experiences are regularly sought by pastors across the denominations. Prayer mountains are popular places where pastors, of Pentecostal as well as non-Pentecostal groups, go to spend time to receive 'grace'. Receiving grace refers to a personal encounter with God and often this confrontation includes typical Pentecostal experiences of the baptism in the Spirit with speaking in tongues, healing, 'receiving messages' and the like. The Pentecostals have added a definite dimension to the traditional Christian life in the region.

Also significant is the immanent presence of God that Pentecostals stress. The Word of God is preached in a dynamic movement of the Holy Spirit. When they preach and pray, they expect a response from the Lord. This expectation is particularly significant for Asians whose religions have a direct bearing in people's felt-needs.

Missionary zeal and commitment is also significant in the Pentecostal movement. Early Pentecostals clearly perceived missions as their divine calling. Although it is not generally true, some Pentecostal churches have been leaders in missions movements. Some large Pentecostal churches in Singapore and Malaysia have initiated missionary endeavours to neighbouring countries.

WHAT THE PENTECOSTALS NEGLECTED

Pentecostalism has continued to exert a strong impact on the Asian church. However, the movement has not given as much attention to the world outside the church.

In oppressive political issues, Pentecostals like some of their Evangelical counterparts, have remained silent. The Pentecostal churches chose to concentrate their attention on 'religious matters only'. Often silence was used by the dictatorial power as an endorsement, while the so-called liberal wing fought hard for social and political issues. Some Evangelical and Pentecostal leaders were even proud of being invited by oppressive political regimes to bless them. Such Pentecostals neglected God's given prophetic mission of the church to the world. Although Pentecostals might not have followed the same methods as politically active Christian groups, their concern and sympathy should have been expressed toward the unjustly suffering masses.

In response to economic injustices in the region, the Pentecostals have also remained largely silent. When labour struggles marred the entire Korean society, it was the Roman Catholics and Christian 'liberals' who raised their voices. The courageous engaged in a David-and-Goliath battle against mega conglomerates and the government. Nevertheless, from its inception, the Pentecostal movement has been surrounded by the poor and under-privileged. With the message of God's power and the presence of miracles, the poor have been nurtured with the spirit of hope. Many 'success' stories shared in

Pentecostal churches can be attributed to the untiring proclamation of God-given hope. Many can testify even today how God turned their lives around through healing and miracles.

In this area of social concern, some Pentecostals have taken a more active role. In Singapore, Teen Challenge, a Pentecostal programme helping drug users, has helped many people. In Malaysia, local churches operate successful rehabilitation programmes. Many big Pentecostal/charismatic churches in Metro Manila are ministering to street children and prostitutes. A Pentecostal seminary in the Philippines and a radio ministry group produced a simple but effective comic booklet to be used for AIDS education in awareness seminars among the youth of the Philippines. A well-known Korean Pentecostal church started a daily newspaper several years ago, and its daily distribution runs to more than a million copies. This newspaper creates and shares a powerful Christian opinion and makes a significant impact in the society. Recently another Korean Pentecostal church opened a facility for women in the community, funding it with 2.5 million US dollars. This same church is also building an impressive multi-million dollar complex for urban youth. A big Pentecostal church has developed an extensive feeding programme in the Philippines. Prayer for the fragile environment was one of several key prayers during the First World Assemblies of God Prayer Congress in Seoul in 1994. In Vietnam, Laos and Cambodia, a US Pentecostal body was invited to operate the social service program such as orphanages and English instruction. There is a recent plan to open a clinic in an underdeveloped region of China. These social programmes all appear impressive and rightly so. However, many of these are not strategic programmes. The efforts to minister in areas of social concern all too often depend upon the ministerial philosophy of a pastor who often fails to understand root causes of social problems, thus leading to short sighted programmes.

FUTURE CHALLENGES

At least three challenges can be identified for the Pentecostal churches in the region as they move into the twenty-first century.

1. MAINTAINING ITS DISTINCTIVENESS AND
   THEOLOGICAL REFLECTION

The Pentecostal Movement has been a spiritually dynamic movement.

Although this chapter has addressed Pentecostal social involvement or lack thereof, Pentecostals need to recognize, nurture, and maximize their spiritual dynamic in encountering political, social, economic, and religious challenges. Power evangelism is what the Pentecostals are known for as signs and wonders are revealed through the power of the Holy Spirit, and Pentecostals take these phenomena as a biblical pattern (e.g., Acts 3:1;16:14; Rom1:16; 1Cor.2:1,4,5). Pentecostals should not be tempted to conform to their established and well recognized Evangelical neighbours. They must remain faithful to their distinctiveness to be effective in their mission and calling.

As the Pentecostal churches mature, we expect serious theological reflection within the Asian context. The traditional anti-intellectualism among the Pentecostals has changed in Asia. Because of a high value given to education itself, Asian Pentecostal leaders are eager to obtain higher education. In the Asian Pacific region, not including India, the Assemblies of God alone have more than 150 Bible schools, and there are at least five schools offering master's programmes. Hence, it is not inconceivable that there will be some creative theological works from among Asian Pentecostal thinkers in the near future.[21]

2.   MISSIONARY AND CHURCH GROWTH MOVEMENT

Pentecostal identity has much to do with a missionary call. Empowerment is perceived as being specifically for the spreading of the good news. Faithfulness to the word and faith in God's power will make Pentecostal missionary work profound and effective. For instance, among Muslims, the most effective way of evangelism is through the power encounter with God.[22] The same can be said for evangelism among tribal groups.[23] As long as Pentecostal churches maintain a high priority on mission, the Holy Spirit will continue to bless and use them. Social involvement should be further explored and implemented in light of the mission of the Kingdom of God.

The Pentecostal churches are known for their effective church growth efforts. While the Asian context is rapidly changing, Pentecostal churches have continually proved that they can turn seeming hindrances into springboards for growth. The rapid church growth of Yoido Full Gospel Church is a fine example. This church has contributed to the worldwide church growth movement through its Church Growth International. Even in the midst of a seeming cessation of church growth, the Pentecostal church invariably moves towards new vitality and growth. Recently, about ten Korean mega-Pentecostal churches, including Yoido, started a fresh prayer movement. Every night, Gethsemane Prayer is held for God's touch in the life of individuals, the family, businesses, churches, the nation and the world. The churches began to reap its immediate results. They regained their spiritual dynamics. Ongoing church growth can be achieved primarily through a spiritual movement, and Pentecostal churches in Korea are testimony to this Pentecostal principle.

As already mentioned, Japanese Pentecostal churches have recently shown that Japan may be a difficult, but not impossible, field for Christian evangelism. The social work which Pentecostals have been invited to establish in former totalitarian countries may gradually open doors for full Pentecostal evangelism. China is another place Pentecostals need to target for a spiritual awakening.

3.   ECUMENICITY AND INTER-RELIGIOUS CONCERNS

Considering the region's religious pluralism, Pentecostals often find a supernatural dimension in other religions. This supernaturalism presents a challenge for a Christian understanding of power encounter. It is not the demonstration of supernatural power alone, but the revelation of truth which will ultimately determine which religion is authentic. As other religions including Roman Catholicism fall into the trap of syncretism with folk religions, there is also a strong possibility for 'folk Pentecostalism'.

Pentecostals should develop an ecumenical sense among Christian groups in working together for the expansion of God's kingdom. At the local level, there are many things Pentecostals can do with other Christian groups. For example, in the northern Philippines, churches are using an Ilocano song book which was compiled by Philippines Assemblies of God. There is a good chance that various Christian groups will join together to revise and eventually come up with a hymn book which will be 'universally' used among Ilocano-speaking Christians. This 'ecumenical' cooperation can expand to social, educational, and economic areas in addition to 'religious' works.

CONCLUSION

Although these challenges are great, the true challenge seems to lie within the Pentecostal churches: self-realization and a sense of its call.

Just like any Christian revival movement historically, the Pentecostal movement has a strong possibility of following the path of secularization and cultural accommodation. There is a powerful weapon within Pentecostalism itself to fight against rising secularism and materialism. The movement has always been a revival movement. As the early Pentecostals perceived, God has poured his 'latter rain' to us for the final harvest. This sense of a unique call will cause the Pentecostals to remain as Pentecostal as possible. With this Pentecostal identity, the movement will not be able to defend traditional Oriental lifestyles and values. It was not called to do that. But it will stand in the forefront to show our loving and powerful God.

It will, however, take more than the simple message of God's power to win billions of Asians for the Lord. Pentecostals have at least three distinctive levels of maturity in the region: 1) Pentecostal churches in an infant stage in countries such as Mongolia, Cambodia, Vietnam, Laos, Tibet, Nepal, China, and hopefully North Korea; 2) Pentecostal churches in struggling areas which need a fresh breakthrough, such as Japan, Thailand and Taiwan; and 3) Pentecostal churches in countries that have enjoyed significant success in the past and face new challenges. This group may include nations like Korea, Singapore, Malaysia, Philippines and Indonesia.

To be on the forefront of God's move in this region, the Pentecostal churches will need to develop leadership for the various ministries crucial to this region. We need to work relentlessly to keep the word 'post-Pentecostalism' from entering into a dictionary.

Notes

1   This term was popularly used to describe abducted and consequently vanished victims under the Marcos' rule in the Philippines.
2   Asian Conference of Third World Theologians, 'Asia's Struggle for Full Humanity: Toward a Relevant Theology', in *Asian Christian Theology,* ed., Douglas J. Elwood (Philadelphia, PA: Westminster Press, 1980), pp. 100–109.
3   See 'Battling the Pedophiles', *Asiaweek*, 25 August 1995, 28.
4   See 'Sex in Asia', *Asiaweek*, 23 June 1995, pp. 36, 40.
5   Ibid., p. 36.
6   Ibid., 39.
7   The animistic orientation of tribal groups has proved to be a vital contact point with the supernatural emphasis of Pentecostalism. The phenomenal growth among the indigenous Pentecostal groups in Indonesia is a good example. I established this thesis, based on the Assemblies of God's ministry among the Kankana-ey tribe, in my recent dissertation, 'Ministry of the Assemblies of God among the Kankana-ey Tribe in the Northern Philippines: A History of a

Theological Encounter' (Ph.D. diss., Fuller Theological Seminary, 1996).

8   See 'The Global Chaebol', *Asiaweek*, 7 April 1995, p. 40.

9   William Dyrness, *Learning About Theology From the Third World* (Grand Rapid, MI: Zondervan Publishing House, 1990), p. 142.

10   See 'Closing in on the Cult', *Asiaweek*, 5 May 1995, p. 37.

11   Steven Piker, 'Buddhism and Modernization in Contemporary Thailand', in *Contributions to Asian Studies* IV (1973), pp. 51–67.

12   Ibid., pp. 64–65.

13   Yong Bock Kim, 'Doing Theology in Asia Today: A Korean Perspective', in *Asian Christian Theology* (Philadelphia, PA: Westminster Press, 1980), p. 317.

14   Ibid., p. 318.

15   Inez Sturgeon, *Give Me This Mountain (Oakland, CA.: Hunter Advertising, 1960), p. 95.*

16   Elva Vanderbout, 'Report on Trip to the Alsados', in *The Missionary Challenge* (Springfield, MO) (April 1954), p. 3.

17   Bong Rin Ro, 'The Korean Church: Growing or Declining?' *Evangelical Review of Theology* 19 (1995), pp. 344–345.

18   He points out Yoido Full Gospel Church in Seoul, Korea as a typical example. It has systematilly organized about 52,000 cell groups for 706,000 members throughout Seoul for Bible study and prayer. Yong Gi Cho claims that the basic strength of his church lies in the cell-group ministry, ibid, p. 346.

19   There are 270 Bible colleges and theological seminaries, including Pentecostals and non-Pentecostals, which yearly produce more than 8,000 graduates. These young and old workers go out and plant a new church in different cities and provinces and go out oversees for mission work.

20   Oscar C. Baldemor, 'The Spread of Fire: A Study of Ten Growing Churches in Metro-Manila' (Th.M. thesis, Fuller Theological Seminary, 1990).

21   Simon Chan, *Spiritual Theology: A Systematic Study of Christian Life* (Downers Grove, IL: Intervarsity Press, 1998).

22   Sobhi Malek, 'Islam Encountering Gospel Power' in *Called and Empowered: Global Mission in Pentecostal Perspective*, ed., Murray W. Dempster, Byron D. Klaus, and Douglas Petersen (Peabody, MA: Hendrickson Publishers, 1991), pp. 180–197.

23   Sunday Aigbe, 'Pentecostal Mission and Tribal People Groups', in *Called and Empowered: Global Mission in Pentecostal Perspective*, eds., Murray W. Dempster, Byron D. Klaus, and Douglas Petersen (Peabody, MA: Hendrickson Publishers, 1991), pp. 180–197.

Chapter Ten

Contextual Perspectives on Pentecostalism as a Global Culture: A South Asian View

Ivan M. Satyavrata

INTRODUCTION

At the very outset I think it is critically important that I clarify the factors which condition both the context and the nature of my approach in this chapter. Critical appraisement of any aspect of a movement should normally be able to build on seminal historiographical or sociological studies. Unfortunately, such resources on the Pentecostal movement in Southern Asia remain very limited to date.[1] May I try to suggest a reason for this even as I clarify my approach to the subject?

In Asia a movement that is less than a thousand years is still in its adolescence. Consequently, it is only in recent years, for instance, that we have begun to produce indigenous histories of the two thousand year old Church in India,[2] and only in the last generation or so that serious attempts have been made to come to grips with critical questions of self-identity.[3] There may be those who feel that the Pentecostal movement in Southern Asia, despite all its strengths, is much too young to produce a history, let alone possess a distinctive culture. In deference to these acknowledged factors I have accordingly chosen to describe the character of the Pentecostal movement in South Asia in relation to the broader South Asian Church, and to look at the wider Pentecostal movement as a South Asian Pentecostal, essentially from the perspective of the dominant indigenous spiritual tradition within the region.

PENTECOSTALISM IN THE SOUTH ASIAN CHURCH

ITS ORIGIN AND DEVELOPMENT

While the origin of Christianity in the Indian sub-continent has been the subject of controversy among historians, the well-attested and uninterrupted tradition which maintains that St. Thomas the Apostle preached, died and was buried in South India is supported by recent scholarly opinion.[4] While the Roman Catholic presence traces its origin to the arrival of Vasco de Gama in 1498, Protestant Missions began with the advent of the Tranquebar Mission in 1706.[5] The origin of Pentecostalism in South Asia presents us with a number of difficulties due to the manifestation of specific charismatic phenomena normally associated with the origin of the movement.[6]

The outpouring of the Holy Spirit at the Mukti Mission of Pandita Ramabai in Pune, India in June 1905 is normally regarded as the origin of the Pentecostal revival in South Asia.[7] According to J. Edwin Orr's account, the Christian bhakti saint, Narayan Vaman Tilak, was with Ramabai in early 1905, from which time she organized special prayer meetings attended by hundreds. He goes on to record what occurred as revival broke out on June 30th. While Ramabai was expounding the eighth chapter of John, her hearers began to pray aloud, girls were stricken by conviction of sin, and there were a variety of manifestations, including the sensation of burning, simultaneous praying with loud crying, and speaking with tongues.[8]

This revival then spread to Gujarat in 1906 where missionaries and Indian Christians alike, of the Christian and Missionary Alliance, experienced similar Pentecostal phenomena. While there were other subsequent incidents of the manifestation of Pentecostal phenomena in other parts of Southern Asia, it has generally been accepted without dispute that the earliest manifestation of Pentecostal phenomena in India was that which occurred at Mukti Mission in June 1905.

If, however, the origin of the Pentecostal movement is traced to the earliest recorded manifestation of glossolalia, prophecy and other charismatic gifts in the modern period, there is reason to believe that the original Pentecostal outpouring in the South Asian region took place at least 45 years before the Mukti Mission outpouring. A major revival broke out in May 1860 in the Tirunelveli district of Tamil Nadu in South India as a result of the ministry of a Tamil evangelist named John Christian Aroolappen.[9] A first-hand witness records his observations following his visit to Aroolappen:

> The 'Spirit' was poured out upon many of those assembled, and there was a great shaking, attended with certain 'gifts', viz. speaking with tongues, seeing of visions, interpretation of tongues and prophecy...the fruits of the Spirit are manifest – there is a hatred of sin of all kinds, casting off of jewels, etc., love and unity, with peace and joy in the Holy Ghost, great love for and searching of God's holy word, with a strong desire for private and social prayer...[10]

Orr adds the comment that this revival was totally unexpected, least of all by the missionaries who had brought the gospel. He adds a word regarding the mixed response, which may well explain why knowledge of this significant event fell into relative obscurity in the years to follow:

> There were tongues, visions, and prophecies, none of which were familiar to the godly clergy of the Church of England. Some reacted against the movement immediately...There were thousands of lasting conversions...[11]

If tracing the origins of the Pentecostal movement in South Asia is a task fraught with difficulties, following its development is even more problematic.[12] It seems clear that the earliest Pentecostal group in India to take on the nature of an organized movement was the Indian Assemblies of God, formed in 1918 by a small group of missionaries, formally constituted two years later as the North India District Council of the Assemblies of God, which included within its jurisdiction what are today Pakistan and Bangla Desh. The South India and Ceylon (today Sri Lanka) District Council of the Assemblies of God emerged a little later, and its genesis is closely linked with the two other large Pentecostal groups in the region: the Ceylon Pentecostal Mission (today known simply as The Pentecostal Mission) started in 1923, and the Indian Pentecostal Church founded in 1933.[13] The Church of God (Full Gospel) in India was started in India in 1936.[14]

In subsequent years, the growth of the Pentecostal movement in

Southern Asia has been influenced by the following factors: i) the spontaneous emergence of new indigenous church movements resulting from the ongoing Pentecostal revival; ii) the advent of new overseas independent and denominational Pentecostal groups in South Asia; iii) the impact of the Charismatic movement upon the established churches, especially the Roman Catholic Church; iv) the emergence of independent healing evangelists and Pentecostal parachurch agencies; v) the consolidation of earlier movements through organization, property acquisition, leadership development and the establishment of educational, social and other holistic ministry agencies.

ITS IDENTITY AND CULTURE

The expressions of Pentecostalism, diverse anywhere in the world, are even more variegated in the South Asian context due to the racial, regional, sociological and linguistic diversities which exist within both church and society. Consequently, the typologies developed in other contexts are not suited to Southern Asia, since most of the categories used elsewhere are inappropriate or irrelevant,[15] and any attempted classification would be problematic. Nevertheless, the following is a suggested provisional classification based on certain broad distinctions among various Pentecostal groups in Southern Asia.

a) Pentecostals with trans-national organizational links – These would denote what are normally classified elsewhere as 'Classical' Pentecostal Movements, and would include groups like the Church of God (Full Gospel) in India, which is linked to the Church of God in Cleveland, Tennessee, and the Assemblies of God in India, which works in close fellowship with the General Council of the Assemblies of God, USA.[16] There are other groups with a much smaller, newer or regional presence, which are included in this category such as the Church on the Rock, Pentecostal Holiness Church, United Pentecostal Church and the Pentecostal Assemblies of Canada.

b) Pentecostals-Charismatics with a national and indigenous identity – These include groups whose origin and practice would place them in the 'Classical' Pentecostal category – such as the Indian Pentecostal Church and The Pentecostal Mission – as well as groups which emerged from the Charismatic movement in the 1960s and 70s, of which a good illustration is the Bombay-based New Life Fellowship.[17] What these movements have in common, despite their many distinctives is their strong indigenous identity and their nation-wide or region-wide influence.[18]

c) Regional/Local Pentecostal and Charismatic churches – This grouping is the most heterogeneous, including Pentecostal and Charismatic fellowships which have regional influence, as well as independent local churches of the congregational type which have become charismatic or local churches which have emerged as a result of the ministry of a charismatic founder-leader. Groups with regional influence are prominent in South India and North-East India.[19] Also included under this category are some charismatic groups which until recently remained on the periphery of the Roman Catholic Church but have now become independent churches with a distinct identity.

d) Catholic Charismatics – While the impact of the Charismatic movement upon the mainline Protestant Church in the region has been minimal, the impact on the Roman Catholic church has been significant, especially in the Bombay and Bangalore areas,[20] and in some southern states. Despite problems caused by significant losses in membership to Pentecostal and independent charismatic groups, the movement continues unabated.

e) Indigenous Pentecostal-Charismatic mission agencies – The emergence of indigenous Pentecostal mission agencies in India is a distinct feature of Pentecostalism in the sub-continent, related to the development and growth of indigenous missions in the church as a whole in the region. A 1988 study revealed that 57 Indian Pentecostal-Charismatic mission agencies with 3661 missionaries have been involved in church-planting in strategic areas where significant numbers of non-Christians are being reached and discipled.[21] The movement has gathered considerable momentum since then.

f) Non-denominational/Para-church Charismatic networks – There are also a large number of para-church organizations and non-denominational networks which have emerged around various charismatic evangelists, prophets and other cult figures.[22] These leaders have large groups of followers in 'mainline' Catholic and Protestant churches. The influence some of these have upon their followers is comparable to that of their cultural counterparts – the Hindu gurus. These constitute a somewhat fluid, but distinct and influential category of those who comprise the charismatic movement.[23]

Regardless of this heterogeneity, it is still possible to distinguish a broad confluence of movements within the region. In allowing the Spirit to liberate them from some aspects of culture while reinforcing other aspects, South Asian Pentecostals have much in common with the broader Christian tradition of the region. In certain other features, however, we observe what are clearly reactionary features of the Pentecostal movement in South Asia, many of which they share with the world-wide Pentecostal movement. Scholars have often drawn attention to this distinctive quality of Pentecostalism – described variously as *sui generis*[24] or 'non-traditional', distinguishing it from traditional 'mainline' or even evangelical Christianity.[25] South Asian Pentecostalism, however, undeniably owes much to the wider Christian tradition in the region. Pentecostal theology and ministerial practice in South Asia have, to a great extent, been shaped by an 'inherited' or 'borrowed' fundamentalist, reformed or neo-evangelical philosophy and ethos.[26]

This does not, however, take away from the distinctive or reactionary nature of the movement, but it is important to stress the fact that South Asian Pentecostalism is as much a part of authentic South Asian Christianity as it is a part of the world-wide Pentecostal movement. It is, however, its distinctives which set it apart from the rest of South Asian Christianity and make it an integral part of the global Pentecostal movement. In the following discussion we describe both dimensions as complementary organic components of a South Asian Pentecostal cultural identity.

1. National and Cultural autonomy – The colonial era and the ensuing struggle for independence witnessed the emergence of deep feelings of national and cultural pride within the Indian sub-continent. The South Asian Church has been engaged in a quest for a culturally indigenous Christian identity from almost a century prior to independence, and possesses a rich theological tradition of its own which the rest of the world is only just beginning to discover.

The same search for self-identity may be observed within the Pentecostal movement despite its youth and the marked western influence in some areas. Several large and growing Pentecostal groups in the sub-continent can boast of genuinely indigenous beginnings. Other movements within the region which have fellowship and support links overseas have thrived, largely because missionary pioneers facilitated the development of and made room for national leadership.[27] Despite the economic and theological influence of foreign independent pentecostal churches and groups upon some pentecostal movements in the region, the vast majority of groups of indigenous origin have succeeded in preserving financial and organizational autonomy.

This vibrant indigenous quality is unfortunately true to a lesser degree when we consider the theology of South Asian Pentecostalism. Due to lack of adequate tools and training, the teaching of smaller independent groups in particular is often determined by the latest 'trend' in North American or European Pentecostalism as expounded by a visiting evangelist or itinerant preacher.

2. *Spiritual Hunger* – Historically, Southern Asia has provided a home for people of all religions, including religious refugees who arrived at its shores escaping persecution on home soil. The traditional hunger and deep reverence for God, religion and spiritual matters have been expressed by South Asian Christians in two ways. In the first place, Christians in the region have manifested a deep and persistent thirst for spiritual revival, of which we see much evidence especially in the last two centuries of South Asian church history. There is secondly, a strong interest in the study of God, as a result of the fact that theological education has always held an important place in the life of the church in South Asia.

Like their fellow Christians in the mainline churches, Pentecostals in South Asia are earnest seekers after God, but may justly be credited with a greater degree of passion. Their ardent thirst for revival is expressed and observed in evangelistic crusades, revival meetings, prayer and fasting and tarrying meetings which constitute an integral and vital part of the Pentecostal culture in the region. At another level, the theological literacy of the Pentecostal constituency in South Asia is relatively high.[28] Pentecostal Bible Schools and Training Institutes of all kinds have mushroomed throughout South Asia in the last two decades, and the interest in higher education is perhaps higher than anywhere else in the two-thirds world.

3. *Caste and Parochialism* – One of the greatest weaknesses of South Asian Christianity is the church's failure to keep caste and regionalism out of the church.[29] The Church union movements in the region while commendable for their achievements, have failed to counteract the powerful forces of caste, regionalism and ethnicism which continue to plague the church, and in some cases, even become institutionalized.[30]

Pentecostals, for the most part, have failed to overcome these deep cultural prejudices despite their experience of the Spirit. The same caste and region based politics that rule the older Christian denominations control the affairs of the larger Pentecostal denominations, and the smaller, independent organizations often fall prey to nepotism.

4. Contextual Relevance among the Poor and socially marginalized – Although Christian missions in the region have traditionally always found greater receptivity among the poor, the upward mobility of Christians has resulted in Christianity eventually becoming more of a middle class movement.[31] In the post-colonial period the leaders within the main-stream of South Asian Christianity inherited a markedly 'colonial' version of Christianity, in which the liturgy, polity, architecture and even theology were distinctly western in flavour. Genuine efforts have subsequently been made both by Roman Catholics and Protestants to contextualize worship and theology, with mixed results. With the exception of a few upper middle class churches in the larger cities, the Pentecostal movement at the grass-roots level remains by and large a movement of the poor, with the vast majority of churches being located in rural areas and urban slums. Contextualization of the gospel among the poor has come somewhat naturally to Pentecostals, due to both historical and sociological factors.

Pentecostalism, in contrast, remained static during the independence struggle, and, furthermore, as a result of the policy of comity,[32] the early Pentecostal missionary efforts were largely relegated to rural areas of the sub-continent. Consequently, in the early stages amongst the largely poor and non-literate, Pentecostals did not feel the need nor did they have the means to develop sophisticated structures of any kind. In keeping with a rural life-style, the worship, practice, buildings and organization were simple and limited to the basic minimum.

The theology and practice of South Asian Pentecostalism were, likewise, marked by simplicity with a reliance on spontaneity and the spoken word appropriate to the non-literate mind-set. The perpetuation of an oral tradition through preaching, testimonies and personal ministry, which is a characteristic of the world-wide pentecostal movement is thus a distinct feature of South Asian pentecostalism as well.[33] This 'contextual relevance' remained an important mark of South Asian Pentecostalism and served it well even as the movement began to make significant inroads into the larger cities in the 1960s and 70s, where it found a high degree of receptivity among urban slums-dwellers and the lower middle class.[34] This 'cultural adaptability'[35] of South Asian Pentecostalism finds mention in Caplan's study in his observation that 'an important reason for the attraction of fundamentalism among the majority of ordinary Protestants lies in the extent to which it accommodates popular beliefs – shared with Hindus – regarding traditionally recognized symptoms of evil in the world'.[36]

5. *Experience-focused Spirituality* – A personal experience of the Spirit is undeniably the central focus of Pentecostal spirituality.[37] This is an integral part of South Asian Pentecostalism and in fact resonates deeply with the dominant religious tradition in the region in which an authentic experience of the divine is at the heart of religion and must be the mark of any true spirituality.[38]

Charismatic excesses are frequently the focus of charges of emotionalism or experiential subjectivity. But the experiential emphasis of Pentecostalism has emerged as a reactionary, but necessary corrective to the cerebral coldness, shallow activism and external formalism of traditional churches.[39] William MacDonald highlights its importance and value to Pentecostals: 'Belief in the availability of God's preternatural power and presence is foundational. It means a theology of God near-at-hand who gives abundant evidence of His powerful presence in the Church.'[40]

In their emphasis on expressive worship, concert and spontaneous prayer, the exercise of spiritual gifts, signs and wonders, exorcism and their ready acceptance of the supernatural, South Asian Pentecostals legitimately affirm their 'Asian-ness'. They also seek to demonstrate with their fellow Pentecostals throughout the world, that biblical truth must be released from its intellectual captivity and certified in practical experience.[41]

6. *Empowerment of the Laity* – Down through the centuries, lay people have played an important role in the mission of the church in the sub-continent, and have often been at the 'cutting edge' of and given leadership to mission work. This is especially true of Protestant Christian missions in the Indian sub-continent from the time of Ziegenbalg onwards.[42]

The Pentecostal revival with its emphasis on the empowerment of every believer, and the bestowal of gifts upon every member of the Body of Christ, has freed lay people for ministry. Although some Pentecostal pastors still struggle with the implications of this, the vast majority of those leading growing churches seem to practise some form of shared ministry and leadership, and are actively involved in equipping lay people for the task.[43]

7. *Ethical Rigorism* – Partly as a result of the influence of the holiness movement, the cultural propensity towards asceticism, and as a reaction to what is regarded as moral laxity in the mainline church, strict legalism may be observed in many quarters of the South Asian Pentecostal movement. Thus, in addition to strict abstinence from

alcohol, tobacco and other intoxicants, dispensing with gold orna-ments is often a requirement for water baptism amongst many groups. White clothing and avoidance of 'worldly' fashions, amusement and entertainment are often closely associated with holiness. The full-time pastors of one of the larger pentecostal groups are required to be celi-bate and live in 'Faith homes' operated by celibate men and women – the pentecostal equivalent of a Catholic or Hindu monastery. This type of ethical rigorism is a characteristic of Pentecostalism in general.[44]

GLOBAL PENTECOSTALISM AND SOUTH ASIAN SPIRITUALITY

In view of the ancient tradition of spirituality in South Asia, the sub-ject of the Holy Spirit is of great interest and attraction in the region. Spirituality pervades much of Hindu philosophy and culture, and this positive orientation to spirituality within Hindu thought has presented the Christian witness in the region with cultural bridges as well as pit-falls. The encounter between these two spiritualities is, however, no longer a purely domestic concern, but is rapidly becoming an issue of global significance.

The rapid growth of Neo-Hinduism in the West through the guru movements and the covert spread of the Hindu monistic worldview via the spread of the New Age movement,[45] makes the emergence of Pentecostal spirituality in this century an event of critical consequence for the renewal of Christian spiritual vitality. The outcome of the engagement between these two spiritualities will undoubtedly be one of the crucial factors which determines the shape of Christianity in the twenty-first century. Some useful insights and lessons emerge from the Christian engagement with the dominant tradition of spirituality in South Asia.[46]

Triumphalism vs. Servanthood – Pentecostal emphasis on spiritual warfare coupled with success stories of unprecedented explosive growth and attested by convincing statistical reports, easily leads to a crusade-like, militaristic spirit and shallow triumphalism. Gary McGee sharply criticizes this tendency among Pentecostal missio-logists, calling for a more realistic assessment of the statistical data and a more Christ-like attitude.[47] The triumphalism which often char-acterizes the Pentecostal mentality can be extremely damaging to the cause of Christ in regions with a history of colonial occupation, in which the missionary endeavour was viewed as part of the imperial expansionist enterprise.

In countries like India, for example, militant Hindu nationalism has arisen as a backlash against the aggressive missionary posture of Islam and Christianity. Pentecostals need to walk humbly in the footsteps of the Servant-King himself and put on the mantle of servanthood in their evangelistic and missionary engagement. While shallow triumphalism creates painful barriers, seekers of truth are always drawn to the truth when it is presented in love and humility.

Mystical monism vs. Trinitarian spirituality – There is an important note of caution for Pentecostals in Claude Welch's words of several decades ago:

> When the Christian speaks of the Holy Spirit, he does not refer to just any spirit or spirituality, certainly not to the spirit of man, or merely to a general immanence of God, but to a Holy Spirit consequent upon the event of objective revelation and reconciliation in Jesus Christ the Son. Where in Christian history the Spirit has not been clearly recognized as the Spirit of the Son...there has arisen what H.R. Niebuhr calls a 'unitarianism of the Spirit...'[48]

This 'unitarianism of the Spirit' or 'pneumatomonism' has, of course, been a danger of Christian mysticism down through the centuries. This tendency towards a 'pnematomonism' may be observed today, not only within contemporary liberal Christian thought in the West and within Indian Christian thought, but in Pentecostalism as well.[49]

Ralph Del Colle's proposal for a trinitarian Spirit-Christology offers a healthy and constructive theological framework for grounding Pentecostal spirituality.[50] Distinguishing his Spirit-Christology construct from the modalist Spirit-Christologies in contemporary western Christian thought, Del Colle believes that an orthodox Spirit-Christology is both verified and enriched by the Pentecostal experience.[51] According to Del Colle, while a Pentecostal-Charismatic spirituality undergirds trinitarian Spirit-Christology, a trinitarian Spirit-Christology deepens and enriches the charismatic life of the church .[52]

Anything less than a robust trinitarian spirituality will find itself in danger of being easily assimilated by the powerful monistic philosophical and theological currents of our day. A short step from an undifferentiated Christian pnematomonism to an un-Christian mystical monism will result in the concepts of divine and human personhood being undermined, the distinction between the Holy Spirit and human spirit being erased, and the uniqueness of Christian spirituality diluted by an overemphasis on divine immanence.[53]

Ascetic Apocalypticism vs. Socio-cultural involvement – Although Pentecostal commitment to social concern has been acknowledged by critics from without,[54] it must be conceded that their excessive apocalyptic orientation sometimes makes Pentecostals theologically averse to pro-active meaningful socio-political involvement. The Pentecostal historian, Gary McGee, draws attention to this:

> Because Pentecostal missions have always been driven in part by the expectation of the imminent return of Jesus Christ, missionaries have generally failed to address the responsibilities of Christians in their societies...[55]

An intrinsic weakness of Hindu mystical spirituality is the lack of any meaningful basis for practical ethical involvement and engagement in socio-political issues.[56] The Christian love ethic in contrast is grounded in the biblical concept of a supremely personal God, whose moral nature constitutes the moral standard for all humankind and the basis for ethical engagement in society. The Pentecostalism ethic, however, is largely negative and often ascetic, sometimes giving rise to a naive cultural imperialism and at other times a cultural escapism similar to ascetic tendencies in much of Hindu spirituality.

There is a growing awareness among Pentecostals that their understanding of the Spirit as the eschatological Spirit who indwells the church today and witnesses to the presence of the Kingdom of God in the world today, is best expressed within the framework of a kingdom theology and a holistic theology of mission.[57] Gary McGee thus makes the following proposal in his summary assessment of the tension between proclamation and social concern in Assemblies of God missiology:

> Continued biblical exposition of the kingdom of God offers Pentecostals the best prospect of developing a holistic theology of mission capable of integrating historic concerns for taking the gospel message to unreached peoples and expressing Christian compassion by ministering to physical and social needs....[58]

He concludes his case for a holistic theology of mission with an aptly-worded challenge: 'The spiritual needs of hundreds of millions of people in our world are too great and the cries of the hungry and the oppressed are too loud for Christians to ignore either, even if one's eschatology chimes that midnight has come.'[59] The apocalyptic eschatological thrust of Pentecostal theology must be balanced by a biblical emphasis on the present reality of the kingdom, and the need for

socio-cultural engagement. The enduring influence and future survival of the Pentecostal movement depends upon the extent to which it
succeeds in permeating, challenging, transforming and owning the
indigenous cultures where the movement has penetrated.

Experientialism vs. Holistic hermeneutic – Most informed people
today would no longer accept the common caricature of Pentecostals
as being anti-intellectual and exegeting their experience rather than
the Bible. Few Pentecostals would, however, deny that in reacting to
the cynicism towards the Bible and the supernatural fostered in many
quarters of academic theology, the average Pentecostal applies a 'hermeneutic of suspicion' when it comes to the intellect and rational discourse about God.

The Pentecostal emphasis on experience is of great value and must
never be compromised, particularly in the context of a post-modern
world with its increasing acceptance of the supra-rational dimensions
of human life and experience. The phenomenal growth and success of
Pentecostalism in the two-thirds world must at least in part be attributed to the importance placed upon religious experience among the
traditional living religions in African and Asian contexts.

In contrast to much of animistic and eastern mystical spirituality,
however, Pentecostal spirituality is both grounded in a revelatory historical event and focused in a revelatory Word. There is, hence, a
pressing need for a spirituality that incorporates the cognitive along
with the experiential in its biblical and theological hermeneutic. The
required corrective and synthesis is perhaps most clearly and suc-
cinctly stated by Stronstad:

> Because man is a creature made in God's image, understanding the
> Bible is always a matter of the mind – of the human intellect...and it is in
> the Word that the human mind encounters the divine mind. Thus, inter-
> pretation must necessarily be a matter of rationality as well as experi-
> ence and spiritual perception...[60]

Pentecostal scholars have already begun to address this need,[61] but a
consensus needs to emerge which will eventually succeed in effecting
change in at least significant sections of the movement . If not, there is
a danger that Pentecostal spirituality in some parts of the world could
deteriorate into superstition, syncretistic mysticism or lapse into the
occult. If Pentecostal spirituality is to survive deeper levels of
encounter with indigenous cultures and spiritualities, it must be
grounded in the Christ-event as recorded in the biblical account, interpretation of which requires both the guidance of the Spirit and an

informed reading of the text.

CONCLUSION

In concluding his analysis of 'fundamentalism'[62] in the South Indian context, Caplan highlights the reasons for the appeal and success of the Pentecostal movement. His verdict is that if western 'fundamentalist' organizations do have a part, the role they play is relatively insignificant. According to his analysis, the unique appeal of the Pentecostal movement is linked partly to its autochthonous, culturally adaptable character, and partly to its identity as an expanding global movement. From the blend of these two factors there seems to emerge an empowering and therapeutic dynamic, that has both existential relevance and practical appeal:

> Fundamentalism can, thus, be seen as a system of knowledge which incorporates indigenous interpretative understanding; which provides everyday knowledge with an authoritative status, both in intellectual terms (as a theology) as well as through being associated with a global, expanding, and powerful religious movement. Furthermore, ordinary individuals whose participation in discourse is limited and constrained by the formalization of orthodox rites...find themselves enfranchised within a fundamentalist setting. They are engaged, heard, listened to, and given support, in many instances rediscovering a new sense of self.[63]

What, then, does it mean to be a Pentecostal? Simply stated – different things to different people! As someone who belongs to different sub-cultures at one and the same time, a variety of different impulses shape, an individual Pentecostal's cultural identity. What about Pentecostalism as a global cultural phenomenon? Pentecostals the world over have much in common, and they must joyfully celebrate this commonality.

To describe this commonality in terms of a global 'culture', however, not only implicitly imposes an artificial homogeneity upon a movement with richly nuanced cultural diversity, it also runs the risk of sectarianism. The Pentecostal movement does not exist for itself, it exists for the purpose of bringing renewal and unity to the church as a whole, and new energy and impetus to her mission.

Notes

1   Clarification is in order: Pentecostals in Southern Asia are by no means theologically naive or untrained and uninformed. In terms of the three phases of
Pentecostal scholarship delineated by the editors of the *Journal of Pentecostal
Theology* in their inaugural issue (*1*, 1992, 3–4), we have successfully negotiated the first phase and have begun to engage in the third phase of critical theological research in various biblical and theological disciplines, although
admittedly, not enough work has been done in what they suggest as the second
phase – a social analysis and descriptive history of the Pentecostal movement
in the region.

2   Until the publication of the Roman Catholic historian, A.M. Mundadan's *History of Christianity in India – I: From the Beginning up to the Middle of the
Sixteenth Century (up to 1542)* (Bangalore: Theological Publications in India,
1984) – the first of a six-volume series on the history of Christianity in India,
produced by the Church History Association of India – the only descriptive
histories of the Church in India were those written by missionaries, C.B. Firth,
An Introduction to Indian Church History [Madras: CLS, 1976] and Stephen
Neill, *A History of Christianity in India: Beginnings to AD 1707* (Cambridge:
Cambridge University Press, 1984).

3   For instance, A.M. Mundadan's *Indian Christians: Search for Identity and
Struggle for Autonomy* (Bangalore: Dharmaram Publications, 1984).

4   For a thorough investigation of the evidence see Mundadan, *History of Chris-
tianity in India – I*, pp. 9–66 cf Leslie W. Brown, *The Indian Christians of St.
Thomas* (Cambridge: Cambridge University Press, 1982), pp. 43–63 and
Firth, *Indian Church History*, pp. 1–17.

5   Firth, *Indian Church History*, pp. 49 f., 131f.

6   It is thus standard practice to trace the origin of the Pentecostal movement to
the earliest recorded manifestation of glossolalia in the modern period. One of
the difficulties we encounter in the South Asian context is that those recording
various manifestations of the Spirit in a revival clearly appear to have had
strong prejudices against certain phenomena, and display a certain reluctance
to record those manifestations which they regarded as inappropriate. For
example, Helen Dyer's account of the revival at Mukti Mission fails to mention the tongues phenomena mentioned in other accounts, but may have
implied it in the vaguely suggestive phrase '...things that are too deep to be
described' *Revival in India* (London: Morgan & Scott, 1907), p. 44. This bias
is also apparent in the tone of G.H. Lang's account of the 1860 Tirunelvely
revival in *The History and Diaries of an Indian Christian: J.C. Aroolapen*
(London: M.F. Robinson & Co., 1939), pp. 158f, 174, 193f.

7   Stanley H. Frodsham, *With Signs Following* (Springfield, MO: Gospel Publishing House, 1946), pp. 16–17.

8   *Evangelical Awakenings in Southern Asia* (Minneapolis, MN: Bethany Fellowship, 1975), pp. 144–145.

9   This is documented by Orr, *Evangelical Awakenings*, pp. 58 f., and recorded
in detail with cautious approval and guarded criticism by G.H. Lang, *The History and Diaries of an Indian Christian: J.C. Aroolapen* (London: M.F. Robinson & Co., 1939), pp. 173ff.

10   Lang, *J.C. Aroolapen*, pp. 198–199.

11 Orr, *Evangelical Awakenings*, pp. 59–60.
12 This is largely due to the fact that not only has Pentecostalism in Southern Asia largely consisted of scattered and spontaneous revival movements (as is the case in other parts of the world as well), but the political changes precipitated by the partition of India and the acquisition of independence, the prevailing ethnic diversity and strong regionalism, and the relative marginalization of the movement in the early years, kept the movement fragmented, scattered and largely unorganized. As a result we have very little by way of reliable records of the growth and development at various stages in different sections of the movement.
13 It is to be noted that while both the CPM (TPM) and IPC had their origin in South India, they have since expanded into other parts of India, where they have engaged aggressively in church-planting efforts.
14 To the author's knowledge, there is no published work to date in which these facts and dates have been documented. Some academic documentation may be found in a few unpublished dissertations. The above sketch is based on the data furnished in Benjamin P. Shinde, *The Contribution of the Assemblies of God to Church Growth in India* (Unpublished M.A. thesis submitted to Fuller Theological Seminary, May 1974), pp. 78–105.
15 Such as for example, Vinson Synan's typology in 'Pentecostalism: Varieties and Contributions', *PNEUMA: The Journal of the Society for Pentecostal Studies* 9:1 (Spring 1987): pp. 32f. or the categories cited in Grant McClung's 'Pentecostal/ Charismatic Perspectives on a Missiology for the twenty-first Century', *PNEUMA: The Journal of the Society for Pentecostal Studies* 16:1 (Spring 1994), p. 12. Worse still is the explicit ethnocentricity in the use of categories such as 'non-white' and 'black-non-white' in some of these classifications, which ironically enough are used to describe sections of a movement that is widely acknowledged to be more 'non-white' than 'white', see Vinson Synan, *The Spirit said 'Grow'* (Monrovia, CA: MARC, 1992), p. 7 cf. p. 5.
16 The Assemblies of God is currently the largest of these groups: a December 31, 1995 Assemblies of God of India Statistics Report indicates that it has over 1500 recognized churches and over 300,000 adherents, registering an annual growth rate of 25%.
17 The NLF which began as a single local church in the early 1970s, according to a March 1996 report, now has a network of close to 1500 house churches in Bombay and over 3000 house churches throughout India.
18 Some of these have begun to reach out to neighbouring countries like Nepal, Bhutan and Bangla Desh, and several have branch churches in Middle Eastern countries as well as North America.
19 By way of illustration, the Sharon Fellowship and Maranatha Revival Church in South India and the Nagaland Christian Revival Church and Full Gospel Fellowship in North East India.
20 Roger Hedlund, *Roots of the Great Debate in Mission: Mission in Historical and Theological Perspective* (Bangalore: Theological Book Trust, 1993), p. 470.
21 Hedlund, *Roots of the Great Debate in Mission*, p. 475f.
22 Perhaps the best-known of these is D.G.S. Dhinakaran's 'Jesus Calls' organization, but there are scores of others with considerable following in the mainline churches.

23 See, for instance, the various degrees of involvement with the Pentecostal movement among CSI members indicated in Lionel Caplan's ethnographical study of the Christian community in Madras: *Class and Culture in Urban India: Fundamentalism in a Christian Community* (Oxford: Clarendon Press, 1987), pp. 215–219.

24 Walter Hollenweger's expression in 'The Critical Tradition of Pentecostalism' *Journal of Pentecostal Theology* 1 (1992), p. 8.

25 Donald W. Dayton, for example, observes that Pentecostalism is: '...precisely not "traditional" Christianity, but a new innovative, renewal movement within the Christian tradition whose distance from traditional Christianity is its greatest strength...' While his point is well taken, he may be overstating his case, 'The Holy Spirit and Christian Expansion in the Twentieth-century', *Missiology: An International Review* 16:4 (October 1988), p. 403.

26 I suspect the same is true in other parts of the world as well.

27 I would cite the Assemblies of God as a good illustration of this, in which a graduate-level institution, Southern Asia Bible College, was established in Bangalore, India, at an early stage in the life of the movement (founded in 1951), with the express purpose of facilitating the emergence of national leadership within the Assemblies of God in Southern Asia. This institution has in fact provided graduate level theological education for leaders in several of the other Pentecostal movements in the region as well. In recent years other independent Pentecostal graduate-level institutions have emerged, including Faith Theological Seminary in Kerala and the COTR Seminary in Andhra Pradesh.

28 Among other things, the region can boast of having the oldest A/G Bible School outside of the USA – Bethel Bible College in Punalur, Kerala, founded in 1927: Gary McGee, *This Gospel Shall Be Preached: A History and Theology of Assemblies of God Foreign Missions to 1959* (Springfield, MO: Gospel Publishing House, 1986), p. 88. The A/G alone has 18 Bible Schools, 44 extension centres and over 2500 Bible students in the region.

29 See Lionel Caplan's ethnographical study, *Class and Culture in Urban India* (Oxford: Clarendon Press, 1987), pp. 149–169; also Sebasti L. Raj and G.F. Xavier Raj (eds.) *Caste Culture in Indian Church: The Response of Church to the Problem of Caste within the Christian Community* (New Delhi: Indian Social Institute, 1993).

30 P. Manoharan refers to this somewhat provocatively as the 'Demon of Communalization' and one of the major obstacles to mission: 'Reflections on the History of Mission in India' in *Debate on Mission: Issues from the Indian Context* (Madras: Gurukul Lutheran Theological College and Research Institute, 1979), pp. 45f.

31 See Caplan, *Class and Culture in Urban India*, p. 18.

32 For a brief explanation of the 'comity' arrangement among missions in India, see Caplan, *Class and Culture in Urban India*, pp. 44f; also Jacob S. Dharmaraj, *Colonialism and Christian Mission: Postcolonial Reflections* (Delhi: ISPCK, 1993).

33 See Byron Klaus, 'A Theology of Ministry: Pentecostal Perspectives', *Paraclete* 23:3 (Summer 1989): 1 and Russell P. Spittler, 'Spirituality, Pentecostal and Charismatic' in *Dictionary of Pentecostal and Charismatic Movements*, ed., Stanley M. Burgess and Gary B. McGee (Grand Rapids, MI: Zondervan Publishing House, 1988), p. 805.

34   This is not to deny or minimize the impact of Pentecostal movement upon the
      upper classes in recent years, particularly in the big cities. See Caplan, *Class
      and Culture in Urban India*, p. 214, for Madras as a case in point of 'Funda-
      mentalist' inroads into big cities in the 1960s and 70s.

35   Vinson Synan's expression: 'Pentecostalism: Varieties and Contributions',
      Pneuma: The Journal of the Society for Pentecostal Studies 9:1 (Spring 1987),
      pp. 44f.

36   Caplan, *Class and Culture in Urban India*, p. 3.

37   Russell Spittler, 'Spirituality, Pentecostal and Charismatic' in *Dictionary of
      Pentecostal and Charismatic Movements*, ed., Stanley M. Burgess and Gary
      B. McGee (Grand Rapids, MI: Zondervan Publishing House, 1988), p. 804.

38   There are several similarities between Pentecostal worship and the devotional
      patterns of followers of the *bhakti* tradition in Hinduism, which needs to be
      studied in greater depth.

39   Caplan, *Class and Culture in Urban India*, pp. 223f.

40   'Pentecostal Theology: A Classical Viewpoint' in *Perspectives on the New
      Pentecostalism*, ed., Russell P. Spittler (Grand Rapids, MI: Baker Book
      House, 1976), pp. 61–62 quoted in Byron Klaus, 'A Theology of Ministry:
      Pentecostal Perspectives', *Paraclete* 23:3 (Summer 1989), p. 1.

41   Klaus, 'A Theology of Ministry', pp. 1ff.

42   See P. Manoharan, 'Reflections on the History of Mission in India', pp. 43f.
      Manoharan blames what he characterises as the 'Demon of Clericalization' for
      the stifling of the laity, which has consequently become an obstacle to mission.

43   Note Roger Hedlund's very valuable observations in this regard: *Roots of the
      Great Debate in Mission: Mission in Historical and Theological Perspective*
      (Bangalore: Theological Book Trust, 1993), pp. 472f.

44   Walter J. Hollenweger, *The Pentecostals* (London: SCM Press, 1972), pp.
      407f.

45   See Lars Johnson, 'New Age – A Synthesis of the Premodern, Modern and
      Postmodern' in *Faith and Modernity,* eds., Philip Samson, Vinay Samuel and
      Chris Sugden (Oxford: Regnum Books International, 1994), pp. 208–251.

46   There is obviously room for a more full-length treatment of the issues listed
      here than we have been able to engage in within the scope of this study. Our
      task in this section has thus been limited to suggesting an 'agenda' for further
      research and reflection.

47   'Pentecostal Missiology', pp. 275ff.

48   'The Holy Spirit and the Trinity', *Theology Today* 8 (April 1951), p. 29.

49   The modalist 'Jesus only' heresy is only an extreme case in point, the 'Jesus'
      in actual effect really designating the Holy Spirit rather than Jesus of Nazareth,
      and thus making it a Spirit-monism or 'Spirit only' doctrine.

50   'Spirit-Christology: Dogmatic Foundations for Pentecostal-Charismatic Spir-
      ituality', *Journal of Pentecostal Theology* 3 (1993), pp. 91–112.

51   'Spirit-Christology', p. 111.

52   'Spirit-Christology', p. 106.

53   A detailed exposition may be found in Ivan M. Satyavrata, 'The Holy Spirit
      and Advaitic Spirituality', *Dharma Deepika* 1:1 (1995), pp. 49, 56–57. An ear-
      lier version of this article was published in *Crux* 27:4 (December 1991).

54   Bonino, 'Pentecostal Missions is More Than What It Claims', p. 284; also
      Hollenweger, *The Pentecostals*, pp. 469 ff. In the South Asian context, social

concern is of necessity an integral part of the mission strategy of the Assemblies of God in Bangla Desh; in India, Pentecostal involvement in social issues has thus far included educational and medical work, child care and vocational training, ministry to street children and the socially marginalized, and urban slum development. Recently, an Assemblies of God church has partnered with World Vision in an effective outreach among *Devadasis* (temple prostitutes) in eastern Karnataka, South India. But this involvement has often been tentative, restricted to specific areas, and has not been altogether without opposition.

55   'Pentecostal Missiology', p. 280.

56   The doctrines of *maya* and *karma*, which lead implicitly to asceticism and fatalism respectively, are, on one hand, escapist and deny value to involvement in the created universe, and on the other, provide no meaningful basis for engagement in social and cultural transformation.

57   See Peter Kuzmic, 'Kingdom of God', *Dictionary of Pentecostal and Charismatic Movements*, pp. 521–526. Also chapters by Gordon D. Fee, Murray Dempster, and Douglas Petersen in *Called and Empowered: Global Mission in Pentecostal Perspective*, eds., Murray W. Dempster, Byron D. Klaus & Douglas Petersen (Peabody, MA: Hendrickson Publishers, 1991).

58   Gary McGee, 'Saving Souls or Saving Lives? The Tension Between Ministries of Word and Deed in Assemblies of God Missiology', *Paraclete* 28:4 (Fall 1994), p. 19; cf Steven J. Land, 'A Passion for the Kingdom', *Journal of Pentecostal Theology* 1 (1992), pp. 39f.

59   'Saving Souls or Saving Lives?', p. 21.

60   'Pentecostal Experience and Hermeneutics', *Paraclete* 26:1 (Winter 1992), p. 28.

61   In addition to Roger Stronstad's article, see also Timothy B. Cargal, 'Beyond the Fundamentalist-Modernist Controversy: Pentecostals and Hermeneutics in a Postmodern Age', *PNEUMA: The Journal of the Society for Pentecostal Studies* 15 (Fall 1993), pp. 163–187, and French L. Arrington's response, 'The Use of the Bible by Pentecostals', *PNEUMA: The Journal of the Society for Pentecostal Studies* 16:1 (Spring 1994), pp. 101–107.

62   In his use of this term Caplan essentially has the Pentecostal movement in view, *Class and Culture in Urban India*, pp. 1f.

63   Caplan, *Class and Culture in Urban India*, p. 245.

Chapter Eleven

'Everybody Bids You Welcome'
A Multicultural Approach to North American
Pentecostalism

David D. Daniels

The globalization of Pentecostalism suggests a future for Christianity where the Mediterranean and European heritage of the Christian church is localized and the multicultural character of the contemporary Christianity is stressed. This new 'future' provides an opportunity for a fresh conception of the character of global Christianity previously viewed as a European religion exported around the world through missions, colonialism, immigration, and 'global culture'. Pentecostalism offers an expression of Christianity which in its origins in North America combines African American Christianity and white American Christianity and includes the presence of Hispanic, Asian American and Native American Christians. In many contexts around the world Pentecostals intersected with local Christian movements, creating local expressions of Christianity and local expressions of Pentecostalism demonstrating dialectical relationships.

The relocation of the epicentre of Christianity from Orthodox Antioch, Catholic Rome, Lutheran Wittenberg and Reformed Geneva to another centre of Christian vitality generates issues beyond the historical ones. This relocation is more than a simplistic dismissal or devaluing of the theological and ecclesial controversies of the previous centres of Christianity. Epicentre relocation provides Pentecostal lenses through which to interpret the Christian tradition.[1]

To make the paradigmatic shift in perspective on global Christianity an interpretation of global Pentecostalism is essential because Pentecostalism is one of the most vibrant expressions of global Christianity is Pentecostalism. Pivotal to this interpretation is the interpretation of North American Pentecostalism, the catalyst of the international Pentecostal movement. To achieve such an interpretation of North American Pentecostalism both regional and global evaluations must be employed.

A regional perspective of North American Pentecostalism could pursue a few trajectories in the historiography of North American religion. The interpretation of Pentecostalism may explore how the movement embodies North American religion. The scholarship of Robert T. Handy and Mark Noll would be central to this thesis, highlighting respectively the revivalistic and democratic characters of North American religion. Another interpretation following the scholarship of H. Richard Niebuhr, C. Eric Lincoln, and Roger D. Hatch would accent the role of race in defining North American religion.[2] Another interpretation following the scholarship of Edith Blumhofer and Grant Wacker would highlight North American Evangelicalism as the key rubric to interpret North American Pentecostalism. Yet another interpretation would stress the multicultural and multiracial character of North American religion.

A global perspective on Pentecostalism also offers a context in which to interpret North American Pentecostalism. The multiculturalism and multi-racialism of North American Pentecostalism emphasizes its position as the intersection of European, African and Hispanic cultures or civilizations.[3] This theme stresses the worldviews and cultures of the peoples who constructed, shaped, and interpreted Pentecostalism. Comparative studies of the cultural histories of African-American and Afro-Canadian, Euro-American and Euro-Canadian, Hispanic-American and Hispanic-Canadian, Asian-American and Asian-Canadian construction and engagement of Pentecostalism are crucial, accenting the multicultural and multiracial dimensions which characterize the Pentecostalist movement in North American.[4] A 'religion in the world' thesis could present the participation of North American Pentecostalism in the construction and engagement of North America, the West, and the modern world. This theme stresses topics such as the North American Pentecostal legitimization or delegitimization of capitalism, consumerism, electoral politics, individualism, racism, sexism, classism, and militarism. The focus would be on the common world that Pentecostalism shapes and is shaped by, taking context as paramount. A 'movement in Christianity' thesis highlights North American Pentecostalist participation in the transformation of contemporary Christianity around the world that is transformed itself by Pentecostal influences from other continents. This theme stresses how North American Pentecostalism impacts such areas as worship, theology, Christian life, ecclesial practices, accenting North American Pentecostalism's production and influence.

In this paper the global perspective will be interpreted under the rubric of multiculturality. The paper goes beyond a discussion of Pentecostal origins and focuses on the development of early Pentecostalism. Multiculturality is being utilized as a framework in which to explore a racial or multi-racial approach to Pentecostalism. The goal is to accent the pivotal role the various racial and ethnic communities, represented in Pentecostalism, played in the formation of the Pentecostal movement. The theme of multiculturality will be employed to highlight the multi-racial construction of Pentecostalism along with the issues and themes generated by this multi-racial reality.

Nascent North American Pentecostalism often developed along racial and ethnic lines with Pentecostal pioneers emerging from the various racial and ethnic communities within North America. Within these multi-racial societies of North America most Pentecostal denominations, like most North American Protestant denominations in general, were later formed, organizing North American Pentecostalism by race. Most North American Pentecostal denominations are predominately associated with a particular race or are organized into race-based, often linguistically defined, judicatories within denominations. Yet the racial divisions shape more that ecclesial organization. Within North American Pentecostalism race informs differences in race relations. The role of women leaders differs according to the predominant race of the denomination; there are more women bishops and pastors within one race than within the others. The strength of institutional networks within North Pentecostalism, such as colleges, magazines, television programmes, and stations is informed by race. The institutional network, which North American Pentecostalism provides to scholars, is also affected by race. More scholars from one race can be employed by Pentecostal institutions because that race supports institutions which need their service. Race also determines the ecumenical involvement of North American Pentecostals which in turn impacts the theological framework that Pentecostal intellectuals employ to articulate their beliefs and practices. Race is only one factor along with polity, theology, class, regionalism or sectionalism, and gender, shaping North American Pentecostalism. However, it remains a singularly defining factor for the development of Pentecostalism in North America.

INTERRACIAL IMPULSE OF NORTH AMERICAN PENTECOSTALISM

The Pentecostal pioneers in the various racial and ethnic communities in North America were often restricted to their respective racial and ethnic communities, although there was a critical cadre of prominent early leaders who crossed the racial divide. The pioneers of white North American Pentecostalism include Charles Parham nationally throughout the U.S., W. Faye Carothers, Howard Goss in the Midwest, and William Durham in the midwest region of the U.S. Florence Crawford worked in the northwest region of the U.S., James and Ellen Hebden in Eastern Canada, Andrew H. Argue in Western Canada, Alice Belle Garrigus in Newfoundland (Canada), A.J. Tomlinson, J.H. King, and Gaston B. Cashwell in the southern region of the U.S. The pioneers of black North American Pentecostalism include African Americans such as William J. Seymour and Charles Harrison Mason nationally throughout the U.S. along with Thomas J. Cox and Magdelena Tate in the South (USA), W.E. Fuller in the Southern and Northeastern States (USA), and Garfield Haywood in the Mid-West (USA); the pioneers of Hispanic North American Pentecostalism include Hispanics such as Juan Navarro and Francisco F. Llorente in the Southwest (USA), Juan L. Lugo in Puerto Rico, and Francisco Olazabal nationally within the United States along with whites such as Henry Ball and Alice Luce in the Southwest (USA). Within the white North American communities ethnicity shaped much of the emergence of early Pentecostalism through pioneers of Italian North

American Pentecostalism such as Luigi Franceson, Giacomo Lombardi, and P. Ottolini in the United States and Luigi Ippolito, Ferdinand Zaffato, Guisippe DiStaulo in Canada, and of Romanian North American Pentecostalism such as Ioan J. Buia. Other communities of ethnic Pentecostalism include the pioneers – Andrew D. Urshan among Iranian Americans and Julian Barnabe among Filipino-Americans and Ioan J. Buia among Romanian Americans. These pioneers carved out successful careers in ministry within their respective racial-ethnic communities. On the one hand this historical development fits the American pattern of Protestant denominational leadership, being race-based. Yet on the other hand, the multi-racial and multi-ethnic composition of Pentecostalism differs from the racial and ethnic composition of the Protestant Reformation religious families who were transplanted to the United States i.e. the predominately white membership and leadership of American Congregational, Presbyterian, Anglican (Episcopalian), Lutheran, and Anabaptist denominations.[5]

While interpreting North American Pentecostalism through racial and ethnic categories illumines the racial and ethnic character of the movement's formation, these categories obscure the multi-racial and multi-ethnic dimensions of North American Pentecostalism with its interracial and multi-racial congregations, interracial denominational leadership, and interracial and multi-racial denominations. While this multi-racial dimension is small, it is critical because it counters the racial pattern of American Protestantism. Central to the multi-racial aspects of the movement is the Azusa Street Revival and William J. Seymour. While other places may compete with Azusa Street Revival for significance in the advancement of early North American Pentecostalism ranging from Parham in Topeka (Kansas) and Houston, Durham in Chicago, Cashwell in Dunn (North Carolina), Mason in Memphis, the Hebdens in Toronto or Argue in Winnipeg (Canada), Juan Lugo in Ponce (Puerto Rico), the Azusa Street Revival serves as a common place which numerous Pentecostal pioneers attended and where many were transformed including Durham, Cashwell, Mason, and Florence Crawford. Thus Durham, Cashwell, Mason and others are connected to the Azusa Street Revival network and consequently receive evangelists and workers who have come from the Revival. The Apostolic Faith paper serves as a key medium to print and reprint information concerning the related experiences of early Pentecostals and their influence.[6]

There is a strong case for the centrality of Los Angeles in the advancement of Pentecostalism because the Apostolic Faith Mission at 312 Azusa Street and even its earlier services on Bonnie Brae were interracial. Douglas Nelson has highlighted this era well. Historian Cecil Robeck has tracked the Seymour's revival from a small all-black revival in February, 1906, to a black revival with a few whites in April, 1906, to 300 whites and about 25 blacks by September, 1906. As Robeck further notes, the official membership was interracial, albeit predominately black, with a 'disproportionate number of whites in leadership positions'. The Azusa Street Revival, according to Robeck, had two periods of high visibility, when the Revival attracted an interracial audience, 1906–1908 and 1911. In Robeck's assessment: 'Clearly, Seymour may be credited with providing the vision of a truly "color-blind" congregation. His was a radical experiment that ultimately failed because of the inability of whites to allow for a sustained role for black leadership.'[7]

Azusa Street Mission provided a model of Pentecostal and Protestant race relations, albeit not the only positive model. From 1906–1908, blacks, whites, Hispanics, and Asians worshipped together at the mission. White leaders such as Florence Crawford, Glenn Cook, R.J. Scott, Hiram Smith, G. W. Evans, and Clara Lum worked alongside Pastor Seymour and other African Americans such as Jennie Evans Moore, Lucy Farrow, and Ophelia Wiley. Early Pentecostalism struggled with its interracial identity during an era in American Christianity and society when most institutions and movements espoused segregation. Pentecostal scholarship notes the insight of Frank Bartleman, a white Azusa Street Mission participant, that at the Revival: 'The color line was washed away in the blood [of Jesus Christ].' Pentecostals counted African Americans, Hispanics, Asian Americans, Native Americans, and whites within their ranks in an era of heightened bigotry and xenophobia when African Americans were legally discriminated against because of their race, Hispanics because of their status, Asian Americans because of their heritage and Native Americans because of their plight. Southern and eastern Europeans as well as Appalachian whites were discriminated against because of their nationalities and class respectively. While Baptist, Methodist, Presbyterian, and Holiness communions marched into racially segregated congregations, associations, and denominational structures from 1865 to 1910, the black and white Pentecostals were pastored and preached to and fellowshipped and worshipped with each other between 1906 and the 1930s.[8]

Even while new racial and ethnic interactions occurred within Pentecostalism, a racialized identity ordering society in terms of white and non-white, shaped the Pentecostal racial experiment. Although multiculturality defined the Pentecostal membership, the small inter-racial denominational leadership consisted basically of whites and African Americans. However, the collapse of the racial experiment as noted above extended to white-Hispanic, Hispanic-African American, and white-African American race relations. The uniqueness of Pentecostalism is that its racial experience differed from the American religious and cultural arrangement, crafting a new racialized arrange-ment on the American religious scene.

The interracial and multiracial impulse of the Azusa Street Revival found a limited expression in North American Pentecostalism in many ways. From New York to California, in the Midwest, and throughout sections of the South, white and black Pentecostals worshipped together in congregations and campmeetings during and after the first decade and more after the multi-racial Azusa Street Revival. In some cases, the interracial pattern of the Azusa Street mission where white Pentecostals participated in black Holiness missions occurred in other cities. In New York City groups of whites along with black missionar-ies bound for the foreign countries worshipped at a black Union Holi-ness congregation pastored by Elder Sturvedant. In Portland, Oregon, Florence Crawford assumed leadership from an African American couple of a Holiness mission in that city. Among Pentecostals in Port-land, '[t]here was no color line. The red, the yellow, the black and the white all worshipped together.' In Memphis, Tennessee Glenn Cook and others preached at Mason's black congregation. According to Stanley Frodsham, 'We did not observe the color line in Pentecostal Assemblies in California' during the early years. Robert Mapes Anderson wrote that 'integrated congregations were common among Assemblies people, especially in the North'. Vinson Synan noted that the practice of biracial worship among poor whites and African Amer-icans existed in parts of the South. Watson Sorrow, a Pentecostal pio-neer, confirmed Synan's assessment recalling 'integrated meetings in various parts of Georgia during the early years'. During her 1917–18 evangelistic tour of Florida, Aimee Semple McPherson attracted blacks and whites. Throughout the winter tour the services were bira-cial. Reflecting on the Florida tour McPherson commented: 'All walls of prejudice are breaking down, white and colored folks at the altar together ... white and colored joined hands and prayed ... people so hungry after God that color is forgotten even here in the Southland.'[9]

In 1924 the Church of God in Christ adopted the Methodist model of establishing a minority conference, specifically a white conference, to unite the white congregations across the United States which belonged to the predominately black denomination. This development was in response to the argument of the white clergy who accepted the anomaly of white congregations in black denominations and being a racial minority within the larger system, yet sought to maximize their presence by uniting under a white administrative unit. The white conference existed until the early 1930s when the predominately black leadership abolished the conference, accusing the white leadership of attempting to form a white separate denomination out of the Church of God in Christ.[10] This denominational structure exhibited the racial experimentation of the Church of God in Christ. The 1924 arrangement was only one of the various interracial experiments that the Church of God in Christ attempted. An earlier design was the interracial or biracial organizational experiment with Howard Goss, Mack Pinson, Rodgers, and Leonard P. Adams, four whites who entered a relationship at different times between 1910 and 1914 with the Church of God in Christ under Mason's leadership. Two arrangements were made: one with Goss, Pinson, and Rodgers, and another with Leonard P. Adams.[11]

Howard A. Goss, who had previously worked with Parham and had defected from Parham's fellowship in 1907 along with some other Midwestern clergy, entered a relationship with Mason seemingly around 1910. Pinson's fellowship initially used the name Church of God, Adams used Church of God in Christ, and Goss used The Church of God in Christ and in unity with the Apostolic Faith Movement. At least by 1913, the Pinson and Goss groups merged within the Church of God in Christ, while Adams remained distinct within Mason's fellowship. By late 1913, the five leaders who would craft 'The Call' for the 1914 Hot Springs meeting, the founding gathering of the Assemblies of God, would be listed on the roster of the Churches of the God in Christ: M.M. Pinson, A.P. Collins, H.A. Goss, D.C.O. Opperman, and E.N. Bell. Pinson's associate, H.G. Rodgers, was also on the roster of 352 Pentecostal leaders in the Churches of God in Christ.[12]

The significance of this expression of the interracial impulse is found in a denominational manual, published in 1918 for the Church of God in Christ, which includes a section entitled: 'equal in power and authority'.[13] The section states:

> Many denominations have made distinctions between their colored and white members. Some advised electing colored officials to preside over colored assemblies, while others have refused to elevate any colored elder to the episcopacy or any other office corresponding to it having equal power with white bishops. This has led to many misunderstandings and has caused the organizing of many separate colored denominations. The Church of God in Christ recognizes the fact that all believers are one in Christ Jesus and all its members have equal rights. Its Overseers, both colored and white, have equal power and authority in the church.

Here is a clear, public statement that the Church of God in Christ is being intentional about embodying the interracial impulse and understands itself as making a political statement against racism and segregation by erecting denominational structures which reflect the oneness in Christ Jesus shared by black and white Christians and which promote racial equality.

As mentioned above the interracial impulse found institutional expression in 1924 with the formation of a white jurisdiction or conference within the predominately African American Church of God in Christ. Some white congregations associated with Adams would participate in the 1924 racial restructuring of the Church of God in Christ. New whites such as William Hoyt would continue to join even after 1914. Clearly there was an interracial impulse within early North American Pentecostalism which informs the organizational and personal relationships between some leading Pentecostal pioneers.[14]

From 1919 to 1924 the Pentecostal Assemblies of the World was an interracial denomination which experience a drastic increase in its African American membership due to the appeal of Garfield T. Haywood, an African American minister whom the interracial denomination elected as general secretary in 1919 and as executive vice-chairman in 1922. Between 1924 and 1937, the denomination first lost a large group of whites, later merged with a white group, and eventually reorganized as a predominately black organization which slotted representation of the white minority at all levels of its structures. The Church of God in Christ and Pentecostal Assemblies of the World built upon the interracial congregational model of Azusa Street and the multiracial intercongregational model of the Pacific Coast Apostolic Faith Movement which Seymour organized in 1906. The biracial support for interracial relations after the 1930s did not emerge again nationally among Pentecostals until the 1950s.[15]

North American Pentecostalism has struggled with race issues from its beginnings. On one hand an interracial impulse which informed the denominational structures of Church of God in Christ and the Pentecostal Assemblies of the World in the 1920s and 1930s was evident at the Azusa Street Revival. On the another hand, a dominant segregationist impulse in the United States mitigated against Pentecostal interracial commitments. Thus, the conversions which occurred in the racial consciousness of whites such as Frank Bartleman, G.B. Cashwell, Jonathan Perkins and others must be balanced against the racist practices of Pentecostal leaders such as Charles Parham.[16] Surprisingly, some whites and African Americans Pentecostal pioneers did work together from 1906 to the 1930s during the height of segregation in the United States, countering the pattern of race relations that dominated the country until the 1960s.

Pentecostalism's interracial vision intensified the biracial vision of some of the holiness networks. Glenn Cook who introduced Pentecostalism to Charles Harrison Mason's black holiness congregation in Memphis and later worked with black pentecostal leader Garfield Haywood had earlier belonged to the biracial Burning Bush movement led by A.G. Garr in Los Angeles. From J.O. McClurkan's biracial network came Mack M. Pinson, H.G. Rodgers, and Leonard P. Adams. Pinson, Rodgers, and Adams from the McClurkan group along with Glenn Cook from the Burning Bush and G.B. Cashwell worked with Charles Harrison Mason and his congregation to introduce the Pentecostal message to Memphis. A local Memphis, Tennessee newspaper depicted the movement as being at least biracial, although two Pentecostal congregations, Mason's and Adam's, remain racially homogeneous.[17]

So if an interracial impulse received vitality from biracial holiness networks as well as the interracial vision of the Black Church, in general, and the African American holiness movement, in particular, it also intermingled with other impulses such as restorationism, pragmatism, and millenarism. How the interracial impulse was fostered and thwarted becomes a question of more than the privileged of white, African American or Hispanic Pentecostalism, debating whether the interracial vision was the preoccupation only of African Americans or ascertaining the nature of white Pentecostal racial prejudice? Pentecostalism must be reconstructed in such a manner that it is interpreted as more than a white movement which welcomed other races.

Early Pentecostalism was an interracial, multi-ethnic phenomenon which emerged from a movement created by African Americans, whites, Hispanics, Asian Americans, and Native Americans, a movement created within the particularities of American Protestantism.

The racial climate of the United States should not be underestimated in its effect of undermining the interracial impulse within early North American Pentecostalism. As segregation became more entrenched in localities and states throughout the country, Pentecostals who had embraced the interracial impulse increasingly encountered difficulties in sustaining their interracial commitments. The anti-interracial pressures were internal as well as external to Pentecostalism. Internally early Pentecostalism attracted leaders who shrank back from the interracial vision. Yet racism also countered the interracial and multi-racial ideal within early Pentecostalism. Parham exhibited racist behaviour and a patronizing attitude toward his black counterparts, especially Seymour. In 1908 blacks withdrew from the Fire-Baptized Holiness Church (later called Pentecostal Holiness Church). In 1913 the Pentecostal Holiness Church dismissed the remaining black congregations. In 1911 Florence Crawford led the withdrawal of many white congregations from the Seymour's Pacific Apostolic Faith Movement. In 1914 a large white group withdrew from the Church of God in Christ. In 1923 Francisco Olazabal withdrew from the Assemblies of God to organize the Latin American Council of Christian Churches (the Assemblies of God had sponsored the first Mexican Convention in 1918). In 1924 the majority of whites withdrew from the fifty percent black Pentecostal Assemblies of the World. And in 1930 the Apostolic Assembly under the leadership of Antonio C. Nava formally withdrew from the Pentecostal Assemblies of the World and was incorporated as a religious body in the California (in 1925 its members had held a national convention for 25 Mexican pastors within the Pentecostal Assemblies of the World).[18]

While segregation among Pentecostals followed the pattern of American Christianity after the Civil War, there were exceptions. As noted above all whites did not withdraw from the Church of God in Christ nor the Pentecostal Assemblies of the World. The majority of the Hispanics in the Assemblies declined to follow Francisco Olazabal; they constituted the Latin American District Council of the Assemblies of God during the 1929 reorganization of Hispanic ministry in the Southwest of the United States. Hispanics, African Americans and whites continued to struggle together to structure their interracial relationships during the height of segregation in the United States.[19]

African American-white relationships were also affected by harassment from local authorities and citizens. White citizens periodically beat Fred F. Bosworth, Dallas (Texas) pastor, for befriending blacks in the early 1900s. The Pentecostal leadership, being strongly anti-Klu Klux Klan, were often the targets of Klan terrorism because of their interracial ethic. There were whites who associated directly with Mason without a white fellowship like Goss's or Adam's as an intermediary. The most prominent white leader in the Church of God in Christ working directly with Mason between 1910 and 1935 was William B. Holt. Holt and his other white colleagues clearly identified with the interracial impulse. According to historian Theodore Kornweibel, Jr., William Holt publicly flaunted the racial etiquette of the segregationist South by hugging Mason and other black clergy as well as greeting them with a holy kiss, engaging in a 'shocking display of interracial intimacy'. This recalls the Los Angeles newspaper reports of blacks and whites embracing each other at the Azusa Street Revival. Kornweibel discovered a newspaper series which referred to 'sworn affidavits [which] reported him [Holt] eating and lodging with blacks and hugging and kissing fellow preachers'. Having been jailed for pacifist activities during WWI, the African American COGIC ministers were released, while their white COGIC counterpart was detained. Thus as the political space became more constrictive, the Pentecostal interracial impulse became less viable.[20]

RACIAL SOURCES OF NORTH AMERICAN
PENTECOSTAL DENOMINATIONALISM

North American Pentecostal denominationalism embraces a variety of polities, ranging from congregational autonomy to presbyterian and episcopal structures. A significant segment within North American Pentecostalism rejects denominational structure altogether, opting for independency. While polity clearly is a major rubric in interpreting the movement, race is still paramount. The majority of North American Pentecostals regardless of their polity are members of denominations where their race predominates. The majority of white and African American Pentecostals are within denominations which are predominately white and African American respectively. The Church of God in Christ and Pentecostal Assemblies of the World are predominately

African American; Asamblea Apostolica de la Fe en Cristo Jesus and Iglesia de Dios Pentecostal are predominately Hispanic; the United Pentecostal Church and the Assemblies of God and the Pentecostal Assemblies of Canada are predominately white; the American Indian Evangelical Church is predominately Native American. While race determines the denominational affiliation of most white and African American Pentecostals in the United States, it differs for Hispanics. The majority of Hispanic Pentecostals in the United States, including Puerto Rico, belong to Hispanic Districts within predominately white Pentecostal denominations such as the Assemblies of God and the Church of God (Cleveland). In Canada, the majority of Afro-Canadians, of Caribbean ancestry, follow the Hispanic example in the United States and belong to the Church of God (Cleveland) and the Pentecostal Assemblies of Canada instead of the few African American Pentecostal denominations with jurisdictions in Canada. Within the denominational leadership of some predominately white Pentecostal denomination are a few non-white leaders such as diocesan or conference heads in the Church of God (Cleveland) who are called overseers.[21]

While North American Pentecostalism has spawned literally hundreds of denominations, it is as much a history of consolidation as fragmentation. Since North American Pentecostalism basically mushroomed in numerical growth as autonomous missions, local assemblies, and small fellowships, the movement embraced different organizational structures through the clustering and non-clustering of these local congregations and small fellowships. Interestingly the outcome has been that almost 90 per cent of Pentecostals in Canada belong to two denominations, the Pentecostal Assemblies of Canada and the Pentecostal Assemblies of Newfoundland and almost 90 per cent of Pentecostals in the United States belong to four denominations, the Church of God in Christ, the Assemblies of God, the Pentecostal Assemblies of the World, and the Church of God (Cleveland). Thus the proliferation of Pentecostal denominations indicates little about the configuration of Pentecostalism and more about American religious liberty. The majority of Pentecostals in North America are organized in these few denominations, exhibiting a high degree of unity. Thus North American Pentecostalism has grown and developed more by unity and less by schism.[22]

A similar account could be sketched regarding gender and ministry in early North American Pentecostalism. As Pentecostalism became institutionalized the social space for women's leadership became constricted, especially within white Pentecostalism as its members sought respectability and identified with white fundamentalism. Yet race coupled with gender seemingly determined the options that Pentecostal women had as leaders. Unlike its Protestant counterparts Pentecostalism during the early twentieth century included denominations which supported the ordination of women such as the United Holy Church, the Church of God (Cleveland), the Assemblies of God, and the Pentecostal Assemblies of the World. The cultural upheaval throughout the American society of the 1920s produced varied responses against women's ordination within the Pentecostal movement. Women pastors came under attack from some quarters for 'usurping authority over men'. Some Pentecostal denominations in North America had always limited clerical authority to males. Some denominations such as the Church of God in Christ and the Church of Our Lord Jesus Christ denied women ordination following their earlier Baptist proscriptions of women, especially the Church of God in Christ. While ordination was denied to women in the Church of God in Christ, the denomination argued that women could be ministers of the gospel, classified as evangelists and 'teaching' missionaries, as 'women in the ministry'. They adopted an arrangement classified as the 'Dual-Sex System'.[23]

The outcome of the debate on women's ordination within North American Pentecostalism has been that more African American women have adopted the model established in 1903 by Magdalena Tate, an African American women who founded the holiness, later Pentecostal, Church of the Living of God, Pillar, Ground and Truth and Alma White, a white women, who founded the holiness Pillar of Fire, the model of women founding and heading denominations that promoted full male-female equality in the church. Consequently, the majority of women founders of Pentecostal denominations are African American. While white women such as Florence Crawford, Aimee Semple McPherson, and Mildred Johnson Brostek are the founders of denominations, the majority of female-headed denominations are led by African American women. The House of the Lord founded by Alonzo Austin Daughtry in 1930 in Augusta, Georgia is one of the few denominations not organized by women which elected a woman as its presiding bishop, Inez Conry who succeeded Daughtry in 1952 and served until 1960.[24] While it is unclear why African Americans founded denominations more frequently than other races and ethnicities in North America, clearly race is a factor. Possibly the difference lies in the involvement of white Pentecostalism in white fundamentalism and the non-involvement of African Americans in larger white fundamentalist and the smaller black fundamentalist movements, creating theological space for black Pentecostal women to adopt the female-led denomination as an option.

Race coupled with class shapes the institutional network of North American Pentecostalism. Following the fundamentalist model of alternative Protestant institutions, white Pentecostalism has become undergirded by an array of institutions beyond the denominational and congregational structures which buttresses white Pentecostalism and indirectly supports African American, Hispanic and Asian American Pentecostalism. These institutions range from Bible institutes and colleges, magazines and journals, and radio and television broadcasts. The Assemblies of God has the largest network of 14 educational institutions, including its seminary, the Assemblies of God Theological Seminary and liberal arts colleges such as Evangel University and Vanguard University of Southern California (formerly Southern California College) as well as a Bible colleges such as Central Bible College and Trinity Bible College. The Church of God has the second largest network with five educational institutions, including its seminary, the Church of God School of Theology, and its liberal arts college, Lee University. While these two major white Pentecostal denominations support such institutions, smaller white Pentecostal denominations are able to support smaller institutes. The major Pentecostal or charismatic educational institutions are Oral Roberts University, with its undergraduate and graduate school divisions, and Regent University, a collection of graduate and professional schools with programmes in theology, law, and communications.[25]

These institutions serve as major employers of white Pentecostal educators, creating a class of Pentecostal theologians and other intellectuals as well as educating generations of Pentecostals. Supporting the educational task is the publishing of teaching material by white Pentecostals to be used in the various courses taught at the different schools. These publications are produced at Pentecostal publishing houses such as Pathway Publishing of the Church of God and Gospel Publishing House of the Assemblies of God as well as independent publishers such as Hendrickson Publishing, Creation House, and Rhema Publishing. Two major journals which publishes works by and about Pentecostals are PNEUMA and the Journal of Pentecostal

Theology. The primary academic conference which explores Pentecostal issues is the Society for Pentecostal Studies founded in 1970. Besides controlling the print media, white Pentecostals and Charismatics own two television networks, Christian Broadcasting Network and Trinity Broadcasting Network. Participators in nationally broadcast white Pentecostal and charismatic television programmes or worship services range from Benny Hinn, Kenneth and Gloria Copeland, James Robison, John Hagee, Jack Hayford, Richard Roberts to Marilyn Hickey.[26]

African American and Hispanic Pentecostalism are less undergirded by institutions beyond denominational and congregational structures than white Pentecostalism. While small, often evening, Bible institutes do exist, African American and Hispanic Pentecostalism have yet to develop educational institutions which support full-time scholars as professors, creating a class of Pentecostal theologians and intellectuals. The African American and Hispanic theologians and intellectuals are often employed by non-Pentecostal institutions or serve as pastors and denominational executives. Denominational publishing houses produce material for laypeople and pastors as well as a few independent publishers such as Pneuma Life Publishing; however, these publishers do not publish scholarly books, except for Mid-Atlantic Publishers and GoodPatrick Press. The Spanish-language magazine *Carisma* is marketed to Hispanics, although it is published by the white-owned Strang Communications. Nationally telecasted programmes and worship services include the ministries of African American Pentecostals such as T.D. Jakes, G.E. Patterson, Richard Henton, and Carlton Pearson along with African American neo-Pentecostals such as Frederick Price, Creflo Dollar, John Cherry, the Timberlakes, Frank Madison Reed, and Paul Morton; these programmes are broadcast on BET (Black Entertainment Television Network) or white-owned Pentecostal/charismatic stations, or a local commercial TV channel.[27]

While a small number of black and Hispanic Pentecostal scholars within predominately white Pentecostal denominations are able to access the institutional networks of white Pentecostalism, the majority of black and Pentecostal scholars, for instance, who are outside these denominations are forced to seek faculty positions in non-Pentecostal educational institutions.

Among all races within North American Pentecostalism there is a predominance of males. The majority of Pentecostal scholars come from a small number out of the more than one hundred Pentecostal denominations, most notably the Assemblies of God, Church of God (Cleveland), and Church of God in Christ. The black and Hispanic Pentecostal scholarly community is experiencing a brain drain as clergy and laity who are scholars have transferred their membership to mainline denominations during their seminary years.

RACIAL SOURCES OF NORTH AMERICAN PENTECOSTAL THOUGHT

The Wesleyan doctrine of sanctification has more adherents among African American Pentecostals than white or Hispanic Pentecostals. This issue emerges out of the theological tradition early Pentecostals carried into Pentecostalism. Broadly defined, two major theological tradition predominated: Wesleyan and Reformed. Church of God in Christ and Pentecostal Holiness Church, reflecting a Wesleyan perspective, teach the doctrine of entire sanctification, while the Pentecostal Assemblies of the World and Assemblies of God, reflecting a Reformed or Keswick perspective, teach the doctrine of progressive sanctification. At least for William Seymour and Charles Harrison Mason the holiness doctrine of sanctification was integral to the doctrine of the Baptism of the Holy Spirit because it made ethics central to Pentecostal teaching rather than glossolalia as initial evidence.[28]

Reformed Pentecostalism attracted more whites and Hispanics than African Americans. 'While two of every three white Pentecostals became Finished Work believers', according to Anderson, by 1936 'only one of eight blacks did so.' This stream consist of the movements associated with holiness Baptists, Alexander Dowie's healing movement, Albert Barnes Simpson's Christian Missionary Alliance, and Charles Parham's Apostolic Faith Mission. The key architect of Reformed Pentecostalism was William Durham. He articulated a theological position called the Finished Work, accenting the atonement and espousing two-stages of grace: justification and the Baptism of the Holy Spirit, and as noted above interpreting sanctification as a progressive process beginning at justification.[29]

Different interpretations of the doctrine of God impacts African American Pentecostalism more than white and Hispanic Pentecostalism, a controversy which basically occurred among Reformed Pentecostals. By the late 1920s, according to Anderson, 'one of every seven' Reformed Pentecostals espoused Oneness, with 'more than nine of every ten' Oneness Pentecostals located in the Mid-West. The major theological issue of this controversy revolved around the doctrine of the Trinity. During the 1910s the Reformed Pentecostal stream split theologically over the interpretation of the doctrine of God in two positions: trinitarian and oneness. Although the vast majority of Pentecostals remained trinitarian, a significant percentage of African American Pentecostals became Oneness Pentecostals, along with some white and Hispanic Pentecostals. In a sense Oneness Pentecostals are not anti-trinitarian; they seek to interpret God in modalistic categories. The Oneness doctrine critiqued the classic Christian doctrine of the Trinity as polytheistic. Oneness advocates claimed that consistent monotheism required the existence of only one God, not three persons in one as espoused by the doctrine of the Trinity. Oneness advocates recognized Jesus as the name of God and asserted that while God expressed Godself in the form of the Father, Son, and Holy Spirit, God was only one person and not three persons in one. The Trinitarians confessed the classic Christian doctrine of the Trinity, rejecting the Oneness doctrine. The major Oneness denominations are the Pentecostal Assemblies of the World among African Americans, United Pentecostal Church among whites, and the Apostolic Assembly among Hispanics, with over 70 percent of all Oneness Pentecostals being African American. Roswith Gerloff argues that the Oneness doctrine of God possibly appealed to people of African descent because of its radicality.[30]

During the 1950s a cadre of healing evangelists emerged, challenging the segregationist ethic of white Pentecostals and other American Christians by rejecting segregated seating in their evangelistic crusades. These included whites such as Oral Roberts and A. A. Allen. These ministers forged a new alliance between black and white Pentecostals against the social norm of race relations. The focus of these healing evangelists was a new accent on demonology, exorcism, and miracles. This new accent formed the core of a revival in Pentecostalism during the 1940s associated with William Branham, a white healing evangelist, and identified by the 1950s as the deliverance movement. The deliverance movement among black Pentecostals emerged from the ministry of Arturo Skinner in the Northeast United States who expanded the traditional black Pentecostal emphasis on healing to include demonology, exorcisms, and heightened the accent on the miraculous. Currently, the strength of the deliverance movement among African Americans is located at the 10,000-plus member

Deliverance Evangelistic Church in Philadelphia founded in 1960 by Benjamin Smith and the 4,000 member Monument of Faith in Chicago founded by Richard Henton in 1963. Among whites the strength of the deliverance movement currently is centered around the crusade ministry of R.W. Schambach and Ron Parsley, two leading white Pentecostal deliverance ministers, and the successors to A.A. Allen. The deliverance movement of the 1950s and early 1960s is the first national interracial experiment within American Pentecostalism since the interracial experiments of early Pentecostalism which had ended by the early 1930s.[31]

The Latter Rain movement emerged in Canada sparked by a revival led by William Branham held in Vancouver, British Columbia during the fall of 1947. Branham's coupling of the gift of healing with the word of knowledge, in this instance revealed knowledge of specific illnesses, impressed faculty members of the Sharon Bible School in North Battleford, Saskatchewan who conducted a revival upon their return from Vancouver. The movement attracted the attention of North American Pentecostals in predominately white congregations such as Myrtle Beall's Bethesda Missionary Temple in Detroit, Michigan, Thomas Wyatt's Wings of Healing Temple in Portland, Oregon and A. Earl Lee's Immanuel Temple in Los Angeles, California. The Latter Rain movement also found adherents among members of the Elim Missionary Assemblies (later the Elim Fellowship) and the Scandinavian-American Pentecostals who constituted the majority within the Independent Assemblies of God.[32]

During the 1970s the 'Word of Faith' movement became a major presence within Pentecostalism. Kenneth Hagin, Sr., a white Pentecostal, and his Rhema Bible Training School led the Word of Faith movement with his message of healing and prosperity as well as salvation in the atonement of Christ appropriated by faith through positive confession. While the healing message reinforced the long healing tradition within Christianity, the prosperity message blessed the entry of some Pentecostals into the middle class as well as legitimating the quest for economic upward mobility among white Pentecostals during the economic growth years of the 1960s and among African Americans during the new opportunities of the post-Civil Rights era. (The original framing of the prosperity doctrine occurred during the late nineteenth century). Frederick Price emerged as the Word of Faith leader among black Christians after establishing the Crenshaw Christian Center in Los Angeles in 1973.[33]

The Neo-Pentecostal or Charismatic renewal movement reflects the racial polarization of American Christianity. Since the Charismatic renewal was often shaped by denominations, which themselves are defined by race in the United States, race became a defining factor within the Charismatic renewal. The Charismatic renewal had a great impact during the 1960s and 1970s among the predominately white Roman Catholic, Episcopal and Lutheran denominations. The leading Episcopal priests were Dennis Bennett of Van Nuys, California, and second Terry Fullam of St. Paul's Church in Darien, Connecticut. The leading Lutheran minister was Larry Christensen of Minneapolis, Minnesota. The leading Roman Catholics were members of two charismatic communities located in Ann Arbor, Michigan and South Bend, Indiana. The most prominent independent congregation was Ralph Wilkerson's Melodyland Christian Center in Anaheim, California.[34]

Neo-Pentecostalism emerges within historic black denominations during the 1970s instead of the 1960s without much interaction with white charismatics. Neo-Pentecostal ministers began occupying major African Methodist Episcopal Church pulpits. The focal point for the movement during the early 1970s was St. Paul African Methodist Episcopal Church in Cambridge, Massachusetts under the pastorate of John Bryant. Bryant sought the Pentecostal experience after encountering African spirituality within African traditional religion in West Africa. By the 1990s, three neo-Pentecostals, Vernon Byrd, John Bryant and James McKinley, were elected bishops within the African Methodist Episcopal Church's fourteen-member bishopric. Within the African Methodist Episcopal Zion Church, the centre was John A. Cherry and his congregation, the Full Gospel African Methodist Episcopal Zion Church in Temple Hills (MD), a suburb of Washington, D.C. The focal point for the movement among black Baptists was Pilgrim Baptist Cathedral pastored by Roy Brown and Paul Morton's St. Stephen's Baptist Church in New Orleans. During this period some college campuses also became centres for the growth of Pentecostalism among black students, particularly through the gospel choirs. During the 1990s two neo-pentecostal black denominations have emerged: Pilgrim Assemblies headed by Roy Brown and the Full Gospel Baptist Fellowship headed by Paul Morton.[35]

Among Hispanics the largest Charismatic congregations within non-Pentecostal denominations are in Puerto Rico with sizable congregations within various denominations ranging from the Southern Baptist Convention and United Methodist Church to the Presbyterian

Church (USA). A significant Roman Catholic charismatic movement exists in Puerto Rico and on the United States mainland.

SOCIAL SOURCES OF NORTH AMERICAN PENTECOSTAL CHARACTER

The race factor within North American Pentecostalism is a constitutive element of the movement. Even before Pentecostalism, race played a key role in the movements which shaped North American Pentecostalism. In early Pentecostalism the African American and white American holiness-healing movements intersected at the Azusa Street revival. Both racially defined movements were diverse with moderate and radical wings. The moderate wings, often remaining and supporting their respective denominations, are represented by leaders such as Bishops Cyrus D. Foss and I.W. Joyce of the Methodist Episcopal Church among whites and Bishops Abraham Grant of the African Methodist Episcopal and Alexander Walters of the African Methodist Episcopal Zion among African Americans. The radical wings were often critical of denominations, represented by such leaders as Daniel Sidney Warner and Benjamin Hardin Irwin among whites and Charles Price Jones and Charles Harrison Mason among African Americans.[36]

The white Holiness movement became divided over independency and come-outerism. The black Holiness movement, however, became divided over the role of slave religion within the movement when Charles Harrison Mason, D.J. Young, and others defended liturgical practices of slave religion deemed biblically sound.[37] Although both movements had wings which embraced Pentecostalism, each movement enters Pentecostalism with a different clustering of issues and which are played out throughout the twentieth-century.

The respective histories of African American and white Pentecostals influence their employment of the dissent and protest tradition within Pentecostalism that was expressed most forcibly in the espousal of pacifism during World War I and to a lesser degree during World War II by African Americans and white Pentecostals. The protest tradition within Pentecostalism included involvement in the civil rights struggle by some African American Pentecostals. William Roberts was a member of the delegation from the Fraternal Council of Negro Churches which went to Washington, D.C. in 1941 to demand justice for African Americans. Robert Lawson joined Adam Clayton

Powell, Jr., and other Harlem clergy in campaigns for black jobs. Along with Mary McCloud Bethune, a Methodist and college president, Arenia C. Mallory, a leader in the Church of God in Christ, was a member of Eleanor Roosevelt's Negro Women's Cabinet which advised U.S. First Lady on issues from the black woman's perspective. Within black Pentecostalism there were clergy and laypeople who were involved in the local civil rights movements of the 1950s and '60s in their cities: Arthur Brazier and Louis Henry Ford in Chicago, Herbert Daughtry and Ithiel Clemmons in New York, Smallwood Williams in Washington, D.C. and J.O. Patterson in Memphis, TN. While the majority of African American Pentecostals rejected involvement in the civil rights movement of the 1950s and '60s, a significant minority did become involved.[38]

Key to the development of North American Pentecostalism after the formative era in the early 20th Century were the alliances Pentecostals formed with other North American Christians. These ecumenical alliances also were often shaped by race, specifically Black Church ecumenism and white conservative ecumenism. During the 1930s the black Pentecostal movement embraced black ecumenism. Black Pentecostal denominations, according to historian Mary Sawyer, slowly joined the Fraternal Council of Negro Churches. The Fraternal Council, founded in 1934, was the major ecumenical thrust of black denominations and black leaders in white mainline denominations of the early twentieth century. The black Pentecostal denominations which joined the Council were the Church of God in Christ, Church of Our Lord Jesus Christ of the Apostolic Faith, Bible Way Church of Our Lord Jesus Christ Worldwide, and The Pentecostal Church.[39]

In 1942 white conservative Christians from various movements as mentioned above – revivalist, fundamentalist, dispensationalist, Holiness, and Pentecostal – formed the National Association of Evangelicals (NAE) to provide a distinct voice for conservative Christians which could be differentiated from the separatist or militant stance of fundamentalists associated with Carl McIntire and his American Council of Christian Churches. The NAE also granted white Pentecostalism respectability and acceptance. The alliance is clearly unequal since for over 60 per cent of the membership of the NAE, for instance, is Pentecostal. The alliance between white Pentecostalism and their Evangelical counterparts eventually offered white Pentecostalism new conversation partners as well access to a larger institutional network such as the flagship institutions of the Fuller

Theological Seminary and Gordon-Conwell Theological Seminary, publications such as Christianity Today and parachurch organizations such Inter-Varsity and Campus Crusade, institutions for the most part identified with the fundamentalist trajectory which reformed fundamentalism into evangelicalism. An extension of white conservative ecumenism was the formation of the Pentecostal Fellowship of North America in 1948, a Pentecostal ecumenical body which denied membership to African American Pentecostals.[40]

During the second half the twentieth century, these racial alliances continued. White Pentecostals assumed prominent roles within white conservative ecumenism through the NAE, marked by the presidency of Thomas Zimmerman and more recently Don Argue of the Assemblies of God. African American Pentecostals assumed prominent roles within Black Church ecumenism through membership of the Church of God in Christ in the Congress of National Black Churches, marked by the presidency of Roy Wimbush of the Church of God in Christ. Among African American Pentecostals, Black Church ecumenism has both liberal and conservative theological wings. The liberal theological wing is associated with the Congress of National Black Churches whose member denominations, except for the Church of God in Christ, belong to the National Council of Churches and the World Council of Churches as well as some who are a part of the Consultation on Church Uniting. The conservative theological wing is associated with the National Black Evangelical Association. The National Black Evangelical Association was founded in 1963 by African American leaders who belong to the NAE but felt frustrated by its racial climate. Prominent African American Pentecostals in the NBEA include William Bentley and George McKinney. While both wings of Black Church ecumenism engage modern black theology on their own terms, this engagement creates commonality between both wings of ecumenism.[41]

Hispanic Pentecostals have joined efforts with other Hispanic Christians in creating new ecumenical initiatives. The most significant initiative has been the Association for Hispanic Theological Education with its headquarters in Decatur, Georgia organized in the early 1990s. The Association includes a cross section of Hispanic Christian educators from conservative Bible Institute teachers to mainline seminary professors, from seminarians to pastors and denominational executives, from Pentecostals to Lutherans to Roman Catholics. Of the approximately 355 members, over 25% identify themselves as members of conservative denominations, including 9 Pentecostal denominations and 10 other conservative non-pentecostal denominations. This is an exciting forum for Hispanic Christians from different theological communions to engage with each other about common issues and challenges.[42]

The Association sponsored a conference on Scripture interpretation hosted by a Pentecostal Bible Institute in Puerto Rico. At the conference a range of new forms of biblical interpretation was presented ranging from liberationist perspectives to other forms, the major absent perspective being the fundamentalist. The Hispanic Pentecostal involvement in the Association reflects their commitment to Hispanic Church Ecumenism.

Studies of the Pentecostal leadership note the occurrence of a cadre of Pentecostals who identify with both twentieth-century theological liberalism and conservatism. While the majority of Pentecostals relate to a popular Pentecostalism, relations between theological liberalism and black Pentecostalism occur on a number of levels. A significant number of African American Pentecostals have become graduates of liberal seminaries from as early as the 1940s i.e. Temple University, Oberlin, and Union (NYC). By the 1960s and 1970s there were African American Pentecostal graduates of from such liberal seminaries as Interdenominational Theological Center (ITC), Howard, Yale, Princeton, Duke, Emory and Harvard. This was coupled with the presence of African American Pentecostals during the 1970s and 1980s on the faculties of liberal seminaries such as Union (NYC), Duke, Harvard, Howard, Emory, ITC, and McCormick. And the first accredited Pentecostal, and only African American, seminary, Charles Harrison Mason Theological Seminary, is a member of ITC, a consortium of African American seminaries affiliated with mainline denominations; Pentecostals who attended Mason are educated in theological liberalism from an African American perspective. Thus, the Church of God in Christ, the sponsor of Mason Seminary at ITC, embraces theological liberalism from a black perspective in the preparation of educated clergy. A number of black Pentecostal leaders are also involved with the ecumenical movement which liberal Protestantism embraces: Bishop Herbert Daughtry participated in some World Council of Churches programmes, Bishop Floyd Perry participated in regional and local ecumenical councils, Rev. Phyllis Byrd served on the staff of the National Council of Churches, and Bishop Norman Quick served as president of the New York City Council of Churches.[43]

Hispanic Pentecostals are also involved in theological liberalism with graduates from McCormick, New York Theological, New Brunswick and Union (NYC). During the 1980s and 1990s Hispanic Pentecostals were on the faculties of liberal seminaries such as New York Theological and Andover-Newton. White Pentecostals are also involved in theological liberalism with graduates from liberal seminaries such as Union (NYC), Harvard, Princeton, Yale, and Emory. Since the 1970s, white Pentecostals have been on the faculties of Union (NYC), Duke, and Emmanuel College, University of Toronto.

Relations between theological conservatism and Pentecostalism also occur on a number of levels beyond involvement in the National Association of Evangelicals. A significant number of white, African American, Hispanic and Asian Pentecostals are graduates of evangelical seminaries such as Fuller, Trinity Evangelical, and Gordon-Conwell. On these faculties Pentecostal scholars, from the various racial communities within Pentecostalism, are members. The David J. DuPlessis Center of Spirituality is even located at an evangelical seminary, Fuller. As mentioned above, Pentecostal involvement in theological conservatism and liberalism represents a small, but significant, minority within the Pentecostal movement, with more Pentecostal seminary graduates embracing theological conservatism.

Since 1983 the Society for Pentecostal Studies has established a relationship with the Commission on Faith and Order (later renamed the Faith and Order Working Group) of the National Council of Churches of Christ. This has allowed for representation from evangelical denominations which were not members of the National Council of Churches. Since 1972 the International Evangelical Church, a Pentecostal denomination with headquarters in Washington, D.C., has been a member of the World Council of Churches. They sent representatives to the Vancouver Assembly in 1983 and to the Canberra Assembly in 1991. Since the early 1990s, they have sent a representative to Faith and Order of the National Council of Churches.[44]

CONCLUSION

In this chapter I have explored the role race has played in the development of North American Pentecostalism. Taking seriously the multiculturality of Pentecostalism encourages the rethinking of the portrayal of the movement. While Pentecostalism advanced more through ethnic and racial leadership, an interracial impulse did exist, inspiring Pentecostal leaders to cross the racial divide. The impulse had historical catalysts, ranging from the interracial vision of the Black Church, the interracial commitments of the black holiness movement, the biracial commitments of some white holiness networks, and the pivotal role played by black holiness congregations in the emergence of Pentecostalism in cities like Los Angeles, Portland, New York City, and Memphis. The interracial impulse did not just evaporate, but internal and external pressures mitigated against it from Pentecostal segregationists to social and governmental harassment of Pentecostal interracialism.

The influence of white conservative Protestantism on white Pentecostals, of black Protestantism on black Pentecostalism, of Hispanic Protestantism on Hispanic Pentecostalism interjected other variables within the construction of North American Pentecostalism. African American women seized the ecclesial space to organize women-led Pentecostal denominations because of the different role black Pentecostalism played in black Protestant conservatism. White Pentecostals adopted the model of white Fundamentalism in erecting an alternative network of institutions to buttress their religious culture. The majority of Hispanic Pentecostalism are members of predominately white Pentecostal denominations, following the model of their Protestant counterparts. The social location of three groups determines the economic resources to which they have access. All three groups engaged in race-based ecumenism: white Pentecostalism in the National Association of Evangelicals with their concern for personal moral issues, African American Pentecostals in the Congress of National Black Churches with their concern for social issues, and Hispanic Pentecostals in the Association for Hispanic Theological Education.

The racial differences in the theological preferences of white and African Americans Pentecostals are difficult to interpret. How does one interpret the predominately African American membership within Wesleyan Pentecostalism, the predominately white and Hispanic membership within Reformed Pentecostalism, and the predominately African American membership of Oneness Pentecostalism? Possibly the indivisibility of the ethics and the Holy Spirit baptism as a frame for an interracial ethic made Wesleyan Pentecostalism appealing to former African American Methodists and Baptists who became Pentecostals. For different reasons white Pentecostals who were former Baptists and Presbyterians and Hispanic Pentecostals who often entered Pentecostalism without connections to the Holiness movement possibly found theological consistency in Reformed Pentecostalism. Oneness Pentecostalism possibly attracted more African Americans because of its radicality. In each case the persuasiveness and charisma of individual Pentecostals pioneers merits consideration.

I have offered a comparative study of North American Pentecostalism from a multicultural perspective, focusing on the role of race. The accent of this study has been on difference; the difference race has played in the construction of Pentecostalism in North America. Other facets of the race also warrant attention. The Pentecostal commonalties deserve study as well as cross-cultural exchanges between the various Pentecostal racial communities.

North American Pentecostalism reflects the capacities within nascent Pentecostalism to reflect and reform the religious cultures which it engages. In the inclusivistic capacity of North American Pentecostalism is located the globality which created the multi-ethnic and multi-racial character of the movement in United States, Canada, Puerto Rico, and around the world.

Notes

1   Such as papal vs. clerical authority, seven ecumenical councils vs. filoque clause, grace vs. works, Christ's lordship over creation vs. two kingdoms, limited vs. unlimited atonement. The history of prophecy, healing, glossalalia, ecstasy, ministry of women and men, and racial equality within the Christian tradition and experience are examples.

2   H. Richard Niebuhr, *Social Sources of Denominationalism* (New York, NY: The World Publishing Company, 1972 [1929]); C. Eric Lincoln, *Race, Religion, and the Continuing American Dilemma* (New York, NY: Hill and Wang, 1984); Roger D. Hatch, 'The Issue of Race and The Writing of the History of Christianity in America' (unpubl. Ph.D. diss., University of Chicago, 1974).

3   Roger Bastide, *The African Religions of Brazil: Toward a Sociology of the Interpenetration of Civilizations* (Baltimore, MD: Johns Hopkins University Press, 1978). Roger Bastide contends that religion in the Americas is the product of three civilizations: Native American, European, African. According to Bastide, these civilizations encountered each other in the Americas and the interaction produced a continuum of religious expressions. Thus, the history of Christianity, for instance, is more than an extension of one civilization, Europe's. With this interaction approach, North American Christianity, including Pentecostalism, is no longer a mere extension of the European Reformations and is best interpreted through north trans-Atlantic studies. North American Christianity, including Pentecostalism, is better reconstructed

within an intercivilizational approach which highlights the impact of non-western cosmologies on the development of North American Christianity and the influences of non-western religions upon it. Bastide employs the term civilization. This paper uses multi-cultural and multi-racial interchangeably.

4   Ronald Takaki, *A Different Mirror: A Multicultural History of America* (Boston, MA: Little, Brown, and Company, 1993); See Neal Salisbury, *Manitou and Providence: Indians, Europeans and the Making of New England, 1500-1643*; Albert Raboteau, *Slave Religion: The 'Invisible Institution' and the Antebellum South.*

5   James R. Goff, Jr., *Fields White Unto Harvest: Charles Parham and the Missionary Origins of Pentecostalism* (Fayetteville, AR: The University of Arkansas, 1988); John Thomas Nichol, *The Pentecostals* (Plainfield, NJ: Logos Books International, 1971 [1966]), pp. 26f., 98f., 109, 116; Ithiel C. Clemmons, *Bishop C.H. Mason and the Roots of the Church of God in Christ* (Bakersfield, CA: Pneuma Life Publishers, 1996); Vinson Synan, *The Holiness-Pentecostal Movement in the United States* (Grand Rapids, MI: William B. Eerdmans Publishing Company, 1971), pp. 165–176; Robert Mapes Anderson, *Vision of the Disinherited* (New York, NY: Oxford University Press, 1982), p. 129; J. Gordon Melton, *Encyclopedia of American Religions* (Gale Research, 1993), pp. 413, 419.

6   Other Pentecostal pioneers connected with the Azusa Street mission are: Glenn Cook, Clara Lum, Frank Bartleman, Lucy Farrow, D.J. Young, A.G. Garr, A.C. Valdez and A.A. Boddy. Robert Mapes Anderson, *Vision of the Disinherited* (New York, NY: Oxford University Press, 1979), pp. 62–78.

7   Douglas J. Nelson, *For Such A Time As This: The Story of Bishop William J. Seymour and the Azusa Street Revival* (Ph.D. dissertation, University of Birmingham [UK], 1981); Cecil M. Robeck, 'Azusa Street Revival' in *Dictionary of Pentecostal and Charismatic Movements*, eds. Stanley M. Burgess et al (Grand Rapids, MI: Zondervan Publishing House, 1988), p. 33.

8   Anderson, *Visions*, p. 70; Frank Bartleman, *Azusa Street* (Plainfield, NJ: Logos Books International, 1980 [1925 rpt.]), 54; James S. Thomas, *Methodism's Racial Dilemma: The Story of the Central Jurisdiction* (Nashville, TN: Abingdon Press, 1992).

9   Anderson, *Vision*, p. 182; Kenneth Gill, p. 42, cites J. C. Vanzandt, *Speaking in Tongues* (Portland, OR: Author, n.d.), p. 32; Anderson, pp. 123, 122, 189; Vinson Synan, *Holiness-Pentecostal Movement*, p. 182; Anderson, p. 124.

10   Lillian Coffey, complier, *1926 Yearbook of the Church of God in Christ* (n.p., n.d, rpt. by Jerry Ramsey), p. 128.

11   Edith Blumhofer, *The Assemblies of God: A Chapter in the Story of American Pentecostalism* (Springfield, MO: Gospel Publishing House, 1989); Paul S. Carter, *Heritage of Holiness: An Eye-Witness History: First Assembly of God Church Memphis, Tennessee* (Memphis, TN: Paul's Press, 1991).

12   Blumhofer, ibid.

13   Eugene B. McCoy, *'Yes Lord': Historical Account of Charles H. Mason and the Church of God in Christ* (n.p. n.d), pp. 33–34.

14   Coffey, *1926 Yearbook.*

15   James L. Tyson, *The Early Pentecostal Revival: History of Twentieth-Century Pentecostalism and the Pentecostal Assemblies of the World, 1901–30* (Hazelwood, MO: Word Aflame, 1992), pp. 181–201, 241–253; also see Morris Ellis

Golder, *History of the Pentecostal Assemblies of the World* (Indianapolis, 1973); David Edwin Harrell, Jr. *All Things Are Possible: The Healing and Charismatic Revivals in Modern America* (Bloomington, IN: Indiana University Press, 1975), pp. 59, 98–99, 201–202.

16   Harold Vinson Synan, *The Holiness-Pentecostal Movement in the United States* (Grand Rapids, MI: Wm. B. Eerdmans Publishing Co., 1971); Jonathan Perkins stated: 'God surely broke me over the wheel of my prejudice.' in Anderson, p. 123.

17   Susie Cunningham Stanley, *Feminist Pillar of Fire: The life of Alma White* (Cleveland, OH: Pilgrim Press, 1993); Stanley (p. 70) quotes an 1879 published statement of Thomas K. Doty: 'Holiness takes the prejudice of color out of both black and white.'; On the McClurkan network see Timothy Smith, *Called Unto Holiness: The Story of the Nazarenes: The Formative Years* (Kansas City, MO: Nazarene Publishing House, 1962), pp. 180–204; David M. Tucker, *Black Pastors and Leaders: Memphis, 1819–1972* (Memphis: Memphis State University Press, 1975), pp. 90–92; Paul S. Carter, *Heritage of Holiness: An Eye-Witness History: First Assembly of God Church Memphis, Tennessee* (Memphis, TN: Paul's Press, 1991), pp. 20–68.

18   Synan, p. 17; Nichol, p. 129; Anderson, p. 140; Eldin Villafañe, *The Liberating Spirit: Toward an Hispanic American Pentecostal Social Ethic* (Grand Rapids: William B. Eerdmans Publishing Co., 1993), pp. 90–92; Kenneth D. Gill, *Toward A Contextualized Theology for the Third World* (New York, NY: Peter Lang, 1994), pp. 52–53, 57.

19   Clifton L. Holland, *The Religious Dimension in Hispanic Los Angeles: A Protestant Case Study* (South Pasadena, CA: William Carey Library, 1974), pp. 345, 350.

20   Theodore Kornweibel, Jr., 'Bishop C.H. Mason and the Church of God in Christ During World War I: The Perils of Conscientious Objection', *Southern Studies: An Interdisciplinary Journal of the South* 26, 4 (Winter 1987), p. 277.

21   Robert Mapes Anderson, *Vision of the Disinherited* (New York, NY: Oxford University Press, 1979); Eldin Villafane, *The Liberating Spirit* (Grand Rapids, MI: Wm. B. Eerdmans Publishing Co., 1993); On congregational level race still defines affiliation. Yet many North American cities include a few interracial and multiracial Pentecostal congregations such as Eglise des Apotres de Jesus-Christ in Montreal (Canada), Brooklyn Tabernacle in Brooklyn, NY, Times Square Church in Manhattan, NY, World Harvest Church in Columbus, OH, Lakewood Church in Houston, and Shiloh Temple in Oakland; although the leadership of these interracial and multiracial congregations is often predominately white.

22   Comparative study of the statistics from the *Yearbook of American and Canadian Churches: 1995*, ed. Kenneth B. Bedell (Nashville: Abingdon Press, 1995).

23   Blumhofer, *Reforming Pentecostalism*; Cheryl Townsend Gilkes, 'The Politics of "Silence": Dual-Sex Political Systems and Women's Traditions of Conflict in African-American Religion' in *African-American Christianity: Essays in History*, ed. Paul E. Johnson (Berkeley, CA: University of California Press, 1994), pp. 80–100.

24   David D. Daniels, 'Pentecostalism', *Encyclopedia of African American Religion*, edited by Larry Murphy, et al (New York, NY and London: Garland

Publishing, 1993), pp. 592–593; Edith Blumhofer, 'Women in Evangelicalism and Pentecostalism' in *Women and Church*, ed. Melanie May (Grand Rapids: William B. Eerdmans, 1991); Black women founders of denominations include: Magdalena Tate, Ida Robinson, Beulah Counts, Magdalene Mabe Phillips, Mozella Cook, Florine Reed, Sammie Lee Dennis.

25 Lewis F. Wilson, 'Bible Institutes, Colleges, Universities' in *Dictionary of Pentecostal and Charismatic Movements*, ed. Stanley M. Burgess et al (Grand Rapids, MI: Zondervan Publishing House, 1988), pp. 57–65.

26 Wayne E. Warner, 'Publications', *Dictionary of Pentecostal and Charismatic Movements*, pp. 742–751.

27 Janice Peck, *The Gods of Televangelism*: *The Crisis of Meaning and the Appeal of Religious Television* (Cresskill, NJ: Hampton Press, 1993).

28 Synan, op. cit.; Cecil M. Robeck, Jr., 'William J. Seymour and "Bible Evidence" ', in *Initial Evidence*: *Historical and Biblical Perspectives on the Pentecostal doctrine of Spirit Baptism*, ed. Gary B. McGee (Peabody, MA: Hendrickson Publishers, 1991), p. 81.

29 Anderson, p. 171; Edith L. Blumhofer, *Restoring the Faith*: *The Assemblies of God, Pentecostalism, and American Culture* (Urbana and Chicago, IL: University of Illinois Press, 1993).

30 Anderson, p. 185; David Reed, 'Origins and Development of the Theology of Oneness Pentecostalism in the United States' (Ph.D. diss., Boston University, 1978); Roswith Gerloff, *A Plea for British Black Theologies* (New York, NY: Peter Lang, 1992).

31 David Edwin Harrell, Jr., *All Things Are Possible* (Bloomington, IN: Indiana University Press, 1975); Daniels, 'Pentecostalism'.

32 Richard Riss, 'The Latter Rain Movement of 1948', *PNEUMA: The Journal of the Society for Pentecostal Studies* 4:1 (Spring 1982), pp. 34–35, 40–41; Joseph R. Colletti, 'Lewi Pethrus: His Influence Upon Scandinavian-American Pentecostalism', *PNEUMA: The Journal of the Society for Pentecostal Studies* 5:2 (Fall 1983), p. 28.

33 Stephen Strang, 'The Ever-Increasing Faith of Fred Price', *Charisma* 10, 10 (May 1985), pp. 20–26; Simon M. Coleman, 'America Loves Sweden: Prosperity theology and the culture of capitalism', in *Religion and the Transformations of Capitalism*, ed. Richard H. Roberts (London and New York, NY: Routledge, 1995), pp. 161–179.

34 Richard Quebedeaux, *The New Charismatics II* (San Francisco, CA: Harper & Row, 1983).

35 Daniels, 'Pentecostalism'.

36 Ibid.

37 Melvin Dieter, *The Holiness Revival of the Nineteenth Century* (Metuchen, NJ, and London: Scarecrow Press, 1980); David Douglas Daniels, III, 'The Cultural Renewal of Slave Religion: Charles Price Jones and the Emergence of the Holiness Movement in Mississippi' (Ph.D. diss., Union Theological Seminary, 1992).

38 Smallwood Williams, *This Is My Story*, (Washington, D.C.: Wm. Willoughby Publishers, 1981); Arthur M. Brazier, *Black Self-Determination; the story of the Woodlawn Organization* (Grand Rapids, MI: Wm. B. Eerdmans Publishing Co., 1969).

39 Mary Sawyer, 'The Fraternal Council of Negro Churches, 1934–1964',

Church History, v. 59 (March 1990), pp. 51–64; a listing on page 53.

40   William W. Menzies, *Anointed to Serve: The Story of the Assemblies of God* (Springfield, MO: Gospel Publishing House, 1971), pp. 177–227.

41   Pam Nadasen, 'Congress of National Black Churches, Inc.', and A.G. Miller, 'National Black Evangelical Association' in *Encyclopedia of African American Religion and Culture*, eds. Jack Salzman et al (New York, NY: Macmillan Press, 1995), vol. 2, pp. 637–638 and vol. 4, pp. 1955–1957 respectively.

42   Interview (1995) with David Cortes-Fuentes, Director of Hispanic Ministries, McCormick Theological Seminary.

43   Daniels, 'Pentecostalism'.

44   Peter Hocken, 'International Communion of Charismatic Churches' in *Dictionary of Pentecostal and Charismatic Movements*, ed. Stanley Burgess, et al (Grand Rapids: Zondervan Publishing House, 1988), pp.463-464.

Pentecostalism as a Global Culture: A Response

Vinay Samuel

The twentieth century has witnessed a global expansion in Pentecostalism. Can we trace common features? Can those features suggest the emergence of a global Pentecostal culture? Are the features of Pentecostalism unique to it? These questions focus on the common features of global Pentecostals. Another question needs to be addressed: What challenges does Pentecostalism encounter in its global phase?

Some common characteristics of Pentecostalism worldwide can be identified. Pentecostals promote indigenous leadership. Their members experience little cultural dislocation. Their churches thrive in rural or urban settings and reflect social mobility in the growing urban middle class among its members. They demonstrate a strong commitment to the stability of family life and generally adhere to traditional gender roles. Their ministry is based on the biblical teaching of the priesthood of all believers. This is increasingly under tension with adoption of historic forms of selection of pastors and their training. In ministry there is an emphasis on healing and deliverance.

There is also evidence of the tension between established but ageing forms of ministry and new forms seeking to meet the needs of fast-changing contemporary cultures. There exists among Pentecostals an awareness of particularities of cultures and context and attempts at new forms of enculturation, though the movement of enculturation is towards emerging contemporary forms rather than traditional ones.

Contemporary churches, particularly urban churches, face multi-cultural influences. Pentecostal churches reflect a greater openness in a multicultural environment. Influences from Asia, Africa and Latin America are as obvious in the life and ministry of Pentecostal churches as are influences from the more affluent West. A strong pragmatic dimension, coupled with openness to spiritual experience, makes Pentecostal churches inclusive, drawing on ideas, models, strategies from anywhere.

The features described above suggest a global culture, as many of the elements are not unique to Pentecostals. It is also increasingly evident that most churches committed to the authority of the Bible, to the wholeness and fulness of the gospel and to the leadership of the Holy Spirit in mission and evangelisation show many of the same elements. The reality most likely is that what we are observing in Pentecostal and evangelical churches is the recovery of a church centred in mission and led by the Spirit.

Some challenges facing the Pentecostal Movement are identified below.

1. The Challenge of Christian Unity

Common features in Christian experience and pastoral and mission practice do not necessarily equal spiritual unity as taught in the New Testament. The global missionary movement of the nineteenth century developed a strong impulse for church unity. This flowered into the ecumenical movement of the early twentieth century which demonstrated the integral relation between mission and Christian unity. As Pentecostalism becomes global, it must draw on its own impulse for understanding Christian unity reflected in its commitment to interracial unity, worship and churches during its founding years in the early twentieth century. Global Pentecostalism can bring a new impetus to the movement for Christian unity with its commitment to mission. Its experience of the ministry of the Holy Spirit brings a much needed dimension to the movement for unity. The democratic principle that shapes Pentecostal church polity and the autochthonous nature of

Pentecostal Churches have much to contribute to the shaping of a new twenty-first century definition for Christian unity. A commitment to Christian unity must become intentional in Pentecostal Churches.

2. The Challenge of Christian Ethics

Human agency is downplayed in much of Pentecostal mission activity. The strong emphasis on the work of the Holy Spirit implies that the Spirit takes over all human activity in a fashion that makes human agency one of obedience to details of action which are gifted. This downplaying of human agency relates to areas of deliverance, health, conversion of unbelievers and miraculous interventions to facilitate evangelism and mission. Along with that Holy Spirit emphasis goes a strong pragmatism which relates to material affluence in this world. The prosperity teaching that continues in many Pentecostal churches sees prosperity as the result and reward for obedience to biblical laws of material abundance. 'Give and you will get more.' The approach is very pragmatic and sometimes mechanistic.

This contemporary pragmatism appears like a Pentecostal version of the Protestant ethic which stresses material prosperity as a result of Christian obedience and does not lay adequate stress on the formation of an ethical/moral character as the result of Christian obedience. This is curious indeed, given Pentecostalism's historical rootedness in holiness teaching.

The marginalising of human agency in mission leads to a much greater emphasis on prayer, on marches for Christ and spiritual warfare where human action is primarily battling in prayer. It can also produce a lack of motivation or energy for commitment to movements of advocacy for social change. This points to the need for a strong recommitment to the development of personal and social ethics shaped by the Pentecostal experience and firmly grounded in the Bible.

3. The Challenge of a Spirituality that addresses socio-political issues

Much of Pentecostalism has emerged from the contexts of economic poverty and social marginalisation. The Pentecostal churches' experience of the gospel in the midst of economic poverty is a key gift to the global church. It has been empowered individuals and families who address their economic poverty through the transformation of their personal and family life. It needs to develop a spirituality that is capable of equipping people to address larger socio-political and cultural issues. The impulse to personal prosperity must be harnessed to produce commitment to economic and cultural transformation which would benefit communities of the poor.

It is here that there is a further challenge to the Pentecostal impulse to holiness. The roots of Pentecostalism in the holiness movement are reflected in the continuing impulse to holiness in Pentecostal teaching. It should be observed that this teaching does not have the same importance as it did two decades ago.

In many Pentecostal contexts, Ivan Satyavrata highlights the danger of a spirituality that is monistically pneumatological. He calls for a Trinitarian spirituality. The quest for spirituality and holiness, when it is shaped by a Trinitarian understanding will stress the challenge to be like Christ in his holiness in this world and fulfill the call to be the Father's stewards in his creation alongside enjoying the ecstasy of the Spirit's involvement in one's life and ministry.

4. The Challenge of the Public square and Civil society

Pentecostal involvement in the public square is highlighted by all the presenters, its interracial impulse in North America, its growing political involvement in Latin America, its protest role in Africa; in contrast the Asian papers see little of such participation and even paint a gloomy picture.

Like other conservative Christians, Pentecostals protest when their freedoms to preach the faith are restricted or threatened in predominantly Islamic contexts. While there is little evidence to suggest that they struggle against oppressive and corrupt social and political structures in countries like Kenya, Zaire and Zimbabwe, Japie Lapourta's case study in South Africa demonstrates Pentecostals' willingness to struggle against evil structures, both political and ecclesial. The need for a civil society in Africa is highlighted by the presenter, reflecting consensus among Africans that issues of governance, leadership and civil society are the most critical for Africa. Pentecostal participation in the development of a civil society for the modern African state is crucial.

In South East and South Asia, the issue of poverty is highlighted, moving beyond the ethical transformation of individuals and families to working with communities as a whole and with the social systems and structures. It is hoped that a Pentecostal spirituality can be maintained while growing in socio-political action.

What theology motivates and shapes Pentecostal social action? The Pentecostal theme of spiritual warfare, the devaluation of all human agency to bring change in society and the strong expectation that all change, healing and transformation is a gift, need be related to a wholistic understanding of mission based on the theology of the Kingdom of God. Christ's rule over all of life mandates Christian involvement in social transformation. How does Pentecostalism draw on its eschatological passion for contemporary social action?

Recent dialogues between Evangelical and Pentecostal/charismatic social activists have demonstrated the overlap in their views and for many are a great encouragement.[1] However, the differences in the way the Kingdom of God is understood and appropriated are significant.

This leads to another issue of the public square which is highlighted in the European paper: the culture of modernity and post modernity.

Older concepts of modernity have fragmented and given way to new modernity or post modernity. The instability of self, the plasticity of language, the suspicion of reason, the rejection of the idea of society replacing it with social change, the search for individual and national identities, the redefinition of the traditional ideas of state rejecting totalitarian or bureaucratic forms all provide a great challenge to Pentecostal spirituality to address these complex issues which are increasingly also the concern of non-western societies. Globalization makes the world very small and draws all nations, communities into its vortex.

5. The Challenge of Religious Plurality

The global Pentecostal movement exists in the context of religious plurality. It is in direct engagement with other religions.

The traditional approach to understanding the belief systems of other religions and developing Christian apologetics to address them is being found to be inadequate. The missionary tradition which developed such resources continues to do so, but finds itself facing resurgent, confident and even hostile non-Christian religions. The challenge is to understand the cultures of non-Christian religions.

Allow me a reference to my own nation of India. The religious culture and cultures of India need to be studied and responded to.

For example, in India Pentecostals and Roman Catholics have drawn on the religious culture of India. It is a selective usage of some features of the religious culture. This has produced impact in the South and the tribal area of India but the effectiveness is minimal in the

Aryan heartland of Central and North India.

In the Indian religious culture, in some parts of India, a 'phenomenon' dominates religious epistemology. A variety of discrete elements – ideas, circumstances, incidents, and feelings join in such a way that together they trigger a sudden experience. This is an effective point of contact with the Pentecostal notions of personal revelation and experience of the Spirit.

The Indian religious culture stresses practical ways of making sense of the world and seeing evidence of God's favour in material prosperity. There is also a reflective element which enables the religious person to make a religious experience his/her own.

Pentecostal mission activity draws on all the above dimensions and is often effective in communicating the gospel. It needs to relate such religious epistemology to the role of biblical revelation and the place of Scripture.

Pentecostals must reflect on the work of the Holy Spirit in other religions and develop a theology of religions that better reflects their own understanding of the work of the Holy Spirit. The work of scholars in other Christian traditions has explored the role of the Spirit in other religions. Whether or not these scholarly explorations have a Christological or Spirit emphasis, it is here that a Pentecostal perspective on theologies of religion can make a fresh and useful contribution.

Note

1   See *Transformation: An International Evangelical Dialogue on Mission and Ethics* (October/December), 1994.

Section III

Issues Facing Pentecostalism in a Postmodern World

Issues Facing Pentecostalism
in a Post-Modern World:
An Introductory Overview

Murray W. Dempster

The term 'postmodern' first crept almost unnoticed into the modern vocabulary in the 1930s to identify a trend in the arts, and later a style of architecture; however, as Professor Stanley Grenz notes, it was in the 1970s when postmodernism gained far-reaching recognition, 'first as the label for theories expounded in university English and philosophy departments and eventually as the description for a broader cultural phenomenon'.[1] One of the common features of postmodernity, whatever else it might be, is its rejection of the modern mind-set which was forged by the foundational epistemology of the Enlightenment with its emphasis on certain and objective knowledge derived from scientific inquiry and autonomous rationality. This rejection of modernity is based on the recognition of interpreters such as Diogenes Allen that modernism is a failed experiment:

> Our intellectual culture is at a major turning point. A massive intellectual revolution is taking place that is perhaps as great as that which

marked off the modern from the Middle Ages. The foundations of the modern world are collapsing, and we are entering a postmodern world. The principles forged during the Enlightenment (c. 1600–1780), which formed the foundations of the modern mentality, are crumbling.[2]

Postmodernism is more than a reaction against modernism and its epistemological assumptions. It represents a paradigm shift in epistemological theory.[3] In the place of epistemological foundationalism, post modernism places perspectivalism, which according to Harold Heie, is 'the view that our claims to knowledge unavoidably reflect our particular perspectives as members of different interpretive communities'.[4] Human knowledge, therefore, is understood as more social than individual, relational than autonomous and reflective of different communities of discourse rather than the monolithic community of scientific and rational inquiry. The metanarratives promoted by the mind-set of modernism are viewed as 'broken myths' which have been replaced by the multiple narratives of various communities vying for acceptance and loyalty in the postmodern world of pluralism and multiculturalism. For some Christian believers, this development is a positive one since it gives the Christian community a place at the table in the cross perspectival discussions about truth, beauty, goodness and human meaning. For others, postmodernism's assumption cannot sustain the intellectual credibility of the Christian witness in the world.[5]

Whether or not postmodernity provides an opportunity for Christian witness has also been debated within Pentecostal ranks but with a unique twist. The shift to a postmodern world has been heralded by some Pentecostal scholars as the philosophical liberation which allows an indigenous Pentecostal theology to emerge free from restrictive Fundamentalist trappings.[6] In contrast, other Pentecostal scholars see postmodern assumptions leading to the relativizing of Christian truth.[7] No matter which side of the controversy Pentecostal scholars and leaders come down on, it is apparent to Pentecostals that the world in which the truth is articulated and ministry is done is marked by increasing globalization, urbanization and multiculturalism. Pentecostals, worldwide, face the challenges of understanding and proclaiming the gospel in a manner appropriate to contemporary questions raised by postmodern assumptions. If truth is verified by communities of discourse, then issues of ethnicities and material culture, gender and sexual identity, religious experience and its linguistic construction, ecumenism and the Other, and hermeneutics and the production of meaning in texts all come to the forefront because communities are constructed around these features which give identities to them. The chapters in this section endeavour to come to grips with the issues of ethnicity, hermeneutics, gender, ecumenism and modernity raised to a new level of importance by postmodernity, although not all the pieces address a particular issue from an explicit postmodern perspective.

Ronald Negron Bueno opens the section with an anthropological study of ethnicity and its bearing on the globalization of Pentecostalism. Bueno begins his analysis with the recognition that the notion of 'ethnicity' itself is not a term that essentializes the nature of an objective reality but instead it is a social and cultural construction which invents a bounded community in the same way that other points of self-referentiality do, such as 'class', 'gender', and 'race'. From this definitional platform, Bueno shows how 'ethnicities' shape religious experience and community identities, how they reflect material culture and disproportionate relations of power, how they relate to the trend of globalization, and the implications of all these intersections for Pentecostal studies. The point that Bueno drives home again and again is that ethnicities are reflective of a culture which, when understood historically, indicates how a community bounded by that ethnic identity responds to the political and economic relations of production and distribution, and to social and communal issues such as kinship, scarcity, powerlessness, and meaningfulness. Ethnicities produce a stock of knowledge tied to social location that function like a set of recipes for dealing with these relations and issues which the movement toward globalization, in Bueno's view, may disregard because globalization embodies the political and economic interests of the powerful. As a consequence of this possibility, Bueno eloquently argues for the re-historicizing of Pentecostal experiences and identities so that the local is empowered to create a dialectic with the global. The study of Pentecostalism in its global context, according to Bueno, needs to take seriously the implications that are embodied in the Pentecostal movement's diverse local ethnic expressions.

In the next chapter by Gerald T. Sheppard, postmodern hermeneutics are described and analysed in general terms in order to provide a clutter-free, yet nuanced, application of these postmodern hermeneutical models of textual interpretation to Pentecostalism and globalization. Interestingly, this applicational task is viewed by Sheppard as an engagement with the '*politics* of scriptural interpretation', a characterization which is cogently illustrated in his three personal testimonies. In the first section of his chapter, Sheppard describes the development of postmodern literary theory since the 1960s, teasing out the hermeneutical implications of such theorists as Michel Foucault, Hans-Georg Gadamer, Jacques Derrida, George Poulet, Ferdinand de Saussure, Steven Best and Douglas Kellner. Although the constructive postmodern proposals of these theorists, and others who build upon and extend their thought, has empowered a fresh rethinking of the disciplines within the academy, and has helped legitimize an array of new approaches to hermeneutics, Sheppard is concerned that these different groups establish some sense of hegemony in order to unite their proliferated voices in shaping public discourse. In his three testimonies, Sheppard demonstrates how his identification with different Christian communities of discourse has led him on his own personal postmodern journey. Marked by differences in educational achievement, racial makeup, political orientation and preaching styles, the various Christian and Pentecostal communities with which Sheppard has been identified were often experienced by him as politicizing agencies. He reflects on his association with these communities from which he forged his identity as an academic, a Christian minister, a proxy voice for the Other, and a Pentecostal.

In her chapter, Janet Everts Powers develops a Pentecostal hermeneutic designed to empower women for vocational ministry. Powers notes that Pentecostal women in the early years of the movement were empowered for ministry by a hermeneutic that drew on the resurrection accounts in Matthew and John, as well as biblical passages such as Joel 2:28 and Acts 2:16–17 which connected the outpouring of the Holy Spirit with the consequence: 'your daughters shall prophesy'. However, this affirmation of women as fully empowered by the Holy Spirit to speak for God was held in tension with the view of male authority in the church, home and society. Thus, the early Pentecostal hermeneutic, according to Powers, both empowered and restricted women. Because of this ambivalence, the number of women in ministry, especially as senior pastors, has been steadily declining. Powers notes that while older women ministers have learned to live with this ambiguity of roles, the younger generation of women called to Pentecostal ministry – whose concerns are often reflected in the work of feminist scholars – find it almost impossible to reconcile their ministry with the traditional hierarchical model of male-female relationships with its emphasis on male authority. Avoiding secular and feminists' grids which often do not resonate fully with the Pentecostal tradition,

Powers maps out the design of a Pentecostal hermeneutic which will empower a new generation of women for ministry in the church. Reclaiming the experientially-oriented hermeneutic of early Pentecostals, Powers performs a narrative exegesis of Mark 5:21–33 to illustrate the legitimate role of narrative in constructing a theology of women, and a historical critical exegesis of I Corinthians 11:2–16 to illustrate the subversive power of the distinction between a teaching text and a historically conditioned text. She concludes by emphasizing the eschatological dimension of biblical texts which connects the reader to the transformation of the Christian community in the already/not yet Reign of God.

The topic of ecumenism within the ranks of Pentecostal denominational leadership in North America has been a hotly disputed issue because, as Cecil M. Robeck, Jr. notes in his chapter, the Ecumenical movement has been defined synonymously with the World Council of Churches (WCC) and its agenda of establishing the world-wide organizational unity of the church. One of Robeck's objectives is to debunk through an appeal to actual source materials this stereotype in order to broaden the Pentecostal understanding of ecumenism as the church heads into the new millennium. By appealing to source material from R.G. Spurling, Charles Fox Parham, Warren Fay Carothers, William J. Seymour, and the founders of the Assemblies of God, Robeck clearly demonstrates that early Pentecostal leaders held the dream of visible Christian unity. Robeck shows that when Pentecostal leaders in the 1940s became more closely aligned with the Fundamentalist movement, some denominations even joining the National Association of Evangelicals, they abandoned the dream of the Pentecostal founders and condemned the Ecumenical movement, forbidding ministers to be in fellowship with the World Council of Churches. Changes in the Ecumenical movement have occurred since the 1940s and Robeck chronicles the broader meaning of ecumenism that has accompanied those developments within the movement itself. He describes the redefined relationship of the WCC, the Roman Catholic Church and a number of Pentecostal churches to ecumenism which make it more inviting for North American Pentecostals to move beyond their limited ecumenical relations with the NAE and the newly formed Pentecostal/Charismatic Churches of North America (PCCNA) to the broader ecumenism offered by the National and World Councils of Churches. Robeck identifies the evangelistic, sociological, and political perils that may await the Pentecostal movement worldwide if its leaders and rank-and-file members do not broaden their ecumenical vision for the visible fulfilment of Jesus' prayer in John 17:21, 'I ask . . . that they may be one . . . so that the world may believe that you have sent me.'

Margaret Poloma, in the next chapter, examines 'The Toronto Blessing' and the unusual manifestations associated with the revival at the Toronto Airport Christian Fellowship (TACF). As a sociologist, Poloma believes that the 'The Toronto Blessing' affords an opportunity to observe a revival in its charismatic moment prior to the processes of institutionalization. She examines the behavioural manifestations – some rather unusual and unprecedented in revival history – from the postmodern emphasis on semiotics in order to interpret what signification the manifestations might represent in constructing and maintaining a Pentecostal world view. Investigating the revival at TACF, Poloma uses the sociological method of a participant observer, gathering her empirical data about the manifestations attributed to Holy Spirit from questionnaires, and reporting her explanations of the manifestations from ethnomethodological accounts – personal testimonies, appeals to Scripture, cross-references to revival history, and ethnotheology – which allow the participants themselves to construct their social reality and interpretive framework for their behavioural responses. Poloma concludes that the Pentecostal/charismatic world view that participants construct draws on the premodern consciousness marked by holism, and holds a balance between the straitjacket of Enlightenment-generated modernism and the chaos of a postmodern de-centered universe.

This section is completed by the provocative and prophetic observations of Harvey Cox, who served as the dialogical partner for this area of Issues Facing Pentecostalism in a Postmodern World. Cox draws on the Diana Ephesian narrative of *Acts* for some biblical insights on the conflicting values represented between Christianity and today's global market culture. Utilizing the 'theology of culture' method of his mentor, Paul Tillich, Cox establishes the premise that the global market culture is the 'form' of a false idolatrous religion with its authoritative metanarrative, its plan of salvation, its missionary force, its eschatology, and its invisible providential 'hidden hand' orchestrating outcomes for the common good. Cox challenges Christian theologians and church leaders to engage in prophetic critique of this 'Market God' with its carnivorous appetite for consumerism and acquisition and with its exacerbating effects of widening the distance between the rich and the poor. Now, as never before, Cox suggests that Pentecostals need to recapture their suspicion of the dominant world order, their resistance to cultural assimilation, their commitment to simplicity and community, all features which marked the early Pentecostal movement. Following the biblical tradition embodied in the Diana Ephesian narrative of *Acts,* Cox prophetically prods Pentecostals to join with other Christians in exposing the Market God as one of the 'gods that are no gods', while speaking out for the integrity of the creation and for justice in the human family.

Notes

1   Stanley J. Grenz, 'Star Trek and the Next Generation: Postmodernism and the Future of Evangelical Theology', in *The Challenge of Postmodernism: An Evangelical Engagement,* ed. David S. Dockery (Wheaton, IL: A Bridgepoint Book, 1995), p. 90.

2   Diogenes Allen, *Christian Belief in a Postmodern World: The Full Wealth of Conviction* (Louisville, KY: Westminster Press/John Knox Press, 1989), p. 2.

3   Although Carl F. H. Henry believes that it is still an open question '[w]hether postmodernism is already entrenched as a decisive historical turning time, or is merely an influential episodic phenomenon...' in 'Postmodernism: The New Spectre?' in *The Challenge of Postmodernism: An Evangelical Engagement,* ed. David S. Dockery (Wheaton, IL: A Bridgepoint Book, 1995), pp. 34–35.

4   Harold Heie, 'The Postmodern Opportunity: Christians in the Academy', *Christian Scholar's Review* 26 (Winter 1996), p. 138

5   See for example the Special Issue of *Christian Scholar's Review* 26 (Winter 1996) on Christianity and Postmodernity which contains a symposium, articles and book reviews all focused on Postmodernism and its implications for Christian thought and practice. Two of the pieces in the symposium reflect in their titles the mixed appreciation for Postmodernism providing an opportunity for Christian scholars to have their voices heard in the academy: Harold Heie's presentation, 'The Postmodern Opportunity: Christians in the Academy', pp. 138–157, is followed by a jointly authored response, Daniel Howard-Snyder and Mark Walhout, 'What Postmodern Opportunity?', pp. 158–167.

6   Timothy B. Cargal, 'Beyond the Fundamentalist-Modernist Controversy: Pentecostals and Hermeneutics in a Post-Modern Age', *PNEUMA: The Journal of the Society for Pentecostal Studies* 15 (Fall 1993), pp. 163–187.

7   Robert P. Menzies, 'Jumping Off the Postmodern Bandwagon', *PNEUMA: The Journal of the Society for Pentecostal Studies* 16 (Spring 1994), pp. 115–120.

Chapter Twelve

Listening to the Margins: Re-historicizing Pentecostal Experiences and Identities

Ronald N. Bueno

I begin with two confessions which will orientate the reader to the various proposals for Pentecostal studies developed in this chapter. First, I am an anthropologist. More specifically, I position myself within historical and political economy approaches and concerns in the field of anthropology. Therefore, when asked to address issues of ethnicity and culture in relation to the 'Pentecostal movement' my first concern was that I did not have original, ethnographic data to elaborate a discussion. My concern was especially acute in that I believe that 'ethnicity' must be understood historically, within specific political and economic relationships and contexts. Ethnicity must be understood as a set of experiences articulated differently within time and space, and in most cases consciously prescribed as sets of 'identities'.

I use ethnicity in this discussion as a modern construct which in most cases primordializes specific social and cultural attributes and creates an imagined, 'authentic', bounded community. The central point of entry for analysis is how 'ethnicities', as well as other points of reference or self-definition – such as 'class', 'gender', 'racial' and other politically invented communities – shape the social relations both of production and of daily life.[1] That is, the principal question is in what ways are ethnicities played out in peoples' daily lives. Or as Michael Kearney states, '[t]he main ethnographic and theoretical issue concerning ethnicity is the cultural construction of person and community.'[2] Thus, I have resolved this initial dilemma by taking a slightly different direction in this chapter: I will focus upon the connections between the political construction of naturalized communities (specifically ethnicity) and the intellectual construction of such images in our basic concepts within Pentecostal studies. More specifically, I will explore how the concepts 'globalization' and 'experience' used by scholars to describe Pentecostal experiences run the risk of homogenizing or erasing historical distinctions between social forms and groups.

Second, I am Pentecostal. I was born, reared and live in El Salvador. Many of the studies I have read on Pentecostalism do not accord with or reflect my experiences in El Salvador. Although that does not cause me to reject, at least initially, many of these works, it does prompt me to ask different questions of the literature in relation to my experiences. Is there a Pentecostal movement, or are there Pentecostalisms? And, what implications do either perspective have on how we understand and study Pentecostalism. Is there a shared 'Pentecostal experience'? In that case, who gets to define what Pentecostal experiences are? And here, as studies on ethnicity specifically remind us, we must maintain an ever present awareness of the risks of assuming authority over speaking *for* and *as* others.

Is there, as Karla Poewe[3] states, a global perspective among Pentecostals? A perspective that is assumed to contain the power to de-patriarchalize, de-colonize, and even under-emphasize ethnic, racial, class and other sets of identities rooted in political and economic contexts. Aside from questioning whether there is a perspective shared by all Pentecostals globally, do we run the risk of under-emphasizing to the fatal degree of erasing these sets of historically and politically constructed distinctions? Is 'routinization'[4] or 'globalization' the same thing as imperialism or hegemony of one set of voices over others?[5] It is here where the intersection of ethnic, other cultural social forms, and Pentecostalisms becomes most vibrant and insightful in understanding the global character of the movement. How do questions of representation and authenticity highlight important aspects of the dialectical process of Pentecostal formation in specific historical contexts? Are Pentecostal experiences routinized and institutionalized at specific times among groups while providing what David Martin states are 'free spaces'[6] at different times and places? To what degree, and under what conditions is the 'freedom' patriarchal, racist, classist, etc., and when is it de-patriarchical, inclusive, etc.?[7] It is this dynamic interplay I want to begin to address in this discussion.

In this chapter I argue that Pentecostal experiences should be examined and understood as specific historical formations within unequal relations of power. That is, studies of Pentecostalism should focus upon how local congregations, movements and individual experiences constitute and shape global processes; how global worship 'styles', liturgical practices and moral codes are integrated, rejected or adapted by localities; how mobile evangelists, pastors and laypersons assimilate to or transform new and old localities; how ethnicity, gender, class and other historically constructed social forms shape Pentecostal experiences and their institutionalization at specific moments in time and space.

To begin to discuss and clarify Pentecostalisms as specific historical formations within political and economic contexts, I will examine how scholars describe and model the growth of Pentecostalism worldwide through their use of the concepts 'global/local' and 'experience'. I will first theorize on the meaning of the central concepts of the 'global' and 'local' inherent in the concept of globalization. In doing so, I hope to provide a more dynamic, historical model which traces operatively the intersections of the local and the global to rescue a socially articulated set of experiences and identities within time and space. Second, I will explore the concept of experience as a theoretical notion that traces the intersection of social processes and individual consciousness. The deliberate emphasis upon this nexus allows us to understand Pentecostal experiences as a set of social and cultural identities negotiated in unequal relations of power.

THEORIZING THE LOCAL AND THE GLOBAL
IN PENTECOSTAL STUDIES

Early in the 1990s globalization became a recurring notion in everyday conversation.[8] New texts and journal issues crossed disciplinary lines and forged new fields out of old ones, including the disciplines of anthropology and religion. Pentecostal studies soon followed with Karla Poewe's edited volume *Charismatic Christianity as Global Culture* and this volume entitled, *The Globalization of Pentecostalism*. Along with the nearly universal focus upon globalization came the universalization of the concepts local and global. The concepts local and global went from geographic markers to reified domains of interaction. That is, the global is now understood as existing apart from the local as an autonomous domain of relationships and identities.

In this section I want to explore the concept of globalization and how Pentecostal scholars have used it to build their stories. I argue that the local and the global should not be merely assumed, but rather should be used as heuristic devices to contextualize global processes within local relationships and institutions. The geographic expansion, and in many cases the globalization of Pentecostalism should be observed and discussed within specific historical localities. We should examine the dynamic intersections between the local and global to explain the specific formations of Pentecostalisms. For example an examination of Marcos Witt's[9] worship style in the context of Latin America may yield informative data of its influence in shaping the experience of Pentecostal worship along class, ethnic or gender lines. Are the differences pronounced and in what ways do they shape people's expressions of worship? How have Carlos Annacondia and Claudio Freidzon[10] shaped people's understanding of closeness to God and/or spiritual anointing. The key struggle remains to explain the geographic growth of Pentecostalism without homogenizing or erasing distinct historically and politically constructed experiences and identities.

Globalization, which only indirectly implies 'localization', most often refers to a geographic expansion of the world. Globalization is described as an amoeba-like movement with no clearly articulated beginnings nor primary agents. Authors discuss trans-world communication systems, international speaking circuits, and even unlocalized relationships, but focus very little upon how these global processes are embodied in and shaped by people. Who is responsible for the creation and/or the continuation of these global forces? How do local populations resist, reshape and/or forcefully or otherwise adopt these global processes?

In Pentecostal studies globalization is discussed primarily in two ways: 1) the 'global' is contrasted with the 'local' and the concepts are understood as naturalized dualisms or essentialized oppositions, and 2) the global is attached to culture to form global culture. In the first instance, the relationship of the local is to the global as simple is to complex, traditional is to modern, collectivist is to individualistic, and even more dangerously, 'authentic' is to diversity or multicultural. These concepts conceived as autonomous, 'naturalized' categories in opposition to one another, paint a picture of the past through our notions of the present. The global is used to reference the present or future while reifying a new and distant other, 'the local'.[11] The local is understood as previous to or in response to the global, not intersecting with the global. That is, we create caricatures of the past through our modern constructions of the present.

The creation of 'tribalism' in Africa is a telling example of how we fabricated distinct ethnic and political groups through our modern constructions, displacing them as active contributors to their histories and from the West. Until recently, most scholarship did not even question the notions that African populations were independent, autonomous, harmonious systems before the arrival of colonialism. Yet much current research highlights the fact that there were expansive trade routes and social networks that extended beyond 'local' populations. Our modern constructions of tradition vs. modern did not allow us to understand African populations outside of ourselves. We created their histories, and thus their ethnicities. Gerald Sider observes that ethnic group formation in the colonial context in Africa – the creation of cultures and peoples – was not so much a product of divide-and-conquer policies as of the much more complex, less specifically planned, and far more resistance-permeated process that he calls 'create and incorporate'.[12]

These dualistic constructions also shaped the way we understood religion in Africa. Terence Ranger states that our 'tradition-modern' opposition served to describe religion in Africa as idiosyncratic, highly ritualistic and systematic.[13] He adds that social analysts were not looking for evidence of regional religious movements or of shared religious experiences outside of the 'tribe' construct before colonial Christianity. He reports that there were many expansive prophetic and purification movements that stretched outside of 'localized groups'. These religious movements spread across these same trade routes and personal networks to shape religious experiences and practices across large geographical terrain long before colonialism and the expansion of Christianity in Africa, many times taking slightly different forms in various populations.

Along with misrepresenting the past, present and even future of these populations, we run a more serious risk of expropriating the voice and agency of 'locals'. Jean and John Comaroff state that '... these stereotypic contrasts are readily spatialized in the chasm between the West and the rest'.[14] They go on to state that in our representations of Others in an 'imagined' past we do not give credence to them as active 'modern actors'. We displace them in time and space from ourselves, inevitably still controlling their stories.

In the same book, *Ethnography and the Historical Imagination,* the Comaroffs give an example of a story originally printed on the front page of the *Chicago Tribune* called 'Mystic Warriors Gaining Ground in Monzambique War'.[15] The report began by stating,

> Call it one of the mysteries of Africa. In the battle-ravaged regions of northern Mozambique, in remote villages where the modern world has scarcely penetrated, supernatural spirits and magic potions are suddenly winning a civil war that machine guns, mortars and grenades could not.[16]

The account continued by describing how several thousand men and boys, sporting red headbands and brandishing spears have instilled great fear in opposing rebel groups and have even caused the army to be in 'awe'. Named after their leader, Naparama – who is said to have been resurrected from the dead – they display on their chests the scars of a 'vaccination' against bullets. Western diplomats and analysts, according to the report, 'can only scratch their heads in amazement'. As the Comaroffs note, the piece ends in a tone of modern authority:

> Much of Naparama's effectiveness can be explained by the predominance of superstitious beliefs throughout Mozambique, a country where city markets always have stalls selling potions, amulets and monkey hands and ostrich feet to ward off evil spirits.[17]

Quite obvious in this newspaper report is the use of stereotypic contrasts, especially between 'traditional' and 'modern' to render a pseudo-historical representation of current events. As the Comaroffs state, the Naparama will never be more than primitive rebels, rattling their sabers, their 'cultural weapons', in the prehistory of an African dawn.[18] Our modern constructions of time and space do not, and cannot, attribute properly to the Naparama political motives, nor can they be credited with the rational, purposive actions that to us constitute history. In this newspaper report, the Naparama are efficiently distanced from ourselves, de-politicized and stripped of significant agency.

In our Pentecostal studies, we must be especially careful to avoid creating contrived pasts for locals by modern dualisms. We must also be extremely careful not to interpret locals' present experiences through these same modern measuring sticks. We must be careful in our classifications of Pentecostal experiences as pre-logical, 'primal' or postmodern that we are not explaining differences as in our own past and thus characterizing their past through our notions of the present. Moreover, through our use of the local and global as naturalized dualisms we run the risk of marginalizing local actors and Pentecostal experiences as in our own past or as insignificant anomalies or more seriously as 'exotic' phenomenon.

In the second instance, Pentecostal scholars use the concept 'global' in relation to culture to form 'global culture'. Global culture, as referred to by many of the authors of Karla Poewe's work, implies a universally shared set of values, experiences and moral expressions that extend beyond personal relations. Poewe herself specifically uses the term 'globality' to describe the transformation of perspective and identity among scientists upon Pentecostal conversion that expresses itself in a 'global culture'. She states that there was a shift in thought and affect toward the world outside of one's 'local' concerns and activities, and that with this shift, there emerged a new mode of knowledge which emphasizes the transnational, international and global.[19] In Poewe's work globality or global culture is used to describe perceived new circumstances which extend literally across 'the world', turning the spreading itself into a noteworthy phenomenon. The global becomes a new realm or domain outside of specific places and people and runs the risk of homogenizing and/or displacing deeply rooted historical and political differences. The use of culture in relation to global also reifies in many cases an understanding of cultures as closed structures and symbols which are static, superorganic and coherent systems.

Culture must be understood as a system of symbols, both of beliefs and practices, in which human beings construct and represent themselves and others, and hence their societies and histories. Culture is a fluent, dynamic system of meanings and actions which are highly contested and negotiated between people in daily life. As Camoroff and Camoroff state, many times these symbols will be woven together into tightly integrated, relatively conscious worldviews, while at other times they remain or become unfixed, relatively free-floating and unclear in their value and meaning.[20]

Marilyn Strathern adds that the concept of culture itself has also become a global phenomenon.[21] She states that the Euro-American perception of the role of culture in human life is being summoned in almost any context and at almost any level of social interaction. The use of the concept of culture is also being employed to describe diversity in human forms of thought and practice. She comments that the use of culture to describe the root of peoples' sense of identity, 'starts behaving in a "global way" – ubiquitous, encompassing, all-explanatory – at the same time as a new and specific phenomenon is designated: global culture'.[22]

As Strathern notes, culture is being used ubiquitously and at worst as synthetic representations; what she calls the 'ethnicization of identity': the perceptions of primordial categorization whose visibility and enactment take away ethnic identity.[23] Cultural differences provide on the one hand a new platform on which to essentialize identity without confronting the other. On the other hand, culture can present ethnicity as a kind of 'cleansed state'.[24] Issues of differences and similarities between groups or cultures as used in the context of 'global' are easily attributed to localized manifestations of lifestyle and community. Cultural uniqueness is essentialized and displaced to the margins.

The term culture, along with the local and global, must be contextualized within social relations. As soon as they are displaced from their original context and used as heuristic devices, culture is taken for granted and local and global manifestations are discussed on their own. Strathern states that the use of globalism conceals the relational dimensions of social life when the concept of culture is globalized on the presumption that cultures manifest a universal form of self-consciousness about identity and when global culture appears to constitute its own context.[25] Poewe's globality definitely reflects the first presumption and comes dangerously close to the second as well. Culture cannot be understood outside of peoples' daily lives, nor can 'global and local relations' be extracted from one another. Global and local relations provide the co-ordinates needed to mark the limits of a field of analysis; however, each term plays off itself; it is ultimately intractable from its relationship to the other. Not only can the global not stand on its own, but it definitely cannot constitute its own conscious identity outside of the local.

What I would like to suggest is that in the study of Pentecostal experiences we should focus upon studying the conjunctures or inter-sections of local and global processes. I am advocating an historical anthropological approach which explores the converging and multiple processes that reciprocally shape and transform subjects and contexts. This task of course is not an easy one, for how do we contextualize fragments of human worlds, reading them without losing their fragile uniqueness and ambiguity? It is not easy to forge units of analysis in unbounded social fields. But it would be false to assume that it is any easier to understand local contexts outside of global processes. All human behaviour is grounded in everyday activity. Even rural and 'peripheral' populations are involved in the making of wider struc-tures and social movements. And macro-historical processes – such as the building of states, the making of revolutions or movements, the extension of global capitalism or global evangelism – have their feet on the ground.

Arjun Appadurai uses the term 'ethnoscapes' to indicate the non-localized, shifting contexts researchers will now have to study.[26] He defines ethnoscapes as the landscape of persons who make up the shifting worlds in which we live: tourists, immigrants, refugees, exiles, guest-workers, and other moving groups and persons.[27] Central to these new landscapes is the changing identity – the ethnoscapes – that around the world are no longer familiar anthropological objects, in so far as groups are no longer tightly territorialized, spatially bounded, historically unselfconscious, and culturally homogeneous.[28] Appadurai promotes a new 'style' of ethnography which will capture the impact of deterritorialization on the imaginative resources of lived, local experiences. The task of the researcher, he suggests, is to unravel a conundrum: What is the nature of locality, as a lived experience, in a globalized, deterritorialized world?[29]

The first step we must take in order to grasp this process is to char-acterize each party as a complex collective, each endowed with its own historicity. And then we can begin to retrace the often barely visi-ble minutiae of their interactions. For it is in the gradual articulation of such different worlds that local and global realities come to define each other and the markers like 'ethnicity', 'culture', 'regionalism', and 'nationalism' take on their meaning. Going back to our example of Africa, it was in the process of colonialization and christianization that ethnic orientations were created and began to define their histories – both as experiences and identities. Pentecostal experiences are understood and expressed in the daily activities of prayer, church

services, and communion with the community of believers. The articulation of Pentecostal believers' identities are constructed within
social relationships as they define themselves and others. They also
intersect at different levels and at different moments with global processes, such as international media, travelling evangelists, and socio-
political developments to negotiate their own histories.

In Pentecostal studies, we should begin to create ethnographic
archives of Pentecostal experiences. That is, we should focus upon the
historical intersection of local and global processes in the shaping of
worship forms and styles, liturgical themes and styles, and questions
of theology, but also examine changes in dress, moral codes, and
behavioural practices. We must understand these expressions as con-
stituting experiences.

Second, we must advocate a call for specificity, for local actors' or
community's point of view, and for a re-focusing upon social relations. Social relations are local and are comprised by what Strathern
calls sociality. By sociality she refers to neither citizen subjects nor
non-animal beings, but to the amalgam of desire, capability, artifact
and embodiment by which people live. She adds that '[t]he idea of
sociality cannot be produced either by generalization or by the purification of other ideas: rather it is brought into existence as an awareness
by what she calls the co-presence of persons.'[30] A central task for Pentecostal studies is to acknowledge and render knowledge local and
restore the presence of people as active participants.

RE-HISTORICIZING PENTECOSTAL EXPERIENCES
AND IDENTITIES

Experience, as an analytical concept, has formed an important part of
the anthropological critique of positivist approaches in the social sciences as well as the basis for a re-examination of the study of religion.
Experience defined as the nexus of social processes and individual
consciousness has questioned the Cartesian dualisms of mind vs.
material, feelings vs. thought, the personal vs. the social and the subjective vs. the objective. Moreover, the concept of experience, as
discussed by Raymond Williams[31] challenges the enlightenment
methodological bias of studying fixed social forms which by definition rest in the past and erase all living presence in social action or
experience. This re-theorizing of experience has the potential of
returning a sense of immanent presence and agency to a previously

held deterministic and structural interpretation of human activity. In this section I want to explore this concept of experience and evaluate its usefulness to the study of Pentecostalism. I suggest that Pentecostal experiences are historical, social constructions richly negotiated by people in their daily lives, and in many cases between people of unequal relations of power. I will first contextualize historically the use of experience in the anthropological study of religion, highlighting its role in restoring a cognitive-emotive, immanent presence to religious life. I will then discuss and critique Victor Turner's and Edward Bruner's[32] use of the concept experience in anthropology in order to provide a new analytical entry point to the multiple, interrelated processes that inform Pentecostal experiences.

The history of anthropological thought on religion is a story laced with expansion and comparative methodologies. Its roots lie in the explanation of other systems of belief and practices by comparison with western, post-enlightenment notions of religion. More specifically, debates were heavily informed by the analytical distinction between what Max Weber later labelled as 'traditional' and world religions.[33] The point of analysis and conclusion for many scholars in the late-nineteenth-century[34] was that both the development of the world religions and, by implication, the decision of an individual or community to convert were part of an inevitable march toward human enlightenment. The history of religion, much like [the] analysis of all culture, was understood as one unilineal, upward evolution, toward greater reason and deeper ethical awareness. It is in this progressive impulse that the impetus for conversion to world religions rests.[35]

Although this view of religious evolution might have reflected or verified assumptions common in the West, it failed to provide a convincing account of religion's cross-cultural reality. How could you explain variation in ritual and ethics among societies that seemed, by other measures, to be at the same 'stage' of development? As anthropological research turned to the study of small-scale societies in the twentieth- century, it became increasingly evident that though some 'primitives' were practical-minded and indifferent toward matters of religion others subscribed to richly elaborate and deeply ethical cosmologies.[36] The focus on small-scale societies in anthropology succeeded in abolishing the myth of religious evolution and the theory of conversion they sustained.

Broader transformations in the theoretical orientations of anthropologists in the study of religion also promoted important shifts in the focus and understanding of religious processes and experiences. Edward Tylor's early studies of religion, and those of other more recognized contributors such as Emile Durkheim, Talcott Parsons, Bronislaw Malinowski, and more recently Robert Bellah,[37] focused primarily upon the structural and functional effects of beliefs and practices upon collective wholes. They focused upon the role of rituals and myths to provide unity, order and harmony among populations lacking the individual, subjective power to abstract knowledge from the 'objective' world. As Adam Kuper states, for Tylor and others, 'religion and perhaps all aspects of cosmology were ultimately epiphenomena of group structure'.[38]

As the twentieth century progressed, two concurrent movements characterized the study of religion in anthropology.[39] One tract of anthropology, as noted in the work of Malinowski, Geertz and others, returned to study those aspects of religion that Tylor had stripped away. Malinowski focused upon the psychological intent and 'healing' of religious adherents. Clifford Geertz, and Claude Levi-Strauss turned to the symbolic and mythological constructions of religion. Pierre Bourdieu and others turned to the rhetorical and metaphorical structures of rituals and beliefs found in religion.[40] Although each scholar added specific foci and elements to Tylor's study of religion, most continued his epistemological conclusion: religion is an illusion or misapprehension.

The second important area in the study of religion in anthropology in the twentieth century was characterized by an epistemological break from 'objective' reality toward an understanding of religion as both structures and sets of subjective experiences. Victor Turner emphasized the importance of religious ritual or performance as an emotional and cognitive experience immanently shaping the beliefs and practices of individuals. Godfrey Lienhardt and Geoffrey White, and many others, turned their gaze toward the importance of religious experiences in shaping people's identities.[41]

Other anthropologists focused upon specific religious experiences, such as conversion as an emotive agent of change. Maurice Leenhardt suggested that conversion entails multiple sets of experiences.[42] Robert Hefner concludes that '... at the very least – an analytical minimum – conversion implies the acceptance of new locus of self-definition, a new, though not necessarily exclusive, reference point for one's identity'.[43] David Jordon, in his analysis of Chinese conversion to Christianity, states, '... conversion is a matter of belief and social structure, of faith and affiliation.'[44] William Merrill and Charles Keyes add that conversion does not need to reformulate one's understanding of the ultimate conditions of existence, but it always involves a commitment to a new kind of moral authority and a new or reconceptualized social identity.[45] In these works, religious experiences are described as multiple processes that are equally internal and social and that shape reciprocally people's sense of identity and actions.

This theorized notion of experience has also informed the study of Pentecostalism. Poewe quotes Wilhem Schmidt with whom Evans-Pritchard was in agreement as saying, '[i]f religion is essentially of the inner life, it follows that it can be truly grasped only from within. But beyond a doubt, this can better be done by one in whose inward consciousness an experience of religion plays a part.'[46] Poewe herself uses this understanding of experience to explain the moment of conversion. She refers to a 'proleptic experience' by which she means 'that profound moment when the scientist experienced the existence of "God" with such "persuasive power" that, from that moment forward, "God's' existence was assumed" '.[47] Jean-Daniel Plüss also refers to many of these same notions of experience by calling for a re-experiencing of the Pentecostal phenomenon through the re-imaging of previous, and for many people removed in time and space, Pentecostal histories.[48] I would like to contribute further to such work, by suggesting that we re-contextualize experiences, and thus identities, within historical and political-economic relationships. That is, I believe we should extend the analysis of and use of the concept of experience to articulate historical relationships and markers of identity – such as 'ethnicities, genders, races, classes, Pentecostalisms' – within unequal relations of power.

In anthropology, perhaps no better work has helped theorize 'experience' than Victor Turner and Edward Bruner's edited volume, *The Anthropology of Experience*.[49] In their work, Turner and Bruner turn to Dilthey's discussion of experience, quoting, '... reality only exists for us in the facts of consciousness given by inner experience'.[50] Thus, according to Bruner and Turner, experience is what comes first. Their focus was upon how 'individuals actually experience their culture, that is, how events are received by consciousness'.[51] Experience is not just sense data, cognition, or products of reason, but also feelings and expectations. James Fernandez[52] adds that experience comes to us not just verbally but also in images and impressions.[53] From this perspective, lived experience, as thought and desire, as word and image, is the primary reality.[54]

Throughout the articles of Turner and Bruner's edited volume experience is understood as distinct from the concept of behaviour. Behaviour is conceptualized as an outside observer describing someone else's actions, as if one were an audience to an event. Behaviour implies a standardized routine that one simply enacts. An experience, on the other hand, is more personal; it refers to an active self, to a human being who shapes an action. The primary distinguishing criterion is that the communication of experience tends to be self-referential.[55]

To Turner and Bruner experience is also analytically separate from but dialectically related to reality and expressions. That is, experience or how reality is understood consciously is distinct from but intimately related to reality whatever that might be and from expressions or how individual experience is framed and articulated in daily life. Experiences can ultimately be understood only individually. They state that although we might try to share others' experiences, we may never completely know another's experiences. People repress or censor, or may not be able to articulate certain aspects of what has been experienced. Thus, Turner and Bruner point to the interpretation of expressions as the entry point to overcome the limitations of individual experiences. They point to Dilthey who understood 'interpreting' to be understanding, interpretation and the methodology of hermeneutics; by 'expressions' he meant representations, performances, objectifications, or texts. To Dilthey, and hence to Turner and Bruner, the analysis of experience can be understood only within social and cultural processes.[56]

The relationship between experience and its expressions is always as problematic to understand and is one of the important research areas in the anthropology of experience. Turner and Bruner state that the relationship is clearly dialogic and dialectical, for experience structures expressions, in that we understand other people and their expressions on the basis of our own experience and self-understanding. But expressions also structure experience, in that dominant narratives of a historical era, important rituals and festivals, and classic works of art define and illuminate inner experience. Once again, we come to the place where culture and experience intersect. More simply stated, experience is culturally constructed while understanding presupposes experience. Dilthey identified this relationship as a hermeneutical cycle to be worked out:

Our knowledge of what is given in experience is extended through the interpretation of the objectifications of life and their interpretation, in turn, is only made possible by plumbing the depths of subjective experience.[57]

Turner and Bruner's analysis of experience ultimately rests upon a construction of the Other based on, what Jay O'Brien and William Roseberry call, 'radical cultural difference'.[58] Experiences, although entirely social and cultural, are immanently individual. Different people's experiences cannot be shared nor fully understood. This hermeneutical conundrum presupposes the radical separation between 'us' and 'them' and creates a problem of crossing boundaries between autonomous cultural objects. Herman Rebel states that such a position 'forecloses on the question of depth to which analysis can go in understanding experience and of the precise ways by which experience enters historical-cultural processes'.[59] Furthermore, such an approach ignores the power relations that made possible and operated our previous interpretations of the other, and neglects a more considered examination of the historical construction of cultural difference within unequal fields of power.

The neglect of politics and sociological features in religious experiences caused by purely 'textual' approaches leads to an inability to recognize how religions like Christianity, or experiences of Pentecostalisms, provide an identity as well as religious faith and a set of rules for life in addition to instruments for the intellectual control of space-time events.[60] The changing social and cultural environment in which Pentecostal experiences so often unfold is not simply a product of material forces. It affects the participators' material well-being but also their sense of self-worth and community and their efforts to create institutions for the sustenance of both. Hefner highlights that this tension between dignity and self-identification in a pluralized and politically unequal world lies at the heart of many testimonials or conversion histories.[61]

Raymond Williams explains what Dilthey calls the hermeneutical cycle as a problem of our enlightenment conceptualization of time and space. He states that '[social] analysis is...centered on relations between ... [the] produced institutions, formations and experiences ... [so] ... that ... only the fixed explicit forms exist and living presence is always, by definition, receding.'[62] That is, experience becomes a unit of analysis only in its having passed from the present in the observable past. Williams states that the study of experience should focus on the reflection upon the immediate in the semi-immediate and years after. Experience is understood in the articulation of its occurrence in mind and/or in conversation with others. We understand experience in reflection, in discussions with others, in journalizing, etc. Thus, the meanings we ascribe to the experience both at its time of occurrence and upon subsequent reflections throughout time are richly imbued by social and cultural process. Our conversion, or receiving of 'the spirit' is understood immediately by its previous presentation, current response of co-participants and later explanation by fellow pastors and/or laity among other factors. But these participants in your experience and the meanings they have ascribed to your experience can be analysed and are entirely contextual. Upon reflection in later years of your experience many new sets of meanings have been ascribed to the event which makes it a new experience to be lived anew with its new social context and participants.

This has great implications for our study of Pentecostal experiences. Although we can assume, in some cases maybe incorrectly as Julie Ma has implied, that a Pentecostal experience is felt on some internal level, it is understood and expressed through our own reflections in prayer or otherwise, conversations with others, journalizing, hearing a sermon or singing a song – to cite but a few examples – all of which are ultimately socially and culturally constructed. In the study of Pentecostal experiences we can analyse the multiple mediums and messages informing events at specific times and place. The conceptual notion of experience can root our studies of Pentecostalism within actors and their dynamic systems of meanings on a very specific level. Furthermore, I suggest that we examine Pentecostal experiences as historically situated within unequal relations of power.

Pentecostal experiences are intimately interrelated with issues of power, and thus with corresponding sets of identities such as class, ethnicity, and gender. The meanings ascribed to Pentecostal experiences are substantively different among poor, female members from that of rich, male members. The co-participants which help shape the experience are distinct, and the remembering and subsequent re-experiencing of such events are lived differently along these lines of power. There are important differences evident among groups of unequal power which should comprise our and their historical accounts of Pentecostalism in specific contexts. We must also be aware of our own positions of power in the re-telling of other peoples stories.

CONCLUSION

In this chapter I have proposed that we should understand and describe Pentecostal experiences, and thus with corresponding sets of identities – such as class, ethnicity, and gender – as historically situated within unequal relations of power. Thus, we must attempt to retrace the intersections of local and global processes in order to understand the multiple histories and identities embodied in Pentecostal experiences. We must be careful to understand the local as active agents in global processes, but also be aware of our own positions of power and those of different actors telling the stories.

Pentecostal scholarship stands at the crossroads of knowledge.[63] With the continuing growth of Pentecostalism worldwide, Pentecostal scholars confront the challenge of describing the spread of its experiences and institutional structures without homogenizing and thus, erasing local experiences and expressions. Pentecostal scholars must strive to recognize local communities as producers of Pentecostal experiences and knowledge. Finally, scholars of Pentecostalism must reconsider their domains of inquiry with in many cases may run the risk of speaking for and as others.

Notes

1   For further work on imagined, politically bounded communities see Bendict Anderson, *Imagined Communities: Reflections on the Origin and Spread of Nationalism* (London: Verso, 1983). For additional work on ethnicity as a historical and political construction please see: Micaela di Leonardo, *The Varieties of Ethnic Experience: Kinship, Class and Gender among California Italian-Americans* (Ithaca, NY: Cornell University Press, 1984) and 'Habits of the Cumbered Heart: Ethnic Community and Women's Culture as American Invented Traditions', in *Golden Ages, Dark Ages: Imaging the Past in Anthropology and History*, ed. Jay O'Brien and William Roseberry (Berkeley, CA: University of California Press, 1991), pp. 234–252; Jay O'Brien, 'Toward a Reconstitution of Ethnicity: Capitalist Expansion and Cultural Dynamics in Sudan', in *Golden Ages, Dark Ages: Imaging the Past in Anthropology and History*, ed. Jay O'Brien and William Roseberry (Berkeley, CA: University of California Press, 1991), pp. 126–138; Gerald M. Sider, *Lumbee Indian Histories: Race, Ethnicity, and Indian Identity in the Southern United States* (Cambridge: Cambridge University Press, 1993).

2   Michael Kearney, *Reconceptualizing the Peasantry: Anthropology in Global Perspective* (Boulder, CO: Westview Press, 1996), p. 179.

3   Karla Poewe, ed., *Charismatic Christianity as a Global Culture*, (Columbia, SC: University of South Carolina Press, 1994), pp. 1–32.

4   Gerard Roelofs uses the term 'routinization' to refer to the diffusion of

Pentecostal experiences as they become institutionalized in his article 'Charismatic Christian Thought: Experience, Metonymy, and Routinization', in *Charismatic Christianity as a Global Culture*, ed. Karla Poewe (Columbia, SC: University of South Carolina Press, 1994), pp. 217–233.

5   D.M. Lima discusses the negative rise of Pentecostalism in Latin America as an extension of US imperialism in her work *Os Demoniôus Descem do Norte* (Rio de Janeiro: Franscico Alves, 1988).

6   David Martin, *Tongues of Fire: The Explosion of Protestantism in Latin America* (Cambridge: Basil Blackwell, Inc., 1990).

7   For further work on the positive effects of Pentecostalism upon gender relations see Elizabeth Brusco, 'Colombian Evangelicalism as Strategic Form of Women's Collective Action', *Feminist Issues* (Fall 1986), pp. 3–13; whereas, for work on the negative effects of Pentecostalism upon gender relations in the workforce and in politics see Leslie Gil, *Precarious Dependencies: Gender, Class, and Domestic Service in Bolivia* (New York, NY: Columbia University Press, 1995). Walter J. Hollenger discusses class relations among Pentecostals in his article 'The Pentecostal Elites and the Pentecostal Poor: A Missed Dialogue?' in *Charismatic Christianity as a Global Culture*, ed. Karla Poewe (Columbia, SC: University of South Carolina Press, 1994), pp. 217–233.

8   For further work on globalization see: M. Featherstone, ed., *Global Culture: Nationalism, Globalization and Modernity* (London: Sage Publications, 1990); Anthony Giddens, *Modernity and Self-Identity: Self and Society in the Late Modern Age* (Oxford: Polity Press, 1991); A.D. King , ed., *Culture, Globalization and the World System* (London: Macmillan Education Ltd., 1991); R. Robertson, *Globalization: Social Theory and Global Culture* (London: Sage Publications, 1992).

9   Marcos Witt is a Mexican song writer, singer and producer of a contemporary worship style called *Alabanza Renovada* (Renewed Worship) that has greatly influenced the style of worship in Latin America.

10   Carlos Annacondia and Claudio Freidzon are two Argentine evangelists who have travelled extensively throughout Latin America conducting 'spiritual revival' meetings.

11   Jay O'Brien and William Roseberry, ed., *Golden Ages, Dark Ages: Imagining the Past in Anthropology and History* (Berkeley, CA: University of California Press, 1991), p. 1.

12   Gerald Sider quoted in Jay O'Brien and William Roseberry, *Golden Ages, Dark Ages: Imagining the Past in Anthropology and History* (Berkeley, CA: University of California Press, 1991), p. 9.

13   Terrence Ranger, 'The Local and the Global in Southern African History', in *Conversion to Christianity, Historical and Anthropological Perspectives on a Great Transformation*, ed. Robert W. Hefner (Berkeley, CA: University of California Press, 1993), pp. 65–98.

14   John Comaroff and Jean Comaroff, *Ethnography and the Historical Imagination* (Boulder, CO; Westview Press, 1992), p. 5.

15   *Chicago Tribune*, Sunday, 9 December 1990, Section 1, p.1 quoted in John Comaroff and Jean Comaroff, *Ethnography and the Historical Imagination* (Boulder, CO: Westview Press, 1992), pp. 3–7.

16   Ibid., p. 3.

17   Ibid.

18   Ibid.
19   Karla Poewe, ed., *Charismatic Christianity as a Global Culture* (Columbia, SC: University of South Carolina Press, 1994), p. 22.
20   Comaroff and Comaroff, *Ethnography and the Historical Imagination* , p. 27.
21   Marilyn Strathern, 'The Nice Thing About Culture is that Everyone Has It', in *Shifting Contexts: Transformations in Anthropological Knowledge*, ed. Marilyn Strathern (London: Routledge, 1995).
22   Ibid., pp. 156–157.
23   Ibid., footnote p. 7, p. 171.
24   Ibid., footnote p. 8, p. 172.
25   Ibid., p. 157.
26   Arjun Appadurai, 'Global Ethnoscapes, Notes and Queries for a Transnational Anthropology', in *Recapturing Anthropology: Working in the Present*, ed. Richard G. Fox, (Santa Fe, NM: School of American Research Press, 1991), pp. 191–210.
27   Michael Kearney refers to these non-localized social fields as 'unmarked regions.' His work, *Reconceptualizing the Peasantry: Anthropology in Global Perspective* (Boulder, CO: Westview Press, Inc., 1996), provides an excellent example of studying 'ethnoscapes.'
28   Appadurai, *Global Ethnoscapes, Notes and Queries for a Transnational Anthropology* in *Recapturing Anthropology: Working in the Present*, p. 191.
29   Ibid., p. 196.
30   Strathern, 'The Nice Thing About Culture is that Everyone Has It', p. 169.
31   Raymond Williams, *Marxism and Literature* (Oxford: Oxford University Press, 1977), *Keywords: A Vocabulary of Culture and Society* (Oxford: Oxford University Press, 1983), pp. 126–129.
32   Victor Turner and Edward M. Bruner, *The Anthropology of Experience* (Urbana, IL: University of Illinois Press, 1986).
33   For a concise review of Weber's understanding of religion see Robert W. Hefner, *Conversion to Christianity, Historical and Anthropological Perspectives on a Great Transformation* (Berkeley, CA: University of California Press, 1993), pp. 3–44.
34   See for example Edward B. Tylor, *Primitive Culture* (London: Murray, 1913) and J.G. Frazer, *The Golden Bough* (London: Macmillan, 1922).
35   Hefner, *Conversion to Christianity, Historical and Anthropological Perspectives on a Great Transformation*, p. 6.
36   Mary Douglas, *Natural Symbols: Explorations in Cosmology* (New York, NY: Vintage Books, 1970); E.E. Evans-Pritchard, *Nuer Religion* (Oxford: Oxford University Press, 1956); Godfrey Lienhardt, *Divinity and Experience: The Religion of the Dinka* (Oxford: Clarendon Press, 1961).
37   E.B. Tylor, *Primitive Culture* (London: Murray, 1913); Emile Durkheim, *The Elementary Forms of Religious Life: A Study in Religious Sociology*, trans. J. Swain (Glencoe, NY: Free Press, 1947); Talcot Parsons, introduction to Max Weber, *The Sociology of Religion* (Boston, MA: Beacon Press, 1963), pp. ix–xvii; Bronislaw Malinowski, *Magic, Science, and Religion* (Boston, MA: Beacon Press, 1948); Robert N. Bellah, 'Religious Evolution', in *Beyond Belief: Essays on Religion in a Post-Traditional World* (New York, NY: Harper and Row Publishers, 1970), pp. 20–50.
38   Adam Kuper, *Anthropology Anthropologist: The Modern British School*

(London: Routledge, 1996), p. 160.

39   Karla Poewe has an excellent review of the study of religion in the social sciences in her article 'Rethinking the Relationship of Anthropology to Science and Religion', in *Charismatic Christianity as a Global Culture*, ed. Karla Poewe (Columbia, SC: University of South Carolina Press, 1994), pp. 324–258. I have fashioned much of this review around her conceptualization of two concurrent movements in the anthropological study of religion.

40   Bronislaw Malinowski, *Magic, Science, and Religion and Other Essays* (Boston, MA: Beacon Press, 1948); Clifford Geertz, ' "Internal Conversion" in Contemporary Bali' in *The Interpretation of Cultures*, ed. Clifford Geertz (New York, NY: Basic Books, 1973), pp. 170–189; Claude Levi-Strauss, *Myth and Meaning: Cracking the Code of Culture* (New York, NY: Schocken Books, 1979); Pierre Bourdieu, *Outline of a Theory of Practice* (Cambridge: Cambridge University Press, 1977).

41   Victor Turner , *The Forest of Symbols: Aspects of Ndembu Ritual* (Ithaca, NY: Cornell University Press, 1967); Godfrey Lienhardt, *Divinity and Experience: The Religion of the Dinka* (Oxford: Clarendon Press, 1961); Geoffrey M. White, *Identity through History: Living Stories in a Solomon Islands Society* (Cambridge: Cambridge University Press, 1991).

42   Maurice Leenhardt, *Do Kamo: Person and Myth in the Melanesian World*, trans. Basia Miller Gulati (Chicago, IL: University of Chicago Press, 1979).

43   Hefner, *Conversion to Christianity, Historical and Anthropological Perspectives on a Great Transformation*, p. 17.

44   David K. Jordon, 'The Glyphomancy Factor: Observations on Chinese Conversion' in *Conversion to Christianity, Historical and Anthropological Perspectives on a Great Transformation*, ed. Robert W. Hefner (Berkeley, CA: University of California Press, 1993), pp. 285–303.

45   William Merrill, 'Conversion and Colonialism in Northern Mexico: The Tarahumara Response to the Jesuit Mission Program' in *Conversion to Christianity, Historical and Anthropological Perspectives on a Great Transformation*, ed. Robert W. Hefner (Berkeley, CA: University of California Press, 1993), pp. 129–163; Charles F. Keyes, 'Why the Thai are Not Christians: Buddhist and Christian Conversion in Thailand' in *Conversion to Christianity, Historical and Anthropological Perspectives on a Great Transformation*, ed. Robert W. Hefner (Berkeley, CA: University of California Press, 1993), pp. 259–283.

46   Poewe, *Rethinking the Relationship of Anthropology to Science and Religion*, p. 237.

47   Ibid.

48   Jean-Daniel Plüss, 'Azusa and Other Myths: The Long and Winding Road from Experiences to Stated Belief and Back Again' *PNEUMA: The Journal of the Society for Pentecostal Studies* 15 (Fall 1993), pp. 189–201.

49   Edward M. Bruner, Introduction to Victor Turner and Edward M. Bruner, eds., *The Anthropology of Experience* (Urbana, IL: University of Illinois Press, 1986).

50   Ibid., p. 4.

51   Ibid.

52   James W. Fernandez, 'The Argument of Images and the Experiences of Returning to the Whole', in Victor Turner and Edward M. Bruner, ed., *The Anthropology of Experience* (Urbana, IL: University of Illinois Press, 1986),

pp. 159–187.

53   Experience as images and impression is an important foundation to Gerard
     Roelofs and Karla Poewe's understanding of metonymy in Pentecostal experi-
     ence in 'Charismatic Christian Thought: Experience, Metonymy, and Routin-
     ization', and 'Rethinking the Relationship of Anthropology to Science and
     Religion', respectively.

54   Bruner, p. 5.

55   Ibid.

56   Ibid., p. 7.

57   Edward Bruner, Introduction to Victor Turner and Edward M. Bruner, ed, *The
     Anthropology of Experience* (Urbana, IL: University of Illinois Press, 1986), p.
     6, quoting Wilhelm Dilthey, Introduction to H.P. Rickman, ed., *Dilthey:
     Selected Writings* (Cambridge: Cambridge University Press, 1976), p. 195.

58   Jay O'Brien and William Roseberry, Introduction to Jay O'Brien and William
     Roseberry, ed., *Golden Ages, Dark Ages: Imagining the Past in Anthropology
     and History* (Berkeley, CA: University of California Press, 1991), pp.
     126–138.

59   Herman Rebel 'Cultural Hegemony and Class Experience: A Critical Reading
     of Recent Ethnological-Historical Approaches', *American Ethnologist* 16
     (1989), p. 123, quoted in O'Brien and Roseberry, ed., *Golden Ages, Dark
     Ages: Imagining the Past in Anthropology and History*, p. 8.

60   Hefner, p. 24.

61   Ibid., p. 25.

62   Williams, *Marxism and Literature* and *Keywords*, p. 128

63   I am borrowing the phrase 'crossroads of knowledge' from Micaela Di-
     Leonardo' introduction in *Gender at the Crossroads of Knowledge: Feminist
     Anthropology in the Postmodern Era* (Berkeley, CA: University of California
     Press, 1991), pp. 1–48. I use the phrase, 'crossroads of knowledge' much like
     DiLeonardo to indicate a crisis of theories and domains of inquiry confronting
     social analysis. But, I am referring to the literal intersection of Pentecostal
     experiences as sets of knowledge.

Chapter Thirteen

Pentecostals, Globalization, and Postmodern Hermeneutics: Implications for the Politics of Scriptural Interpretation

Gerald T. Sheppard

The complex subject of this essay will be treated in two main parts. In the first part, I will sketch at a high level of generality the development of postmodern theory in the humanities since the 1960s. In the second part, I will try to counter the detached impersonal tone of this topic by offering something typically Pentecostal: three 'testimonies'. My hope there is to illustrate by a few cross-sections from a single life some hint of what is at stake for Pentecostals in the dense topic of post-modern hermeneutics.

In general, on this theme of postmodern hermeneutics, Pentecostals will be treated as belonging to a diverse variety of Christian groups that are socio-historically more 'submodern', than premodern, anti-modern, or postmodern. Among other strengths, Pentecostals can nurture a sophisticated understanding of cultural, racial, and religious differences at the lower as well as the upper strata of society. A profound Christian experience, freed somewhat from a fixation with modernity, may allow Pentecostals to perceive more profoundly than some others the larger intellectual challenge to reinterpret Christianity constructively through its premodern, modern, and postmodern transformations. Pentecostals can be promodern without being modernists, find positive links with premodern Christians without being 'precritical', and see afresh the limits of modern criticism without uncritically joining self-labelled 'postmodernists' who pander to a nihilism based too one-sidedly on its love-hate relationship with modernity. So, for example, Pentecostals may be inclined to gain far more insight from modern proverbs in the 'wisdom' of secularity than from the equally modern and pious prophecies of the Christian Right. Once Pentecostals learn that they are not simply a movement which arrived 'suddenly from heaven', as an early history of Pentecostals claimed, they can conjoin with a larger body of ecumenical Christians who must rewrite the history of Christianity from the bottom up, reopen the ancient Christian quest for the 'literal sense' of Scripture, and seek a renewed and robust confessional theology, one that takes as seriously the real presence of the Holy Spirit in history as it does the history of institutions.[1]

THE DEVELOPMENT OF POSTMODERN THEORY IN THE HUMANITIES SINCE THE 1960S

Most 'postmodern' theories of hermeneutics build upon radical criticisms of modernity that arose in the social, political, and intellectual unrest of the 1960s, though these criticisms do not lack earlier precedents. In the last half of the nineteenth-century and in the opening decades of the twentieth, older modern theory retained its ascendancy only by undergoing thoroughgoing modifications by theorists, such as Freud (1886–1939), Nietzsche (1844–1900), and Marx (1818–1883).[2] These late modern 'fathers of suspicion' rejected many earlier modern assumptions, including for example the nineteenth-century, Victorian literary ideal of 'serious modern realism' as found in the novels of Thomas Carlyle, Charles Dickens, William Thackary, Lord Macaulay, Charlotte Brontë, and Benjamin Disraeli.[3] In his lectures of 1894–1895, Frederic Harrison, a prominent literary interpreter of Victorian literature opines, 'For good or for evil, our literature is now absorbed in the urgent social problem and is become but an instrument in the vast field of Sociology, – the science of Society.'[4] Harrison can no longer name a single contemporary English novelist 'of accepted fame', comparing the present intellectual disequalibrium to circumstances attending the earlier transition from the Post-Reformation Classical Period to the Modern Age.

> We are like men under the glamour of some great change impending. The spell of a new order holds us undecided and expectant. There is something in the air, and that something is a vague and indescribable sense that a new time is coming. Men felt it in France, and indeed all over Europe, from 1780 until 1790. It was an uncertain and rather pleasing state of expectancy. It did not check activity, nor enjoyment, nor science. But it diverted the profounder minds from higher forms of imaginative work.[5]

Harrison's words should forewarn us about the difficulty we, too, may have in assessing contemporary changes, since by looking back we now see only a major adjustment in Harrison's time within the Modern Age and not a shift befitting the analogy with the rise of new epoch. Yet, as Harrison began to realize, late modern criticisms would seek to ground the older modern project less in realistic narratives or metaphysics and more in social-scientific or psychological analysis of the deeper structures of conflict, such as the interplay between the ego, the id and the superego, class struggle, or the unconscious will to power.

By the 1960s even the late modern 'fathers of suspicion' had themselves become suspect. Events in very different historical settings and from unrelated points of view began to converge in support of a general critique of late modern perspectives across the spectrum of the humanities. For instance, the failure of the Communist Party to support the student revolts of 1968 in France led many intellectuals to question the objective nature of Marxist economic materialism. Feminists pointed to conspicuous signs of Freud's own misogyny in his evaluation of unconscious elements in dreams, in his psychological theories based on gender differences, and in his preoccupation with the Oedipal Complex. Though Nietzsche's incisive critique of 'virtues' anticipates post-modern deconstruction, his own version of nihilism and the will to power stood in the shadows of its Nazi appropriation by philosophers as noteworthy as Martin Heidegger. For many, this evidence led to profound questions about modern perception itself, rather than to hope that it might be simply refined, augmented, or better applied.

On this basis, a number of theorists began to propose that the

Modern Age had somehow played itself out. They often tried to express this 'feeling' with an admixture of concrete judgements regarding the present and wide-eyed poetic speculation about the future. So, John Lukas wrote in 1970, with blunt confidence, 'Our civilization is in ruins because our ideas about civilizations are in ruins.' But when he turns to the future, his language suddenly becomes laden with metaphors,

> The outlines of things are blurred, and we have grown accustomed to the curious coexistence of winter and summer, of night and day. We experience little physical suffering and little spiritual joy. The contrast between illness and health, adversity and happiness is less striking. We have progressed from child's life to a state of the world in which we are all adolescents now. And this painful mental state of adolescence (a word whose ritual origin from Latin contains elements of pain) marks our condition half a thousand years after the waning of the Middle Ages, at the time of the passing of the Modern Age.[6]

A few years earlier Michel Foucault had, likewise, stated in words nearly oracular,

> [T]he impression of fulfillment and of end, the muffled feeling that carries and animates our thought, and perhaps lulls it to sleep with the facility of its promise... and makes us believe that something new is about to begin, something that we glimpse only as a thin line of light low on the horizon—that feeling and impression are perhaps not ill founded.[7]

In the decades since 1970, scholars have openly debated whether the most recent theories simply reflect modifications in our late modern understanding or if they herald a genuine, pervasive, epochal shift in our 'form of knowing' (Foucault). If we think this last assessment is more likely, as I do, then we still must ask whether we are at the present moment in a period of transition or have already crossed over into an as yet ill-defined Postmodern Age. After a remarkably penetrating assessment of postmodern proposals, Steven Best and Douglas Kellner conjectured in 1991,

> At this point, it seems premature to claim that we are fully in a new postmodern scene, though one might see postmodern culture and society as new emergent tendencies which require a new theoretical and political response and thus a reconstruction of social theory....We may be living within a borderline or traditional space between the modern and the postmodern.[8]

By speaking of the postmodern as 'emergent', Best and Kellner wisely allow for the uneven impact of any epochal shift on levels of social and historical self-consciousness. They agree that these new 'tendencies' exceed the older modern paradigm and will require us to find new theoretical, political, and, I would add, theological responses.

Since the postmodern prognosis assumes an epistemic change in how we view the world, a systemic shift in the history of human consciousness, then a definition of 'postmodern' may be premature, as is implicit in the inadequate label itself. Certainly, the term 'postmodern' may mislead us into thinking we can ignore the fruits of modern criticism or into understanding it only as a reaction to modernity itself rather than as a challenge for us to renegotiate afresh our relationship to the premodern. If, for instance, we consider the continued value of modern literary theory for postmodern proposals, we see that the newer criticisms can be 'deconstructive' of modern theory without being merely destructive or uncritically dismissive. For example, much remains valuable in Hans-Georg Gadamer's brilliant pursuit of 'the hermeneutic universalism'. While Gadamer accepted the negative results of Kant's *Critique of Pure Reason*, he also sought, as had Kant, another foundation within the practical reason of modern hermeneutics which 'has nothing to do with any metaphysical conclusion'.[9] In a late modern mode, Gadamer conjoins Schleiermacher's earlier modern effort to derive from the arts and human sciences a singular 'general hermeneutic' for literature. By granting a modern notion of 'history', Gadamer situates the hermeneutical problem of literary interpretation at the intersection of two 'historical horizons', that of the text and that of the reader. If in a postmodern mode we now raise elemental questions about the historical dimension of texts, Gadamer's insights will, nonetheless, still prove helpful in many respects, especially his attempt to understand the 'effective history' of textual interpretation over the centuries. His proposal will probably be far more persistently useful than, by comparison, the strategies of late modern structuralists.

Similarly, late modern literary criticism faces formidable challenges by scholars such as Jacques Derrida. Derrida 'decentres' or 'deconstructs' each interpreter's proposed 'centred structure' of a text by exposing the circular logic required to overcome the semantic 'gaps' or 'aporia' characteristic of any 'text'. The semantic 'gaps' of any text leave room for an almost infinite number of possible structures. Each structure is justified, to some degree, only by the reader's own sleight of hand and cannot by reason alone sustain a modern theory of universals that requires our consent, such as metaexegetical theories of history, author's intent, reference, deep structure, meaning as a presence in the text, or any other intrinsic order to linguistic elements indicative of a text's form and content.[10] Postmodern critics generally repudiate all modern assumptions about universal ideas of history, foundationalist theories of reference, 'dualistic' modes of description, claims to find the presence of a definitive surface or deep structure within a text (in literary, anthropological, or any other mode of interpretation), metaphysical arguments in support of a theory of transcendence, or essentialist semantic theories based on the singularity of an author or a subject matter. Against structuralist and phenomenological approaches, there is no singular 'centre' or 'presence' in a text as something genetic and indispensible to its proper interpretation. Therefore, there remains no neutral, innocent, nor objective stance from which we can describe the proper interpretation of 'texts' in and of themselves. How interpretation is anything more than 'free play' remains a major point of contention. Yet, Derrida, George Poulet, and many others certainly allow for the practical necessity of choosing some 'centre' in any specific reading, even if it constitutes only a 'function' of a text rather than the only proper choice.[11] In my own words, we might put this matter in economic terms — if I can do all things with texts, what things are profitable? What centred 'text' do I want to interpret among the textual possibilities of any text and why?

Recent studies in 'semiotics' build on Ferdinand de Saussure distinction of 'sign', 'signified', and 'signifier' to demystify our understanding of all texts and human actions as 'signs'.[12] On the one hand, images on television or in simulations on the screen can be hyperreal, creating a world more compelling and as complex as historical life in the older modern sense. 'Signs' may have no external referent or the referential capacity of signs may seem entirely secondary to some other dominant intertextuality to which they also belong. Hence, the vision of 'reality' itself, as a concrescence of signs, may seem mostly dependent on the semiotic game we choose to play with them, without anything to commend our judgement beyond certain qualities of the sign. From the perspective of globalization, we may ask if the world has not already been divided by wealthy nations between those who have the privilege to choose among many games and those for whom a terrible game have already been chosen, as their only economic, moral, and political option? On the other hand, apart from a loss of confidence in modern objective theories of reference, we may suspect that signs conventionally have their own subtle codes for the exchange of power? These codes may arise as a byproduct of an even more complex socio-biology, with its own deterministic and evolutionary dimensions, pertinent to any given epoch. Can those who master these codes use images to confine, define, manipulate, reward, and punish us? The problem, then, becomes one of both who can take advantage of the socially constructed, dominant function of signs, and of how we can find lines of escape within these games or push the games to their limits in order to change them entirely? For example, the commercialization of the Internet, as a projector of images and seductive virtual realities, gives us only a blink in the direction of its global economic and political power. Within this semiotic milieu, how can a desire for freedom and liberation find its voice in response to the hyperreality, commercialization, and costly escapism of a postmodern world of images?

At a minimum, many if not the majority of scholars in 'the First World' [itself an admittedly ill-chosen modern term] agree that the last three decades present us with a period of messy, divergent hermeneutical disequalibrium, perhaps symptomatic of the dawn of a Postmodern Age. If we speak in such an audacious manner about the future, we cannot assume that 'better' conditions lie ahead of us, our perception of them may be only *different*. One obvious sign of our uncertainty about the future occurs in the term 'postmodern' itself. In conventional English usage, 'post' is an ambiguous prefix, capable of signifying a position *ahead* in time or *behind* in space ('postaxial'). What this term states unequivocally is only what it situates as no longer dominant, namely, the 'modern'. Furthermore, Best and Kellner conclude, '[N]o postmodern theory has formulated an adequate political response to the degraded contemporary conditions they describe.'[13] Conversely, many scholars rightly fear that a naive postmodern criticism, eschewing the task of mediating older positions within modernity, has allowed for the reemergence of the most strident voices of older modern fundamentalisms – religious and otherwise – racisms, sexisms, and even Fascist options, which the best of modern criticism had successfully called into question. As these voices gain temporary credibility in 'First World' nations who have disproportionate advantages of wealth and formal education, then their disciples will through Christian 'missions' and non-Christian exploitation undoubtedly prey upon other economically more vulnerable nations and socially marginalized people wherever they may be.

A major reason constructive postmodern proposals have been slow in appearing is precisely that they depend for their integrity on development and shareability of a newer variety of 'regional' hermeneutics spawned since the 1960s. Besides the fresh reformulation we see today in matters of theory in all the older disciplines of the academy, we see new resources globally in work coming from the Third World, from feminism in rich variety (including, for example, Afro-American 'womanist' literature), from socially marginalized racial communities, from sub-modern groups (such as Pentecostals where entirely new self-descriptions have appeared only in the last two decades), from sexual minorities, and so forth. These regional expressions must have time enough to gather fresh data and to design an analysis that does justice to that data so that they themselves can move into the public arena for more than merely polemic reasons. Then, these different groups can connect their work and strategies of analysis with a wider public discourse, establishing some 'hegemony' with other groups, so that society is not just a 'heteronomous ensemble of isolated practices'.[14] As an example of such hegemonies, we might recall Martin Luther King's courageous linking of his own movement against racism to the anti-Vietnam War movement or how some First World, Anglo-feminists have conjoined anti-racist or other liberationist movements, or even the choice Pentecostals make between publicly joining forces with conservative Anglo-evangelicals and the Republican Party or with Afro-American churches and their predominance alliance with the Democratic Party or with diverse Hispanic church communities whose political associations far exceed these boundaries and include other alternatives such as democratic socialism. A genuinely global postmodern hermeneutical theory will become possible only when hegemonies among these and other groups can generate a wide ranging public discourse. In anticipation of that possibility, we have already begun to hear, however prematurely, of postmodern philosophical analysis, postmodern novels and literary theory, postmodern architecture, postmodern theatre, postmodern art, postmodern music, even postmodern furniture, and, certainly, various proposals on a 'postmodern use of the Bible'.[15]

THREE 'TESTIMONIES'

In terms of postmodern theory, the following testimonies will self-consciously transgress the proper limitations of a modern 'historical' account, without intentionally changing 'facts' in so far as they coincide with a modern historical mode of understanding. In terms of Christian theology, 'testimonies' are admittedly an exercise in the sharing of faith with one's sisters and brothers, while seeking, at the same time, to say back to God what God already knows. Just as the Bible assumes prayer addressed to God is usually meant to be over-heard, with criticism and discernment, by one's sisters and brothers, a testimony addressed to one's sisters and brothers is also meant to be overheard by God.[16] Each is a learned as well as a visceral expression, equally indebted at its best both to the worldly wisdom (what Joseph Hall in the seventeenth-century called 'Solomon's Divine Arts' of 'politics, economics, and ethics') and to the Gospel of Jesus Christ that will seem like 'folly' to the world. We, therefore, agree fully with Feuerbach that 'all theology is anthropology', when seen, in the words of Paul Lehmann, 'as a reflex of Christology'.[17] Any transcendental or universal claim made by a testimony, therefore, derives not from the efficacy of practical reason, but solely from the real subject matter to which it points, God's own revelation of humanity in this specifically economic and political sense.

Most of us raised in Pentecostal churches know well the uses and abuses, the profundity and the folly, of publicly stated 'testimonies', deriving from older worship traditions as diverse as slave religion and Methodist-Holiness practices. With modernization and a routinization of charisma, many such 'marginal rituals' (including also foot-washing, the ring shout, the holy dance, group singing 'in the Spirit', and the Jericho march, as just a few examples) have gradually disap-peared. 'Testimonies' from the congregation usually belong to a par-ticular place in the worship service and since anyone could testify at that particular time, they entailed some risk. I realize they can be senti-mentally pious, full of false promises of deliverance, subtly manipula-tive, and self-serving. While I would want to defend the importance of marginal rituals, beyond baptism and the Eucharist ('communion' among most Pentecostals), to mark a variety of transformations and moments of hope within any church, my aim here is not to presume what forms they may need to take. Even in Pentecostal churches, the testimony time has often been replaced with 'announcements' whereby laypeople inadvertently testify as they promote some church activity, or by the 'coffee hour', where people accidentally share their faith. This theological idea of testimony (or its synonym, 'witness') was inherited by Christians from the Jewish reception of God's revelation (Deut. 29:28–29) by means of inspired human testimonies to the Torah (e.g., Deut. 31:26; 32:46; Jos. 24:26–27) to which we find the proper response, 'We are witnesses' (Jos. 24:22), taken up in the words of the risen Lord, 'You shall be my witnesses' (Acts 1:8; cf. Luke 24:48; John 24:24–25). From its non-theological origins in the courts, in the report of spies, in the informal appeals to what has really happened in daily life as well as in formal attestation to contracts, covenants, and wills, we are reminded, as Jews have always known, that a promising testimony deserves critical discernment rather than uncritical acceptance. For that reason, I have added to each of the following testimonies a brief comment about interpretive criticism of it, to some degree a testimony upon a testimony, as a propadeutic along those lines.

Each of the following three testimonies come from my experiences in New York City as an Assistant Professor of Old Testament at Union Theological Seminary between 1976 and 1985 because I experienced there one of the richest confluences of cross-cultural and racial differences as they touch on my identity as a Christian.

TESTIMONY 1: 'WE FEEL LIKE WE KNOW YOU NOW.'

With my doctoral dissertation from Yale University in hand, I searched for a full-time teaching position. Years earlier I had been ordained as a minister in the Assemblies of God, while I worked as a youth minister and was finishing my M.Div. at Fuller Theological Seminary. At Fuller, a beloved professor, William Sanford LaSor, advised me repeatedly to change my ordination to Presbyterian so I might be able to teach someday at an 'evangelical' seminary at a time when we did not know of any Pentecostal seminaries in the United States. During my doctoral work at Yale, a mentor again told me to switch denominations; otherwise, 'no one will understand you'.

In 1976 I became a candidate for a position at Union Theological Seminary in New York City. After a long day of interviews about the Bible, tradition history, and theology, I remember my sense of awe when I sat down with Raymond Brown, James Cone, and others in the oak-lined faculty dining room. I thought of others who had probably sat around this same table, including Reinhold Niebuhr, Paul Tillich, and Dietrich Bonhoeffer. Donald Shriver, the new president of Union, said, 'Jerry, we feel like we know you now. By the way, what denomination are you?' Having established some rapport, I stated bluntly, with a smile, 'I am a Pentecostal.' I watched the startled looks, Shriver's mouth dropped open in amazement. Just before anyone could recover, I added, 'In fact, I am an ordained Assemblies of God minister.' Pushing his chair back from the table in surprise, Shriver asked, 'Jerry, tell us, what does this mean?' The perfect question for a Pentecostal, right out of Acts 2:12!

I said, 'We Pentecostals believe that God demands that you pray well. If in your effort to meet God's demands, you ever find yourself reduced to silence, or moaning, or groaning, or to some form of inarticulateness through which you hope in faith that the Holy Spirit prays back to God the prayers God demands, then you know what it means for me to be a Pentecostal.' They seemed satisfied enough and nothing more was said about it in my interviews.

Some Critical Discernment of Testimony 1

In my own way, I tried to be faithful to my Pentecostal heritage by putting the subject of 'glossolalia' in a language that any Christian ought to value. But did I do justice to Pentecostal tradition? Certainly not. The trans-racial, trans-cultural understanding of William Seymour at Azusa Street deserved better representation in my comments. I could have recalled details about Perpetua, Tertullian, and Cyprian centuries ago or could have commented on the significance of Pentecostal-like movements in Christianity across the centuries of what Donald Gelpi has aptly called 'a history of divisive enthusiasm'.[18] I could admit my suspicion that glossolalia, as the modern linguistic study by William Samarin has shown, is mostly a learned liturgical metalanguage rather than speaking a foreign language without the benefits of study, but that observation alone would not decide its relation to the miraculous.[19] My comment could not do justice to the prolific new studies on the roots of Pentecostals in Afro-American churches, in the Holiness movement, in slave religion, or within an equally richly diverse set of Hispanic cultures, besides the robust Korean and other cultural representations. I know that glossolalia plays a different and often minor role in Afro-American churches compared with Anglo-Pentecostal churches. Today I could even discuss the Blumhardts as 'socialist' Pentecostals who influenced Karl Barth and comment on the political and theological implications of glossolalia, thanks to the recent work of Frank Macchia.[20] My reply to Don Shriver at Union Seminary only scratched the surface, and was at best just a scratch. It erred too glibly on the side of piety, and I confess my failure.

What has happened to Pentecostal identity since the decline of the Modern Age? One important element is that Pentecostals from their beginnings in this century self-identified as a 'movement' that testified specifically against the 'formalism' and 'denominationalism' of other Christian Protestants. Now we have Pentecostal organizations that participate fully as denominations among others. Complicating the matter further, we have seen since the 1960s what I would now call 'postmodern' movements of the Jesus People and the Charismatic Renewal that likewise crossed both denominational lines and social strata. Are such charismatics that we now meet across the same table at any ecumenical dialogue 'real' Pentecostals, even though they lack membership in 'classical Pentecostal' denominations? If not, then we, as Pentecostals, need to become much more articulate about what distinguishes us from others. Particularly for Anglo-Pentecostals, I fear that we have been seduced by the promise of social validation from older modern conservative evangelical institutions, so that we now want to identify only with those charismatics who are politically conservative evangelicals and dismiss the rest as 'liberal'. In a postmodern situation, those distinctions will no longer suffice. By focusing instead on the interracial hope signaled in the Azusa Street revival, or on the Holiness traditions, or on an interracial political eschatology like that of C.H. Mason, our priorities and choices would look remarkably different.[21]

Apart from the sensational occurrence of prophecy and glossolalia, Pentecostals have been well aware of their successes among the lower classes and marginalized races. As a 'submodern' group in the modern period, we did not feel at home in the modern world; we were either ignored by the modern 'liberals' as uneducated and culturally vacuous or condemned by modern 'fundamentalists' for emotionalism and doctrinal ignorance. Our responses to our own social gains and access to education have, not surprisingly, been quite varied. Some of us found in postmodern liberation theology and canonical or literary approaches to Scripture an alternative way to move beyond the older modern theological boundaries, left and right. Yet, we are painfully aware that we remain today sharply divided along racial lines. The dismantling of the Pentecostal Fellowship of North America, founded partly on a legacy of racism and fundamentalism by Anglo-Pentecostals in association with the National Association of Evangelicals, is one recent positive response. Yet, in many other respects we have failed to honor the positive dimensions of race and class that belong to our Pentecostal heritage. On the one hand, Anglo-Pentecostals from Jimmy Swaggart to Jim Bakker have, at least in North American 'mainstream' culture, become household names conveying a sad image of persons who naively and comically imitate their fantasies of what the upper classes enjoy. On the other hand, we are equally foolish if we romanticize poverty, the atrocities of racial prejudice, the lack of access to economic resources and formal education.

In the here and now, what is a 'Pentecostal?' Generalizations are dangerous because groups labeled 'Pentecostal' differ so substantially among other Protestants within their specifically Afro-American, Asian (with significant differences between Korean, Thai, Chinese, and others), Hispanic (with significant cultural differences between Cubans, Puerto Ricans, Costa Ricans, and so forth), and Anglo-American settings. Perhaps even the claim in my testimony, 'I am a Pentecostal', violates the older Pentecostal self-understanding of a Christian movement which aimed to call all churches to a restoration of their Apostolic faith, to a re-formation of their holiness as a prophetic counter-cultural stamp, and to a transformation of lives by the power and guidance of the Holy Spirit in our midst. Perhaps I would have been more true to my upbringing and more properly scandalous had I identified myself at Union as a 'Spirit-filled Christian', to use older, more popular Pentecostal language. Of course, the original idea was not to deny that every Christian had been baptized *by the Holy Spirit* 'in Christ', but to endeavor to express the hope that we might also be a living vessel that had been filled to overflowing with the Holy Spirit *by Jesus Christ* in a way that challenged the present order of things. Hence, any Christian who joined that exercise of faith-in-action becomes 'Pentecostal'. It is, thus, far more a political-spiritual matter, than a matter of denominational affiliation.

TESTIMONY 2: 'AM I A MISSIONARY?'

During my first year as an Assistant Professor at Union, I remember vividly an event in May, 1977. James Forbes, an Afro-American Pentecostal, had been hired that same academic year to teach homiletics. At his suggestion, I was invited to preach a commencement address at a Bible Institute connected with a major Afro-American Pentecostal church pastored by Jesse Winley in Harlem. I recall walking through the rotunda of Union, with my brand new doctoral academic gown draped over my arm and with a briefcase in my other hand. Malcolm Warford, a junior administrator at that time and now a seminary president, accidentally saw me and asked, 'Where are you going?' I enjoyed how odd my answer might sound to him, 'Mac, I am going to preach the commencement address at the unaccredited Bible Institute of The Soul Saving Station for Every Nation.' 'Where is that?' he asked. 'Oh, it's about five blocks northeast of here up on 125th Street.' He smiled with approval and said, 'You must have a wonderful ministry with those people.' I walked to the church and preached the commencement address. Afterwards, a long line of people warmly greeted me. One woman, a little overweight, hugged and nearly suffocated me with her affection, then asked, 'Brother Sheppard, tell me now, where do you teach?' I responded, 'I teach at Union Theological Seminary?' She added, 'Where's that?' I told her while pointing in the direction of the seminary, 'It's about five blocks south of here on Broadway.' She assured me, 'You must have a wonderful ministry with those people.'

Some Critical Discernment of Testimony 2

From the perspective of an administrator and a friend at Union Theological Seminary, I was representing the seminary in ministering to an Afro-American Church, and from the perspective of this Pentecostal Church I had been accepted as a 'brother' enough so that this dear woman could view me as her representative to Union Seminary. The five blocks that separated those two institutions could have been ten thousand miles in terms of what each of these two people knew about the other. Many at Union Seminary probably saw me as able to bring a 'critical' understanding of the Bible to such 'pre-critical' or 'biblicist' or, even mislabeled, 'fundamentalist' churches. The members of the Soul Saving Station could see me as a 'sanctified' or 'Spirit-filled' missionary to a 'non-Pentecostal', 'unspiritual', 'unsanctified', and perhaps even 'God forsaken' seminary. Pastor Jesse Winley and the congregation at the Soul Saving Station were actually not just concerned about the quality of their worship services, but also ran a drug rehabilitation program, a day care, a Bible Institute, and various other socially uplifting programs that would rival those of Riverside Church next to Union Seminary.[22] While some members of Riverside Church and many students at Union would assume the Soul Saving Station only emphasizes piety, I suspect members of the Soul Saving Station might have underestimated the piety of most of my students at Union.

Serious hermeneutical misunderstandings on both sides left me wondering, 'Whose missionary am I?' Maybe I am an unworthy missionary to both. When I think of positive and negative connotations of 'missionaries', I realize that I might do more harm than good to each; God's grace and hidden providence might be my only sure hope of success. I would prefer to be seen as a liberator, thanks to the Gospel, to both sides. Furthermore, how accurately can I describe the one community to the other so that they can, in some way, see themselves working together as sisters and brothers in Christ? Postmodern hermeneutics ought to make that bridge easier and a necessary one to cross from the side of the seminary, if only for its own intellectual integrity.

My testimony is admittedly too self-serving, pretending more agility at either place than I really felt I had managed. It is true that by retaining my own minority consciousness, I often have felt like a missionary at any place where I have taught, today at an epicenter of Canadian culture and politics, Emmanuel College of the United Church of Canada. This circumstance of feeling like a missionary in the most privileged of places reminds me of a serious conversation I had many years ago with an Assemblies of God missionary who encouraged me as a student at Bethany Bible College to become a missionary to France. Regarding such possibilities, a major concern raised in ecumenical dialogues has been the charge that Pentecostals proselytize, based on the assumption that we steal 'sheep' (a telling term itself) from other denominations. However, Samuel Solivan, who teaches at Andover Newton Theological Seminary, has rightfully called attention to what might be called the proselytizing by other denominations of some of the most talented young people from Pentecostal churches when they attend a seminary or doctoral program. Solivan points to Puerto Rican seminary students at Union Theological Seminary in New York City who find themselves seduced by financial support from major Protestant denominations at precisely the time they are viewed with suspicion by their home churches. They may end up pastoring small, struggling, inner-city Presbyterian or Methodist churches in Hispanic neighborhoods where large Hispanic Pentecostal churches are thriving. Yet, they are treated as second-class citizens in their new denominational affiliations. This identity crisis has led at times to depression and even to suicide. They become prophets without honor in any country.

What I find most encouraging by some Anglo-Pentecostal missionaries in Latin America are evangelistic efforts accompanying programs invested in social development along with strong national leadership and participation. Latin America ChildCare seems to me to be just such an example. In the United States, a Pentecostal effort like Teen Challenge that works with drug addicts and people in the inner-cities comes closer to what is often a requirement of Afro-American or Hispanic Pentecostal churches within a situation that demands a similar response on a daily basis. Here, however, we face a major political problem. Will Pentecostals that win new educational and economic opportunities be able to retain a minority conscious-ness, a counter-cultural suspicion, a street wisdom that will allow them the imagination to avoid the older modern choices of 'liberal' and 'conservative?' Can we find enough acceptance based on a shared spiritual faith to allow for the necessary disagreements we must have with each other about what missionaries ought to do? Can we be liber-ationist without being merely liberals, and can we be preservers of indigenous culture and tradition without being uncritical conserva-tives? May God give us grace in our participation in such ventures, courage to pursue them despite the mistakes we will all make, and the wisdom to prepare carefully so we might be more a sign of hope rather than of triumphalism and arrogance.

TESTIMONY 3: 'I HAVE SINNED.'

Several years ago in New York City, I dropped my ordination in the Assemblies of God to become an elder in the Church of God in Christ (Memphis, Tennessee). This shift was not a noble one, since these Afro-American Pentecostal churches in New York City had much more to contribute to this eccentric academic than I could ever give back to them. Bishop Ithiel Clemmons made the transition easy and sharing the platform with two other elders, Alonso Johnson and David Daniels, both brilliant Afro-American doctoral students, made this experience extraordinary. As part of my own contribution, I taught courses in Bible at the O. M. Kelly Bible Institute at Clemmons' church in South Brooklyn. Likewise, I made some even more awk-ward efforts to connect with the impressive Hispanic Pentecostals in New York City, including 'Juan 3:16' in the Bronx with its huge con-gregation and exhilarating tambourine band. I thank God for the open-ness, generosity, and forgiveness of these communities as I have tried to participate in some measure with them on their own terms.

But my testimony here mostly concerns something I discerned in listening to two Pentecostal sermons. We have been taught, at least in theory, that we must judge the prophets, but whether or not preaching seems especially 'anointed' or prophetic, it deserves as much discernment as any other congregational 'prophecy' or 'interpretation of tongues'. Hence, we must be critical rather than passively accepting of what we hear from a pulpit. Along these lines, I remember what might be called a preaching contest at Clemmons' church. Three women each delivered three minute sermons one after the other, though of course we did not actually vote on one over the other except in our hearts. None of these women had been to seminary or sat in my M.Div. subsections on historical criticism. Yet, their sermons were not 'uncritical' in how they used the Bible. They were so impressive that I fantasized having some of my best M.Div. students to whom I could turn and say, 'Now, you're next!'

Of course, not every sermon I hear in Afro-American Pentecostal churches avoids the familiar pitfalls, but I will never forget one sermon that Bishop Ithiel Clemmons preached on the anointing of Saul to be king. After recalling the complexity of the people's desire for a king, Clemmons came to that scene when all the people gathered together at Mizpah for Saul's anointing as king of Israel (1 Sam. 10:20–27). On this auspicious moment, the prophet Samuel takes the center stage in order to introduce the person God has chosen for their king, but Saul himself has suddenly disappeared. What the servants discover is that 'he has hidden himself among the baggage' (v. 22). So, Clemmons described in detail the particularities of Saul's unique situation and not uncritically: he avoided making naive historical references, even if he did not show much interest in the prebiblical traditions (a preoccupation of modern scholars) behind the scriptural account. Then, he raised a question about whether we on such occasions might not be found 'hidden among the baggage'. In a powerful oscillation between sermonic words and counterpoint by the musicians, Clemmons played out the permutations of our own responses to the question, 'what baggage have you chosen to hide behind?' The baggage might be prejudice, shame for our sins, false humility, spiritual pride, fear of the social system, lack of courage, irresponsibility, or unwillingness to join with others to seek the renewal of this church and this proud and degraded city. Ever since that sermon, I often think of myself as Saul, an over privileged and not very faithful leader in ancient Israel, summoned by God to perform a service the people ought not to have even desired. Worse than that, I am often found 'hiding among the baggage' (including my own prejudices, my insecurity, and my Pentecostalism) when God calls upon me to be of service. It challenges me to confession, to rejoice not in the failure of others, and to seek to live by God's grace and mercy rather than my own machinations.

By contrast, I remember another Pentecostal sermon, one by Jimmy Swaggart who represented for me, I should confess, the worst combination of narrow-minded fundamentalist dogmatism and superspiritual Pentecostalism. When Swaggart was caught with a prostitute by a minister whom he had self-righteously condemned earlier, he repented on national television with the words: 'I have sinned.' I do not want to underestimate the sincerity of his confession, nor do I feel morally superior to him. What disappointed me was not his words, which I respect, but his use of the biblical account of King David. Swaggart had opportunely chosen a phrase, 'I have sinned', in the biblical presentation of David's response after his killing Uriah and his taking of Bathsheba for his wife was exposed by the prophet Nathan. What makes these words significant intertextually is their occurrence both in the narrative of 1 Samuel 12 (cf. v. 13) and in the penitential Psalm 51 (cf. v. 4), with a superscription further linking it to this specific event in David's life. Swaggart's selection of biblical texts was neither naive nor uncritical. He knew, as became clear later in his sermon, that despite committing a horrendous sin, David remained honored by God and became in Christian interpretation a type of Christ. David still could be 'the king' despite his mistake. Swaggart admitted there were some negative consequences, but could not see the internal destruction of his own kingdom, like that of David, as one of them (cf. 2 Sam. 12:10–11; Ps. 51:18–19;). Moreover, Swaggart cleverly tells us to view his own failure as historically and morally analogous to David rather than Saul who prays the same, 'I have sinned' (1 Sam. 15:24) and lost his leadership that very day.

Some Critical Discernment of Testimony 3

I have not the slightest question about which sermon by these two Pentecostal preachers rings true to my own hearing of the Gospel. At stake for me is the question, in a postmodern period, of how we can properly interpret biblical interpretation, both today and in the centuries past. In other words, how can we discern 'the politics of exegesis', or how can we refine our ability to reject, for example, biblical interpretation in support of the Spanish conquistadors in favor of a Gospel

understanding of the pedagogy of the oppressed?[23] The problem cannot be solved by acceptance of modern historical 'methods' of interpretation, nor is it merely an academic matter. If anyone tries to
resolve this problem by making a modern distinction between piety
and politics, rights and ritual, we ought to respond in utter disbelief. If
the recent postmodern attack upon modern theories of universals has
done anything, it has called the bluff on easy modern dichotomies of
theory and practice, politics and piety, meaning and significance. We
also know that we might, through a creative act of misreading, *hear* a
testimony to the Gospel even in the most self-serving and apostate sermon, in the same way the cursings of a drunk on the street inadvertently bears testimony to the same.

If we focus less on what we might hear in spite of what a preacher
tries to say and more on how a Pentecostal sermon uses Scripture to
testify to the Gospel, then we can consider the relation of these Pentecostal sermons to the premodern, modern, and postmodern debates
over the use of Scripture in preaching and theology. The late James
Washington first suggested to me that most Afro-American preaching
and Pentecostal sermons might best be described as 'submodern'.
These preachers had usually been uninvited guests who fed off the
crumbs that fell beneath the table of the older modernist debates. They
were not premodern because they did participate piecemeal in the
modern debates. Moreover, the climate of opinion established by
modern discourse influenced every level of society. Both Swaggart
and Clemmons had more formal training than most Pentecostal
preachers. Swaggart often mouthed the words of fundamentalist
theologians, without being a consistent student of fundamentalist-
evangelical hermeneutics. Clemmons had been educated in the
postliberal climate of both Union Theological Seminary and New
York Theological Seminary, so he had studied modern 'liberal' historical criticism without pretending to be a biblical scholar, but he knew
how to use the biblical text as a realistic narrative testifying to the
revealed reality of the Gospel. Both could speak in everyday language
to a range of formally educated and uneducated people in their pews.

Swaggart and Clemmons made significant critical decisions about
how they found continuity with the premodern tradition of Christian
preaching. Swaggart assumed the modern stance of reading the Bible
as an inerrant reference to ancient history. He sought, therefore, to
argue from legal precedence about the consequences of immorality by
drawing an analogy between himself in the present and the historical

David. His case was like that of David so that we ought, in Swaggart's opinion, to be able to accept Swaggart's willingness to accept only minimal consequences when he faced discipline by leaders within the Assemblies of God for flagrantly doing exactly what he had preached against. In this respect, he remained a moralist without adequate appeal to the Gospel. By contrast, Clemmons appealed to the figural interpretation at the heart of the literal sense, a premodern conception he maintained through an awareness of how modern criticism can be used to sustain the Scriptural text instead of reconstructing an histori-cal analogy. In Clemmons' sermon the depiction of Saul's human weakness rendered a revelation of reality within which we find our-selves today as figures. In my own mind, I find resonance with Hans Frei's proposals regarding 'the literal sense' of Scripture.[24] We had to examine ourselves and explore the family resemblance or lack of it between a pattern of meaning in the biblical text and similar moments in the pattern of our own lives. He assured us of God's grace to Saul, afterwards the prophet Samuel returned to Saul and joined him in wor-shipping God (1 Sam. 15:31), so that we too ought to be open to self-critical judgement and accept the consequences for failures in our own conduct without being paralysed in our continuing service to others.

In brief, postmodern criticism forces us to renegotiate the present debate over the literal sense of Scripture by a fresh appeal to premodern interpretation as well as an awareness of the limits of mod-ern historical criticism. Rather than opting for a fundamentalist histor-ical apologetic in defence of Scripture, we need to reopen prior questions about what Scripture *is* and how we interpret Scripture scripturally. Instead of using modern historical criticisms simply to reconstruct prescriptural traditions or an ancient social-history, as valuable as that still proves to be, we must ask how we can accurately employ those same resources to sustain a scriptural text that is shared between the pulpit and the pew, and how we can heighten the realism and avoid harmonizing away the differences in the Scripture's own testimony to the Gospel. However unaware Clemmons might have been about all of the hermeneutical issues that morning, he illustrated a way to move beyond the fundamentalist-liberal options and demon-strated the impact of postmodern theory already evident in preaching today.

CONCLUDING REFLECTIONS

It is important to underscore the point, as I conclude my critical and personal reflections on Pentecostal hermeneutics, that even earlier Anglo-Pentecostals who were the most tempted to become modern fundamentalists could occasionally criticize modern historicisms, left and right, for its investment in either an apologetic 'past tense' of Scripture or for offering only a cafeteria of options among 'biblical' traditions reconstructed from the Bible's prehistory. A popular expression of this position once circulated widely within the Assemblies of God, perhaps originating in J. Roswell Flower's 1925 address to the graduating class at Central Bible Institute. It described 'fundamentalists' and 'modernists' (old liberals) as 'the Pharisees and Sadducees of our day'. The liberals are 'Sadducees' because they pick and choose what they believe is true, while the fundamentalists are 'Pharisees' because they believe it is all true but 'only in the past'.[25] This illustrates well some awareness of the limitations of the modern options. By contrast, Flower and other Pentecostals could describe the Pentecostal investment in 'the present tenses' of Scripture, rooted in 'holiness' expressions from the nineteenth century.

Another sign of the submodern disposition of Pentecostals can be seen in Eric Lund's Spanish essays on hermeneutics, translated into English in 1934 for use in Assemblies of God Bible Institutes by P.C. Nelson, a prominent Anglo-Pentecostal leader in the United States. Eric Lund, a Baptist missionary from Sweden to Spain and, then, to the Philippines, had become, by the late nineteenth and early twentieth century, one of the most prolific biblical scholars in the Spanish language. His essays on hermeneutics were originally published in two editions of *Revista Homiletica* but show no awareness of the current modern debates over 'higher criticism'. Instead, they speak from the perspective of a post-Reformation tradition of systematized 'rules of interpretation', including attention to Hebraisms and symbolic language so that pastors would not confuse 'the literal sense' of Scripture with literalistic readings. The English translation went through four editions (the 4th, 1941), complete with pictures of both Eric Lund ('author') and P.C. Nelson ('translator') in the opening pages.[26] Meanwhile the Spanish edition was reprinted in 1941 under the title, *Hermeneutica: o sea Reglas de Interpretación de las Sagrada Scripturas* and continues to be used to this day among many Pentecostals in Spain, in Latin America, and among Hispanics in the United

States. The subtitle of Nelson's English translation, once again, betrays Nelson's own influence from a modern climate of opinion: 'The Science and Art of Interpreting the Bible'.

The importance of this book lies in Nelson's effort to translate a Spanish book to serve in Pentecostal Bible institutes as a hermeneutical textbook instead of choosing from among the dozens of other readily available fundamentalist books on this same subject. While Anglo-Pentecostals of this period often treated Hispanic Pentecostalism paternalistically as a culturally inferior, missionary wing of their own churches, they looked to that very same segment of their churches for a primary book on hermeneutics. The 'sub-modern' character of Anglo-Pentecostals found compatibility in this study by Lund because it was more practically valuable than the current English options which called for a choice between using either a modern fundamentalist 'historico-grammatical exegesis' or a modern liberal 'higher criticism'. Here we see an early sign of the benefits in terms of hermeneutical theory of globalization for Anglo-Pentecostals, decades before our present consideration of this subject. Today we might look similarly to Latin American liberation theologians and to the publications of North American Hispanic Pentecostals, like Eldin Villafañe, for lessons in hermeneutics that go beyond that of conservative evangelicals or even most Anglo-Pentecostal efforts.[27] I must end where I began in the second paragraph of this essay, though with the assurance that Pentecostals have already begun to contribute significantly to the signs of hope for an uncharted postmodern future of the Christian Church.[28]

Notes

1   Cf. David D. Daniels, 'Teaching the History of U.S. Christianity in a Global Perspective', *Theological Education* 29 (Spring 1993), pp. 91–111. I found the other essays in that volume particularly helpful, as are the 'case studies' in *The Globalization of Theological Education*, ed. Alice Frazer Evans, Robert A. Evans, and David A. Roozen (New York, NY: Orbis Books, 1993).

2   Besides the standard secondary literature, see William Lloyd Newell, *The Secular Magi: Marx, Freud, and Nietzsche on Religion* (Cleveland, OH: Pilgrim Press, 1986).

3   Besides the standard secondary literature, see William Lloyd Newell, *The Secular Magi: Marx, Freud, and Nietzsche on Religion* (Cleveland, OH: Pilgrim Press, 1986).

4   See similarly the description of 'realistic mimetic' literature in Erich

Auerbach, *Mimesis: The Repesentation of Reality in Western Literature*, trans. Willard R. Trask (Princeton, NJ: Princeton University Press, 1968 [orig. in German, 1946]).

5   Harrison, *Studies in Early Victorian Literature*, pp. 36–37.

6   John Lukacs, *The Passing of the Modern Age* (New York, NY: Harper & Row Publishers, 1970), pp. 2, 10.

7   Michel Foucault, *The Order of Things: Archaeology of the Human Sciences*, a trans. of *Les Mots et les choses* [1966] (New York, NY: Vintage Books, 1973 [orig. 1970, Random House]), p. 384.

8   Steven Best and Douglas Kellner, *Postmodern Theory: Critical Interrogations* (New York, NY: Guilford Press, 1991), p. 280.

9   Hans-Georg Gadamer, *Truth and Method* (New York, NY: Seabury, 1975 [orig. in German, 1960]), pp. xxiv–xxv.

10   Outstanding overviews of the literary debate since the 1970s include Frank Lentricchia, *After the New Criticism* (Chicago, IL: Chicago University Press, 1980); M. H. Abrams, *Doing Things with Texts: Essays in Criticism and Critical Theory* , ed. Michael Fischer (New York, NY: W.W. Norton, 1989); and Jonathan Culler, *On Deconstruction: Theory and Criticism After Structuralism* (Ithaca, NY: Cornell University Press, 1982). In my view, the most impressive overview is that of Best and Kellner, *Postmodern Theory: Critical Interrogations* (see n. 8). For an incisive constructive effort at postmodern criticism, see Calin Falck, *Myth, Truth, and Literature: Towards a True Postmodernism* (Cambridge: Cambridge University Press, 1994 [2nd. ed.]. 1989 [1st. ed.]). For an excellent criticism of both modern and postmodern criticism, see Anthony J. Cascardi, *The Subject of Modernity* (Cambridge: Cambridge University Press, 1992).

11   'Structure, Sign, and Play in the Discourses of the Human Sciences', 271, in *The Structuralist Controversy: The Languages of Criticism and the Sciences of Man* (Baltimore, MD: John Hopkins University Press, 1972). See the discussion similarly of Derrida in Lentricchia, *After the New Criticism*, pp. 75–78.

12   As just one example, see the essay by Ferdinand De Saussure, 'The Linguistic Sign', in *Introducing Semiotics: An Anthology of Readings*, ed. Marcel Danesi and Donato Santeramo (Toronto: Canadian Scholars' Press, 1972), pp. 36–46, and the elaboration by Marcel Danesi, in a way that moves beyond Marshall McCluhan, in his *Message and Meanings: An Introduction to Semiotics* (Toronto: Canadian Scholars' Press, 1993).

13   Best and Kellner, *Postmodern Theory*, p. 285.

14   Chantal Mouffe, 'Toward a Theoretical Interpretation of "new Social Movements" ', in *Rethinking Marx*, ed. Sakari Hanninen and Leena Paldan (New York, NY and Bagnolet: International General IMMRC, 1984), p. 142.

15   Edgar V. McKnight, *Post-Modern Use of the Bible: The Emergence of Reader-Oriented Criticism* (Nashville, TN: Abingdon Press, 1988).

16   For a more detailed account of 'prayer' as something meant to be overheard, see Sheppard, 'Psalms: How to Read a Book that Seems Intent on Reading You', *Theology News and Notes [Special Issue in Memory of William Sanford LaSor]* 46 (1992), pp. 45–47; and 'Enemies and the Politics of Prayer in the Book of Psalms', in *The Bible and Liberation: Political and Social Hermeneutics*, ed. Norman Gottwald and Richard Horsley (Maryknoll, NY: Orbis

Press, 1993), pp. 376–391.

17   Paul Lehmann, *The Transfiguration of Politics: Jesus Christ and the Question of Revolution* (London: SCM Press, 1975), p. 231.

18   Cf. Donald Gelpi, *Pentecostalism: A Theological Viewpoint* (New York, NY: Paulist Press, 1971).

19   William Samarin, *Tongues of Men and Angels: the Religious Language of Pentecostals* (New York, NY: Macmillan, 1972).

20   Frank D. Macchia, *Spirituality and Social Liberation: The Message of the Blumhardts in Light of Wuerrtemberg Pietism* (Metuchen, NJ: Scarecrow Press, 1993).

21   Ithiel C. Clemmons, *Bishop C H Mason and the Roots of the Church of God in Christ* (Bakersfield, CA: Pneuma Life Publishing, 1996).

22   For a personal account, see Jesse Winley, with Robert Paul Lamb, *Jesse* (Pittsburgh, PA: Whitaker House, 1976).

23   On the biblical interpretation of the conquistadors and issues raised by it for biblical interpretation in Latin America today, see Leif Vaage, 'Text, Context, Conquest, Quest: The Bible and Social Struggle in Latin America', in *Seminar Papers of the Society of Biblical Literature, Annual Meeting 1991*, ed. Eugene H. Lovering, Jr. (Atlanta, GA: Scholars Press, 1991), pp. 357–365, and for the primary documents, see *History of Latin American Civilization: Sources and Interpretation. Vol. 1: The Colonial Experience*, ed. Lewis Hanke (2nd ed.; Boston, MA: Little, Brown, and Company, 1973).

24   Hans W. Frei, *The Eclipse of Biblical Narrative: A Study in Eighteenth and Nineteenth Century Hermeneutics* (New Haven, CT: Yale University Press, 1974).

25   *The Pentecostal Evangel*, 13 June 1925.

26   Eric Lund, *Hermeneutics or The Science and Art of Interpreting the Bible* , trans. P. C. Nelson (Enid, Oklahoma: Southwestern Press, 1934), with an 'Introduction' by Donald Gee. To the 2nd edition, 1938, Nelson added an appendix, 'Helps and How to Use Them', which included word studies, some geographical information, annotated lists of Bible translations and commentaries [with no mention of any conflict with 'liberal' historical criticism], and a Scripture index. The 3rd edition in 1941, had a further chapter by Nelson on 'Rhetorical Figures'. A 4th edition was published posthumously in 1948.

27   Eldin Villafañe, *The Liberating Spirit: Toward an Hispanic American Pentecostal Social Ethic* (Grand Rapids, MI: Wm. B. Eerdmans Publishing Co., 1993 [initially pub. in 1992 by University Press of America]).

28   For my own more programmatic assessments of current issues in Bible and theology, see 'How Do Neoorthodox and Post-neoorthodox Theologians Approach the Doing of Theology Today?', in *Doing Theology in Today's World*, ed. John Woodbridge and Thomas Edward McComiskey (Grand Rapids, MI: Zondervan Publishing House, 1991), pp. 437–459; and 'Biblical Interpretation After Gadamer', *PNEUMA: The Journal of the Society for Pentecostal Studies* 16 (Spring 1994), pp. 121–141.

Fourteen

'Your Daughters Shall Prophesy': Pentecostal Hermeneutics and the Empowerment of Women

Janet Everts Powers

In the early days of Pentecostalism, women ministered in nearly every area of the growing movement. Women preached, taught the Bible, administrated educational institutions, conducted evangelistic campaigns, founded local congregations and denominations, proclaimed the gospel on the mission field and wrote or edited numerous books and periodicals.[1] Both Pentecostal and Holiness churches ordained women in great numbers around the turn of the century. Although the numbers of women ordained declined after 1920, in 1995 over 50 per cent of all women who had ever been ordained were from Pentecostal and Holiness backgrounds. Only 17 per cent of all women ever ordained came from other major Protestant denominations.[2] These figures commanded the attention of the mainline denominations, and in the 1990 report of the National Council of Churches it was noted that the Assemblies of God, the largest Pentecostal denomination, had led the way in affirming the ministries of women.[3]

Despite the large numbers of women ordained in the history of Pentecostalism, the current picture is not necessarily encouraging for Pentecostal women. Although the number of credentialed women ministers is growing in the Assemblies of God, the number of those progressing to full ordination is decreasing. Women are serving in ministries that are peripheral to the central work of the gospel. Few are senior pastors or serving on the mission field and many are now past retirement age. It has become rare for women to preach from Assemblies of God pulpits on Sunday, and the number of female models for younger women to follow is declining.[4] Voices from both inside and outside Pentecostalism are concerned about this trend. Most of the work on women in Pentecostalism either sees the egalitarianism of the early days as an ideal or emphasizes how unliberating Pentecostalism, with its emphasis on male authority, really is.[5] But both these stances fail to recognize the dynamics that have characterized Pentecostal discussions about women in ministry from the beginning of the movement. Using the Bible as the basis for these discussions, Pentecostals have affirmed women's ability to speak for God as fully empowered vessels of the Holy Spirit, but have also accepted traditional attitudes about the place of women in society.[6]

At the beginning of the century, Pentecostals had to defend their practice of ordaining women against accusations that it was unbiblical and did not respect the divine order for male and female. Pentecostals vigorously defended women's rights in the preaching of the gospel on the basis of biblical passages like Joel 2:28 and Acts 2:16–17 and the resurrection accounts in Matthew and John. Christ commanded women to go and bear witness to his resurrection, and the Holy Spirit empowered them to bear this witness on the day of Pentecost, who were they to withstand God? But, in general, they still saw the woman as the 'weaker vessel' who was under the authority of the man in the home and in matters of church government.[7] This stance enabled them to defend their practice as biblical and give women far more freedom in ministry than any of the major Protestant denominations.

It is only in recent years, after the mainline denominations opened the ordained ministry to women, that Pentecostals have been accused of having a restrictive stance on the ordination of women.[8] Feminist scholars have begun to study Pentecostal women ministers, and the way they function in the church. Their critique of Pentecostal practices has created a whole new set of accusations that Pentecostals have not been equipped to answer. One of these feminist scholars is Elaine Lawless, who has published several studies on Pentecostal women preachers in poor rural areas.[9] Lawless has tremendous sympathy for the women she studies and interviews, and these interviews provide fascinating material on the way women preachers understand their calls and their ministries. But she does not have much understanding of Pentecostalism or the Bible, and some of her conclusions are marred because she does not understand the religious context within which these women operate.[10] Despite these weaknesses, her work raises questions about the Pentecostal understanding of women's ministry which have to be answered in contemporary American society. A feminist theologian who has a far better understanding of the religious context of Pentecostalism is Mary McClintock Fulkerson. She studied Pentecostal women preachers because she was interested in hearing the voices of women who appropriate the traditions of Christianity very differently from feminists and still feel empowered as women.[11] She based a great deal of her study on the work of David Roebuck, a Pentecostal scholar from the Church of God, who has studied the waning of women's voices in Pentecostalism. All of these studies raise questions about the way the Pentecostal understanding of women's ministries restricts women who pursue ministries within Pentecostal churches.

The concerns of these feminist scholars are reflected in the younger generation of Pentecostal women ministers. Older women ministers, who are represented in the scholarly studies mentioned above, genuinely approve of a biblically based subordination of women, and have adjusted their way of understanding their ministry to fit into this traditional model. But younger women ministers are finding it difficult to reconcile their call to ministry with denominational and theological restrictions on the ministry of women.[12] It is important that scholars from within Pentecostalism address these questions, since they understand the dynamics of Pentecostalism and are less likely to try to fit Pentecostalism into a secular or feminist grid which ends up misunderstanding or distorting the tradition. This call for serious investigation of this issue by scholars inside the movement is not to suggest that those outside the tradition have nothing to offer. But unless suggestions for change come from within the tradition and are faithful to a Pentecostal hermeneutic, they are not likely to effect a lasting change in attitudes.

Pentecostal scholars have suggested several reasons for the decline in the number of women ministers in Pentecostalism: institution-alization, the professionalization of the ministry.[13] Pentecostal atti-tudes towards changes in American cultural attitudes toward women[14] and the intrusion of Reformed/Evangelical theology into Pentecostal thinking about women.[15] Probably the most penetrating analysis is offered by David Roebuck in a paper entitled 'Go and Tell My Brothers'. In this paper he suggests that 'the limitations on authority ... inherent in the doctrine of Spirit-baptism combined with the anti-culturalism of Pentecostalism' have contributed to the decline of women's ministries.[16] This paper intends to build on Roebuck's thesis and examine how the unique dynamics of Pentecostal biblical herme-neutics have contributed to both the empowering of and the restric-tions on women ministers. It was their reading of the Bible that gave Pentecostal women the freedom to preach and made Pentecostals such vigorous defenders of women ministers. If Pentecostals are to answer the questions raised by those outside the tradition and continue to defend the rights of women in the gospel, they will need to draw on the rich tradition of their own unique hermeneutic.

A unique factor in Pentecostal hermeneutics is the vital role that spiritual experience plays in biblical interpretation.[17] The early Pente-costals saw themselves as recovering and re-entering the biblical real-ity; they participated in and appropriated biblical events in their own lives.[18] The Spirit would confirm correct interpretation by giving the interpreter experiences corresponding to biblical manifestations.[19] New experience could also give fresh insight and Scripture could take on a new meaning. But experiences, beliefs and practices all had to be tested by the Word of God.[20] Because of this hermeneutic, the Pente-costal interpreter did not have to worry about the hermeneutical gap between what the text meant to the original reader and what it means now. The Holy Spirit was at work in the original author's life and is at work in the life of the believer reading the text, so a bridge is created between the text and the reader which makes the text accessible to everyone. This Spirit-led interpretation also opens up the possibility of multiple interpretations of a text.[21] The point of this Pentecostal read-ing was not the experiences themselves, but experiencing life as par-ticipation in the biblical story.[22] For Pentecostals, the aim of Bible study is to discover the will of God and act on it.[23]

This Pentecostal hermeneutic is much closer to what Hans Frei calls pre-critical interpretation than it is to the historical-critical method.[24] So it is not surprising that this hermeneutic also gives a very high value to biblical narrative. For Pentecostals the Bible is not a textbook of theological or historical propositions, but a story about redemption in Jesus Christ by the Holy Spirit.[25] So Pentecostals look to biblical narrative to discover a pattern of experience and assume that this narrative has normative theological value.[26] The story of the Bible has continuity with the past and with the future consummation of the kingdom, so the power of the age to come is now available to the church through Pentecost.[27] The ending of a story is perhaps the most crucial element in determining the meaning of a story, so Pentecostals often determine the meaning of biblical passages and their own experience in the light of the coming kingdom of God.[28] Pentecostal hermeneutics offers a paradigm which asserts that right experience leads to right doctrine, so Pentecostals are much more concerned with locating their experiences in the biblical narrative than with determining theological propositions based on the biblical text.[29]

Pentecostals have always upheld these hermeneutical truths when defending their understanding of Spirit baptism and the charismatic manifestations of the Spirit. But when the discussion shifts to women ministers, Pentecostals are often hermeneutically inconsistent. On the one hand they have affirmed that, because women have an experience of the Spirit that is identical to that of men, parallel with the experience of the church on the day of Pentecost and compatible with the experience of other women in the Bible, they must be empowered to preach the gospel, just as men are. But Pentecostals have failed to carry this narrative and experiential hermeneutic into discussions on the position of women in society and the church. This ambiguity has meant that Pentecostals have expanded the traditional ecclesiastical roles of women and allowed them to preach as ministers empowered by the Spirit and, at the same time, have never been certain if this Spirit-empowering gives women the ability to assume positions of authority.[30] If Pentecostals want to answer the questions that have been raised by the feminist critique of their tradition, they need to recover the Spirit-empowered dynamic of their narrative hermeneutic and apply it to the biblical passages that affect their understanding of women ministers.

WOMEN EMPOWERED

Pentecostalism emerged out of the Wesleyan-Holiness tradition at the end of the nineteenth-century. This background strongly influenced the egalitarian models of ministry in early Pentecostalism. Wesley thought that experiences of the Holy Spirit were crucial for the church and his theology promoted charismatic leadership. His emphasis on charismatic qualifications for ministry opened up new opportunities for women, and by 1761 women were serving as itinerant ministers and local preachers in the Methodist movement.[31] In America, Wesleyan holiness had a strong influence on the revivalism and social activism of the nineteenth-century. Within this American Holiness movement three main lines of argument were used to support the equality of women. The first was the Pentecostal argument based on Joel 2:28 as it was repeated in Acts 2:16–17.[32] Phoebe Palmer asserted that the baptism of the Holy Spirit qualified women to preach and prophesy. Her view was extremely influential because of her powerful ministry and her position as editor of the major Holiness periodical.[33] A second argument was based on the results of sanctification in the life of the believer. Since, by virtue of redemption, women were released from the curse of sin and the inferiority associated with that curse, the effects of that curse were no longer applicable to the community of the redeemed and restored in Christ. The third argument for the equality of women was based on Galatians 3:28, and the unity of male and female in Christ.[34] Because the early Pentecostals placed such a strong emphasis on Spirit baptism and the Spirit's empowering of believers for ministry, when they championed the right of women to minister, they used the Pentecostal argument almost exclusively. They saw Joel's prophecy in Acts 2:16–17 as an adequate explanation and justification for the prophetic ministry of women. They did not worry about the verses which said that women should be silent, because these verses did not refer to the preaching of the gospel.[35] The Pentecostal understanding of glossolalia was crucial to their understanding of the qualifications of women ministers.[36] Glossolalia was a supernatural gift, and the actions of one who had been baptized in the Spirit were considered the actions of God rather than the actions of a human speaker. Because a woman minister preached under the control of the Holy Spirit, early Pentecostals were able to ignore the traditional qualifications for ministry. They saw authority vested in the manifestation of the Spirit, rather than in the human speaker.[37]

This early Pentecostal apologetic for women's ministry is seen quite clearly in the preaching of Maria Woodworth Etter, one of the most famous early Pentecostal woman ministers. In her sermon on 'Women's Rights in the Gospel', Etter uses scripture to exhort her sisters in Christ to 'use [their talents] for the glory of God'. The key scripture passage is the prophecy of Joel in Acts 2:18–19, but she also uses the resurrection narratives and the story of the woman at the well in John 4 to show that Jesus clearly commanded women to spread the gospel. The examples of women who prophesied in the Old Testament, and the women who worked with Paul are held up as examples for Pentecostal women to imitate. She dismisses the passages on the silence of women as having less authority than the passages like Galatians 3:28 where women are seen as equal to men, and I Corinthians 11:5 in which it is clear that women pray and prophesy in the churches Paul founded. This gift of prophecy is the greatest gift, and God has promised it to women. Her clear focus is the importance of preaching the gospel, and she urges women not to let pleas of weakness hold them back from obeying God's command and allowing him to speak through them.[38]

Maria Woodworth Etter appeals primarily to the Pentecostal argument from Scripture and makes very little reference to the Pentecostal understanding of Spirit baptism. But present day women Pentecostal preachers understand their call more in terms of the Pentecostal understanding of Spirit baptism. This emphasis on Spirit baptism can be clearly seen in the call narratives and sermons which Elaine Lawless analyzes in her book, *Handmaidens of the Lord*. Lawless was surprised by the number of women preachers and women pastors, nearly all of whom were Pentecostal, in central Missouri, and who described themselves as 'called to preach'.[39] As Lawless interviewed them she discovered that in Pentecostalism the weight of this call from God to preach is so profound that it outweighs the fact that women are not usually granted equality in authority in this very traditional cultural setting.[40] Women who insist that God has called them to preach can use their call to provide freedom from the normal expectations of the culture in which they live.[41]

Women who have succeeded as preachers and pastors have well-developed call narratives and use these narratives to legitimate their ministry.[42] Typical elements in a woman preacher's call narrative include: 1) A clear perception of difference from other people, 2) a conviction about her sinful nature, 3) an attraction to revival or missionary work, 4) a concrete account of her conversion and call to preach, and 5) the construction of an alternative life strategy. But the most crucial aspect of the call narrative is the part that convinces the woman that it is indeed God who is calling her. Almost every woman talks about how others discouraged her, and she put God to the test by setting up a situation to determine God's wishes. These 'ritual disclaimers' convince her and her listeners that she is following God's call because God's power overcame her resistance, hesitation and inadequacies; they are proof that God has selected her.[43] Anyone familiar with biblical literature can see that these women are familiar with the pattern of prophetic call narratives in the biblical text and understand their own calls in the light of these narratives. They see their ministry as prophetic and Spirit empowered.

Lawless also points out that in worship services these women use many strategies to reinforce this idea that it is God who is working through them. During one service, the sermon starts with a Scripture reading, a clear signal that the message that follows is inspired by God. Throughout the sermon, nearly everything that is said is framed in terms of God's word, and at the end of the sermon there is a disclaimer that this sermon is just a plain simple message from God. When there is a message in tongues, the woman preacher reinforces her authority by giving the interpretation the flavour of biblical language; it is clear that the voice speaking is not herself, but God.[44] Fulkerson points out that women preachers use the word 'anointing' to describe the way that God uses them in preaching. The Scripture used in preaching becomes the living word of God, and the congregation's response to the living word confirms that God is working through the preaching. They use call narratives and other forms of testimony in much the same way. These narratives proclaim God's mighty work as it intersects with their own story. The goal of these stories is to invite others into a mutual reality in which God works in human lives. The participatory, Spirit-led nature of Pentecostal worship gives women's testimonies and preaching a platform.[45]

The Spirit-based hermeneutic of Pentecostalism, which is seen in both the way Scripture is read and in the importance of testimony, 'levels access to the privilege of preaching'.[46] If God is the speaker, then anyone can be used as God's vessel. Since the same Holy Spirit is in the woman as in the man, the experience of Pentecost means that the new age, in which women can be the mouthpiece of the Lord, has arrived.[47] But this Pentecostal argument depends less on the Scriptures that empower women than it does on the Pentecostal understanding of baptism in the Holy Spirit. Pentecostal women ministers understand their lives in the light of biblical narratives about prophetic calls and the doctrine of Spirit baptism. This prophetic understanding of ministry empowers women as mouthpieces of the Lord, but does not empower them as women.

WOMEN RESTRICTED

Central to the issue of women in ministry is the question of what constitutes legitimate spiritual authority. The Pentecostal answer to this question is what has produced the restrictions on the ministry of women in Pentecostal circles, even as the doctrine of Spirit baptism empowered them.[48] In the doctrine of Spirit baptism, the authority for ministry resides in the manifestation of the Spirit rather than in the human vessel. So, although this doctrine gives women the right to preach, it says nothing about the nature of women's authority.[49] 'While this understanding of ministry allowed for... a significant place for women within the movement, it did not impart to female ministers the authority of a ministerial office'.[50] This distinction meant that from the beginning of the movement, tension existed concerning the nature of women's authority and their right to a ministerial office.[51]

Among Charles Parham and his disciples, most of whom came out of the Holiness movement, it was normal for men and women to minister as equals and women were crucial to the initial spread of the Pentecostal revival.[52] But even at Asuza Street, the reading of the Acts 2 account was conditioned by a cultural understanding that women had a separate and limited sphere of activity. 'Spirit-baptized women had the right to preach, because the authority to preach resided in the Holy Spirit, but they were still distinct from men and under the authority of men'.[53] As the revival spread into Protestant traditions that had not been affected by the egalitarian theology of the Holiness movement, Pentecostals were influenced by other social and theological assumptions about women.[54] Churches like the Church of God, which had existed before the revival, embraced the revival, but retained their existing forms of government and policies about women.[55] It was not until 1990 that the Church of God granted women equal standing with men as licensed ministers. In the Assemblies of God, E.N. Bell argued that women should not have the authority of ministerial office because there was no instance in Scripture of women having authoritative rule in the church.[56] Bell's position became the dominant view in the Assemblies of God despite the fact that ordained women were among the founding ministers of this denomination.[57] However, this view was never the only one in the Assemblies of God, and its congregational polity meant that women continued to preach, pastor and perform sacraments.[58] In 1935, the Assemblies voted to ordain women ministers,[59] but until 1977 there were official distinctions between male and female ministers. By 1990, when the Assemblies of God published a position paper which indicated that there was no convincing evidence to restrict the ministries of women who had been called and gifted by God,[60] the number of younger women seeking ordination in the denomination was decreasing.[61]

This ambivalence toward the authority of women ministers comes through clearly in Lawless' interviews with Pentecostal women pastors. In their call narratives, Lawless sees the tension between their belief in the God-given inferiority and submission of women to men and their belief in the individual's equality before God.[62] These narratives are 'carefully couched and framed within the religious belief structure of the group'.[63] When women speak about their calls, they highlight the ideas that legitimate their ministry, like their absolute dependence upon God and their submission to God and man.[64] Lawless also sees these themes highlighted in the sermons these women preach. The most common themes of Pentecostal women preachers are the importance of absolute surrender to God and the importance of salvation. Although she concedes that men also use these themes in their sermons, Lawless thinks that these themes 'seem to reflect the concerns of women who are accustomed to passivity, submission, fear and feelings of unworthiness and inadequacy'.[65] Although it is standard for both male and female preachers to defer to God's authority at the beginning of a sermon, women must pay a deeper type of deference.[66] Submission as a theme is also seen in the women's self-denigrating speech and their insistence that they are always submissive to male authority in the church and in the home.[67] These women know that they cannot usurp the authority of men. The God-given hierarchy of the home prevails in the church as well.[68]

Although women from outside the Pentecostal tradition notice the same themes in the stories and sermons of Pentecostal women preachers, they differ radically in their interpretation of these themes. Lawless has by far the most condescending interpretation. Although she acknowledges that these women see their radical submission as a means of gaining freedom, she thinks this equation of submission and freedom is peculiar to women and shows their fear of provoking an angry God with their disobedience.[69] She thinks that these women accept the blame often given to them for Eve's sin, feel worthless and sinful and are not convinced of their own salvation. But she also admires these women for the way they have created alternative narrative patterns that 'neutralize the power of the standard socio-cultural script', because any rescripting of a life story is a comment on the status quo that calls it into question.[70] Fulkerson's interpretation is both more sympathetic to the Pentecostal context in which these women operate and more insightful. Like Lawless, she admires the way these women have used the theme of dependence on God to rescript their lives and create a place of authority in the church even as men oppose them. But she does not see the language of self-denigration as a language of self-hatred. Instead she suggests that this is the language of true identity in the face of the world's estimation of them as 'nobodies' and a culture that subordinates them to men. It is dependence on God, not men or society, that sustains these women. They find the promises of God more powerful than the texts on female submission and are willing to act accordingly. This kind of faith is anything but passive.[71]

Both these feminist scholars know that one of the dynamics which holds these women in a position of submission to men is the Pentecostal reading of the Bible. The Pentecostal belief in the infallibility of the entire canon means that all texts about women need to be obeyed. According to the Pentecostal reading of the biblical texts, men should have authority over women and the hierarchical order of the family is part of the divine order.[72] This Pentecostal commitment to the authority of the Bible also means that the scriptural directives that insist on women being silent in church are taken literally. Lawless observes that Pentecostal women preachers justify their position behind the pulpit by referring to Acts 2:16–17 (although she gets the reference wrong) and agreeing that they are just 'handmaidens of the Lord' going about saving souls in these 'last days'. She then makes the interesting point that these women choose the term 'handmaiden', a word which characterizes the women as caretaker and servant, rather than the word 'daughter', which is found in the same verses. So even the texts which empower women preachers are interpreted in a way that acknowledges their submission to both God and men.[73] Both Lawless and Fulkerson are clearly disturbed by this reading of Scripture, although Fulkerson is able to see that the Pentecostal reading of Scripture also allows women to claim the status of ministry.[74] Both these women also seem to assume that as long as Pentecostals believe in the infallibility of the Bible and read it literally, the ministry of women in Pentecostal churches will be restricted. Is this assumption necessarily true?

USING A PENTECOSTAL HERMENEUTIC
TO EMPOWER WOMEN

In the early days of the Pentecostal movement, Pentecostals had to defend their doctrine of Spirit baptism against accusations that it was unbiblical and based on highly questionable experience. They also had to defend the right of Pentecostal women to preach. So they brought the issue of women ministers under the umbrella of the doctrine of Spirit baptism and defended Spirit baptism at the same time that they defended the women who preached this doctrine. By doing so they did not have to re-examine cultural assumptions about the role of women and were able to leave traditional interpretations of passages about women alone. This interpretive approach was actually a very efficient apologetic tactic. The doctrine of Spirit baptism was at the heart of the Pentecostal movement. If the way Pentecostals explained Spirit baptism had lost its persuasive power, the movement would have lost its most important distinctive and might have eventually died out. A new movement within the Christian church can challenge only so many traditional doctrines at one time. Challenging the traditional and cultural understandings of the position of women might have jeopardized the success of the movement. As it was, the Pentecostal doctrine of Spirit baptism empowered women to minister decades before other denominations even considered whether or not to ordain women as ministers. Until the last few decades, championing the rights of women in the gospel by defending the distinctive Pentecostal doctrine of Spirit baptism served both women and the Pentecostal movement well.

In the process of developing and defending this doctrine of Spirit baptism, Pentecostals also developed a rather sophisticated hermeneutic. But Pentecostals never applied every aspect of this hermeneutic to passages about women. The hermeneutic that defended the Pentecostal understanding of Spirit baptism had four distinct elements. 1) It affirmed the vital role that experience plays in interpretation.[75] 2) It insisted on the value of narrative texts in developing theology.[76] 3) It refused to accept the traditional distinction between teaching passages and narrative passages, which assumed that since Paul's writings were 'teachings' they were more authoritative than the narratives of the gospels and Acts.[77] 4) It saw the significance of the eschatological dimensions of Pentecost – that the church was meant to be a community being transformed by the power of the age to come which would reflect the reality of the coming kingdom.[78] But only the first element, the importance of experience in interpreting the text, was ever applied to biblical passages about women. If Pentecostal scholars are to answer the types of questions raised by feminists outside the tradition about the ministry of women, they need to reclaim the hermeneutic that was used to defend the doctrine of Spirit baptism in early Pentecostalism and apply it to biblical passages about the role of women.

What would exegesis based on such a hermeneutic look like? The examples which follow will try to show how a Pentecostal hermeneutic can be used to illumine passages about women in the New Testament. The first passage examined, Mark 5:21–43, will be used to show how narratives about women can be used to develop a theology about women. The second passage examined, I Corinthians 11:2–16, will illustrate how refusing to make a distinction between teaching texts and historically conditioned texts can undermine the basis of the doctrine that the woman is submissive to the man in ministry situations. Both texts will be used to show how an eschatological understanding of the text can lead to transformations in the Christian community.

MARK 5:21–43

Pentecostals have always made use of the gospel texts, like the resurrection narratives and the story of the woman at the well, in which Jesus tells women to tell others about him. But they have been blind to the theological significance of other gospel texts about women. One of the most important gospel texts about women is found in Mark 5:21–43. Pentecostals have often used the story of the woman with a flow of blood to show the importance of faith for healing. They find encouragement for the belief that the power of God can raise people from the dead in the story of Jesus and Jairus' daughter. But they have not realized that these texts also have something to say about the status of women in the Christian community.

It is almost certain that the early church placed these two stories together because of the message they conveyed about the status of women,[79] a literary device called *inclusio*, a story within a story, relates them. This literary device is common in Mark, who often uses *inclusio* when the stories he is telling indicate that Jesus is opposing standard Jewish practices and reinterpreting Torah. Most of the *inclusio*s in Mark, for instance the stories of the cleansing of the temple and the cursing of the fig tree, are not found as *inclusio*s in Matthew and Luke. But the stories of the woman with the flow of blood and the raising of Jairus' daughter are found as *inclusio*s in all three synoptic gospels (Matthew 9:18–26, Luke 8:40–56). This universal synoptic witness would indicate that all three gospel writers knew that these two stories belonged together and should be interpreted in light of each other. Both these stories are commentaries on the blood taboo laws of Leviticus 15:19–33. Taken together they indicate that in Christ women are freed from the restrictions of Torah and are given a new status as daughters of God.

The story of the woman with a flow of blood is quite clearly set against the backdrop of Leviticus 15:25–30. For twelve years she has been in a state of cultic impurity that would have infected anyone who touched her or anything that she had touched. This kind of impurity would not only have drained her finances, but would have isolated her socially, since she could not have participated in any kind of public worship or public gathering. By approaching Jesus in a crowd, she is violating religious law, for everyone whom she touches or who touches her will be made unclean as well. When she touches Jesus her impurity should have been transferred to him. Instead, she is instantly healed of her disease. When Jesus calls her out of the crowd, she is afraid because she has so obviously violated Torah and fears that both Jesus and the crowd will condemn her for her actions. But Jesus commends her and calls her 'daughter'. With his words, Jesus restores her to the community and establishes her kinship with him as one who has done the will of God (Mark 3:35). When Jesus cleanses the leper in Mark 1:40–44, he commands the leper to fulfil the requirements of Torah: to go to the priest and offer for his cleansing what Moses commanded as a proof to the people. But here Jesus does not even hint that the woman needs to do anything further, even though Leviticus 15:28–30 indicates that she should make atonement for her unclean discharge. She is completely freed from the requirements of Torah and the curse of her illness.

At first glance, the story of the raising of Jairus' daughter has little to do with the blood taboo laws of Leviticus 15:19–33. But when it is placed in juxtaposition with the story of the woman with a flow of blood, the significance of this story is changed. At twelve years of age, a Jewish girl was considered a marriageable adult woman, because at twelve years of age her regular menstrual cycle would have begun. So Jairus' daughter is not a little girl, but a woman who is subject to the cultic restrictions of Leviticus 15:19–24. Even when a woman's flow of blood was not associated with illness, she was considered 'sick with her impurity' (Leviticus 15:33). In a culture which saw sickness and death as one of the results of sin, this means that a woman's normal menstrual cycle is part of the curse on sin. So when Jesus touches Jairus' daughter, he runs the risk of contracting the impurity associated with women and the curse associated with that impurity. In the same way that he ignored the issue of cultic impurity in dealing with the woman with the flow of blood, he ignores the restrictions of the blood taboo laws when he takes Jairus' daughter by the hand, raises her from the dead and restores her to her family and community.

It is quite clear that in these two stories, Jesus shows that the blood taboo laws which had restricted women in Judaism are no longer valid in the Christian community. The wall of the temple that divided women from men is abolished. Not only is he not concerned about contracting the curse of impurity associated with women, he reverses this curse and turns it into a blessing. In these two stories, Jesus blesses women as women and includes them as full members in the Christian community that constitutes his family. Lawless' observation that Pentecostal women preachers refer to themselves as 'handmaidens' rather than as 'daughters'[80] is interesting in light of this understanding of Mark 5:21–43. Handmaidens are servants who have a right of access to the Father only because of their faithful service. But daughters can approach their father just because they are daughters and are therefore accepted for who they are. Early Pentecostals sensed that in Spirit baptism, the status of women had been changed. An early Pentecostal article stated:

> Before Pentecost, the woman could only go into the 'court of women' and not into the inner court. The anointing oil was never poured on a woman's head but only on the heads of kings, priests and prophets. But when the Lord poured out Pentecost, He brought all those faithful women with the other disciples into the upper room, and God baptized them all in the same room and made no difference. All the women received the anointed oil of the Holy Ghost and were able to preach the same as men.[81]

But they grounded this new status in the baptism of the Holy Spirit rather than in the new community established by Jesus which was to reflect the coming kingdom of God. They knew that 'the church was a movement from the outer court to the inner court to the holy of holies', but they did not see the implications of this understanding of the church for women.[82] Recognizing that the new status of women is grounded in Christ as well as Pentecost, means that the truth Paul proclaims in Galatians 3:28, 'There is no more male or female; for you are all one in Christ Jesus', is meant to be realized in concrete ways in the Christian community.

I CORINTHIANS 11:2–16

When traditional Protestant churches have argued that the women are supposed to be subordinate to men and are therefore excluded from the ministry, they have traditionally turned to the Pauline epistles to find support for this argument. The most crucial passage for this understanding of the relationship between male and female is found in I Corinthians 11:2–16. It is argued that here Paul clearly states that the man is the head over the woman, and that this means women are to be subordinate to men. But this traditional interpretation is by no means the only way to understand this passage. And even if this passage is understood in this traditional way, it is not obvious that it therefore has enough authority to override other teachings about men and women found in the New Testament. But Pentecostals have, in general, accepted this interpretation of this passage and have granted that other passages need to be interpreted in the light of this teaching. In doing this, Pentecostals have accepted a hermeneutical premise that they do not accept in discussing Spirit baptism with traditional Protestants – that there is a clear distinction between the didactic portions of Scripture and the purely narrative portions and that doctrine should be constructed from these didactic portions and not from narrative accounts. Too often Pentecostals who wish to show that this passage is not meant to restrict the ministry of women accept this hermeneutical premise and try to argue with traditional Protestants on their own hermeneutical ground. They would be far more effective if they used their own hermeneutic, one which has successfully defended their doctrine of Spirit baptism against traditional interpretations of the role of the Spirit in the Christian community.

The first thing that Pentecostals need to point out about this passage is that it assumes that women pray and prophesy in public worship. Early Pentecostals like Maria Woodworth Etter were not hesitant about using this passage to support the ministry of women,[83] and modern Pentecostals should follow their example. They should also point out that Paul is not speaking directly to the question of authority relationships between men and women, he is explaining to the Corinthians that women who pray and prophesy ought to wear veils. In support of this directive Paul uses two arguments: 1) that the man is the 'head' of the woman and that woman is the glory of man, and 2) that it is disgraceful and improper for a woman to pray to God with her 'head' uncovered. By pointing out Paul's obvious intention, Pentecostals can reinforce the obvious point that Paul is writing letters that speak to specific occasions in the churches he founded. This contextual reality means that the epistles are historically conditioned and are not any more valid for doctrinal purposes than the historical narratives of the gospels and Acts. They can also prevent some of the worst exegetical abuses of this passage. Too often exegetes who want to use this passage to support the position that women are supposed to be subordinate to men, ignore Paul's adhoc intentionality and treat his supporting argument about the man being the 'head' of the woman as though it is the main point of the passage. When they then turn around and use their understanding of the headship argument to prove that women should not preach, they are contradicting the clear intentions of the text.[84]

Once the basic purpose and context of this passage is established, it is possible to turn to the actual exegesis. This passage is full of exegetical difficulties, most of which cannot be dealt with here.[85] Two of these difficulties are especially relevant to the issue of women ministers. The first is that the meaning of 'head' is not at all obvious. In the passage Paul seems to be using it both metaphorically and literally, and it is not always clear whether any given usage is literal or metaphorical. Nor is the metaphorical meaning all that clear; it can be understood as a metaphor for 'authority over', 'source' or 'unifying factor'. An examination of other Pauline passages seems to suggest that all three are possible. All of the exegetical difficulties inherent in this passage culminate in I Corinthians 1:10: 'That is why a woman ought to have *exousia epi* her head, because of the angels'. The word *exousia* is traditionally translated as 'veil', even though the Greek word means 'authority'. The traditional view that sees this passage as referring to the subordination of women understands this to means that a woman should have a sign of her submission to her husband's authority on her head. The problem with this view is that there is no evidence in the New Testament or related literature of *exousia* ever being used in this passive sense or of the idiom *exousia epi* referring to an external authority other than the subject of the sentence.[86] So this expression needs to be understood in a way that admits that the woman is being granted authority over her own head, perhaps that she is being given the right to preach as long as she does wear a veil, since both men and women are under God's authority when they preach.[87] The expression 'because of the angels' is equally puzzling. The suggestion that it refers to the spiritual guardians of the old world order that is passing away makes sense. If this is the case, the Corinthian women are being told that, even though they are free from the old order as members of the new community of Christ, they should wear veils when prophesying out of deference to the customs of the society in which they live.[88] Whatever else this verse means, it is clearly granting women the right to pray and prophesy in public worship.

It is astonishing that Pentecostals have allowed their opponents to use a passage which offers clear support to the rights of women in the gospel to argue that women ministers are unbiblical. Even if this passage does place restrictions on the ministry of women, they are restrictions in matters of dress; in no place does this passage imply that women should not preach in public worship. The restrictions seemed to be based on one of two principles: 1) that one should not break convention if that would distract from the glory of God in worship, 2) that being God's eschatological community in the present age does not mean that all distinctions between the sexes are obliterated.[89] Here the eschatological understanding of Pentecostals can help articulate what this passage might be saying to the church. It is clear that the realization of Joel's prediction that 'your daughters shall prophesy' is one of the signs that the last days have arrived. So the church needs to reflect the realities of the coming age of the kingdom in its worship and community practices and encourage its daughters to prophesy. But they cannot ignore the conventions of the society they live in or pretend that all distinctions between men and women have been removed by the presence of the Holy Spirit. Women who preach or pray in public worship need to have a clear sign that their authority comes from God and need to behave in ways that do not distract from the glory of God when the community is at worship.

SUMMARY CONCLUSION

The hermeneutic of Pentecostalism has empowered women for almost an entire century. Although feminist scholarship and the questions of a younger generation of Pentecostals have challenged some of the traditional Pentecostal arguments about women, these questions can be answered by a hermeneutic that is thoroughly Pentecostal. It is vitally important that Pentecostals use their own hermeneutic to empower Pentecostal women and not the hermeneutic of feminism. Feminist scholars offer a cultural critique of patriarchal religion and are concerned with empowering women culturally. But Pentecostals have always been concerned with empowering women spiritually. When Pentecostal women ministers insist that they are not feminists, they are making an important statement about the source of power in their ministries. Pentecostals have always resisted secularization, because they know that they get their power from radical dependence upon God. Pentecostal women preachers are far more concerned with continuing to receive direct experiences of the Spirit than with gaining cultural power, because without the Spirit's anointing they would have no empowering for ministry. Feminism simply cannot offer Pentecostal women the kind of power they value; a Pentecostal hermeneutic can.

Especially disturbing from the Pentecostal perspective is the assumption of feminist scholars that as long as Pentecostals believe that the Bible is the infallible word of God and read it literally, women will be oppressed by that reading. They ignore the obvious fact that it was a literal reading of Scripture that empowered Pentecostal women in the first place. If Pentecostal women continue to be empowered, they will be empowered by both the Word and the Spirit. This empowerment by Word and Spirit is why it is so important that Pentecostals apply their distinctive hermeneutic to the biblical texts about women. When they do so they can augment the Pentecostal argument that empowers women as ministers, with arguments from Scripture that empower women as women. The sanctification argument, that by virtue of Christ's atonement, the curse and inferiority of women is broken, is clearly supported by Mark 5:21–43. Pentecostals have always used a very similar argument for healing in the atonement, so it would not even require a major shift in thought patterns to extend this argument to empower women as women. Pentecostals claim that in the pouring out of the Spirit, the power of the age to come is being poured out on the church. So the Pentecostal community also needs to examine Scripture to find out how this coming kingdom can be realized in concrete ways in the church. One of those ways is certainly that they encourage their daughters to prophesy in fulfillment of Joel's prophecy. Another way is allowing the 'neither male nor female' of

Galatians 3:28 to change the way that Pentecostal brothers and sisters relate to each other. As Pentecostals search the Scriptures for answers to the questions that are being raised about the status of women in the church, they will be able to come up with solutions inspired by the Spirit and grounded in the Word that will truly empower Pentecostal women.

In the past few years, Pentecostals have been looking at the history of women in their tradition and becoming discouraged by trends that seem to indicate that women are losing their distinctive place in Pentecostalism. They see the intrusion of Reformed theology into Pentecostal thinking about women and blame the Charismatic Renewal or the increasing acceptance of Evangelical theology for the decline of women's ministry in Pentecostal churches.[90] Others suggest that the anti-cultural stance of Pentecostalism, which saw the change in women's roles in this century as anti-biblical, is responsible for this change. It can be seen in the backlash among Pentecostals against denominational statements which affirm women's ministries.[91] It is also possible to blame the waning of revival for this trend. In revival, spiritual power reigns and social patterns are disrupted, so woman who have spiritual power can operate autonomously. But when revival wanes, the original social and religious patterns are restored.[92] Pentecostal scholars are good at analysing the problem, but few seem to be offering distinctively Pentecostal solutions.

But there is also reason for Pentecostals to have confidence in their tradition and the way that it has empowered and continues to empower women in ministry. Pentecostals should not forget that over half of all women ever ordained come from their tradition or closely related traditions.[93] The two most famous women ministers of this century, Aimee Semple McPherson and Kathryn Kuhlman were both Pentecostal. Several Pentecostal women ministers are well-known around the world today: Daisy Osborn, Gloria Copeland (although some Pentecostals would prefer not to claim her, she clearly relies on a Pentecostal understanding of ministry) and Marilyn Hickey. All of these women have powerful ministries and are influencing the Pentecostal church in significant ways. No other Protestant denomination has produced a woman minister who can claim to have influenced the church the way that Pentecostal women have.

Recently, I was able to attend a Marilyn Hickey encounter at Faith Christian Center in Holland, Michigan, and observe the dynamics of her ministry.[94] Like all the women in the studies of Lawless and

Fulkerson, she has a well developed call narrative and uses it to vali-date her ministry. Every time she speaks, she stresses that it is God who is working through her, that she can do nothing without him. She uses this radical dependence on God to encourage others, both male and female, to move out into ministry. If God can use her, he can use any yielded vessel. She stresses the importance of holding on to your dreams and trusting God to work through you: 'I don't go by what peo-ple say I can't do!'[95] But in many ways she did not fit the pattern of the women ministers Lawless interviewed. She spoke on the subject of the family at every service, but never once used self-denigrating language or spoke about female submission, even though she spoke often about being dependent on and submissive to God. It was clear that she was empowered not only by the Spirit, but by her knowledge of the Bible. She used Scripture in her call narratives and empowered people in the congregation by calling them out and giving them scriptural passages. She never said anything that suggested that the Bible restricted her ministry. The women Lawless and Fulkerson used in their studies are not the only models available for Pentecostal women. The ministry of a woman like Marilyn Hickey should give Pentecostals reason to be encouraged about the potential a Pentecostal understanding of minis-try has for the empowering of women.

Notes

1   David G. Roebuck, 'Go and Tell My Brothers: The Waning of Women's Voices in American Pentecostalism' (Paper presented at the Twentieth Annual Meeting of the Society for Pentecostal Studies, 1990), p. 2.

2   Barbara Brown Zikmund, 'Women and Ordination', in *In Our Own Voices: Four Centuries of American Women's Religious Writing*, ed. Rosemary Radford Ruether and Rosemary Skinner Keller (San Francisco, CA: Harper & Row Pub-lishers, 1995), p. 299.

3   Susan Hyatt, 'Your Sons and Your Daughters: A Case for Pentecostal-Charismatic Egalitarianism with Special Emphasis on *Kephale* in the Pauline Literature' (M.A. Thesis, Oral Roberts University, 1993), p. 55.

4   Deborah M. Gill, 'The Contemporary State of Women in Ministry in the Assemblies of God', *PNUEMA: The Journal of the Society for Pentecostal Studies* 17 (Spring 1995): pp. 34–36.

5   Mary McClintock Fulkerson, *Changing the Subject: Women's Discourses and Feminist Theology* (Minneapolis, MN: Fortress Press, 1994), p. 285.

6   Roebuck, 'Go and Tell My Brothers', p. 14.

7   Ibid., pp. 7–8.

8   Ibid., p. 14.

9   Professor Elaine Lawless has published several studies which all have

remarkably similar conclusions. The one which I found most interesting and informative and have used throughout this paper is: Elaine J. Lawless, *Handmaidens of the Lord: Pentecostal Women Preachers and Traditional Religion* (Philadelphia, PA: University of Pennsylvania Press, 1988).

10   Lawless simply lacks basic biblical knowledge and so fails to understand the dynamics of Pentecostal churches. For example, she states that it is Paul who asserts that Joel's prophecy has come to pass in Acts 2:28–29 and that he repeats himself in Acts 9:16–17 (obvious misreferences) (p. 153). She is surprised that all three women whose sermons she analyses use the story of the children of Israel and how they became back-slidden (pp. 132–133) and that two themes – sacrifice and sin/salvation – are so common (pp. 112–113). She sees the fact that these women preachers derive everything from the Bible as a sign that they cannot present these directives as their own (p. 114). No one who sat in Pentecostal services on a regular basis would be surprised by any of these themes or see them as unique to women's sermons. Probably more damaging to her basic thesis is her assumption that in the Bible, preaching is described as a male role (p. 85). She does not seem to realize that most Pentecostals (especially not the Assemblies of God, which is the denomination the women in her study are affiliated with) would not agree with this nor that Pentecostalism is quite distinct from fundamentalism in this. 'Oddly enough, even in the face of their obvious heresy, it is the strong connection these women maintain with a conservative fundamentalism that enables them to acquire the position of power and authority in a church as pastor and provides the means for them to maintain that position' (p. 145). She accuses these women of not seeking 'liberating scriptures to revise theologies' (p. 145) because she does not recognize that they are doing this to some extent already, but doing it in a way that is completely separate from the feminist agenda.

11   Fulkerson, *Changing the Subject*, pp. 3–6.

12   Roebuck, 'Go and Tell My Brothers', p. 16.

13   Hyatt, 'Your Sons and Your Daughters', pp. 46, 56; Roebuck, 'Go and Tell My Brothers', p. 1.

14   Roebuck, 'Go and Tell My Brothers', pp. 1, 15.

15   Hyatt, 'Your Sons and Your Daughters', pp. 57–58; Roebuck, 'Go and Tell My Brothers', p. 1.

16   Roebuck, 'Go and Tell My Brothers', p. 2.

17   Hyatt, 'Your Sons and Your Daughters', p. 79.

18   Steven J. Land, *Pentecostal Spirituality: A Passion for the Kingdom* (Sheffield: Sheffield Academic Press, 1993), pp. 72–73.

19   Hyatt, 'Your Sons and Your Daughters', p. 82.

20   Land, *Pentecostal Spirituality*, p. 74.

21   Fulkerson, *Changing the Subject*, pp. 250–251.

22   Land, *Pentecostal Spirituality*, p. 74.

23   Ibid., p. 74.

24   Hans W. Frei, *The Eclipse of Biblical Narrative: A Study in Eighteenth and Nineteenth Century Hermeneutics* (New Haven, CT: Yale University Press, 1974), pp. 24–25.

25   Land, *Pentecostal Spirituality*, pp. 74–75.

26   Roger Stronstad, *The Charismatic Theology of St. Luke* (Peabody, MA: Hendrickson Publishers, 1984), p. 5.

27   Land, *Pentecostal Spirituality*, pp. 72, 79.

28   Ibid., pp. 72–73.

29   Hyatt, 'Your Sons and Your Daughters', pp. 83–84.

30   Roebuck, 'Go Tell My Brothers', p. 3.

31   Hyatt, 'Your Sons and Your Daughters', pp. 3–5.

32   Ibid., pp. 10, 14.

33   Ibid., pp. 14–15; Roebuck, 'Go Tell My Brothers', p. 9.

34   Hyatt, 'Your Sons and Your Daughters', pp. 22–23.

35   Fulkerson, *Changing the Subject*, p. 254.

36   Ibid., p. 245.

37   Roebuck, 'Go and Tell My Brothers', pp. 5–6.

38   Maria Woodworth Etter, *Signs and Wonders God Wrought in the Ministry for Forty Years* (Tulsa, OK: Harrison House, reprint of 1916 edition), pp. 210–216.

39   Lawless, *Handmaidens of the Lord*, pp. 12–13.

40   Ibid., p. 163.

41   Ibid., p. 131.

42   Ibid., pp. 66–68.

43   Ibid., pp. 76–84.

44   Ibid., pp. 102–109, 114.

45   Fulkerson, *Changing the Subject*, pp. 271–277.

46   Ibid., pp. 252–253.

47   Ibid., p. 253.

48   Hyatt, 'Your Sons and Your Daughters', p. 46; Roebuck, 'Go and Tell My Brothers', p. 3.

49   Roebuck, 'Go and Tell My Brothers', p. 3.

50   Ibid., p. 7.

51   Ibid., p. 3.

52   Hyatt, 'Your Sons and Your Daughters', pp. 34–44.

53   Roebuck, 'Go and Tell My Brothers', pp. 7–9.

54   Hyatt, 'Your Sons and Your Daughters', p. 45.

55   Ibid., p. 50.

56   Roebuck, 'Go and Tell My Brothers', p. 12.

57   Hyatt, 'Your Sons and Your Daughters', pp. 51–54.

58   Roebuck, 'Go and Tell My Brothers', p. 13.

59   Hyatt, 'Your Sons and Your Daughters', p. 54.

60   Roebuck, 'Go and Tell My Brothers', p. 17.

61   Gill, 'The Contemporary State of Women in Ministry in the Assemblies of God', pp. 34–36.

62   Lawless, *Handmaidens of the Lord*, pp. 145–146.

63   Ibid., p. 86.

64   Fulkerson, *Changing the Subject*, p. 263.

65   Lawless, *Handmaidens of the Lord*, pp. 111–112.

66   Ibid., p. 93.

67   Fulkerson, *Changing the Subject*, pp. 266–267.

68   Lawless, *Handmaidens of the Lord*, p. 152.

69   Ibid., pp. 130–133.

70   Ibid., pp. 68–69.

71   Fulkerson, *Changing the Subject*, pp. 289–298.

72   Fulkerson, Changing the Subject, pp. 254–255.
73   Ibid., pp. 254–255.
74   Ibid., pp. 287–288.
75   Hyatt, 'Your Sons and Your Daughters', pp. 79, 82; Land, *Pentecostal Spiritu-ality*, pp. 72–74.
76   Stronstad, *The Charismatic Theology of St. Luke*, p. 5
77   Ibid., p. 6.
78   Land, *Pentecostal Spirituality*, pp. 72, 76.
79   I have been teaching this interpretation of the text for the last eleven years. I am not quite sure when I first realized that, if these two stories were a comment on Leviticus 15, they had something significant to say about the new status of women in the Christian community. Frank Kermode has an interesting analy-sis of the narrative shape of these stories and suggests that the cleanliness laws of Judaism are important to interpreting these stories in *The Genesis of Secrecy: On the Interpretation of Narrative* (Cambridge, MA: Harvard Uni-versity Press, 1979), pp. 131–135. At the 1984 meeting of the Southeastern Society of Biblical Literature, I remember that Dan Via pointed out that the words 'daughter' and 'twelve years' functioned as key words, which tied these two stories together. If my memory serves me correctly, I talked about this pas-sage with Mary Ann Tolbert at the same meeting. Her article on 'Mark' in *The Women's Bible Commentary* (London: SPCK Press, 1992) reflects a somewhat similar reading of these stories. Other than these acknowledgements it is impossible for me to state the sources for my reading of this passage.
80   Lawless, *Handmaidens of the Lord*, p. 154.
81   Quoted in Roebuck, 'Go and Tell My Brothers', p. 7.
82   Land, *Pentecostal Spirituality*, p. 75.
83   Etter, *Signs and Wonders God Wrought in the Ministry for Forty Years*, p. 210.
84   Here I am using Gordon Fee's analysis of the way a scholar uses Pauline texts to show that the gifts of prophecy and tongues have ceased. My point is that exactly the same sort of exegetical moves are made by those who wish to show that women should not be ministers. This analysis is found in: Gordon D. Fee, *Gospel and Spirit: Issues in New Testament Hermeneutics* (Peabody, MA: Hendrickson Publishers, 1991), pp. 75–78.
85   An excellent Pentecostal exegesis of this passage can be found in: Gordon D. Fee, *The First Epistle to the Corinthians* (Grand Rapids, MI: Wm. B. Eerdmans Publishing Company, 1987), pp. 491–530.
86   Fee, *The First Epistle to the Corinthians*, p. 519.
87   Morna D. Hooker, 'Authority On Her Head', *New Testament Studies* 10 (1963–1964), pp. 210–216.
88   G.B. Caird, 'Paul and Women's Liberty' *Bulletin of the Johns Rylands Library* 54 (1972), p. 278.
89   Gospel and Spirit, p. 14.
90   Hyatt, 'Your Sons and Your Daughters', pp. 57–77.
91   Roebuck, 'Go and Tell Your Brothers', pp. 15–17.
92   Hyatt, 'Your Sons and Your Daughters', pp. 47–48; Lawless, *Handmaidens of the Lord*, pp. 160–161.
93   Zikmund, Women and Ordination , p. 299.
94   This encounter took place from April 28, 1996 to April 30, 1996. She spoke in both morning and evening services each day. I probably observed for a total of

about 18 hours. I also spoke to members of her staff when I had questions or needed a point clarified.
95   Marilyn Hickey in the morning service on April 29, 1996.

Chapter Fifteen

Pentecostals and Ecumenism in a Pluralistic World

Cecil M. Robeck, Jr.

Each year the world celebrates the end of one year and the beginning of another. It does so with resolutions, late night vigils, singing, dancing, fireworks, parades, and other festive, or even liturgical acts. The beginning and ending of centuries bring about similar celebrative moments in our common human history. If these frequent historical hinges can serve as significant points of celebration and reflection, how much more can the coming of a new millennium? It is the coming of this new millennium which has motivated Christians around the world to bring a positive closure to the present millennium through their Decades of Harvest, Decades of Destiny, Target 2000, AD 2000, even Pope John Paul II's Apostolic Letter *Tertio Millennio Adveniente*.[1] Such moments fill us with anticipation on the one hand and apprehension on the other. Just what does the future hold for our collective human history?

Such fears, dreams, questions, and hopes touch the lives of Christians and non-Christians alike. The second millennium AD has had its times of hope as well as despair for the entire world. But it has been particularly significant for the church. This millennium has seen the Eastern and Western parts of the church torn asunder. It has shattered any real semblance of visible unity in every facet of the church, East or West. Where once stood a single visible church, now stand a multiplicity of denominations, a myriad of congregations who are often unwilling to speak even with those who constitute their nearest Christian neighbours. They appear to value different authorities, use opposing methodologies, embrace conflicting values, and sometimes even seem to preach different gospels. When we add the various concerns laid before the church by different nations, racial and ethnic groups, genders, age groups, classes, and the like, any thought of a shared consensus, conviction, narrative, or consciousness seems absolutely elusive. The modern world seems to have abandoned us. The Newtonian world of cause and effect seems to have betrayed us at times. The Darwinian promises which education, medicine, science, and technology, even of democracy, dangled before us a century ago, bringing hope and optimism for a brighter future, no longer seem to exist.

Two images from Scripture seem to describe the present situation fairly well. Today seems to be a day like the days of the judges in which it was said that '... all the people did what was right in their own eyes' (Judges 17:6b, NRSV). But it also captures elements of Jesus' own prediction when he pointed to a day in which some would draw attention to a messianic figure in one place while others would direct attention to a messianic figure elsewhere (Matthew 24:23; Mark 13:21; Luke 17:21). Ultimately there seem to be so many answers, that there appear to be *no answers at all*. Everything seems merely to be relative to everything else, with no overarching point of correlation. There appears to be a lack of a centre.

The end of the present millennium coincides with the end of 500 years in which the Protestant movement has splintered into pieces. It is, therefore, extremely difficult for us to imagine that there ever existed 500 years in which there was essentially one church in the East and another in the West. It is virtually impossible for us to conceive of an entire millennium in which the church was essentially undivided. All we have before us is the reality of visible division, entrepeneurialism, and individualism, as well as a lack of understanding, cooperation, or even of appreciation for one another. The legacy which has culminated in suspicion and fear between us, is the legacy of the second half of the Second Millennium AD. There seems to be no shared vision of unity, not even between Christians. There is simply the proliferation of division or the careful construction and maintenance of ever higher boundaries between us, often in the name of purity (2 Corinthians 6:17a), with no discernible recognition or acknowledgment of the need for cooperation between us, to say nothing of reconciliation.

The Pentecostal movement, like her older Christian siblings who identify themselves with one or another ecclesial family, has also contributed to this confusing and contradictory morass. A movement whose earliest leaders once believed that Christian unity might be their ultimate gift to the church seems, in subsequent years, to have lost its way with regard to this vision. Instead of maintaining relationships with older churches in such a way that their unique message of Pentecost could be heard and appreciatively appropriated by these older churches, Pentecostals have often broken with them, frequently adopting sectarian positions, attitudes, and behaviours.[2]

In its first century of existence, then, the Pentecostal movement has repeatedly found its message of reconciliation compromised through external condemnations and internal discord. It has demonstrated the fact that 'truth' claims are frequently more important than love and acceptance within the household of God, by such factors as its inability and continuing unwillingness to resolve tensions and differences in doctrine over the nature of the Godhead and of Christian baptism.[3] It has fought over the issue of sanctification, when and how it takes place and what constitutes true holiness, to such an extent that the entire discussion has rendered the reality which is being described, as profane.[4] Pentecostals have appealed to their organizational structures in such a way as to guarantee a lack of cooperation at any significant level.[5] They have taken on national, regional, even political identities in such a way as to leave no room for God in any alternative position.[6] The movement has split over when and how to keep the Sabbath.[7] Its constituents have alienated one another over issues related to war and peace.[8] The movement has been divided over racial and ethnic biases and bigotries,[9] over the limits of legitimate fellowship with the non-Pentecostal world,[10] even over the correct way to butcher a chicken.[11] These are but a few of the issues which have imperilled the contribution that Pentecostals have sought to make to the larger church.[12] What is noteworthy about these divisions is that none of them is new. They have all appeared before. Pentecostals have not been creative in their divisions. They have been extremely predictable.

In a real sense, then, the Pentecostal movement has managed, in just less than a century, to contribute to nearly as many different divisions as it took the rest of the church a millennium to produce. By ignoring lessons which could have been learned from the historic churches, the Pentecostal movement has not lived up to its potential, nor has it achieved the hopes and dreams of its pioneers. Like the Christians it often criticizes, it has contributed to the fragmentation and pluralization of the Christian portion of the contemporary global context.

PENTECOSTALS AND THE QUEST FOR CHRISTIAN UNITY

The earliest literature of Pentecostalism is replete with the dream of visible Christian unity. R.G. Spurling, founder of the Christian Union, forerunner to the Church of God (Cleveland, TN), claims to have lamented frequently the 'strife and confusion' which he identified with the denominational diversity around him. 'Above all this din of strife and confusion', he wrote, 'I hear Christ praying in John 17:21, that they may all be one'. He knew that some would argue that the answer to Jesus' prayer had already come. It could be found in the spiritual unity of all Christians. It was something that was essentially invisible. But, he argued, '... our reason says not so'. Spurling's concern was a logical one, based in the need for tangibility. 'Christ said the world might believe', he argued, 'but there is not a unity that the world can see. No, it is not the unity which Christ wanted by any means, but a confusion that He does not want'.[13]

Like Spurling, Charles Fox Parham was troubled by the confusion of denominationalism, the divisions he observed at the turn of the century, and he came to believe that God had anointed him to be 'an apostle of unity'. Unity did not come through the establishment of 'concentration camps', (a term he used to describe denominations) but rather, through the work of God among those who were '... baptized by the Holy Ghost into one Body, the gloriously redeemed Church ...'. The true Elijah, (a less than humble self-designation) would lead this redeemed Church into fruitful evangelization in such a way as to result in a single, restored, visible, Pentecostal Church.[14]

Warren Fay Carothers served as the Field Director for Charles F. Parham's Apostolic Faith Movement. He was completely committed to the restorationist historiography which was so prevalently embraced among early Pentecostal leaders. The 'restoration of Pentecost', he argued, ultimately meant 'the restoration of Christian unity'.[15] This restoration of unity was a hope and an expectation on which Carothers acted, first by calling for a central role for Parham's Apostolic Faith Movement, then by entering the newly formed Assemblies of God. He called for them to reach out to other Pentecostals as well as to the larger church in concrete acts of fellowship. Ultimately, he conducted a series of Unity Conferences even as he left his active involvement in ecclesiastical leadership and pursued a long and fruitful judicial career.[16]

Drawing in part from the work of Charles F. Parham, William J. Seymour, the African-American pastor of the famous Azusa Street Mission in Los Angeles, affirmed in no uncertain terms that 'The Apostolic Faith Movement' did not desire to fight 'men or churches', but rather it wanted 'to displace dead forms and creeds' on the one hand and 'wild fanaticism' on the other, with 'living practical Christianity'. Among other things, he asserted, this movement stood for 'Christian Unity everywhere'.[17]

Even the Assemblies of God shared the view that something unique was happening in the Pentecostal movement, yet its founders viewed themselves as standing in full continuity with other Christians. In its originating meeting, the Assemblies of God unanimously adopted a resolution which vehemently denied that its membership desired to establish themselves into a 'sect'. What they meant was that they had no intention of ever becoming 'a human organization that legislates or forms laws and articles of faith and has unscriptural jurisdiction over its members and creates unscriptural lines of fellowship and disfellowship....' Such bylaws and creeds would only serve to separate Christians, they argued, and such actions would inevitably stand 'contrary to Christ's prayer in St. John 17, and Paul's teaching in Eph. 4:1-16', which the members of the founding Council claimed to 'heartily endorse'.[18] The world needed to see more than such narrowness emerge among Pentecostals. Their membership from 1920 onward in the Foreign Missions Conference of North America (later the Foreign Missions Division of the National Council of Churches, USA) and from 1921 onward in the International Missionary Conference (later the Mission & Evangelism Department of the World Council of Churches) was fully consistent with their stated concerns.

By the 1940s, however, following their rejection by many of their progenitors in the Wesleyan-Holiness movement,[19] as well as by the Fundamentalist movement for which they clearly had sympathies,[20] such visions of visible Christian unity had begun to fade. With the desire to be accepted by evangelical leaders, and the partisan pressures brought to bear upon Pentecostals by the anti-Pentecostal American fundamentalist Carl McIntire, a number of Pentecostal leaders abandoned the foundational dream of early Pentecostal leaders, and bowed to the increasing pressures to conform to American evangelical interests.[21] In the process, they chose to condemn the formal Ecumenical movement, and they spread their concerns throughout their missionary churches world wide.[22]

As we near the close of the present millennium, few Pentecostals are aware of these historic positions regarding Christian unity. Few Pentecostals understand what ecumenism is, and the so-called 'Ecumenical movement' is ill-defined. Typically many Pentecostals seem to believe that the World Council of Churches *is* the Ecumenical movement, but the movement is much more than that. Pentecostal periodicals typically report only the negative news regarding the work of conciliar churches and councils, while describing only the positive news about their own alliances and constituencies.[23] It appears that Pentecostals generally assume that all ecumenism is (1) an attempt to compromise doctrinal standards to the lowest common denominator in such a way as to affirm not only questionable forms of Christian expression, but also the classic religions of the world, in a human scheme to embrace all of humankind[24] in a (2) relativistic international organization that will usurp the rights and freedoms of existing denominations in such a way as to promote 'unity' at the expense of 'truth', or at least of genuine Christian faith and life, an organization which will[25] (3) ultimately and inevitably be united with the Roman Catholic Church in such a way as to form the infamous Babylon of Revelation 17 and 18 out of which a voice from heaven has cried, 'Come out of her, my people, so that you do not take part in her sins ...' (Rev. 18:4b, NRSV).[26]

Such an understanding of ecumenical realities, of course, seems to be quite foreign to the earliest vision of Pentecostals, even if their views could be judged as triumphalistic. It raises questions about the nature of apocalyptic literature, about the role of Scripture, and about what constitute legitimate hermeneutical methodologies. It appears to impose upon the text certain fears, prejudices, and entire theological systems which are foreign to the earliest Pentecostal impulses toward visible unity, rather than to allow the text to reveal its own treasures to the interpreter. Such an understanding of ecumenical realities at the close of the current millennium reveals much more about the nature and extent of Pentecostal insecurities, fears, and misunderstandings than it does about the ecumenical realities it attempts to describe. On the whole, Pentecostals have not kept up with ecumenical developments over the past half-century. They do not understand what ecumenism is, and as a result, they do not trust it.[27]

THE NATURE OF THE ECUMENICAL DISCUSSION

The term 'ecumenism' is based upon the Greek noun 'οι' (*oikos*), meaning 'house' or 'dwelling'. By extrapolation, it has also come to refer to a 'household'.[28] In a sense, then, to engage in business pertaining to the household is to engage in a form of ecumenism. But different people view the extent of the household differently. Some view it narrowly as referring to things pertaining to a single family, while others view it in extended family terms. The Greek noun (*oikoumene*) is clearly a derivative of '*oikia*'. It, too, lies behind the definition of 'ecumenism', and its meanings extend beyond the single dwelling and its inhabitants, to all of 'humankind' even to the whole of the 'inhabited earth, the world'.[29] Thus, the term 'ecumenism' has come to encompass a variety of meanings, depending upon the concerns of those who have chosen to use this term.

As the so-called 'Ecumenical movement' lumbers toward the next millennium, it is struggling to do justice to its acknowledged calling and concern. There are those within the movement who view their calling in narrowly defined terms, as moving toward some form of visible unity shared by all Christians, perhaps in some form of organic, if not organizational unity.[30] The discussion surrounding this position is highly theoretical, technical, and theological. It moves very deliberately and very slowly. It frustrates many who are interested in immediate solutions. Most frequently, this position is elaborated by various Orthodox leaders, although this is not a position which is of interest solely to them.

At a second level may be found many Christians who are more action-oriented, and who are interested in the integrity of humanity. 'We were human before we were Christian', they remind us, 'so we must stand in solidarity with all humanity'. These Christians tend to emphasize our common bonds with other people, including non-Christians, who frequently share the same hopes, dreams, and aspirations and are subject to many of the same fears, disappointments, and injustices as are their Christian counterparts. Some of them emphasize the need for unity for the sake of mission.[31] Others focus their attention more specifically on raising the level of human dignity for all humanity, from the street children in Calcutta, India or Lima, Peru, to the Arab women in the Middle East, to the victims of racial injustice in the United States or South Africa, to the victims of war in the former Yugoslavia. They are also frequently driven by their Christian convictions to work toward world peace, and their concern to work for human dignity by fighting poverty as well as a range of social injustices is intended, in part, to deprive entire nations of their reasons for entering into social and political conflict, or even the invasion of another country.

This group of Christians also looks frequently for similarities between their own Christian faith and piety and the faith and piety expressed within other religions through their non-Christian cultures. They see the Holy Spirit at work within culture, including the Spirit's presence in the religions which other people pursue. In recent years the idea that the world is merely a global village has gained credibility as we have watched as one market economy has impacted another in very different parts of the world. Regional conflicts which have threatened world peace even in far-flung regions of the world have also pointed in this direction. The issue of religious toleration has also emerged as a factor with global implications, not merely in the Middle East, but elsewhere as well. To what extent must Christians learn to live within a culturally and religiously pluralistic setting? Does the need to do so mean an end to evangelization altogether, or does it mean an end to certain types of evangelization? Where should they draw the lines of toleration? Those within this discussion come down on the issue in varying ways. Some are clearly convinced of the uniqueness of Jesus Christ and the particularity of the Christian message that he alone 'is the way, the truth, and the life' (John 14:6). But there are others who have decided, at least for themselves, that there may be a legitimacy to the idea of multiple paths to God.[32]

A third group of action-oriented Christians within the Ecumenical movement is committed to the idea that ecumenism cannot stop either with the church, or with humanity, but must take into consideration the impact of human sin and inhumanity upon the whole of creation. They tend to look beyond the mere interactions of the human species with one another, and ask questions of the impact of the human species on the world around them. Their convictions, as Christians, point to the obvious global implications of human sin and greed. What impact, for instance, does war have on the environment, through the use of atomic weaponry, chemical warfare, and scorched earth policies? What impact does the burning of fossil fuels, the razing of rain forests, the over-farming of land, or the over-use of pesticides have on the world around us? These are no longer regional questions, but our answers to these questions impact the whole of the world around us. This group, then, is concerned to ask the questions of the stewardship of the earth.[33] What does it mean for us to stand in solidarity with God's creation, even if we are stewards?

It may not be readily apparent, but the funnel produced by these three positions which define ecumenism narrowly as (1) intra-Christian relations, more broadly as (2) Christian-human relations, or more broadly yet as (3) Christian-creation relations, is an ever expanding one. These three groups are not mutually exclusive, nor are the interests of those who participate in one or another group necessarily limited to the concerns being emphasized by a particular group. There is considerable movement across such distinctions as, indeed, there should be. But in recent years there has been a blurring of such distinctions and the bases for such distinctions until many have been confused about the meaning of the term 'ecumenism' itself.

THE WORLD COUNCIL OF CHURCHES AND ECUMENISM

The World Council of Churches is one place where these different views of ecumenism are being held in tension. Its programme on Justice, Peace, and the Integrity of Creation clearly attempts to give expression to the concerns of the second and third groups, and to a lesser extent to the first group.[34] The Commission on Faith and Order has given primary expression to the first group, and secondary support to some of the concerns of the programme on Justice, Peace, and the Integrity of Creation. The discussions between the various member churches has not always been easy, but in light of the global realities which face us at the end of the present millennium, they are essential.[35]

If the World Council of Churches, as one international expression of the modern Ecumenical movement, began with the hope of bringing all Christians into a single organizational structure with one another, that ideal was short lived.[36] To be sure, there are those who still seem to argue toward that end in one way or another,[37] but given the fact that neither the Roman Catholic Church (the world's largest denomination) nor the majority of the Pentecostal/Charismatic Renewal (the world's second largest ecclesial family of Christians and by far the fastest growing Christian movement worldwide) are members of the World Council of Churches, such an expectation is probably unreasonable and clearly not accomplishable by the World Council of Churches as it presently stands. Thus, in recent years the World Council of Churches, through its Commission on Faith and Order, has focused its attention on two major projects which, if accepted by the churches of the Council, would bring a greater level of visible Christian unity through mutual recognition. The first of these is the search for a common creed as a common expression of Apostolic Faith.[38] The second is a project which has sought for convergence on three important church-dividing issues; baptism, eucharist, and ministry.[39]

The status of the discussion on the possibility of a common creed currently lies with the various denominations. The last truly ecumenical creed, that is, the last creed which was adopted by the one, undivided church, was the Nicene-Constantinopolitan Creed, approved by the Council which met at Constantinople in AD 381. This creed was later modified, unilaterally, by the Church in the West through the insertion of the so-called *filioque clause* in AD 589 when the addition was affirmed by the Council of Toledo. Because of the unilateral character of this addition, the Commission on Faith and Order has submitted a study which is based upon the earlier version of the creed to the denominations of the World Council of Churches. It is currently being studied by the churches in a process known as *reception*.[40]

More difficult to accomplish has been the work toward some type of mutual recognition of the sacraments and/or ordinances of baptism and the eucharist, and on the mutual recognition of the ministry of one another. What has resulted from this discussion is not an agreement, but a convergence statement, which has been commended to the various denominations for review and reception. The churches have been asked to articulate the extent to which they can recognize in this study 'the faith of the Church through the ages', to spell out how these churches might respond to other churches who also recognize it as 'an expression of the apostolic faith', and to give expression to the ways in which each church can be guided by the text in matters related to 'worship, educational, ethical, and spiritual life and witness'.[41]

The Commission on Faith and Order has played a critical role in making possible the presence of the Orthodox churches and the Roman Catholic Church in the discussions of the World Council of Churches. The Roman Catholic Church is not a member of the World Council of Churches, but it does hold membership in the Commission on Faith and Order. The Orthodox churches are members of the World Council of Churches, but they hold their membership in the Council somewhat tenuously. What made their membership even possible was the adoption of the so-called 'Toronto Statement' of 1950 published as a 'Statement on "The Church, the churches and the World Council of Churches" '.[42] Important to that document are the affirmations of what the World Council of Churches *is not*, and what it cannot do, as well as a spelling out of the assumptions which underlie the formation of the Council.[43]

In spite of all of this work, the World Council of Churches today is seeking to find its way through a new quest for 'Common Understanding and Vision'. This new emphasis, led in large part by the General Secretary, Dr. Konrad Raiser, is an outgrowth of discussions which first emerged in 1989. Four major areas are being explored at the present time. They include (a) 'the nature and task of the WCC as a *fellowship of churches*; (b) the role of the WCC within the *one ecumenical movement*; (c) forms of representation, participation and communication within the fellowship of the WCC; and (d) steps towards an integrating ecumenical vision'.[44] What this suggests is that the World Council of Churches has begun more accurately to see itself merely as one portion of the much larger Ecumenical Movement. Ecumenism is, in fact, taking place at a variety of levels and in many different ways around the world. In one sense, anywhere where the churches are actively pursuing issues within the household of God, or of humanity, or of creation, with a Trinitarian or at least a Christological centre out of which their concerns and actions have emerged and on which they are based, some level of ecumenism is taking place. It may begin as interdenominational cooperation, but inevitably it must move beyond that. Thus, Pentecostals are already participating in the larger ecumenical movement when they reach out to cooperate with, and to coordinate efforts to meet the mutual concerns of, other believers, or when, in the name of Christ they cooperate with other believers on issues of justice, peace, or even ecology. They simply do not understand that they have already made an ecumenical commitment when they do these things.[45]

A ROMAN CATHOLIC APPROACH TO ECUMENISM

The issue of the Roman Catholic Church is more complicated, for it has not entered the ecumenical world easily, nor has it done so by joining the World Council of Churches. As late as 1928, Pope Pius XI, in his Encyclical *Mortalium Animos,* spelled out the reasons that the Apostolic See had never allowed its 'subjects' to participate in the assemblies of non-Catholics: 'for the union of Christians can only be promoted by promoting the return to the one true Church of Christ of those who are separated from it, for in the past they have unhappily left it'. What this communicated was that Rome was pure, that all of Protestantism had sinned against Rome by leaving it, and that any reconciliation with Rome would be on Roman terms. Not only did Pope Pius XI deny any complicity in the division which occurred at the time of the Reformation by announcing that the 'Spouse of Christ has never been contaminated, nor can she ever in the future be contaminated', he also announced that all who were not members of the mystical body of Christ were not 'in communion with Christ its head'.[46] Thus, it was clear that only in the Roman Catholic Church was salvation really possible.

With the advent of the Second Vatican Council in 1962, and with the insistence of Pope John XXIII that the Latin term *aggiornamento*, meaning 'updating', 'modernization' or 'adaptation', would govern the actions of the Council, came many changes to Roman Catholic self-understanding. The emphasis on the church became one on the People of God. While it was the case that the church *subsisted* in the Catholic Church, the Council noted that 'many elements of sanctification and of truth are found outside its visible confines'.[47] More importantly, the Council noted that 'men of both sides were to blame' for the separation which had occurred at the time of the Reformation, and that it was inappropriate to view those persons who were now outside the Roman Catholic Church as in some way guilty of the sins of their forebears. They were from this point onward to be accepted as 'brothers. For men who believe in Christ and have been properly baptized are put in some, though imperfect, communion with the Catholic Church'.[48]

More recently, the *Directory for the Application of Principles and Norms on Ecumenism* issued by the Vatican in 1993, has spelled out in more specific terms the ways in which the Roman Catholic Church understands the one ecumenical movement in which it participates, and outlines guidelines for interchange between Catholics and other non-Catholics.[49] Pope John Paul II has built on these documents of Vatican II and subsequent years to reaffirm the commitment of the Roman Catholic Church to the ongoing ecumenical quest in his most recent Encyclical *Ut Unum Sint,* issued May 30, 1995. He is fully aware of the unfinished business left over from the Reformation, including discussions on (1) the relationship between Scripture and Tradition, (2) the nature of the eucharist, (3) ordination, (4) the role of the magisterium, and (5) the place of Mary in the Church.[50] He moves beyond the language of mere 'ecclesial communities' when referring to Christians other than the Orthodox, to the language of 'Christians',[51] and he even invites mutual reflection on the nature of the papacy.[52]

The Vatican, therefore, offers another perspective on ecumenism. Because of its belief in the uniqueness, priority, and authority which exists in the papacy, it has been unwilling to join the World Council of Churches. Where does the ultimate authority in the church rest? Is it in a Council where representatives are supposed to speak on behalf of their respective denominations but sometimes do not? Or is it in the papacy who is said to funtion as the Vicar of Christ and which is at home in the magisterium? Can the Roman Catholic Church view itself as simply another denomination? It seems very unlikely that it can, given its theology and the present situation. Thus, John Paul II offers a vision of ecumenism which views the ministry of the Bishop of Rome, perhaps in a new way, as providing 'a service of unity' on behalf of the whole church.[53] He is well aware that this suggestion 'constitutes a difficulty for most other Christians, whose memory is marked by certain painful recollections' and to the extent that 'we [Catholics] are responsible for these', he notes, 'I join my Predecessor Paul VI in asking forgiveness'.[54]

John Paul II is fully cognizant of the fact that the World Council of Churches has suggested a new study on the subject of 'a universal ministry of Christian unity'[55] and he wants to work with that notion. The Vatican also cooperates with the World Council of Churches through a Joint Working Group made up of members from the Roman Catholic Church and from the World Council of Churches. Thus, even though the Roman Catholic Church offers a different version of the ecumenical vision, John Paul II seems not to want to offer his vision as something which is exclusive of the vision shared by so many other Christians.

WHAT DOES THIS CHANGE IN ECUMENISM MEAN FOR PENTECOSTALS?

In the contemporary world, a great deal of conversation is going on regarding the nature of Christian unity and what definition might best be given to the idea of ecumenism. As one Pentecostal noted three decades ago, 'Pentecostals as a whole have tried to disregard the entire movement toward organic church union for a long time'.[56] It could be equally affirmed that for at least the past three decades, Pentecostals on the whole, have assiduously avoided participating in anything which they believed might move them toward some form of 'organic church union' even among themselves. There are exceptions, to be sure. The *Iglesia Pentecostal de Chile*, the *Misión Iglesia Pentecostal* (also from Chile), the *Igreja Evangélica Pentecostal 'O Brasil para Cristo'*, the International Evangelical Church, the *Iglesia de Dios* from Argentina, the *Missão Evangélica Pentecostal de Angola*, and the *Iglesia de Misiones Pentecostales Libres de Chile* are all members of the World Council of Churches.[57] But in the end, ecumenism does not begin and end with the World Council of Churches or with the Roman Catholic Church. As early as 1967, the editor of the *Church of God Evangel* portrayed the National Association of Evangelicals in ecumenical terms when he wrote 'The National Association of Evangelicals is a fellowship in a truly ecumenical and biblical setting, offering to the world a visible demonstration of the unity of believers in Jesus Christ.'[58]

The formation of the Pentecostal/Charismatic Churches of North America (PCCNA) in Memphis, Tennessee, October 17–19, 1994 was significant, in part, because it adopted as its first resolution a 'Racial Reconciliation Manifesto' titled 'Pentecostal Partners'. The PCCNA thereby claimed that its membership would seek new partnerships 'in the Spirit of our Blessed Lord who prayed that we might be one' (John 17:21). It went on to pledge a commitment to 'the reconciliation of all Christians regardless of race or gender as we move into the new millennium'.[59] These are, in fact, ecumenical statements and commitments.

Pentecostals need to become more alert to the fact that they already function in an ecumenical manner with an ecumenical agenda. They have, however, chosen to engage in a limited ecumenism rather than a broader ecumenism such as is being offered by various National and World Councils of Churches, and they are clearly not yet tripping over one another to accept the invitation of John Paul II, even to meet him at the foot of the cross in prayer. In spite of this reality, Pentecostals need to understand that the larger or broader forms of ecumenism of the World Council and the Vatican have major implications for who the

Pentecostal Movement is and what it does. By engaging in dialogue with these other forms of ecumenism, Pentecostals can become aware of the implications of these larger discussions for their lives and ministries. These implications include the following concerns:

1. Pentecostals who choose to ignore other Christians and other Christian organizations, and who do not participate in the process of intra-Christian discussion, can be said to argue that there are other parts of the Body of Christ for which they have no need. In a sense, they have turned against sister and brother, and have chosen to travel alone. In an increasingly pluralistic age, when there are increasing calls in the world at large to limit the role of the church or to disarm the ability of the church to engage in such things as evangelism, this does not seem to be a wise move. It seems to be arrogant, self-serving, and condescending. It violates the sense of what the Apostle called the Corinthians to embrace, the full Body of Christ, with Christ being the one Head of the one Body (1 Cor. 12:12–27).

2. Pentecostals who choose to ignore the larger church have a tendency to move steadily toward sectarianism. Even if they do not end up in sectarianism, they run the risk of being labelled as sects and thereby, of being marginalized from their own sisters and brothers. It is largely because of the International Roman Catholic-Pentecostal Dialogue which has been taking place since 1972 that in 1993 Cardinal Cassidy, President of the Pontifical Council for Promoting Christian Unity, made the following statement:

> We must be careful... not to confuse the issue by lumping under the term 'sect' groups that do not deserve that title. I am not speaking here, for instance, about... Pentecostals.... The Pontifical Council has had fruitful dialogue and significant contacts with certain... Pentecostals. Indeed, one can speak of a mutual enrichment as a result of these contacts.[60]

On the opposite extreme are the places where contacts between Pentecostals and Roman Catholics have been most difficult, that is, in countries where Pentecostals have been a minority expression of faith while Roman Catholics or others have been a majority expression. Cardinal Ahumada Archbishop of Mexico City complained in a 1991 report that 'The Christian sects are most numerous', and went on to note that 'the majority are Pentecostals....'[61] Such designations result from a lack of contact, and are ultimately not helpful to Pentecostals, because they raise concerns among those who do not know them about what Pentecostals are doing when they minister to people at large.

3. Pentecostals who choose not to build relationships with other

people who claim to be Christian run the risk of being charged with intolerance, with proselytism, or of inciting the rhetoric of 'Holy Wars'. The discussion of what constitutes proselytism is a major discussion which is currently going on in ecumenical discussions within the World Council of Churches, the Orthodox Churches, and the Roman Catholic Church. One of the reasons is obvious. Pentecostals have been engaged in evangelistic activities for nearly a century, and they have been very successful. Unfortunately, Pentecostals on the whole are not engaged in most discussions on proselytism. They are not defining the term. They are not condemning the activity. They are not attempting to be understood. They are not seeking a hearing or defending their position in such a way as to change the nature of the discussion. As the world becomes smaller, members of other world religions are looking to ecumenical groups for help in putting a stop to evangelism, increasingly being defined as proselytism, among their members. The lack of Pentecostal input into these discussions makes this a very dangerous state of affairs.[62]

Without the input of Pentecostals, the discussions can have the effect of placing limitations on what Pentecostals can do in some places. The Orthodox in the former Soviet Union have sought to block any type of evangelization within that territory which is not indigenous to the area. Their openness to the sensitivities of the new nationalism simply adds another risk factor to the issues.[63] In Italy, the bishops are accusing the cults of embarking on a dangerous path using 'violent methods' (*metodi violenti*). Among these 'cults' they number members of the Assemblies of God.[64] In Brazil, the rhetoric of a 'Holy War' has been raised regarding Pentecostals.[65]

Some Pentecostals may choose to interpret all of this as though they are suffering for the sake of righteousness. And for some it may well be. But the question needs to be asked, would that rhetoric be softened were those against whom it is being aimed to sit down at a table and speak with their accusers?

4. Pentecostals who choose not to be sensitive to or to recognize an existing Christian presence in a particular region and who, therefore, incur the wrath of the majority group, run an enormous risk of becoming just like their oppressors when they move into majority status. Pentecostals have yet to prove that their claims to sanctification and the baptism of the Spirit really do make a difference in the way they will govern when it is their turn. If the Presidency of Rios Montt in Guatemala is any indication of what might happen,[66] it does not

bode well for Pentecostal leadership in the political arena. If the participation of leadership from the Apostolic Faith Mission in South African governance during the reign of apartheid is any indication of what might happen, it does not bode well for Pentecostal leadership in the political arena.[67] Within the next fifteen years, Pentecostals will begin to emerge as major political and social players in many Latin American countries. In order to avert still hotter rhetoric, even the possibility of turning the region into something like Northern Ireland, or the Middle East, the time for talking is now, not then.

By engaging the larger ecumenical worlds in discussion, Pentecostals have a great deal which they can gain. First, they can gain a truly global perspective. Many Pentecostals live in very regional worlds, with strong boundaries and high walls. Some North American Pentecostals need to realize that there are Pentecostals elsewhere in the world who, for instance, support a socialist, or even a communist party agenda. Some anti-ecumenical Pentecostals need to hear from those Pentecostals who have had positive ecumenical contacts and experiences. All Pentecostals need to listen to one another as well as to all others who claim the name 'Christian' in order to be truly catholic in their experience.[68]

By engaging the larger ecumenical worlds in discussion, Pentecostals have the sheer numbers to shift the balance of power on certain issues, be they social, political, ecumenical, or even theological. But without that interchange, they will never be able to test out their theories. If they are as good as Pentecostals claim that they are, Pentecostals should not fear to put them to the test. Pentecostals speak a great deal about power, about possessing the power of the Holy Spirit. But when it comes to dealing with other Christians they frequently act as though they were powerless. In the World Council of Churches it is frequently the Orthodox Christians who take positions which Pentecostals would support most strongly. Both the Orthodox Christians and Pentecostal Christians might be very surprised by the joy of finding each other in such discussions.

In North America, especially in the United States where there is an uneasy and incomplete separation of Church and State, and where there has been a major rise in the number of Muslims and Buddhists in particular, the issue of toleration of religions other than Christianity will soon move well beyond being a moot point. Place next to that the kinds of social changes which are going on in the areas of family, of gender issues, of immigration, the secularization of culture with its marginalization of religion, and the like, and it becomes readily apparent that all Christians are in need of greater wisdom.

Pentecostals will continue to face a growing pluralization in a range of areas. Engaging other Christians in discussion, even if they be Christians with whom Pentecostals have some deeply rooted disagreements, may be the best way, perhaps ultimately the only way to face the issues which confront them. It may be that by engaging in such discussions, Pentecostals may also help other Christians to see more clearly the central features of what it is that Christianity is all about, and in turn, help everyone establish themselves in a relationship to that centre. It will also help them embrace boundaries which have real meaning.

Notes

1   These are but a few of the many programmes which churches and Christian communities have spawned during the last decade of the Second Millennium AD. Their intent seems to be to provide closure to the present era and to function as a foundation for a new one. His Holiness, John Paul II has suggested in his Apostolic Letter *Tertio Millennio Adveniente*, released November 10, 1994, a three year celebration with precisely this agenda.

2   The history of how Pentecostal churches came into being at the turn of the century has two sides. Pentecostals often recite the fact that they were asked to leave the churches they believed that they were called to renew. Members of the historic churches often recite the fact that Pentecostal believers split their churches because of their unwillingness to submit to properly constituted authority The truth lies, undoubtedly, somewhere in the middle. But it is difficult for either side of this century-old divide to admit the truth or legitimacy of the other perspective. One example of this can be documented from both sides. The Pentecostal version of the split in the Holiness Church of Los Angeles may be found in Mrs. R.L. (Clara) Davis, *Azusa Street Till Now: Eyewitness Accounts of the Move of God* (Tulsa, OK: Harrison House, 1989), pp. 21–26. The Holiness Church version may be found in Josephine M. Washburn, *History and Reminiscences of the Holiness Church Work in Southern California and Arizona* (New York, NY: Garland Publishing, Inc., rpt. 1985), pp. 376–378, 383–385, 388–390.

3   David K. Bernard, *The Oneness of God* (Hazelwood, MO: Word Aflame Press, 1983); David K. Bernard, *The New Birth* (Hazelwood, MO: Word Aflame Press, 1984); Billy Sunday Myers, 'Was Jesus God's Son Before the Incarnation?' *The Church of God Evangel* 38:17 (June 21, 1947), pp. 8–9; L.L. Green, 'Is Water Baptism in Jesus' Name a Bible Doctrine?' *The Church of God Evangel* 41:48 (February 10, 1951), p. 14; Gregory A. Boyd, *Oneness Pentecostals and the Trinity* (Grand Rapids, MI: Baker Book House, 1992); James L. Tyson, *The Early Pentecostals: History of Twentieth Century Pentecostals and The Pentecostal Assemblies of the World, 1901–1930* (Hazelwood,

MO: Word Aflame Press, 1992); Fred J. Foster, *Their Story: 20th Century Pentecostals* (Hazelwood, MO: Word Aflame Press, 1965, 1981).

4   Frank Bartleman, *How Pentecost Came to Los Angeles: As It Was in the Beginning* (Los Angeles, CA: F. Bartleman, 1925), pp. 145–153; 'The Great Revival at Azusa Street Mission–How It Began and How It Ended', *Pentecostal Testimony* 1:8 (no date), pp. 3–4; 'The Second Work of Grace People Answered', *Pentecostal Testimony* 1:8 (no date), pp. 7–9; 'History of Pentecost: Divisions of Pentecost', *The Faithful Standard* (November 1922), pp. 8, 14.

5   J. Roswell Flower, 'The Snare of Sectarianism', *Pentecostal Evangel* #1537 (October 23, 1943), pp. 1, 7–9, 12–13; H. A. Gross, 'Whither Are We Bound, Brethren?' *Herald of Faith* 9:6 (June 1944), pp. 21–22; Joseph Mattson Boze, 'Too Big to Bag: A Vigorous Attack on the Assemblies of God?' *Herald of Faith* 10:6 (June 1945), pp. 20–32, especially p. 28; Lester F. Sumrall, 'International Pentecostal Conference in Switzerland', *Pentecostal Evangel* #1726 (June 7, 1947), p. 6; Lewi Pethrus, 'No Pentecostal World Organization', *Herald of Faith* 12:7 (July 1947), p. 7; Donald Gee, 'Are We Too Movement Conscious?' *Pentecost* 2 (December 1947), inside back cover.

6   Cf. Dr. F.P. Möller, *Church and Politics (A Pentecostal View of the South African situation)* (Braamfontein, South Africa: Gospel Publishers, no date), which claimed Pentecostal support for the status quo in Apartheid South Africa over against the likes of Frank Chikane, *No Life of My Own: An Autobiography* (Maryknoll, NY: Orbis Books, 1988). Both men were ministers in the same denomination, the Apostolic Faith Mission of South Africa. Similar situations can be found in the relationships between Pentecostal groups in North and South America, and especially between North American Pentecostal denominations and certain autochthonous groups from Latin America. See Manuel J. Gaxiola-Gaxiola, 'Latin American Pentecostalism: A Mosaic within a Mosaic', *PNEUMA: The Journal of the Society for Pentecostal Studies* 13:2 (Fall 1991), pp. 115–123; Douglas Petersen, 'The Formation of Popular, National, Autonomous Pentecostal Churches in Central America', *PNEUMA: The Journal of the Society for Pentecostal Studies* 16:1 (Spring 1994), pp. 23–48, especially pp. 34–37.

7   For Pentecostal groups which observe a seventh-day sabbath see the Directory of Sabbath-Observing Groups (Fairview, OK: The Bible Sabbath Association, 1957, 1974), pp. 184–188. Groups such as the Assemblies of God treat those who press such opinions on others as persons 'adding conditions to salvation', thereby making them subject to discipline by the group. See the Bylaws of the General Council of the Assemblies of God, Article IX.B.2.b in *Minutes of the 45th Session of the General Council of the Assemblies of God* (August 10–15, 1993) (Springfield, MO: General Secretary's Office, 1993), p. 166.

8   Frank Bartleman, *Two Years Mission Work in Europe: Just Before the World War 1912–14* (Los Angeles: F. Bartleman, no date), pp. 54–55; Jay Beaman, *Pentecostal Pacifism: The Origin, Development, and Rejection of Pacific Beliefs among the Pentecostals* (Hillsboro, KS: Center for Mennonite Brethren Studies, 1989).

9   See Cecil M. Robeck, Jr., 'Historical Roots of Racial Unity and Division in American Pentecostalism', unpublished paper delivered as a keynote address to Pentecostal Partners: A Reconciliation Strategy for 21st Century Ministry, Memphis, TN (October 17, 1994), 54 pp.

10   Cecil M. Robeck, 'A Pentecostal Looks at the World Council of Churches', *The Ecumenical Review* 47:1 (January 1995), pp. 63–64.

11   Joseph Colletti, 'Ethnic Pentecostalism in Chicago: 1890–1950', (Ph.D. diss., University of Birmingham, 1990), pp. 155–160; Louis De Caro, *Our Heritage: The Christian Church of North America* (Sharon, PA: General Council, Christian Church of North America, 1977), pp. 64–65. The argument revolved around the interpretation of Acts 15:28–29.

12   Other issues which have raised consternation between Pentecostals have included the treatment of divorce and remarriage among clergy, the role of women in ministry, positions on the security of the believer, differences in eschatological understandings, etc.

13   R.G. Spurling, *The Lost Link* (Turtletown, TN: no publisher, 1920, rpt. 1971), p. 20.

14   Charles F. Parham, *A Voice Crying in the Wilderness* (Baxter Springs, KS: Apostolic Faith Bible College, 1902, rpt. 1910), pp. 61–65.

15   W.F. Carothers, *The Baptism with the Holy Ghost and Speaking in Tongues* (Houston, TX: W.F. Carothers, 1906–07), p. 25.

16   Cecil M. Robeck, Jr., 'The Assemblies of God and Ecumenical Cooperation: 1920–1965', Wonsuk Ma and Robert Menzies, eds., *Pentecostalism in Context: Essays in Honor of William W. Menzies*, Journal of Pentecostal Theology Supplement Series 11 (Sheffield, England: Sheffield Academic Press, 1997), pp. 107–150.

17   These statements may be found in most issues of *The Apostolic Faith*, the irregular newspaper published by the Azusa Street Mission. They also appear in a single page handout which was distributed to visitors at the mission.

18   'Preamble and Resolution of Constitution', in *Minutes of the General Council of the Assemblies of God in the United States of America, Canada and Foreign Lands held at Hot Springs, Ark. April 2–12, 1914* (Findlay, Ohio: The Gospel Publishing House, 1914), p. 4.

19   A brief survey of Wesleyan-Holiness periodicals such as *The Burning Bush*, *The Gospel Trumpet*, *The Free Methodist*, etc. is sufficient to document this claim. See above, note 2 for one such example.

20   Typical of Fundamentalist treatments of Pentecostalism were H. A. Ironside, 'Apostolic Faith Missions and the So-Called Second Pentecost', (New York, NY: Loizeaux Brothers Inc., Bible Truth Depot, 1911), 15 pp. ; R.A. Torrey, 'Is the Present "Tongues" Movement of God?' (Los Angeles: Biola Book Room, 1915), 15 pp., and Benjamin B. Warfield, *Counterfeit Miracles* (1918; London, England: The Banner of Truth Trust, 1972). Pentecostal teaching was condemned by the Fundamentalists in 1928. See 'Report of the Tenth Annual Convention of the World's Christian Fundamentalist Association: Chicago, 13–20 May, 1928', *Christian Fundamentalist* 12 (June 1, 1928), p. 9. See on this topic Russell P. Spittler, 'Are Pentecostals and Charismatics Fundamentalists? A Review of American Uses of These Categories', in Karla Poewe, ed., *Charismatic Christianity as a Global Culture* (Columbia, SC: University of South Carolina Press, 1994), pp. 103–116.

21   On this point see my forthcoming article, 'The Assemblies of God and Ecumenical Cooperation: 1920–1965', pp. 132–147. Cf. C.M. Robeck, Jr. 'National Association of Evangelicals', in Stanley M. Burgess and Gary B. McGee, eds. *Dictionary of Pentecostal and Charismatic Movements* (Grand

Rapids, MI: Zondervan Publishing House, 1988), pp. 634–636, especially pp. 635–636 where I suggest several areas in which Pentecostals compromised their original positions in keeping with broader evangelical consensus.

22 Robeck, 'The Assemblies of God and Ecumenical Cooperation: 1920–1965', pp. 123–124.

23 This is readily apparent especially through the 1980s in the news digest sections both in the *Pentecostal Evangel* of the Assemblies of God and in the *Church of God Evangel*.

24 Dr. Harold Carpenter is quoted as saying that the Commission on Faith and Order of the World Council of Churches has made room in the 'ecumenical faith' for 'such religions as Animism, Hinduism, Buddhism, and Islam', based upon the concept of 'the cosmic Christ'. In '"Unity of the Faith..." a Faculty Panel Discussion', in *Contending for the Faith: The Theological Journal of Central Bible College* (Fall 1995): p. 3. This 'journal' is printed as the latter pages of *The Bulletin: The Official Magazine of Central Bible College* (Fall 1995), a quarterly publication of the President's Office. A similar statement is made in Opal L. Reddin, 'Church Unity,' *Enrichment* 1:2 (Spring 1996): p. 69.

25 'The Pentecostals and Church Unions', *Church of God Evangel* 42:33 (October 20, 1951), p. 15 quotes Bishop J. A. Synan, Senior Bishop of the Pentecostal Holiness Church and then Chairman of the Pentecostal Fellowship of North America as saying that Pentecostals will steer away from church union because 'it involves sacrificing of individual convictions'.

26 Clyde C. Cox, 'The Vatican Ecumenical Council', *Church of God Evangel* 63:2 (March 26, 1973), p. 18; Clyde C. Cox, 'The Church Unification Movement', *Church of God Evangel* 63:10 (July 23, 1973), p. 18; George L. Britt, 'The Scarlet Woman', *Church of God Evangel* 48:30 (September 30, 1957), pp. 4–5, 10; James A. Cross, 'Answers from the WORD', *Church of God Evangel* 54:13 (May 25, 1964), p. 11. In August 1995, the Assemblies of God reaffirmed its Bylaw which disapproves of ministers or churches participating in any of the modern ecumenical organizations in such a way as to 'promote the Ecumenical Movement', in part because they maintain that 'the combination of many religious organizations into a world superchurch will culminate in the religious Babylon of Revelation 17 and 18'. See the Bylaws of the General Council of the Assemblies of God, Article IX.B.11.c in *Minutes of the 46th Session of the General Council of the Assemblies of God* (August 8–13, 1995) (Springfield, MO: General Secretary's Office, 1995), p. 149.

27 See on this lack of trust, Cecil M. Robeck, Jr., 'A Pentecostal Assessment of "Towards a Common Understanding and Vision" of the WCC', *Mid-Stream: The Ecumenical Movement Today* (anticipated in 1997), 34 pp.

28 'oikia', Walter Bauer, William F. Arndt and F. Wilbur Gingrich, *A Greek-English Lexicon of the New Testament and Other Early Christian Literature* (Chicago, IL: The University of Chicago Press, 1957, 1979), pp. 559–560.

29 'oikoumene', Bauer, Arndt, and Gingrich, *A Greek-English Lexicon of the New Testament*, p. 563.

30 Paul A. Crow, Jr., 'Ecumenics as Reflections on Models of Christian Unity', *The Ecumenical Review* 39:4 (October 1987): pp. 397–398.

31 John A. Mackay, *Ecumenics: The Science of the Church Universal* (Englewood Cliffs, NJ: Prentice-Hall, Inc., 1964), pp. 6–7.

32 S. Wesley Ariarajah, *The Bible and People of Other Faiths* (Maryknoll, NY:

Orbis Books, 1989), pp. 19–28, 58–71; S. Wesley Ariarajah, *Gospel and Culture: An Ongoing Discussion within the Ecumenical Movement* (Geneva: WCC publication, 1994); S. J. Samartha, *One Christ–Many Religions: Toward a Revised Christology* (Maryknoll, NY: Orbis Books, 1991), pp. 92–111; Raimundo Panikkar, *The Unknown Christ of Hinduism: Towards an Ecumenical Christophany* (Maryknoll, NY: Orbis Books, 1964, Revised and Enlarged, 1981); and Paul F. Knitter, *No Other Name? A Critical Survey of Christian Attitudes toward the World Religions* (Maryknoll, NY: Orbis Books, 1986), pp. 145–231.

33   Janice Love, 'JPIC and the Future of the Ecumenical Movement', *The Ecumenical Review* 42:1 (January 1991): pp. 107–119; Wesley Granberg-Michaelson, 'An Ethics for Sustainability', *The Ecumenical Review* 42:1 (January 1991), pp. 120–30. By noting that these last two categories are more action-oriented than is the first, I do not mean to infer that they are not theologically developed, I merely wish to suggest that their interest in acting out their theology moves much more quickly than does that of the first group. Cf. 3.2. Report of Section I: 'Giver of Life–Sustain Your Creation!' Michael Kinnamon, ed. *Signs of the Spirit: Official Report, Seventh Assembly* Canberra, Australia, 7–20 February 1991 (Geneva: WCC Publication/Grand Rapids: Wm. B. Eerdmans, 1991), pp. 54–71.

34   *Costly Unity* (A World Council of Churches consultation on Koinonia and Justice, Peace and the Integrity of Creation) (Geneva: The World Council of Churches, 1993).

35   One of the largest tensions within the World Council of Churches at the present time is the concern to integrate theology and action, unity discussions and the interest of JPIC. Symptomatic of this tension is Georges Tsetsis, 'What Is the World Council's Oikoumene?' *The Ecumenical Review* 42:1 (January 1991): pp. 86–89. He clearly reminds the Council of the Constitutional mandate which it carries, 'to call the churches to the goal of visible unity in one faith and in one eucharistic fellowship ...' from 7.13 Constitution and Rules, Constitution, III. Functions and purposes, 1, in Kinnamon, *Signs of the Spirit*, p. 358.

36   More recently terms such as 'Conciliar Fellowship' have tended to dominate the discussion. Cf. Aram Keshishian, *Conciliar Fellowship: A Common Goal* (Geneva: WCC Publications, 1992).

37   This is particularly true within the Orthodox tradition, and one may construe the argument of George Tsetsis in this way. See above, note 35.

38   *Confessing the One Faith: An Ecumenical Explication of the Apostolic Faith as It Is Confessed in the Nicene-Constantinopolitan Creed (381)* Faith and Order Paper no. 153 (Geneva: WCC Publications, revised 1991).

39   *Baptism, Eucharist and Ministry* Faith and Order Paper No. 111 (Geneva: WCC Publications, 1982).

40   For a significant discussion of the *filioque* issues see Theodore Stylianopoulos, 'The Filioque: Dogma, Theologoumenon or Error?' Theodore Stylianopoulos and S. Mark Heim, eds. *Spirit of Truth: Ecumenical Perspectives on the Holy Spirit* (Brookline, MA: Holy Cross Orthodox Press, 1986), pp. 25–28. Pentecostal interests in this discussion appear in the same volume by Gerald T. Sheppard, 'The Nicean Creed, Filioque, and Pentecostal Movements in the United States', pp. 171–186. On the notion of 'reception' see William G.

Rusch, *Reception: An Ecumenical Opportunity* (Geneva: Lutheran World Federation/Minneapolis: Fortress Press, 1988).

41   *Baptism, Eucharist and Ministry*, p. x.

42   This important statement is most easily accessible in W.A. Visser 't Hooft, *The Genesis and Formation of the World Council of Churches* (Geneva: World Council of Churches, 1982), pp. 112–120.

43   Notable among these for Pentecostals are the statements that 'The World Council of Churches is not and must never become a superchurch', that 'The purpose of the World Council of Churches is not to negotiate unions between churches, which can only be done by the churches themselves acting on their own initiate', that 'The World Council cannot and should not be based on any one particular conception of the Church', that 'Membership in the World Council of Churches does not imply that a church treats its own conception of the Church as merely relative', that 'Membership in the World Council of Churches does not imply the acceptance of a specific doctrine concerning the nature of Church unity', that 'The member churches of the Council believe that conversation, cooperation and common witness of the churches must be based on the common recognition that Christ is the Divine Head of the Body', etc.

44   Konrad Raiser, 1. Report of the General Secretary, *Central Committee of the World Council of Churches: Minutes of the Forty-Sixth Meeting* Geneva, Switzerland, 14–22 September 1995 (Geneva: World Council of Churches, 1995), p. 19. General Secretary, Konrad Raiser has, in fact, suggested a major shift in the framework through which the World Council of Churches might work, in his *Ecumenism in Transition: A Paradigm Shift in the Ecumenical Movement?* (Geneva: WCC Publications, 1989, 1991).

45   Cecil M. Robeck, Jr., 'Taking Stock of Pentecostalism: The Personal Reflections of a Retiring Editor', *PNEUMA: The Journal of the Society for Pentecostal Studies* 15 (Spring 1993), pp. 35–60, especially pp. 39–45.

46   Pope Pius XI, '*Mortalium Animos*', in Claudia Carlen, IHM, *The Papal Encyclicals 1903–1939* ([Wilmington, NC]: McGrath Publishing Co., 1981), p. 317.

47   'Dogmatic Constitution on the Church (*Lumen Gentium*)', 8. Cf. 'Decree on Ecumenism (*Unitatis Redintegratio*)', p. 4. All quotations from documents originating in the Second Vatican Council are from Austin Flannery, O.P., ed. *Vatican II: The Conciliar and Post Conciliar Documents* (Collegeville, MN: The Liturgical Press, 1975, revised, 1984). The verb 'subsists in (*subsistit in*)' has been difficult for some Pentecostals to understand because it sounds as though it were a synonym for 'is'. The discussions on the Latin term which was used in the official text of *Lumen Gentium* 8, however, hold significant ecumenical implications. Had the framers of this passage desired to equate the Church with the Roman Catholic Church, they would have chosen to use the verb 'to be', in this case, *est*. Indeed, there was considerable discussion on which verb should ultimately be chosen, but in the end, the verb *est* was overwhelmingly rejected by the bishops, 'thereby deliberately leaving open the question of the one relation of the one Church to the many Churches'. This affirmation would later find its way into *Unitatis Redintegratio* 4 where its implications for ecumenism would be further mined. Thus, the Bishops of the Second Vatican Council chose to endorse a new, open, ecumenical stance which enabled them to view others who shared a trinitarian baptism as fully Christian even if they were not in full communion with Rome. For an analysis

of the discussion over this important verb, see Aloys Grillmeier, 'The Mystery of the Church', in Herbert Vorgrimler, ed., *Commentary on the Documents of Vatican II* (London/New York: Burns & Oats/Herder and Herder, 1967), I. pp. 149–151.

48   'Decree on Ecumenism (*Unitatis Redintegratio*)', 3, in Flannery, *Vatican II*, 1, 455.

49   *Directory for the Application of Principles and Norms on Ecumenism* (Vatican City: Pontificium Consilium ad Christianorum Unitatem Fovendam, March 25th, 1993).

50   Encyclical Letter *UT UNUM SINT* of the Holy Father JOHN PAUL II on Commitment to Ecumenism (Vatican City: Libreria Editrice Vaticana, 25 May 1995), Section 79. Hereafter denoted *Ut Unum Sint*, 79.

51   *Ut Unum Sint*, 13.

52   *Ut Unum Sint*, 96. Pentecostals might do well to think about such a possibility, not necessarily in theological terms, but in symbolic and/or official terms. The highly visible nature of the papacy, with over 900 million followers, citizens of every nation, for instance, might allow the occupant of this office to be encouraged by another 400+ million Pentecostals, to take a unique and proactive role in maintaining peace, or in functioning as an arbitrator in international peace talks. The Pope might also be called on to make unique contributions wherever human welfare and dignity are at stake.

53   *Ut Unum Sint*, 94.

54   *Ut Unum Sint*, 88.

55   *Ut Unum Sint*, 89.

56   'Pentecostal View of the Ecumenical Movement', *Church of God Evangel* 56:34 [5] (October 31, 1966), p. 8.

57   The *World Council of Churches: Yearbook 1996* (Geneva: WCC Publications, 1996), lists all member churches, among which these Pentecostal denominations are to be found.

58   '25th Anniversary Covenant', *Church of God Evangel* 57:11 (May 22, 1967): p. 3.

59   'Pentecostal Partners: Racial Reconciliation Manifesto', Sections VII, VIII, and XI, in *PNEUMA: The Journal of the Society for Pentecostal Studies* 17:2 (Fall 1995), p. 218.

60   Edward Idris Cardinal Cassidy, 'Prolusio', in the Pontifical Council for Promoting Christian Unity's *Information Service*, no. 84 (1993/III–IV), p. 122.

61   Cardinal Ernesto Corripio Ahumad, Archbishop of Mexico City's statement was originally part of a *Regional Report of North America* dated April 5, 1991. It forms part of the Preamble to The Working Group on New Religious Movements, ed., *Sects and New Religious Movements: An Anthology of Texts from the Catholic Church, 1986–1994* (Washington, D. C.: United States Catholic Conference, Inc., 1995), p. 4.

62   Cecil M. Robeck, Jr., 'Mission and the Issue of Proselytism', *International Bulletin of Missionary Research* 20:1 (January 1996), pp. 2–8, outlines some of the definitions and the status of the discussions which are taking place on this topic in a variety of ecumenical circles. Cf. Cecil M. Robeck, Jr., 'Evangelization or Proselytism of Hispanics? A Pentecostal Perspective', *Journal of Hispanic/Latino Theology* 4:4 (1997), pp. 42–64. The Final Report of the International Roman Catholic-Pentecostal Dialogue released in 1997 is

the first place in which Pentecostal discussions of these issues with other Christians is made explicit.

63   See, for example, the 'Message of the Primates of the Most Holy Orthodox Churches', *Ecumenical Trends* 21:4 (April 1992), pp. 57–60.

64   Orazio Petrosillo, 'I vescovi italiani attaccano le sette Metodi violenti', in the *Messaggero* [Rome], date and page unknown at this time.

65   This phrase has been attributed to Bishop Sinesio Bohn, in Gary Haynes, 'Brazil's Catholics Launch "Holy War"', *Charisma* 19:10 (May 1994), pp. 74–75.

66   David Martin, *Tongues of Fire: The Explosion of Protestantism in Latin America* (Oxford: Basil Blackwell, 1990), pp. 254–255; David Stoll, *Is Latin America Turning Protestant? The Politics of Evangelical Growth* (Berkeley, CA: University of California Press, 1990), pp. 180–217.

67   Nico Horn, 'The Possibilities of the Rediscovery of the Black Roots of Pentecostalism for South African Theology', *Azusa: Theological Journal* 1:1 (March 1990), pp. 20–42, especially pp. 28–29.

68   Cecil M. Robeck, Jr., 'Southern Religion with a Latin Accent', *PNEUMA: The Journal of the Society for Pentecostal Studies* 13:2 (Fall 1991), pp. 102–103. Cf. also Cecil M. Robeck, Jr., 'Evangelicals and Catholics Together', *One in Christ* (1997), 29 pp. in which I lay out a series of guidelines which may be of use to Pentecostals and non-Pentecostals alike as they meet to discuss their common concerns.

Chapter Sixteen

The 'Toronto Blessing' in Postmodern Society: Manifestations, Metaphor and Myth

Margaret M. Poloma

I am entering territory where even angels should fear to tread. Not only am I a mere mortal, but I am a sociologist whose discipline and data are clearly more modern than postmodern. Even thinking about discussing the controversial manifestations that have characterized, at least in many minds, the so-called 'Toronto Blessing' should make me tremble, but trying to frame these activities with the nebulous theories that wear the postmodern label should have me shaking as wildly as the most demonstrative pilgrim to the Toronto Airport Christian Fellowship. Be that as it may, I am foolhardy enough to think that postmodern thought can indeed provide a framework within which to understand better the phenomenon that will go down in the history of the Pentecostal/charismatic movement as the 'Toronto Blessing'.[1]

The Toronto Blessing is the latest phase of the Pentecostal/charismatic movement that began early in the twentieth-century and is now said to account for one out of four Christians worldwide. Beginning in

North America with the Azusa Street Revival in Los Angeles (1906–13), rekindled through the Latter Rain movement (1948), entering mainstream Christianity through the charismatic movement (1960s and 1970s), and modified by the Third Wave (1980s), the Pentecostal/charismatic movement has experienced periodically a fresh outpouring of charisma just when the forces of institutionalization loomed to quench its free spirit. The Toronto Blessing, one stream of a larger revival movement spreading across the globe, is still in its 'charismatic moment', presenting an unusual opportunity to observe the process through which unusual religious experiences are socially framed.[2] For those who are unaccustomed to the phenomena that have accompanied many earlier revivals, including Pentecostal revivals, and are now a hallmark of the Toronto Blessing, the following description by Leslie Scrivener, a reporter from the *Toronto Star* (October 8, 1995), shortly after Hurricane Opal had spewed its wrath on the East Coast of North America, may prove instructive:

> The mighty winds of Hurricane Opal that swept through Toronto last week [were] mere tropical gusts compared with the power of God thousands believe struck them senseless at a conference at the controversial Airport Vineyard church. At least with Opal, they could stay on their feet. Not so with many of the 5,300 souls meeting at the Regal Constellation Hotel. The ballroom carpets were littered with fallen bodies, bodies of seemingly straitlaced men and women who felt themselves moved by the phenomenon they say is the Holy Spirit. So moved, they howled with joy or the release of some buried pain. They collapsed, some rigid as corpses, some convulsed in hysterical laughter. From room to room came barnyard cries, calls heard only in the wild, grunts so deep women recalled the sounds of childbirth, while some men and women adopted the very position of childbirth. Men did chicken walks. Women jabbed their fingers as if afflicted with nervous disorders. And around these scenes of bedlam, were loving arms to catch the falling, smiling faces, whispered prayers of encouragement, instructions to release, to let go.

Thousands of pilgrims continue to flock to the Toronto Airport Christian Fellowship from around the world for regular nightly renewal services or specially scheduled topical conferences. Often these pilgrims 'catch the fire' (a popular expression at TACF) and take a spark back home to their local churches. TACF leaders as well as leaders from other ministries impacted by the Toronto Blessing also travel throughout the world to support local efforts to 'catch the fire' of the renewal (as this revival has come to be called). According to an article in *Charisma*, the renewal fires that were sparked in Toronto have now spread to the United Kingdom (especially England, where an estimated 5,500 British churches have been affected), German-speaking European countries, Indonesia, Africa, Russia, South America, Japan, Australia, and Korea, in addition to countless sites in both the United States and Canada.[3] This list is but a partial one, with new reports of the spread of the blessing coming regularly over the Internet.

What initially attracted the media's attention were the unusual manifestations described earlier in the *Toronto Star* article. Some leaders of the renewal have playfully dubbed them God's 'advertising signs'. While it is beyond the scope of social science to attribute supernatural origin to these 'signs', postmodernism's emphasis on semiotics signals the potential of postmodern thought for understanding these unusual manifestations and the culture in which they are found. Semiotics – the study of representations or signs – is not an end in itself, but rather, 'semiotic analysis requires movements beyond the sign to a conceptualization of culture as a system of signification within which the signs are elements'.[4] The experiences associated with the manifestations and their interpretations can provide rich data for understanding the construction and maintenance of the Pentecostal world-view which underlies this global religious culture.[5]

The task I set for myself in this discussion is threefold. First, I will present limited quantitative data on reported incidences of various physical/bodily 'signs', including the more common ones of falling, speaking in tongues, laughing, shaking, and jerking, as well as the more controversial 'animal sounds' of lions, chickens and dogs, together with some simple description of the role they may play in the construction of a Charismatic world-view. Second, I will supplement these 'positivistic' data with information collected through qualitative procedures that are more in accord with postmodern methodological dictates. The latter, based on participant observation, personal accounts secured from the Internet, testimonies given at renewal services, and open-ended interviews, permit me to focus on the meanings ascribed to the physical manifestations. It is through methodologies which allow the observer to see beyond seemingly apparent and objective realities that postmodernism offers the challenge to probe the meaning of even seemingly meaningless behaviors. Finally, I will attempt to gaze into my sociological crystal ball to assess the implications of this renewal for the larger Pentecostal/charismatic movement in postmodern societies.

CONSTRUCTING A POSTMODERN THEORY:
A HEURISTIC EXERCISE

There is little agreement at present about the nature and essence of so-called postmodern theory, and I can do little more within the space constraints of this chapter than to point out the lack of consensus that exists among its scholars. Problems of definition and conceptualization are compounded by the different languages of discourse and attendant issues and agendas set for scholars of diverse disciplines. Artists have a different language and agenda than do most anthropologists; philosophers struggle with issues quite different from most sociologists; poets often have a different world-view from that of historians. Even scholars who seemingly embrace the same spirit and drink from the same well are impacted by the divisive forces of postmodernism that they seemingly share in common. Sociologist Norman Denzin describes the diversity as follows:

> *Postmodernism* refers to many things. In the arts, architecture, and humanities, it signifies recent aesthetic developments that challenge conventional modernist conceptions of structure, meaning, beauty and truth. In the social sciences, it connotes a non-totalizing, anti-foundational form of theorizing about the social world. Temporally, it refers to a period in world history extending from the end of World War II to the present era. As a new historical era, postmodernism is most often defined theoretically in terms of the emergences of multinational forms of late capitalism. . . . More important, as the object of social inquiry, postmodernism refers to a new form of society, one that has been radically transformed by the invention of film and television into a visual, video culture.[6]

Postmodern scholarship itself appears to have fallen victim to the very fragmentation its proponents insist is the hallmark of postmodern society.

Postmodernism in its present state is hardly a satisfactory resolution of the philosophical issues that have plagued thinkers for centuries, but it can be used as a heuristic tool to counter some of the problems of modern social theory and research. Postmodernism depicts a culture that is clearly fragmented, devoid of deep emotions, and superficial. It challenges the dogmatism and absolutism of the 'scientism' that has come to characterize much of modern science. Most importantly, its methodologies allow researchers and scholars to take seriously the kind of phenomena experienced by those who, as participants describe the process, 'swim in the river of renewal'. In its best 'minimalist dress' it recognizes that realities are multiple and that they are constructed socially.[7] It is with a focus on social constructionism – rather than on deconstruction – that I am employing postmodern thought to discuss the physical manifestations experienced by thousands and thousands of people worldwide through the Toronto Blessing.

BEGINNING WITH FACTS: SOME SURVEY FINDINGS

METHOD AND MEASUREMENT

A questionnaire was first included in the August 1995 issue of *Spread the Fire*, a magazine sent to persons who have visited the Toronto Airport Christian Fellowship to keep them informed of activities and to provide testimonies/teachings relevant to the renewal. It was also included in the October 1995 'Catch the Fire Again' and November 1995 'Healing School' programmes. Nine hundred and nine (909) useable questionnaires were returned. Although the survey instrument was structured to allow for computer analysis, respondents were encouraged to send any additional material that they wished. Twenty-four per cent [24 %] included supplemental materials. The letters, diary pages, and testimonials that accompanied many of the questionnaires provided qualitative data to complement the statistics.

Questionnaires were returned from twenty countries, with the majority of the responses coming from the United States (54%), Canada (28%), and England (11%). Although these three countries do supply most of the visitors to the Toronto Airport Christian Fellowship (TACF), other countries – especially non-English speaking Asian ones who make up a visible minority at many meetings – are noticeably missing from this sample. Visitors represent over forty denominations and sects, with more than one in four (26%) indicating that their church affiliation is either independent, nondenominational, or inter-denominational. Seventeen percent (17%) of the respondents are members of Pentecostal denominations or sects, fifteen per cent are either Anglican (Canada and England) or Episcopalian (U.S.), eleven per cent are members of Vineyard Christian Fellowships, and six per cent are Baptist (of one stripe or another). Seventy-four percent (74%) reported that their pastors had visited the TACF. The profile of the 'average' respondent thus far is that of an American (most likely to be from California, Colorado, New York, Ohio, or Pennsylvania) who belongs to a non-denominational church that is likely to be charismatic in worship style and teaching.[8]

The demographic profile of the respondents is skewed toward being married (71%), female (58%), middle-aged and having a college diploma. The average age is forty-five years (with a median of forty-three), and the mean education is fifteen years of formal schooling, with a median and mode of sixteen years. Eighteen per cent (18%) of the respondents were church pastors and another four per cent were the spouses of pastors; thirty per cent indicated that they were church leaders. The demographic profile indicates that those who completed the questionnaire tend to be well-educated and mature individuals, the majority of whom are involved in church leadership.

Following the demographic section of the questionnaire, respondents were asked: 'If you have experienced one or more of the following manifestations, please place a check mark on the appropriate line to indicate whether this experience occurred before, during or after your first visit to the Toronto Airport Vineyard'. The manifestations listed were: speaking in tongues, resting in the spirit, roaring like a lion, holy laughter, dancing in the spirit, jumping up and down, drunk in the spirit, deep weeping, 'birthing', uncontrolled shaking of an arm or leg, deep bending from the waist, rolling on the floor, thrashing on the floor, uncontrolled jerking of bodily limbs, and 'other (please describe)'. When these items were combined to form a scale, scores ranged from zero to fourteen, with a mean of three and a half and a median of three for manifestations experienced while visiting TACF.

SUMMARY OF FINDINGS

In reviewing the incidence of the various manifestations prior to a first visit to TACF, it appears that the vast majority of the respondents had experienced at least one of the manifestations in question. Fifty-nine percent (59%) reported having one, two, or three different physical manifestations, and only seven per cent indicated having no personal experience with any physical manifestation in question at the time of their first visit to TACF. This finding is a reflection of the fact that ninety-five per cent of the respondents self-identified as Pentecostal/ charismatic Christians. Only one per cent indicated that they had no personal experience of any of the manifestations – either before, during or after visiting TACF. As may be seen from the Table, two particular manifestations were more likely to have been experienced before this initial visit than during the TACF visit: glossolalia or 'tongues' and 'resting' or being 'slain' in the Spirit. These two practices have been common fare for many charismatics and Pentecostals throughout the twentieth-century. Other manifestations, although reported in earlier American revivals, have not played a noteworthy part in the contemporary Pentecostal/charismatic movement. These include roaring, 'birthing', shaking, thrashing, rolling on the floor, deep bending, uncontrolled jerking, and laughter.[9] The accompanying Table suggests that although the respondents were not strangers to physical manifestations accompanying religious experiences, many experienced new manifestations for the first time at TACF.

FREQUENCIES OF MANIFESTATIONS (N=909)			
	Before Visit	**During Visit**	**After Visit**
Tongues	87%	23%	24%
Resting in spirit	70%	45%	30%
Roaring like lion	4%	12%	12%
Holy Laughter	38%	32%	26%
Dancing in spirit	34%	17%	15%
Jumping up and down	19%	17%	12%
Drunk in spirit	24%	27%	19%
Deep weeping	46%	32%	21%
'Birthing'	12%	22%	16%
Shaking of arm/leg	22%	35%	23%
Bending from waist	10%	29%	23%
Rolling on floor	9%	13%	9%
Thrashing on floor	7%	18%	9%
Uncontrolled jerking	11%	25%	16%
Other*	3%	23%	6%
Mean index scores	Mean=3.9 s.d.=2.8	Mean=3.5 s.d.=3.0	Mean=2.5 s.d.=3.0

* Included among the 'other' manifestations were uncontrolled shaking of head, being stuck to the floor, groaning/grunting, vibrating, feeling heat/energy, barking, screaming, and running.

IN SEARCH OF MEANING: ETHNOMETHODOLOGICAL ACCOUNTS IN SOCIAL CONTEXT

Whatever else they are, the physical manifestations accompanying the renewal are regarded as signs that the Spirit of God is moving in powerful ways as this century draws to a close. Nightly, in the church auditorium and often in the parking lots, restaurants, and hotel lobbies, people can be seen laughing and rolling, falling and jerking, shaking and grunting, as onlookers stand around praying, 'Give them more, Lord-more, Lord-more, Lord'. In this playful atmosphere it is not surprising that one of the meanings given to the outbreak of these phenomena is that 'God is playing with his kids'. But while one person may be lying on the floor consumed with laughter, the person lying next to her may be heaving sighs from deep weeping. Metaphors, therefore, will be mixed (as they often are in religious thought), with 'playfulness' being replaced with 'power' as the underlying explanation for some manifestations. John Arnott, pastor of TACF, offers the following hypothesis on the violent shaking that can often be seen at TACF:

> People often shake when the power of God hits them. Why are we so surprised that physical bodies react to God's power? It is a wonder to me that we do not explode and fly apart. God's power is real power – the *dunamis* of heaven.[10]

As noted in still another popular explanation, the manifestations are much like a flashing sign saying, 'Spirit at work ... Spirit at work ... Spirit as work....' Whether a sign of God's power or his playfulness, the manifestations first and foremost are regarded as *signs* or even sacraments.[11] Although spokespersons for the Toronto Blessing, coming as they are from non-liturgical traditions, would be hesitant to use the term *sacrament* for these phenomena, their attributions fit well the accepted definition for the term as 'a visible sign of inward grace'. Whether the *signs* of semiotics or the *sacraments* of ecclesiastical theology, the physical manifestations that are part of the Toronto Blessing are important elements for understanding the process of reality construction.

I would like to examine briefly, accounts from four different social discourses through which order is being brought out of the seeming chaos caused by the more unusual manifestations: personal testimonies, biblical exegesis, historical context, and finally ethnotheology. Each may be regarded as an ethnomethodological account – as methods used by the participants themselves to construct their social reality regarding physical manifestations. Of the four methods of accounting for the manifestations, the *primary* one is that of personal testimonies based on personal experience. The other three methods–biblical hermeneutics, revival history, and ethnotheology – are *secondary* accounts in that they employ the primary accounts to construct interpretations fitting into the existing Pentecostal/charismatic world-view.

PRIMARY ACCOUNTS: PERSONAL TESTIMONIES

Testimonies are regularly given at renewal services, often while the interviewee is 'manifesting' before an amused audience, that highlight how lives have been changed through the Toronto Blessing. While the interviewee may be laughing, jerking, or exhibiting some other physical sign, the focus of the questioning is on what has come to be called the 'fruits of the renewal'. The narratives include countless stories of personal spiritual refreshment, inspirational reports of increased holiness, wholeness, and healing, and tearful accounts of repentance, forgiveness, and restored relationships. These narrations based on personal experiences and interpretations are the primary material from which other secondary accounts develop.[12]

I have elected to provide ethnomethodological accounts for four of the more controversial manifestations: three from prophetic mime (roaring, crowing/clucking, and barking) and Spirit drunkenness. Some physical manifestations, although unfamiliar to those outside the Pentecostal/charismatic movement, are well-known experiences for those who claim to be Spirit baptized. The most common is tongues or glossolalia, an experience regarded by many as a litmus test for being Spirit-filled. Falling under the power of the Spirit (being 'slain in the Spirit' or 'resting in the Spirit') has also been experienced by many veteran Pentecostal/charismatic believers, as have jerking and shaking. These relatively familiar manifestations stand in stark contrast to prophetic mime and drunkenness, with the latter providing new charismatic script for the reality construction process, just as the older manifestations provided a reality construction challenge for Pentecostals of generations past.

PROPHETIC MIME: THOSE 'ANIMAL SOUNDS'

As I have already noted, many of the physical manifestations experienced during the Toronto Blessing, for the most part, are not new to revival history. Most had been experienced in early American revivals, including the Azusa Street revival that birthed Pentecostalism, and more recently at Association of Vineyard churches in both North America and in England beginning in the late 1970s.[13] Although it is continually being modified, the basic construction of social reality around glossolalia, being slain in the Spirit, and, to some extent, jerking and shaking occurred much earlier in Pentecostal/charismatic history. It was the 'animal sounds' that provided a fresh challenge for the renewal.

John Arnott often tells of his first encounter with roaring, a phenomenon that broke out at TACF about five months after the manifestations first began. Arnott was away and called to see how things were going at his church, when someone told him that a man 'roared like a lion last night'. He immediately asked questions like, 'did he hurt anyone? was it demonic? did he attack anybody?' and finally 'did you stop it?' The person on the other end of the phone responded negatively to each query, concluding with the assessment, 'We felt it was from the Lord.' Arnott recounts the rest of the story as follows:

> When I arrived back in Toronto later that week, the man who had roared was still at our meetings. I interviewed him in front of the church. He was Gideon Chiu, a prominent Cantonese Chinese leader from Vancouver, Canada, a pastor's pastor, very honored and well-respected. He shared what he was feeling and how he had come to Toronto desperately hungry for more of God. Suddenly this meek and mild pastor started roaring again, right in front of everyone. He moved back and forth across the front of our church, roaring and lunging like an angry lion, crying, 'Let My people go! Let My people go!'
>
> Then he came back to the microphone and testified that the Chinese people have been deceived by the dragon for hundreds of years, but now the Lion of the tribe of Judah was coming to set His people free. Our church immediately exploded into volumes of praise as they bore witness to what the Spirit of God was saying.[14]

Crowing rooster and clucking hen sounds soon followed the roaring lions in renewal services. On one occasion during testimony time at a TACF service, a man who was clucking like a chicken came up to the microphone as he struggled to share what he believed God was saying to him. He would try to speak, but a clucking noise would interrupt. He stammered and clucked (much like a stutterer might stammer with a speech impediment), and then he would begin again to try to speak.

The prophetic message that finally emerged in this struggle was a simple one: 'God is saying that I am going along the ground scratching like a chicken for whatever little I can find while he has set a banquet table. He is telling me to feast at the banquet table'. The banquet table image is a biblical metaphor, one that would have been an acceptable message for this visible sign.

By the time some people began to bark at renewal meetings, the TACF (then still a member of AVC) was coming under increasing fire from the Association of Vineyard Churches under the leadership of John Wimber for the animal sounds. At one meeting I attended, a man who had just given a testimony about how God had changed his life through the renewal was prayed for, as is customary after such testimonies. He fell to the floor and began barking. The minister in charge of the meeting that night was already interviewing another person. He interrupted his line of questioning, turned to the audience and said, 'I don't hear anything, do you? Tell me there is no barking going on right now'. The audience laughed. The minister continued saying, 'We are not trying to create a theology of roaring or falling – or barking. But I recently asked a woman who was barking what she was doing and she replied, "I see the Master coming". We do know that Jesus is coming again'. The elephant in the centre of the room –in this case, sounds of a yelping puppy – was dealt with and the focus went back on the person giving the new testimony.

A particular animal sound, or any other manifestation, is not automatically given a set interpretation. Sometimes the interpretation may come from someone hearing the sound rather than the person giving it. Recently a woman shared her experience at a conference she attended at TACF with members of St. Luke's Episcopal Church in Akron, Ohio. An account of a barking dog was part of a longer testimony about a remarkable emotional healing this woman received while at the conference in Toronto. Included in her opening statement was the following self-description:

> I am thirty-six years old, and I have not really lived. I have existed and survived. When I was twelve years old, I gave up all hope of being emotionally accepted and belonging, and I went inside the walls of a castle and disappeared. The pain of rejection was too great, so little Sharon went inside and big Sharon was created on the outside to cope with what was going on in the inside. *(Audiotape from the March 31, 1996 service at St. Luke's Episcopal Church)*

Sharon shared a series of visions she had while at the TACF conference, all of them related to the emotional healing that took place as 'little Sharon' was freed from this captivity created by fear of rejection and as 'big Sharon' correspondingly became less angry and more receptive. One scene involved the Heavenly Father carrying her out of the castle in which she was imprisoned into his castle. As the Father carried her in she heard cries of 'Alleluia' both in her vision as well as from a person somewhere in TACF's auditorium. She continued her testimony as follows:

> Now this is the strangest thing – suddenly this man started barking. At the exact time he began to bark, I saw a picture and heard a dog barking in my vision. I had a dog when I was in the fifth grade, and my parents had him destroyed while I wasn't around. I never got to say good-bye, and I didn't know how bad that hurt me. And in this picture a dog runs in and starts jumping and barking. That man will never know why he was barking! (Laugh) God was returning my dog to me, and the child in the picture really perked up. She was able to walk. It was so healing. And in my picture, I looked around, and suddenly all the signs and smells came to life...

We see in these accounts how the interpretation of the animal sounds began by soliciting the meaning ascribed to the action by the actor and then evaluating it. If the outcome is judged to be good, the story is accepted not so much for the animal sounds as for the phenomenon it is said to represent. As Arnott has noted, 'These sounds are most often made in the context of prophecy, vision, and revelation'.[15] The sounds and gestures are regarded as being a means through which God is speaking to people, not unlike the way a donkey was reportedly used to speaking to Balaam in the biblical account (see Numbers 22:21–39). Put another way, the animal sounds can be regarded as visible signs of a fresh work of the Holy Spirit, much like glossolalia became the preeminent sign for the earlier Pentecostal/charismatic movement.

Spirit Drunkenness

'Drunkards in the Spirit' could be observed from the onset of the Toronto Blessing at TACF in January 1994. Guy Chevreau reported an account of his wife's experience in one of the first books to be published on the Toronto Blessing:

> She was down on the floor, repeatedly, hysterical with laughter. At one point, John Arnott, the senior pastor prayed that she would stay in this state for forty-eight hours. She was that, and more – unable to walk a

straight line, certainly unfit to drive, or to host the guests that came for dinner the next evening.

Guy Chevreau has often recounted this story of the dinner guests who came to find nothing prepared and a hostess who was acting very strangely. He went out to buy fish and chips, and when he returned, the table was still not set for dinner. As he began setting the table, Janis (Guy's wife) began portioning out the fries on the table and tossing the fish from the container to their guests – all the while thinking this was incredibly funny.[16]

Janis Chevreau described her own state and feelings both before and after her experiences at TACF when she appeared on the Donahue Show in September 1995. She and her husband had been co-pastoring a Baptist church just outside Toronto when they heard about what was happening at the then-Toronto Airport Vineyard. Both were having a very difficult time with the work they were doing when they decided to pay a visit to the renewal:

Janis Chevreau: We went about a week into it. I was too desperate to be sceptical. We were having a hard time in the church we were working at, and we just decided to go because I had been away the weekend prior with two friends who had been taken by this the week it had begun. And they laughed the whole weekend, and I thought, 'Well', I said, 'God, I really need you, but I don't think I want that'. But we went the first day, and when it came time for prayer, someone prayed for us and I just – my knees got all wobbly and wiggly, and I just kind of fell over, and next thing I know, I woke up and was just in a fog. And I thought, 'Well, I don't know what this is but that's okay'. And I went home and we got invited back a day later, we went up to pray again. And they invited pastors and wives who kind of burned out, and that was us, so we jumped up. And they prayed for us, and the men came forward, and there was (sic) about 50 men, male pastors, and about two of us women, and he didn't get over to me and I was on the floor, and that began the laughter for about four hours.

Phil Donahue: You laughed for four hours?

Janis Chevreau: Four hours. . . . There was an intense – I would describe it as joyfulness. I will just briefly tell you I'm a very uptight person. I'm not someone who has a lot of fun as a rule. I'm very serious about life, I saw the heavy side of it. . . . And to see me there (in that state of Spirit drunkenness) was absolutely a miracle in itself. But, yeah, it's just such an intimate time of having fun. . . . But there was some embarrassment. I was always trying to cover my face and crawl under chairs. . . . . You're conscious of what's going on, but everything is funny. It just doesn't matter. So I was trying – I was embarrassed a bit, because I thought, 'What am I doing? Am I that much in need? Do I need people's opinions of me, or what is it?' So I'd go home each time, wondering what this was about, but there was also – I would go home and literally that first night, there was a joy that came over me. Our circumstances hadn't changed – and there were some hard circumstances we were in – I had a lot of pain, but it lifted right off. And I walked around for months with it lifted.

In his book *The Father's Blessing,* John Arnott told of how people in another congregation were being affected somewhat similarly by Spirit drunkenness. A pastor from Quebec shared how children and adults were experiencing outward manifestations of being drunk while being changed inwardly:

> Every time they go down, it's like they had another glass of booze, but it isn't that at all. It's the Lord's Spirit. If it was just limited to that, I guess that would not necessarily be special in and of itself, but it goes much, much further. While people are under the Spirit they are delivered of all sorts of problems. They go into the heavenlies. They come back, and they are no longer the same. They are transformed.[17]

At the 'Catch the Fire' conference held in Dallas in August 1995, I had an opportunity to observe as a participant another incident of Spirit drunkenness. The young woman who had picked me up at the airport came over to greet me during the prayer ministry time. As she hugged me long and hard, I began quietly praying for her and she suddenly crashed to the floor – her keys going one direction and her camera another. I gathered her belongings and sat on the floor next to her for nearly an hour, watching as she jerked, shook, writhed, and at times seemed to be pulling in a rope with hand motions made in the air. In her case there was no laughing; her face often looked pained, but the pain would dissolve into a look of peace. Pained pulling on the rope; then peace – more pulling – and peace.

As the crowd began to get quite animated in the hotel ballroom and danced around the room as they worshipped, I began to be concerned for my new friend's and my own safety on the floor in the midst of all the active celebration. I motioned to a young man and asked him to help me get the young woman on her feet. As we stood her up, the laughter began. She seemed to be in such a drunken stupor that I decided to have her brought up to my hotel room for the night. She was aware of her state but seemed to be enjoying it too much to do anything about it. It took three of us and a wheel chair to get her out of the auditorium and up to my room.

The next morning I asked the young woman what she had experienced. She responded, 'There was a lot of junk inside me that I didn't even know was there. Jesus was pulling out hatred, anger, bitterness, resentment from the depths of my stomach. It just kept coming and coming. Jesus was pulling on what seemed to be yards and yards of ribbon in which these negative feelings were attached. I really did not know I had those ugly feelings within me'. I then asked why she thought God allowed her to get so drunk in the Spirit. She replied, 'It was probably an anesthetic. It was the only way I could stand it as God removed all that stuff from within me'.

As with the examples of prophetic mime, there is no single explanation given by those who experience Spirit drunkenness. Some, like Janis Chevreau, are filled with joy; others offer prophetic words; still others find it a time of worship and praise. As rational beings in a culture still heavily influenced by Enlightenment thought, humans are quick to move beyond simple experiential narratives in an attempt to uncover more systematic explanations. Initial social- scientific attempts to find patterns, however, have not been successful. Psychiatrist John White began his investigation with the assumption that he would uncover some patterns when he studied the manifestations exhibited in John Wimber's gatherings in the mid-1980s and reports:

> But the more I have interviewed affected people and pondered their stories, the more mysterious the matter has become. To force my observations into a coherent theory is at present impossible. I suspect that even rigorous research would not clarify the matter.[18]

BUILDING ON THE EXPERIENTIAL ACCOUNTS: SECONDARY INTERPRETATIONS

BIBLICAL EXEGESIS

Pentecostal/charismatic Christians are also Evangelical Christians for whom the Bible is regarded as the 'Word of God'. The primacy of the Bible is beyond questioning, although reconstructing the meaning of the Bible is as troubling for them as it has been for Christians throughout history. While not particularly concerned with a formal study of hermeneutics, they are very responsive to questions raised about whether or not their experiences are biblical. The early Pentecostals reflected on their experiences – particularly glossolalia and healing – and developed doctrines that served as distinguishing marks for the newly developed sects based on their interpretation of the Scriptures. The leaders of this renewal movement appeared to be more laid back and less eager to defend the manifestations by proof-texting the Bible. Nor were they eager to silence the manifestations when no biblical text could be found to support them. Instead they listened to testimonies and judged by the fruits – and the effects, for the most part, were deemed to be good.

Although no systematic theology has been developed by renewal leaders (systematic theologians they are not), there is much theologizing by inference and metaphor. Some such activity may be found in the testimonials presented earlier. Spirit drunkenness may have been reported in the book of Acts, God seemed to speak to Balaam through a donkey, there are Scripture passages about laugher and joy, Jesus is often referred to as the Lion of Judah, and so on.

When the manifestations began to spread in Vineyards in both North America and England, the Association of Vineyard Churches issued the following statement in its September/October 1994 Board Report:

> We are willing to allow 'experiences' to happen without endorsing, encouraging or stimulating them; nor should we seek to 'explain' them by inappropriate 'proof-texting'. Biblical metaphors (similar to those concerning a lion or a dove, etc.) do not justify or provide a proof-text for animal behavior. There are some manifestations while socially uncomfortable (i.e., they wouldn't seem 'decent and in order' in most church context today), have biblical precedent ... The absence of a proof-text, however, does not necessarily disallow an experience. If so, none of us could go to Disneyland, use computers to write messages, or have worship bands. The point is, don't try to defend unusual manifestations from biblical texts that obviously lack a one-to-one correspondence with a current experience.[19]

This secondary level of reality construction proved to be even more controversial than firsthand accounts. It is difficult to argue with a personal account and interpretation of a religious experience. Countless people were giving testimonies at TACF as well as at conferences and in churches throughout the world about how the manifestations were accompanied by significant life changes.[20] Yet the tentative explanations of the physical manifestations offered by TACF pastor John Arnott was one of the major reasons given by the AVC for the dismissal of the Toronto church. In retrospect it appears that any discussion of the more controversial manifestations by the leadership that made use of the Bible – even if as metaphor – was unacceptable to the parent organization.

MANIFESTATIONS IN REVIVAL HISTORY

When Guy Chevreau and his wife Janis were touched by the Toronto Blessing, Chevreau, whose Th.D. was earned with a focus on Christian spirituality, initially was left confused but intellectually curious. As Chevreau reports: '[W]hile sitting on the floor during one of the ministry times at the Airport Vineyard, I surveyed the bodies laid out everywhere, and leaned over to a newly-made friend and said, "All of this makes applesauce out of a fellow's theological apple carts" '.[21] Drawing his inspiration from John White's *When the Spirit Comes with Power,* Chevreau used Jonathan Edwards and the experiences of the First Great Awakening to conclude that what he was seeing was indeed 'a well-travelled path'.

Patrick Dixon, a well-known doctor, church leader, author, and broadcaster, did a similar historical analysis for British readers. His work included a much wider sampling of unusual religious experiences in history, weaving together 'two different but not entirely separate strands of historic Christian experience'. These two strands were the *mystical,* with its 'gradual alternations in conscious state through meditation and contemplation', and the *charismatic,* with its 'more rapid alternations in conscious state associated with tongues, sudden loss of strength, unusual body movements and other outward manifestations'.[22]

While Chevreau and Dixon provided an overview of similarities and differences between past revivals and the current Toronto Blessing, Richard Riss began to write a current history of the revival using the Internet as a medium. Riss, a part-time instructor at a Bible college and a doctoral student at Drew University, has painstakingly gathered details about the revival which can be found in his manuscript 'A History of the Worldwide Awakening of 1992–1995'.[23] Using the medium of the 1990s, Riss joins Chevreau and Dixon in countering the early Pentecostal/charismatic movement's reluctance to record events for history. Historical accounts, both classic and contemporary, have been important sources of legitimation as this religious drama continues to unfold.

ETHNOTHEOLOGY: THEOLOGY CONSTRUCTED BY THE PEOPLE

Reality construction is necessarily a social process – a process that has a new facilitator in cyberspace. Through the Internet, a medium not available in earlier revivals, Christian discourse by the laity has been ongoing about the Toronto Blessing. Global Resources Ministries (http://www.grmi.org), an Internet service that focuses on providing information on renewal and related topics, has been playing a particularly significant role.[24] It is from the Usenet <new-wine@grmi.org> that I have selected an example of this third type of secondary reality construction which I have called *ethnotheology,* or a theology by the people.

On the Internet just as outside cyberspace, the process often begins with an unresolved issue. For example, on August 15, 1995, Dan reported:

> On Sunday night we had a special Communion and Healing service at our church. An unusual phenomena (at least to us) took place. Our pastor prayed for healing in one of the men who had come forward. Very shortly after, this fellow who had been prayed for noticed that the palms of his hands were covered with oil. It was a thick covering of oil. He grabbed our pastor and asked him what it meant. Our pastor felt his hands and was quite amazed at the literal covering of oil which had not been there just moments before. Then it was noticed that this oil was actually appearing all over the visible skin of this fellow. Has anyone else seen or heard of something like this? Does anyone know what this means?

An answer was soon in coming from John, who had seen similar things and offered a biblical explanation that seemed acceptable to others on the list. 'The application of oil speaks of Holy Spirit anointing', says John, so this oil 'could be a sign that a special anointing had been given by the Holy Spirit'. Others seemed to concur that oil was a 'sign' of a special anointing in this exchange of messages.

Trying to assign meaning to the manifestations is a subject that comes up on the Internet from time to time, but one on which limits are placed. Cautionary warnings are interspersed with the explanations warning about the dangers of assigning prophetic significance to all manifestations. Most of those involved in the discussion are careful to state that they are simply sharing their own observations, experiences, and opinions – yet these are the very ingredients out of which an experiential theology of manifestations may emerge in a more systematized way.[25] Those involved in the New-Wine discussions appear to be reluctant, at least for now, to make the Pentecostal error of a rigid interpretation of any manifestation, even of tongues. As Doug (April 16, 1996) notes;

> The rigid assignment of meaning to manifestations has been a source of great division within the Body for at least 80 years, perhaps longer. One issue that comes immediately to mind is the assertion that the primary evidence of baptism in the Holy Spirit must be accompanied by speaking in tongues. This has been a barrier that divided many segments of the Pentacostal (sic) tradition from the rest of the Body for many years.

A POSTMODERN ASSESSMENT OF THE TORONTO BLESSING

One of postmodern theory's challenges to social science is to take human experience seriously – in fact, to see it as foundational to any study of culture. Culture, as anthropologist Victor Turner reminds us, is more than structures and norms; his 'anthropology of experience' emphasizes the role experience, including emotions, plays in the ongoing construction of culture. Culture, an ongoing dramatic human production, is thus never static. In Turner's words: 'The social world is a world in becoming not a world in being ... and for this reason studies of social structure *as such* are irrelevant'.[26] The Pentecostal/charismatic subculture is no exception; it too is an ongoing production that continues on the stage set by Azusa Street. It is a drama that is being invigorated by the newest waves of renewal, but one that cannot be understood without a careful examination of bodily expression, emotions, and the cognitive processing of its significance by participants.

Postmodernism may provide more than a simple framework for analysing the Pentecostal/charismatic movement. The charismatic world-view is a curious combination of the premodern and modern that may paradoxically be a good fit for the emerging postmodern world while simultaneously protesting its seeming chaos. With all the talk in so many arenas about 'paradigm shifts', the Pentecostal/charismatic world-view actually has the potential for providing a dramatically different model from the modern one. It offers the promise of a substitute for the Aristotelian logic, Cartesian dualism, and Marxist materialism that have been pillars of modernist thought. What Richard Quebedeaux noted about the Charismatic Movement of the 1970s is equally true for the Toronto Blessing movement:

> Charismatic renewal has rejected the liberal, nonsupernatural god who really isn't there anyhow, but it has also rejected the rational

evangelical god of the intellect – the great giver of propositional truth – in favor of a God you can feel, respond to, and love, the God who *cares* about our present and our future. It is the knowledge of this God, given through the experience of his Holy Spirit, that has bound charismatics together.[27]

A crucial component of the maintenance of an alternative world-view is the Pentecostal/charismatic movement's image of person. The Toronto Blessing demonstrates a holistic view of person – an integration of body, cognition, emotions, will, and spirit – that has all but been lost in the materialism, rationalism, and technologies of modernism. This model moves away from the limited and limiting Cartesian mind-body dichotomy that has dominated Enlightenment thought, a perspective affecting religious as well as secular thinking. Its world-view offers a creative response to both the straight-jacket of modernism and the abyss of postmodernism. Whether this latest venture of the Pentecostal/charismatic movement will be successful in retaining its distinctive perspective or whether it accommodates to the larger world-view of western society remains to be seen.

APPENDIX
Description of Select Manifestations

Birthing – Going through the motions of labor (twitching and convulsing as if due to contractions) with reports that the person is 'birthing' some new ministry.

Blowing – Walking around blowing and puffing strongly.

Chopping – Flailing at the air like a karate wrestler.

Dancing in the Spirit – seemingly uncontrolled dancing, sometimes in a trance-like state.

Drunk in the Spirit – person appears to be inebriated but reports to be in touch with God.

Deep bending – aerobic-like deep bending forward (and sometimes backward).

Falling, 'slain by' or 'resting in' the Spirit, or 'doing carpet time' – falling to the ground as the body goes limp feeling the presence of God.

Fluttering eyelids – with eyes closed the eyelids seem to be trembling.

Groaning and travailing – steady cry of moaning and anguish sounding like a deep lament.

Heat – feelings of warmth or tingling in certain parts of the body.

Inability to speak – speaker loses ability to concentrate and is unable to talk.

Jumping – uncontrollable bouncing up and down as if on a pogo stick.

Laughing – deep uncontrollable laughter sometimes going on for hours.

Prophetic mime – people acting out animal movements and/or sounds, including 'roaring ,' 'barking' and 'crowing.'

Running or twirling – running around the room as if being chased; twirling or spinning.

Shaking – Being dishevelled like a rag doll being shaken by some big, unseen hand.

Shouting and yelling – screaming for no apparent reason.

Stuck to the floor – falling down and experiencing immobilization so as to be unable to get up.

Notes

1   The revival that has been underway since January 20, 1994 at the Toronto Airport Christian Fellowship (formerly the Toronto Airport Vineyard) was first called the 'Toronto Blessing' by the British press. Leaders involved in this revival have come to prefer and use either the term 'Father's Blessing' or simply 'Renewal' to refer to this charismatic happening. I will use the term 'Toronto Blessing', 'renewal', and 'revival' interchangeably. The latter term has been avoided by most leaders in response to critics who have argued that more 'salvations' (i.e. first-time conversions) will take place during a 'genuine' revival than have taken place through the Toronto Blessing.

2   The Toronto Blessing had its institutional roots in John Wimber's Association of Vineyard Churches (AVC), the denomination to which the TACF belonged until its ouster in early December 1995. The manifestations experienced during this renewal differ primarily in intensity and transferability (from one congregation to another and one person to another) from those experienced in Vineyard Christian Fellowships since the late 1970s. Many Vineyard churches (estimated to be about half of the over 600 VCFs that make up the AVC) had been impacted by the early Toronto Blessing with fresh waves of these more intense manifestations. Some Vineyard Christian Fellowships remain part of the renewal movement described in this article, but many have backed away from it after the dismissal of TACF from the AVC. Partners in Harvest, an association of former Vineyards and other autonomous churches, is the institutional embodiment of this stream of the renewal. A number of independent ministries are also part of a larger renewal movement, including that of Claudio Friedzon (Pentecostal Assemblies of God in Argentina), Rodney Howard-Browne (ex-patriate South African evangelist now in the U.S.), and Benny Hinn (a former independent evangelist now with the Assemblies of God in the U.S.). While these ministries operate independently of each other,

many people involved in the renewal have been refreshed by more than one stream.

3 Diana Doucet, 'The "Blessing" Sweeps the Globe', *Charisma,* (November 1995), p. 63; and Clife Price, 'A Revival Without Walls', *Charisma,* (November 1995), pp. 54–58.

4 M. Gottdiener, 'Semiotics and Postmodernism', in *Postmodernism & Social Inquiry*, ed. D.R. Dickens and A. Fontana, (New York, NY: Guilford Press), pp. 155–181.

5 For further information, see, David Barrett, *World Christian Encyclopedia* (New York, NY: Oxford University Press, 1982); Harvey Cox, *Fire From Heaven: The Rise of Pentecostal Spirituality* (Reading, MA: Addison-Wesley Publishing Company, 1995); and Karla Poewe, ed., *Charismatic Christianity as a Global Culture* (Columbia, SC: University of South Carolina Press, 1994).

6 Norman K. Denzin, 'Postmodernism and Deconstructionism' in *Postmodernism and Social Inquiry*, eds., David R. Dickens and Andrea Fontana (New York, NY: Guilford Press, 1995), pp. 182–202. For further discussion see also Walter Truett Anderson, *Reality Isn't What It Used to Be* (San Francisco: Harper, 1990); David S. Dockery, ed., *The Challenge of Postmodernism* (Wheaton, IL: BridgePoint, 1995); David Ray Griffin, ed., *Varieties of Postmodern Theology* (Albany, NY: State University of New York, NY, 1989); Houston Smith, 'Postmodernism and the World's Religions' in *The Truth about the Truth: De-Confusing and De-Constructing the Postmodern World*, W.T. Anderson, ed., (New York, NY: G.P. Putnam's Sons, 1995): pp. 205–213; and Ernest Gellner, *Postmodernism, Reason and Religion* (London: Routledge, 1992).

7 A precursor to postmodern thought in sociology may be found in the social constructionist framework described by Peter Berger and Thomas Luckmann, *The Social Construction of Reality* (Garden City, NY: Doubleday & Company, Inc., 1966). The new sociological postmodern theories – particularly those in 'softcore' or 'minimalist' dress – are not as new as they first appear. Those found at the 'hardcore' end of the spectrum seem to carry these earlier theories a step beyond into the very absurdity of extreme relativism that allegedly characterizes the postmodern world. As Houston Smith (Ibid., 1995, p. 211) astutely notes: 'Perspectivalism becomes absurd when the obvious fact that we look at the world from different places, hence different angles, is transformed into the dogma that we therefore cannot know things as they actually are.'

8 The vast majority of the respondents (95%) had self-identified as being 'charismatic, Pentecostal, or full gospel' Christians. They were also likely to belong to congregations in which 90% or more of the members were Pentecostal/charismatic Christians.

9 For a brief discussion of each of the more common manifestations, see Appendix.

10 John Arnott, *The Father's Blessing* (Orlando, FL: Creation House, 1995), p. 153.

11 See Peter Hocken's 'Theological Reflections on the "Toronto Blessing" ' (Paper presented at the 1996 Annual Meeting of the Society for Pentecostal Studies. Wycliffe College: University of Toronto, 1996). Hocken discusses the relationship between the physical and spiritual in the Toronto Blessing, noting

there is much to be gleaned from the physical manifestations for those seeking to understand the renewal.

12   For further discussion and results of survey data see Margaret M. Poloma, 'By Their Fruits ... :A Sociological Assessment of the "Toronto Blessing"' (paper presented at the Annual Meeting of the Society for Pentecostal Studies, 1996, and available from the Toronto Airport Christian Fellowship Bookstore; 272 Attwell Drive; Toronto, Ontario, Canada M9W 6M3).

13   For an excellent discussion of the manifestations that could be found in Vineyards around the country prior to the Toronto Blessing, see Canadian psychiatrist John White, *When the Spirit Comes in Power* (Downer's Grove, IL: InterVarsity Press, 1988). In it (p. 158) can be found the story of John Wimber's introduction to 'unusual manifestations' on Mother's Day, 1978, over fifteen years before the onset of the Toronto Blessing.

14   John Arnott, *The Father's Blessing* (Orlando, FL: Creation House, 1995), pp. 168–69.

15   Ibid., p. 40.

16   Guy Chevreau, *Catch the Fire* (London: Marshall Pickering, 1995). See especially pages 13 ff.

17   John Arnott, Ibid., p. 146.

18   John White, Ibid., p. 104.

19   Exactly what constituted 'proof texting' came to be a thorny issue between the AVC and the Toronto Airport Vineyard (now TACF). John Arnott's discussion of the animal sounds in *The Father's Blessing* (a book whose first edition bears the endorsement of AVC founder John Wimber) became one of the reasons for the Toronto church's ouster from the larger fellowship. It seems that discussion of the manifestations were to be off limits – something that is difficult to do when a dog may be barking, a lion roaring, or a Spirit-drunk preacher is trying to deliver a sermon.

20   For further discussion and illustration, see Margaret M. Poloma, 'By their Fruits ...' 1996. Ibid.

21   Guy Chevreau, *Catch the Fire* (London: Marshall Pickering, 1994), p. 70.

22   Patrick Dixon, *Signs of Revival* (E. Sussex: Kingsway Publications, 1994), pp. 115–16.

23   Richard M. Riss, *A History of the Worldwide Awakening of 1992–1995,* 11th ed., (October 15, 1995), <http://www.grmi.org/renewal/Richard_Riss/history.html>.

24   For further information see Kim A. Lawton, 'Christians in Cyberspace', *Charisma,* (May 1996), pp. 52–65.

25   See <http://www.grmi.org/pub/new-wine/articles/manifest> on the Internet, for unpublished work on the manifestations,

26   Victor W. Turner, *Dramas, Field, and Metaphors: Symbolic Action in Human Society* (Ithaca, NY: Cornell University Press, 1974), p. 33.

27   Richard Quebedeaux, *The New Charismatics II* (San Francisco: Harper & Row Publishers, 1983), p. xiv.

'Pentecostalism and Global Market Culture': A Response to Issues Facing Pentecostalism in a Postmodern World

Harvey G. Cox

Now about that time, the Christian movement gave rise to a serious disturbance. There was a man named Demetrius, a silversmith who made silver shrines of Diana and provided a great deal of employment for the craftsmen. He called a meeting of these men and the workers in allied trades, and addressed them. 'Men', he said, 'you know that our high standard of living depends on this industry. And you see and hear how this fellow Paul with his propaganda has perverted crowds of people, not only at Ephesus but practically in the whole province of Asia. He is telling them that gods made by human hands are not gods at all.'

Acts of the Apostles 19:23–27

Pentecostals at the beginning of the 21st century AD are not the first Christians to have to cope with the opportunities and pitfalls of a worldwide culture. The culture into which Christianity was born was that of the Pax Romana. It was, as far as the people who lived in it at the time, a 'global' culture. But no sooner had it began its mission in the first century AD, than the young Christian movement found itself in conflict with a powerful combination of global religious and commercial interests. The account in *Acts* of the sharp conflict that arose between the followers of Paul and the local alliance of idol merchants and priests of Diana at Ephesus has some important lessons to teach us about the present relationship between Christianity and the values represented by the emerging global market culture.

First, this passage helps us recognize that the realms of economics, culture, morality and religion are not as separate as we sometimes think. The world market is not just an economic artifact. Any economy requires social and cultural institutions that make such an economy possible. Different kinds of economies spawn different types of personalities and engender different values. Feudal man and early industrial man differ from technological man and post-industrial man. A 'culture' is merely the pattern of values and meanings by which a society exists, and a culture in which 'market values' assume predominance displays its own characteristic meanings and values. Economy and culture are ultimately not separable.

Secondly, this passage reminds us that there is always an equally integral relationship between religion and culture. The great Protestant theologian Paul Tillich, who was my own teacher, wrote that 'religion is the substance of culture, and culture is the form of religion'. Religion and culture are not separate spheres. Religions express themselves through cultural creations, and the stories and patterns of a culture incarnate the meanings and values that constitute the real operational religion in any society. A religion – whether true or false – without linguistic, ritual, artistic and ethical forms through which to express itself remains mute. But cultural forms remain empty and powerless unless they convey meanings that guide human life, whether for good or for evil.

This integral relationship between religion and culture means that Pentecostals today, like all Christians, must develop a critical theology of culture. The earliest Christians had one, as the idol makers at Ephesus discovered when Paul told the people that the gods they were serving were no gods at all, and they realized that if the people believed what Paul was saying, then their own 'high standard of living' would be endangered. Christian theology if it is truly biblical theology must always be prophetic. It must constantly expose those points at which any culture engenders false values which are destructive to God's will for the human community. One of the biggest mistakes theologians make today is to think of the economy merely as a neutral system of production and distribution mechanisms that has little direct relevance for religion or Christianity. Religion, it is sometimes imagined, deals only with the 'spiritual' or ethical dimension of life, while the economy deals with the material side. Or, theologians naively think they should be concerned exclusively with the just *distribution* of what an economy produces – which is indeed one very important concern – but not with the moral values an economic system breeds and promotes.

In responding to the previous papers of this consultation I would like to focus on 'Christianity and Economic life' in the tradition of the 'theology of culture' method I learned from Tillich. This response takes the form of a Christian theological analysis and critique of the religious assumptions and values, the 'gods made with hands', that characterise the emerging global market culture. My thinking here is also influenced by the famous essay of Max Weber, written in 1920, 'The Protestant Ethic and the Spirit of Capitalism'. However, my purpose here is not just descriptive. As a Christian theologian I also wish to suggest that the 'market religion' which is the substance of this global market culture is, from a Christian perspective, clearly a form of idolatry – a 'false religion' – but that instead of confronting it and challenging it as the early Christian did at Ephesus, Christians today all too often collude with it, and sometimes even sacralize it.

There is nothing idolatrous about markets as such. Markets have had a place in every human civilization on record and surely have a legitimate place in our emerging world civilization. Indeed their value for increasing the supply and quality of products, reducing inflation in some situations, and opening new kinds of relationships between nations has been demonstrated. But there is an enormous difference between the way markets have operated in the past and the way the market functions today. In the past, markets have always performed *along with* and have most often been *guided by* other strong institutions such as moral traditions, legal restrictions, and, especially, religious world-views. Today in more and more places all over the globe, these restraints are becoming increasingly weaker and less effectual.

Consequently, just as a truly global market has emerged for the first time in human history, that market is functioning without those guideposts, and it has become the most powerful institution of our age. Even nation states can often do little to restrain or regulate it. More and more the market is seen not as a creation 'made by human hands', but gives the appearance of being merely 'natural', just 'the way things are'. For this reason, the 'religion' the market generates often escapes criticism or even notice. It becomes invisible. My thesis is that the emerging global market culture generates a value-laden, 'religious' world-view. It is also my view that theology must make people aware of those values and of how they coincide with or contradict Christian values.

There is much disagreement today about the global world market and its culture. But there is also some agreement. The following are some of the characteristics of the global market culture about which both its advocates and its critics agree.

1.) Global market culture uproots traditional forms of work, family and community. In doing so it also undermines traditional belief systems and moral norms. Some people welcome this change because it contributes to 'progress' while others lament the erosion of 'traditional values', but all agree that the process is universal and inevitable wherever global market culture spreads.

2.) Global market culture produces enormous new wealth, but tends to polarize populations between a relatively small group of those who reap the benefits and a much larger group which is excluded from its bounty. For example, in June 1996 the U.S. Census Bureau reported that the gap between affluent Americans and everyone else was wider now than at any time since the end of World War II. In the nation that presents itself as the prime model of a market economy the chasm between the incomes of the well-to-do and the lower three-fourths of the population has been steadily increasing. Advocates and opponents of the global market economy tend to disagree on how long this polarization will last. Advocates claim it is only a temporary phase and that at some future point everyone will be drawn into the benefits. Critics say this is a false promise, that an unregulated, 'free' market economy will always produce enormous disparities, and that these disparities will only grow worse over time.

3.) The relationship of a market economy to democracy is a disputed point. Its advocates say that by dissolving traditional, semi-feudal and corporate-state structures the so-called 'free market' also makes political freedom possible. Others claim that when the market becomes this powerful it 'marketizes' politics as well. The result is that the democratic idea of 'one person one vote' is replaced by 'one dollar one vote', and what appears to be a democracy becomes in fact a plutocracy, where the wealthiest groups control the society. In the United States, for example, although theoretically anyone can be elected to the Senate, with a few exceptions, only people with private fortunes or who are financially supported by special interest groups with vast financial resources have much chance of being elected. Consequently, a majority of U.S. Senators are millionaires.

The religion of market culture exhibits all the qualities of a more classical religion. It has, for example, what is now called a 'master narrative', a story or 'myth' (in the technical sense) about the origin and course of the human enterprise; a 'plan of salvation', which teaches what is wrong with human history and how to redeem it; an army of dedicated (albeit well-paid) missionaries: advertising profession. It even has an eschatology which was recently explicitly spelled out by Francis Fukayama in his book *The End of History,* which describes the victory of world capitalism as a kind of secular Kingdom of God. Most importantly, the market culture also has a 'god', what Adam Smith once called the 'hidden hand', under whose benevolent, if sometimes mysterious guidance, all things eventually work together for the common good.

This God of the Market is obviously not the God and Father of our Lord Jesus Christ. Our problem as Christians today is that although we oppose idolatry in general terms, it is often difficult to notice the most obvious and invasive forms of idolatry, maybe because they do not announce themselves as 'religious'. We are faced with a formidable theological task. We need to uncover and unmask the service of false gods, even – indeed especially – when they mask themselves in secular disguises. We need to appreciate the market for what it can do, but question it when it begins to dictate human values and meanings.

The early Christians have much to teach us. They also lived within a complex relationship to the global culture of their time, just as we do today. On the one hand they took advantage of the *pax romana* to carry the gospel across the empire. They wrote in koine Greek, the lingua franca of the day. Christians have often told the story of how they stood up against the imperial religion of the day. But we sometimes forget that they also found themselves in conflict with the market culture of their time. This conflict is why the Bible reports that they caused such a 'a great disturbance' at Ephesus and were accused of threatening the 'high standard of living'. The issue was idolatry just as certainly as it was in their conflict with the emperor cult. An 'idol' is any human creation which is made into a value that displaces the pre-eminence of God. Also an idol, in the biblical view, is hollow. It poses as something it is not. It makes promises it cannot possibly fulfill. These first century Christians exposed the false promises of the idols. They saw that the idols of their time were promising people life and community, salvation and well-being, but that those idols were in reality completely powerless. They were 'not gods at all'. So Paul and his followers proclaimed in the name of the God revealed in Jesus Christ that gods made of human hands could not deliver on their promises. There was bound to be a great disturbance.

Today the relationship between the now much larger Christian movement and the global market god with all its promises is even more complex. The emergence of a global technological culture has made a truly global Christian movement possible for the first time. Christians use the hardware and software of the global culture to make the gospel known. Just as Paul made use of ships, the Greek language, references to classical poetry, letters, and his Roman citizenship to travel with the good news, so Christians benefit from the worldwide travel and communications technologies of today. Just as the *pax romana,* guaranteed by the emperor cult and the Roman legions, provided the space for the expansion of the early church, so today's global village makes possible a global church.

But while the first century Christians said both 'yes' and 'no' to the global culture of their time, today's Christians mainly just say 'yes'. Occasionally here and there Christians challenge the hegemony of the Global Market God. The churches of the USA have insisted that human genes should not be marketed. Christians have advocated a simplification of lifestyle so that the goods of the earth can be shared more equitably. Christians in Latin America and elsewhere have strenuously opposed the imposition of an international market economy on their more traditional ways of living. Both the World Council of Churches and the Pope have issued statements reminding Christians that there are important virtues the market does not nurture, but mostly discourages, virtues Christians value such as compassion, cooperation and tenderness. In many churches pastors warn their people against being swept away by the empty promises of consumerism and acquisition.

But very frequently Christian churches are reluctant to cause any 'disturbance' about the Market God, and even contribute to its grow-ing power. Most often they do so by simply trying to ignore consumer culture and all its patently nonchristian values. They concentrate on the 'spiritual' and leave the 'material' to others. But what they forget is that Christianity is a radically embodied and even in one sense 'ma-terial' faith. God created the material world and found it originally good. Also, the Bible has much to say about economics. The Jewish Law protects the poor and those without families from the greed of the rich. The prophets issue stern warnings against the privileged and powerful. In Jesus Christ, God actually enters the material world and clearly casts his lot with those on the bottom of the social and eco-nomic hierarchy. The Bible is anything but a merely 'spiritual' book. And it repeatedly warns against the terrible dangers of following after the gods of the market. There may be some religions in which it would be acceptable to ignore the economy itself, i.e., the ways in which the goods of the earth are produced and distributed; or there may be reli-gions in which one might not take any interest in the values spawned by an economy and the world-views it promotes. But Christians can-not ignore these things and remain true to the Bible.

At worst, certain Christian movements actually promote and even sacralize the false values of the Market. In a church in America I once heard a preacher tell his people that if they were rich and successful it meant that God had looked with favour on them, and that poor people were poor because they lacked sufficient faith. In a church in Brazil I once heard a woman give a testimony in which she thanked God that although she once did not have a colour TV, now she had one. Rather than helping her to question the consumer way of life, which is the main rival of Christian faith today, her church seemed to strengthen and undergird those values. It is hard to reconcile her testimony, how-ever sincerely meant, with the values announced by Jesus in the Ser-mon on the Mount.

Christianity and the religion of the global Market also have different views of nature. For Christians, 'the earth is the Lord's and the fullness thereof, the sea and all that is therein'. God is the only real owner of the earth, the sea, the sky. God makes human beings his stewards and gardeners. But God retains title to the earth. The logic of the market religion is quite different. Human beings, more particularly those with the money to do so, own anything they buy (and everything is for sale), and they can dispose of it as they choose.

A terrible collision awaits the human race if the religion of the

Market God continues to go unchallenged, a future quite different from the rosy one predicted in the promises of the global market forecasts. It would be impossible for the entire population of the earth, now about four billion people, to live at the same level of consumption of the elites in industrially developed countries. If they did, the planet's resources would run out very quickly. There is an absolute contradiction when an economic system whose inner logic is based on infinite growth continues to dominate a finite plant. The Market God literally knows no limits. But the earth's supply of clean air, drinkable water, arable soil and minerals and fossil fuel is limited. Infected by the pathology of the Market logic which celebrates 'growth' above all else, some Christian groups point to their growth, rather than their faithfulness to the gospel, as the hallmark of their success.

The global market culture favours individualism, not community. It prefers mobility, not rootedness. It needs to be able to shift people wherever production requires them. It is hampered only when individuals have deep ties to families, local traditions and particular places. Therefore it wishes to dissolve these ties. In the Market's eyes, all places – and indeed all people – are interchangeable. The Market prefers a uniform, homogenized world culture with as few inconvenient particularities as possible. We can discern a foreshadowing of what the Market God has in store for us in the indistinguishable airports, luxury hotels and glistening downtown business areas of the major cities of the global culture. Even food and music and dress, which used to exhibit some distinct local cultural qualities, are becoming uniform in the global culture. Where particularities survive they are rapidly becoming merely folkloristic, exotic reminders of what used to be. Parodies of local custom are preserved to lend a pseudo-'authentic' flavour to places which have themselves been transformed into commodities in the world tourist market.

But Christianity need not become a mere acolyte in the temple of the Global Market God. The early Christians did not shrink from telling the Ephesians that their gods were 'no gods at all'. They did not hesitate to announce and demonstrate a way of life based on sharing, not vicious competition. In Acts 4:32 to 5:12 we read of the common purse Christians required, and of the sorry fate of Ananias and Sapphira, who preferred to accumulate rather than share. In a blow against all levelling and homogenizing, the descent of the Spirit at Pentecost in Acts showed how people could respect and affirm cultural particularities, including different languages, and still live together in a vibrant Spirit-filled community. They were consistently unwilling to make compromises with the corrupt religious culture of their day. Paul and Peter and many others died rather than allow Christianity to become yet one more sub-cult in the imperial religious system, which at that time spanned the known world. The result of this early Christian resistance was that when the 'global culture' of Rome cracked and fell, Christians were ready to build a new culture to replace it.

There was a time when Pentecostals warned themselves and anyone else who would listen not to become entangled and dependent on the 'things of this world'. Pentecostals were suspicious of the passing fads of stylish clothings, the latest hair-do, glitzy new consumer products. They were also – as it turns out rightly – suspicious that the powerful new mass media could be a seductive lure, tricking people into the empty values of the consumer market culture. Perhaps it is time for a rebirth of that ethic of simplicity, that suspicion of 'the things of this world', for which the early Pentecostals were so famous.

Christians are not against a world culture as such. The vision of a single world family stems from the biblical teaching that we are all descended from the same ancestors, and that Jesus Christ died to redeem the whole world, not just one class or nation or race, and that the Holy Spirit was poured out at Pentecost on 'all flesh'. Christianity, however, envisions a world culture built from the bottom up by the gentle action of the Holy Spirit, not a culture imposed from the top by an imperial religion or a wealthy elite. The gospel clearly requires a 'preferential option for the poor', not an economic system which rewards the few and excludes the many. Christianity is not against markets, but it is unalterably opposed to allowing The Market and its false ethic to dictate the meaning of life; and the gospel stands in dramatic opposition to the dominant values of the currently reigning global market culture.

But will Christians in this global economy manage to resist it as the early Christians did theirs? The question is still an open one. If Christians ignore the obvious fact that the global economy has spawned not just a new kind of society but a new culture with its characteristic religion, then Christianity will fail in its prophetic task. But Jesus said, 'You cannot serve God and Mammon'. And what is 'Mammon' but Money (as it is translated in the New English Bible), that is growth and productivity and consumption raised to the level of a religious system?

In the next century Christians will have to develop ways of living marked by communal sharing, not by individualistic accumulation. For Pentecostals this means that there must be more sermons on Acts 5 ('They had all things in common') as well as on Acts 2. Christians will have to speak out for the integrity of the creation against its despoilers. And we will have to expose the false claims of the 'gods that are no gods'. in the debased ethic of the global market. If we can be faithful to this calling, God may permit us to create something new, just and beautiful in place of the debilitating religious culture of the present world age when it finally collapses, as it one day surely will.

Index

Abeysekera, Fred G., 64
Abrams, M.H., 311
Adams, Anna, 141
Adams, Leonard P., 229, 231, 233
Adeney, David H., 115
Africa, 53, 109, 170, 254, 256, 272, 365
African Methodist Episcopal Church (AME), 242
African-American, 9, 98, 161, 222, 223, 227, 228, 232, 233, 234, 235, 236, 237, 238, 242, 244, 245, 247, 296, 299, 301
Afro-Brazilian, 143
Afro-Canadian, 234
Agora, 26
Aigbe, Sunday, 202
Albrecht, Daniel E., 68
Alford, Delton, E., 111
Allen, A.A., 239, 240
Allen, Diogenes, 261, 267
Allende, Salvador, 141
America Latin, 42, 53, 74
American Indian Evangelical Church, 234
Anderson, Bendict, 284
Anderson, Gordon, 111
Anderson, Robert S., 95, 96, 97, 104, 113, 250, 251
Anderson, Walter Truett, 384
Angeles City, 187
Anglican, 196
Anglo-evangelicals, 296
Animistic people, 53, 188, 194, 201
Annacondia, Carlos, 271, 285

Anthropological, 276, 278
Anthropologists, 268, 278, 381
Anthropology, 268, 271, 279
Apartheid, 162, 165
Apostolic Faith Mission (AFM), x, 128, 151–169, 227, 354
Apostolic Faith Movement, 342
Appadurai, Arjun, 276, 286
Argentina, 134, 135, 148
Argue, Andrew H., 225, 226
Argue, Don, 244
Ariarajah, S. Wesley, 358
Armenia, 134
Arnott, John, 370, 372, 374, 377, 378, 384
Aroolappen, John Christian, 205
Arrington, French L., 26, 67, 68, 83
Asamblea Apostólica de la Fé en Cristo Jesús, 234
Asia, 53, 128, 170, 183–202, 254, 256, 301
Asia Charismatic Theological Association, 66
Asia Pacific, x
Asia Pacific Theological Association (APTS), 60, 66
Asian American, 222, 227, 232, 236
Asiaweek, 202
Assemblies of God, 36, 37, 42, 112, 137, 165, 194, 199, 232, 234, 235, 236, 238, 265, 298, 303, 304,

313, 314, 321, 342
Assemblies of God Theological Seminary (AGTS), 9, 236
Assemblies of God, India, 205, 206, 218
Assemblies of God, Sri Lanka, 205
Association for Hispanic Theological Education, 244, 247
Association of Pentecostal and Charismatic Bible Colleges, 67
Atkinson, William, 67
Aubrey, Roger, 140
Aulen, Gustav, 20, 28
Australia, 58, 365
Azusa Street, 5, 30, 31, 34, 37, 39, 45, 47, 54, 112, 154, 163, 166, 167, 226, 227, 228, 233, 242, 298, 300, 321, 342, 364, 372, 381
Azusa Street Mission, 35, 155, 157, 158, 159, 160–162, 164

Baker, Robert O., 67, 68
Bakker, Jim, 301
Baldemor, Oscar C., 202
Baldwin, James, 98, 114
Ball, Henry C., 225
Bangalore, xi, 207
Bangkok, 187
Bangla Desh, 205
Baptist Charismatic churches, 58
Baptistic Pentecostals, 16

Barratt, Thomas Ball, 98
Barrett, David, xvii, 44, 47, 51, 112, 145, 147, 384
Barth, Karl, 11, 27, 28, 117, 299
Bartleman, Frank, 227, 230, 249, 356
Bastian, Jean Pierre, 133
Bastide, Roger, 248
Beall, Myrtle, 240
Beaman, Jay, 356
Belize, 137
Bell, E.N., 229, 321
Bellah, Robert, 279, 286
Bennett, Dennis, 241
Bentley, William, 244
Berger, Peter L., 182, 384
Berkhof, Hendrikus, 13, 27, 117
Bernard, David, 355
Best, Steven, 264, 292–293, 295, 311
Bethesda Missionary Temple, 240
Bethune, Mary McCloud, 243
Beyer, Harald, 148, 149
Birmingham, England, 135, 153
Black Holiness movement, 228, 242
Blumhardt, Christoph, 20, 21, 22
Blumhardt, Johann, 20, 22
Blumhofer, Edith W., 65, 68, 96, 97, 113, 114, 223, 249
Boddy, Alexander, 98, 249
Bombay, 206, 207
Bong Rin Ro, 68
Bonhoeffer, Dietrich, 153, 154, 298
Bonnie Brae, 227
Bosch, David J., 33, 34, 49, 117
Bosworth, Fred F., 233
Bothner, Matthew S., 148
Bourdieu, Pierre, 279
Bourguigon, Erika, 111
Bouvard, Marguerite Guzmán, 148
Boyd, Gregory A., 355
Boze, Joseph Mattson, 356
Branham, William, 239, 240
Brazier, Arthur, 243

Brazil, 109, 134, 135, 136, 137, 138, 140, 141, 142
Breckenridge, Charles, 34
Britain, 174
British Assemblies of God, 42
Brostek, Mildred Johnson, 235
Brown, Leslie W., 217
Brown, Raymond, 298
Brown, Roy, 241
Brumback, Carl, 11, 27, 56
Brunei, 191
Bruner, Frederick, 32, 49
Brunner, Edward, 12, 117, 280–282, 286, 288
Brunner, Emil, 27
Brusco, Elizabeth, 133, 137, 147, 285
Bryan S. Smith Institute, xv
Bryant, John, 241
Buddhism, 191, 192, 354
Bueno, Ron Negron, 263
Buia, Ioan J., 226
Bultmann, Rudolph, 78, 83, 117
Burdick, John, 133, 140, 146
Burgess, Stanley M., 146
Byrd, Phyllis, 245
Byrd, Vernon, 241

Caird, G.B., 336
Calcutta, India, 345
Calvin, John, 118, 153
Cambodia, 129, 184, 186, 198, 201
Cameron, William Bruce, 112
Campo Alegre, 140
Campos, Bernardo, 123
Campus Crusade, 244
Canada, xi, 226
Caplan, Lionel, 210, 216, 219, 220
Cargal, Timothy B., 62, 67, 68, 221, 267
Caribbean, 109, 131
Carísma, 237, 365
Carothers, W. Faye, 225, 265, 341–342, 356
Carpenter, Harold, 358
Carter, Paul S., 250
Carter, Richard, 114
Casanova, José, 149

Cascardi, Anthony, 311
Cashwell, Gaston B., 225, 226, 280
Caste, 209
Catholic, 25, 34, 131–138, 139, 212
Catholic charismatics, 13, 58, 206, 241, 242
Caveness, Barbara, 68
Central America, 134, 137
Central Bible College, 236
Central Bible Institute, 309
Centro de Investigaciones Culturales y Estudios Lingüísticos (CINCEL), x, xv
Cerillo, Augustus Jr., 93, 94, 95, 96, 97, 105, 112
Ceylon, 205
Ceylon Pentecostal Mission, 205
Chacón, Arturo, 149
Chan, Simon, 65, 202, 354
Chao, Jonathan, 114
Charismatic Movement, xiii, 96, 108, 364
Charismatic Renewal, xiii, 214, 300
Charismatics, 13, 382
Charles Harrison Mason Theological Seminary, 9, 11, 245
Cherry, John A., 237, 241
Chevreau, Guy, 374–375, 379, 385
Chevreau, Janis, 375, 377, 379
Chikane, Frank, 169, 356
Chile, 134, 135, 136, 138, 139, 141, 142
Chilean, 134, 135, 139, 148
China, 129, 183, 184, 187, 189, 191, 198, 279, 301
Chiu, Gideon, 372
Cho, Paul Y., 65
Cho, Yong Gi, 196
Christian and Missionary Alliance, 204
Christian Broadcasting Network, 237
Christiansen, Larry, 241
Christological, 13, 15, 19, 122
Christology, 15, 16, 120,

155, 213, 297, 348
Church of England, 205
Church of God (Cleveland),
  233, 234, 235, 238, 341
Church of God (Gull Gos-
  pel), India, 205, 206
Church of God in Christ
  (COGIC), 229, 230, 231,
  233, 235, 236, 238, 243,
  245, 304, 315, 321
Church of God School of
  Theology (Cleveland, Ten-
  nessee), x, 9, 236
Church of Our Lord Jesus
  Christ, 235, 243
Church on the Rock, 206
Clark, Matthew S., 146
Classical Pentecostals, 25,
  96, 108, 165, 196, 206,
  300
Clayton, Allen, 28
Cleary, Edward, O.P., x, 127,
  128, 146, 147, 148, 149
Clemmons, Ithiel, 243, 304,
  305, 307–308, 312
Coffey, Lillian, 249
Coleman, Simon M., 251
Colletti, Joseph, 251, 357
Colombia, 141
Comaroff, Jean and John,
  273, 274, 285, 286
Commission on Faith and
  Order, 246, 347
Cone, James, 153, 155–157,
  158, 168
Confessing Church, 153
Conry, Inez, 235
Conversion, 13, 14, 15, 16,
  36, 138, 140, 142, 144,
  175, 255, 283
Cook, Glenn, 227, 228, 249
Copeland, Kenneth and Glo-
  ria, 237, 332
Costa Rica, vii, x, xiv, xv,
  121, 122, 301
Costa Rica Study Center, xv
Cox, Clyde C., 358
Cox, Harvey, ix, xiii, xiv,
  xvii, 18, 28, 68, 117, 133,
  145, 146, 266
Cox, Thomas J., 225
Crawford, Florence, 161,
  225, 227, 228, 232, 235
Creation, 21, 22, 24, 75, 122,

178, 346
Creation House, 44, 45, 236
Crentes, 137, 140
Criollo, 134
Crow, Paul A., 358
Culler, Jonathan, 311
Cunningham, R, 28

Dalton, Robert Chandler, 56
Damen, Franz, 147
Danesi, Marcel, 311
Daniels, David D., xi, 130,
  250, 251, 252, 304, 310
Daughters, 264, 323, 326,
  327, 331
Daughtry, Alonzo Austin,
  235
Daughtry, Herbert, 243, 245
Davis, Clara, 355
Davis, Elmer, 112
Davis, Merle J., 41, 42, 50
Dayton, Donald, 15, 19, 28,
  95, 113, 146, 219
De Saussure, Ferdinand, 294,
  311
Dealy, Glen C., 147
Decade of Harvest, 338
Del Colle, Ralph, 213
Deliverance Evangelistic
  Church (Philadelphia),
  240
Dempster, Murray W., ix,
  xiv, 29, 45, 63, 68
Denzin, Norman, 366, 384
Derrida, Jacques, 264, 293,
  311
Dharmaraj, Jacob S., 219
di Leonardo, Micaela, 284
Dialetic, 178
Dieter, Melvin, 251
Dispensationalism, 24, 75,
  178
DiStaulo, Guisippe, 226
Dixon, Patrick, 379, 385
Dockery, David S., 384
Dollar, Creflo, 237
Doornfontein, Johannesburg,
  159, 162, 166, 167
Doucet, Diana, 384
Douglas, Mary, 286
Dowie, Alexander, 19, 20
Drogus, Carol, 137
Du Rand, J.F., 169
Duff, Alexander, 34

Dunn, James D.G., 67
Durham, William H., 161,
  225, 226, 238
Durkheim, Emile, 279
Dutch Reformed Church,
  162
Dyer, Helen, 217
Dyrness, William, 202

East Asia, 183–202
East Timor, 185, 191
Eastern Orthodox, 155
Ecumenical movement, 165,
  245, 265, 344, 345, 346,
  349
Ecumenical organizations,
  165
Ecumenism, 4, 25, 26, 40,
  47, 175, 200, 225, 262,
  263, 265, 338–362
Ecumenism, black, 111, 243,
  244
Edinburgh, 34
El Salvador, xi, 141
Elbert, Paul, 59
Elim, 240
Emmanuel College, 303
Episcopal, 241
Ervin, Howard M., 56, 59
Eschatology, 4, 8, 12, 21, 23,
  24, 25, 35, 36, 37, 38, 39,
  40, 47, 56, 117, 214, 257,
  254, 300, 324–325, 330
Escobar, Samuel, 133, 134,
  146
Ethics, 71, 151, 158, 175,
  214, 255
Ethnicity, 153, 166, 262,
  263, 268, 269, 270, 272,
  276, 283, 284
Ethnography, 269, 273, 276,
  277
Ethnotheology, 156, 266,
  370, 371, 380–381
Etter, Maria Woodworth,
  318, 319, 328, 334, 336
Eucharist, 297
European Pentecostal, 109,
  128, 170–182
European Pentecostal Theological Association, 128
European Pentecostal/Char-
  ismatic Research Association, x, 11, 58

Evangel University, 236
Evans, G.W., 227
Everts, Janet Meyer, 28
Exegesis, 5, 13, 40, 47

Fackre, Gabriel, 152, 167
Faith Theological Seminary, 219
Falck, Calin, 311
Falwell, Jerry, 137
Farrow, Lucy, 159, 227, 249
Faupel, D.W., 26, 66
Featherstone, M., 285
Fee, Gordon D., 13, 27, 60, 63, 67, 336
Feminism, 291, 296, 315, 325
Feminist scholars, 315, 323, 331
Feminist theology, 157, 315
Fernandez, James, 287
Filho, Elias Dantas, 64
Filioque clause, 347
Fire-Baptized Holiness Church, 232
Firth, C.B., 217
Fleming, David, 59
Flora, Cornelia Butler, 146
Flower, Alice Reynolds, 36
Flower, J. Roswell, 36, 37, 112, 309, 356
Forbes, James, 301
Ford, Louis Henry, 243
Foster, Fred J., 356
Foucault, Michel, 264
France, 303
Franceson, Luigi, 226
Free market economy, 189, 389
Frei, Eduardo, 141, 316
Frei, Hans, 308, 312, 334
Freidzon, Claudio, 271, 285, 383
Freire, Paulo, 71, 72, 73, 74, 81
Freston, Paul, 133, 140
Fujimori, Alberto, 141
Fukayama, Francis, 390
Fulkerson, Mary McClintock, 315, 320, 323, 333, 334, 335, 336
Fullam, Terry, 241
Fuller Theological Seminary, viii, x, xi, 44, 243–244,

246, 298
Fuller, W.E., 225
Fundamentalism, 10, 11, 24, 26, 118, 208, 216, 235, 236, 243, 244, 247, 262, 265, 295, 300
Fundamentalists, 9, 11, 12, 54, 79, 86, 103, 300, 309, 342

Gadamer, Hans-Georg, 264, 293, 311
Garr, A.G., 131
Garrard-Burnett, Virginia, 135, 147, 148
Garrigus, Alice Belle, 225
Gause, Hollis R., 83
Gaxiola, Manuel, 132, 356
Gee, Donald, 40, 50, 56, 356
Gelpi, Donald, 312
Gender, 137, 138, 263, 269, 270, 283, 284, 339, 354
General Council of the Assemblies of God, 206
Gerloff, Roswith, 172, 173, 180, 181, 182, 239, 251
Germany, 174
Gill, Deborah Menken, 61, 69, 333, 335
Gill, Kenneth, 132, 147, 250
Gill, Leslie, 133
Glazier, Stephen D., 146
Global culture, 171, 173, 174, 177–180, 222, 272, 274, 275, 394
Global market culture, 266, 386–395
Global Pentecostalism, 4, 16, 17, 48
Globalization, viii, xiii, xiv, 2, 47, 142, 269, 270, 271
Glossolalia, 11, 12, 16, 17, 18, 19, 21, 22, 23, 25, 56, 87, 96, 111, 117, 120, 121, 159, 160, 161, 171, 175, 196, 197, 205, 238, 299, 300, 318, 369, 372, 377
Goff, James R., 64, 66, 96, 97, 113, 249
Golder, Morris Ellis, 250
Gomez, Jorge, 112
Goodman, Felicitas D., 111
GoodPatrick Press, 237
Gordon-Conwell Theological

Seminary, 244, 246
Gospel Publishing House, 42, 45, 50, 60, 236
Goss, Howard, 225, 229, 233
Gottdiener, M., 384
Grant, Abraham, 242
Great Awakening, 35, 379
Green, L.L., 355
Grenz, Stanley J., 261, 267
Griffin, David Ray, 384
Groome, Thomas, 72, 73, 78, 82, 83
Gros, Jeffrey, 141, 149
Guatemala, 134, 135, 136, 139, 143, 353
Gujarat, 204
Guthrie, Woodie, 94
Guynes, Delmer R., 45
Guynes, Eleanor R., 45

Ha, Kim Chi, 193
Hagee, John, 237
Hagin, Kenneth Sr., 240
Handy, Robert T., 223
Hanson, Paul B., 68
Harper, Michael, 180, 181, 182
Harrell, David Edwin Jr., 250, 251
Harrington, Hannah K., 68
Harris, Jan, 112
Harrison, Frederic, 290, 291, 311
Harter, Hans, 173, 180
Hastie, Eugene H., 37
Hatch, Roger D., 223, 248
Hauerwas, Stanley, 168
Hayford, Jack, 237
Haynes, Jeff, 149
Haywood, Garfield T., 225, 230, 231
Healing, 4, 7, 19, 20, 21, 22, 23, 24, 25, 117, 120, 121, 123, 176, 194–195, 196, 197, 238, 239, 253, 377
Hebden, James and Ellen, 225, 226
Hedlund, Roger, 218, 220
Heffner, Robert, 279, 282, 286
Hegel, G.W.F., 72
Heie, Harold, 267
Henry, Carl F.H., 267
Henton, Richard, 237, 240

Hermenuetics, 5, 12, 118, 119, 166, 215, 262, 296, 309, 310, 371
Hermenuetics, Pentecostal, 12, 27, 54, 58, 63, 111, 264, 265, 313–337
Hermenuetics, postmodern, 63, 262, 263, 264, 289–312
Hesselgrave, David J., 32, 49
Hickey, Marilyn, 237, 332–333, 336
Higginbotham, Evelyn Brooks, 148
Hilton, David, 28
Hindu spirituality, 207, 212, 214
Hinduism, 191, 212, 213
Hinn, Benny, 237, 383
Hispanic, 222, 223, 225, 227, 232, 234, 235, 236, 296, 299, 301, 309
Hocken, Peter D., 65, 252, 384
Hodges, Melvin L., 33, 42
Hoekendijk, Johannes Christian, 153, 154
Hoff, Paul B., 139–140, 148, 149
Holdcroft, Thomas L., 56
Holistic, 5, 20, 21, 24, 25, 75, 214, 215, 382
Hollenweger, Walter J., xvii, 18, 24, 25, 27, 28, 29, 96, 111, 113, 145, 152–154, 167–168, 181, 219, 220, 285
Holm, Randall, 111
Holt, William B., 233
Hong Kong, 189, 190
Hooker, Morna D., 336
Horton, Harold, 56
Horton, Stanley M., 26, 56, 66
Horton, Wade H., 56
Howard-Brown, Rodney, 383
Hoyt, William, 230
Hunter, Harold, 58, 59, 60, 61, 66
Hyatt, Susan, 333, 334, 335, 336

Idígoras, Luis, 148

Igorots, 188
Illich, Ivan, 32, 49
Immanuel Temple (Los Angeles), 240
Incarnation, 121
India, xi, 199, 203, 204, 205, 213, 216, 257
Indian Pentecostal Church, 205, 206
Indigenous Pentecostal, 127, 205
Indonesia, 129, 183, 184, 185, 186, 196, 365
Industrialization, 190
Interdenominational Theological Seminary, 9
Inter-Varsity, 244
Ippolito, Luigi, 226
Ireland, Rowan, 133, 136, 140, 146, 147, 148
Ironside, H.A., 356
Islam, 191, 256

Jacobson, Douglas, 26
Jakes, T.D., 237
James, William, 112
Japan, 182, 183, 184, 187, 190, 191, 192, 196, 200, 201, 365
Jerusalem, 109
Jesus People, 300
John Paul II, 147, 338, 349, 351
Johns, Cheryl Bridges, 82, 83, 84
Johns, Jackie David, x, 6, 68, 82, 83, 84, 120
Johnson, Alonso, 304
Johnson, Lars, 220
Johnston, Douglas, 149
Jones, Charles Edwin, 146
Jones, Charles Price , 242
Jordon, David, 279, 287
Journal of Pentecostal Theology (JPT), 12, 27, 59, 82, 217, 236
Joyce, I.W., 242
Justice, 18, 21, 22, 346

Kamikuishiki, 192
Kankana-ey tribal people, 194, 201
Kay, William, 181
Kearney, Michael, 269, 284,

286
Kellner, Douglas, 264, 292–293, 295, 311
Kendrick, Klaude, 64, 95, 113
Kepel, Gilles, 142
Kermode, Frank, 336
Keswick, 16
Keyes, Charles, 280, 287
Killing Field, 186
Kim, Ij-Jin, 181, 182
Kim, Yong Bock, 202
King, A.D., 285
King, J.H., 225
Klaus, Byron D., xiv, 45, 63, 219
Klu Klux Klan, 233
Kock, W. De, 167
Korea, 184, 189, 190, 191, 193, 195–196, 198, 201, 365
Korean, 109, 197, 200, 299, 301
Korean Presbyterians, 196
Korean War, 184, 186, 189, 191
Kornweibel, Theodore, Jr., 233
Kraiss, Wayne, xvi
Kuhlman, Kathryn, 332
Kuper, Adam, 279, 286
Kurtz, Lester, 149
Kuzmic, Peter, 48, 51, 221

La Hora, 147
Lake, John G., 159
LaLive d'Epinay, Christian, 133, 141
Land, Steven J., 12, 27, 75, 82, 83, 123, 334, 335, 336
Lang, G.H., 217
Laos, 129, 184, 198, 201
Latin America, viv, 141, 170, 254, 256, 271, 303, 309, 354
Latin America ChildCare, xv, 303
Latin American Council of Christian Churches, 232
Latin American District Council of the Assemblies of God, 232
Latin American Pentecostalism, 109, 127,

Latin American
Pentecostalism, *cont.*, 128
Latin American Theological
Fraternity, xv
Latourette, Kenneth Scott, 50
Latter Days, 16, 17
Latter Rain movement, 240,
364
Lawless, Elaine, 315, 319,
320, 322, 323, 327, 332,
333, 334, 336
Lawson, Robert, 242
Lawton, Kim A., 385
Le Roux, Pieter Louis, 159
Lederle, Henry I., 146
Lee University, 236
Lee, Earl A., 240
Leenhardt, Maurice, 279,
287
Lehmann, Paul, 297, 312
Lentricchia, Frank, 311
Leone, Mark P., 111, 114
Levine, Daniel, 146, 147
Levi-Strauss, Claude, 279,
287
Lewis Wilson Institute for
Pentecostal Studies, xv
Liberation Theology, 72, 80,
300, 310
Liberation, black, 156, 166
Lienhardt, Godfrey, 279, 287
Lima, 345
Lima, D.M., 285
Lincoln, Eric C., 223
Lombardi, Giacomo, 226
Los Angeles, 33, 134, 227,
233, 247
Love, Janice, 359
Lovett, Leonard, 96, 113
Luce, Alice, 225
Luckmann, Thomas, 384
Lugo, Juan 1., 225
Lukas, John, 292, 311
Lum, Clara, 161, 227, 249
Lund, Eric, 309, 312
Luther, Martin, 20, 118, 120,
153
Lutheran, 120, 241

Ma Jungja (Julie), x, 65, 129,
283
Ma, Won Suk, x, 5
Macchia, Frank D., x, 3, 4,
27, 29, 120, 121, 299, 312

MacDonald, William G., 56,
211
Machado, María das Dores
Campos, 138
Machismo, 138
Mackay, John A., 358
MacRobert, Iain, 96, 113,
168
Malaysia, 184, 186, 189,
191, 196, 198, 201
Malek, Sobhi, 202
Malinowski, Bronislaw, 279,
287
Mallory, Arenia C., 243
Manila, 187, 198
Mann, Arthur, 113
Manoharan, P., 219, 220
Maranatha Revival Church,
218
Marianismo, 138
Mariz, Cecília, 133, 138,
140, 147
Market economy, 389
Market religion, 388,
390–392
Martin, David, 19, 28, 99,
105, 114, 132, 133, 146,
149, 270, 285
Marx, Karl, 72, 73, 290
Marzal, Manuel, 133, 147
Mason, Charles Harrison,
225, 226, 228, 229, 233,
238, 242, 300
McClung, Grant L., x, 4, 5,
45, 50, 51, 65
McClurkan, J.O., 231
McCoy, Eugene B., 249
McDonnell, Kilian, 13, 27
McGavran, Donald A., 41,
43, 44, 50
McGee, Gary B., 32, 40, 42,
45, 49, 50, 56, 64, 66, 146,
212, 214, 220, 221
McGlasson, Robert T., 43
McIntire, Carl, 343
McKinley, James, 241
McKinney, George, 244
McKnight, Edgar V., 311
McPherson, Aimee Semple,
92, 228, 234, 332
Melodyland Christian Cen-
ter, 241
Melton, J. Gordon, 249
Memphis, Tennessee, 226,

247
Menzies, Robert P., 14, 15,
28, 61, 62, 67, 68, 69, 120,
267
Menzies, William W., 64, 66,
145, 251
Merrill, William, 280, 287
Methodist, 297, 318
Methodist Episcopal Church,
241, 242
Metz, Johann Baptist, 152,
158, 167
Mexico, 134
Mid-Atlantic Publishers, 237
Middle East, 345, 354
Míguez Bonino, José, ix,
xiii, xiv, 7, 27
Miller, Daniel, 147
Mindanao, 185, 191
Minjung theologians, 157
Minjung theology, 193
Missiology, German, 34, 153
Modernism, 12, 118, 261,
262, 263
Modernists, 290, 309
Möller, F.P., 356
Mongolia, 129, 183, 184,
201
Monism, 213
Montanist, 89, 111
Montanus, 111
Monument of Faith Church
(Chicago), 240
Moore, Jennie Evans, 161,
227
Moravianism, 35
Morton, Paul, 237, 241
Mouffle, Chantal, 311
Mount Fuji, 192
Mouroux, Jean, 144, 149
Mu, Ahn Byung, 193
Mukti Mission, 204
Mundadan, A.M., 217
Muslims, 191, 199, 354
Myanmar, 129, 183, 185,
191
Myers, Billy Sunday, 355

Nadasen, Pam, 252
Nam-dong, Sum, 157, 168
Narrative, 55, 62, 151–169,
265, 291, 317, 319, 320,
324, 325, 339
Narrative theology, 62,

151–169
National Association of
    Evangelicals (NAE), 41,
    243, 246, 265, 351
National Black Evangelical
    Association, 244
National Council of
    Churches, 244, 246, 265,
    313, 351
Native Americans, 222, 227,
    232, 234
Navarro, Juan, 225
Navarro, Marysa, 148
Neill, Stephen, 217
Nelson, Douglas J., 96, 113,
    168, 227
Nelson, P.C., 26, 309–310
Neo-Hinduism, 212
Neo-Pentecostals, 142, 237,
    241
Nepal, 129, 184, 191, 201
New People's Army, 185,
    191
Newbigin, Lesslie, 42, 43
Newell, William Lloyd, 310
Newfoundland, 234
Newsweek, 141
Nicaragua, 134
Nichol, John Thomas, 40,
    50, 95, 113, 249
Nida, Eugene A., 42, 146
Niebuhr, H. Richard, 223,
    218, 298
Noll, Mark, 223
North Korea, 184, 201

O'Brien, Jay, 282, 284, 285
Olazabal, Francisco, 225,
    232
Olongapo, 187
Oneness, 15, 239
Oneness Pentecostal, 15, 25,
    238, 239, 248
Opperman, D.C.O., 229
Oral Roberts University, 236
Orr, J. Edwin, 204, 205, 217,
    218
Orthodoxy, 12, 58, 75, 77,
    79, 81, 82, 83, 179, 344,
    347–348, 350, 353, 354
Orthopathos, 12
Orthopathy, 75, 77, 79, 81,
    82
Orthopraxis, 13, 75, 179

Orthopraxy, 76, 77, 79, 81
Osaka University, 192
Osborn, Daisy, 332
Osborne, Grant R., 67
Ottolini, P., 226
Oxford Centre for Mission
    Studies, xvi

Pacific Coast Apostolic Faith
    Movement, 230, 232
Pakistan, 205
Palma, Anthony D., 56
Palmer, Phoebe, 318
Panama, 137
Pannenberg, Walter, 28
Parachurch agencies, 206
Paraclete, 81
Parham, Charles F., 54, 56,
    65, 96, 97, 109, 159, 161,
    225, 226, 232, 265, 321,
    341, 356
Parousia, 12, 121
Parsons, Talcott, 279
Pathway Publishing, 236
Patten, Rebecca, 68
Patterson, G.E., 237
Peace, 18
Pearlman, Myer, 26, 65
Pearson, Carlton, 237
Peck, Jane C., 251
Pentecostal Assemblies of
    Canada, 206, 234
Pentecostal Assemblies of
    Newfoundland, 234
Pentecostal Assemblies of
    the World, 230, 231, 232,
    233, 235, 239
Pentecostal Bible Institute
    (Puerto Rico), 13
Pentecostal Bible Institute
    (Santiago, Chile), 139
Pentecostal Fellowship of
    North America, 41, 244,
    300
Pentecostal History, 85, 86,
    91, 92, 93, 94, 97, 98, 99,
    101, 110, 116
Pentecostal Holiness Church,
    206, 232, 238
Pentecostal missiology, 4,
    30, 31, 32, 33, 34, 35, 36,
    37, 39, 41, 42, 43, 45, 47,
    48, 58, 62, 63, 116
Pentecostal Origins, 86, 96,

98
Pentecostal pastors,
    136–139, 142, 211, 224,
    253
Pentecostal spirituality, 13,
    20
Pentecostal theology, 4, 8, 9,
    10, 11, 12, 13, 14, 15, 16,
    17, 18, 24, 25, 26, 62
Pentecostal, politics, 70,
    140–141, 197
Pentecostal, women, 64, 68,
    69, 138, 224, 235,
    313–337
Pentecostal/Charismatic
    Churches of North Amer-
    ica (PCCNA), 351
Pentecostal/charismatic,
    Europe, 128, 129, 171,
    172
Pentecostal-charismatic,
    black, 58, 153
Pentecostalism Latin Ameri-
    can, 19, 131–150
Pentecostalism North Amer-
    ica, 130
Pentecostalism, African
    American, 9, 130, 237,
    238, 239, 304
Pentecostalism, globalization
    of, vii, xiii, xiv, 2
Pentecostalism, North Amer-
    ican, 130, 222–252
Pentecostalism, Romanian,
    226
Pentecostalism, South Asia,
    129
Pentecostals Brazilian, 42
Pentecostals South Asia, 129
Pentecostals, hispanic, 109,
    130, 238, 239, 244, 245,
    246, 247, 303, 304, 310
Pentecostals, popular, 94
Pentecostals, reformed, 16,
    238, 239
Pereira de Queoroz, Mariá
    Isaura, 149
Perkins, Jonathan, 230
Perry, Lloyd, 245
Peru, 134, 141
Petersen, Douglas P., ix, xiii,
    3, 26, 45, 63, 132, 137,
    148, 356
Philippines, x, 68, 184, 185,

Philippines, *contd.*, 186, 188, 191, 198, 200, 201, 309
Pickett, Wascom, J., 43
Pietism, 35
Pietists, 145
Piker, Steven, 202
Pilgrim Baptist Cathedral, 241
Pinnock, Clark H., 67
Pinson, Mack, 229, 231
Piper, O.A., 78, 83
Plüss, Jean Daniel, x, 128, 182, 280, 287
PNEUMA, 12, 26, 27, 28, 29, 50, 58, 59, 63, 112, 146, 147, 148, 149, 218, 221, 236
Pneuma Life Publishing, 237
Pneumatology, 12, 16, 119, 122, 155, 176
Poesis, 71
Poewe, Karla, xiii, xvii, 269, 271, 274, 275, 280, 284, 285, 287, 288, 384
Poloma, Margaret, xi, 38, 114, 121, 266, 385
Pomerville, Paul A., 45
Poorta, Japie La, 128, 169
Portland, 161, 247
Postmodernism, 12, 261–267, 292–296, 364–367, 381
Postmodernity, 257, 261
Pousson, Edward K., 45
Powell, Adam Clayton Jr., 243
Praxis, 6, 9, 11, 12, 13, 71, 72, 73, 74, 76, 80, 81, 82, 116, 120
Praxis of Geist, 72
Presbyterian, 241
Price, Charles S., 92
Price, Fred, 237, 240
Programa Integral de Educación de las Asambleas de Dios (PIEDAD), xv
Progressive history, 96
Prostitution, child, 187
Protestant Missions, 34, 35
Protestantism, European, 172
Puerto Rico, 134, 141, 226, 235, 241, 242, 301, 303
Puritanism, 35

Quebedeaux, Richard, 251, 385
Quick, Norman, 245

Racial reconciliation, 351
Racism, 23, 96, 154, 161, 162, 164, 166, 224, 231, 232, 295, 300
Raiser, Konrad, 348, 360
Ramabai, Pandita, 204
Randall, Ian, 181
Ranger, Terence, 272, 285
Read, William R., 42, 50
Rebel, Herman, 282
Reconciliation, 340
Reddin, Opal L., 358
Redemption, 6, 18, 19, 20, 21, 22, 23, 24, 70, 122
Reed, Frank Madison, 237
Reformation, 119, 145, 349, 350
Reformed theology, 54, 332
Reformed/Evangelical, 316
Regent University, 58, 59, 236
Regnum Books International, xvi
Rhema Bible Training School, 240
Rhema Publishing, 236
Richardson, William Edwin, 61
Ricoeur, Paul, 182
Ring Ro, Bong, 196
Riss, Richard, 251, 379, 385
Riverside Church, 302
Robeck, Cecil M, xi, 25, 29, 64, 69, 112, 140, 147, 149, 168, 227, 265, 356, 357, 358
Robert, Dana L., xiii, xvii
Roberts, Oral, 239
Roberts, Richard, 237
Robertson, Roland, 182
Robinson, Brian, 111
Robison, James, 237
Rodgers, H.G., 229, 231
Roebuck, David, 68, 315, 316, 333, 334, 335, 336
Roelofs, Gerard, 284, 288
Roennfeldt, Ray C.W., 68
Rolim, Francisco C., 133
Roman Catholic, vii, 35, 112, 165, 197, 205, 206, 265,

343, 346, 347–350, 351, 352, 353
Roman Catholicism, 131, 191, 200, 210
Roman Catholic-Pentecostal Dialogue, 165, 352
Roseberry, William, 282, 285
Russia, 365

Sahliyeh, Emile, 149
Salisbury, Neal, 249
Samarin, William, 299, 312
Sampson, Cynthia, 149
Samuel, Vinay, x, xiv, xvi, 130
Sanctification, 25, 77, 117, 122, 340
Santiago, Chile, 139
Saracco, Norberto, 64, 132
Satyavrata, Ivan M., x, 129, 220, 256
Sawyer, Mary, 243, 251
Schambach, R.W., 240
Schipani, Daniel, 80, 84
Schmidt, Wilhem, 280
Scrivener, Leslie, 364
Second Coming, 94
Sectarianism, 352
Secularization, 142, 175, 177–179, 201, 354
Segregation, 160
Segundo, Juan Luis, 27, 121
Seoul, vii, 190, 195, 198
Sepúlveda, Juan, 132, 135, 148
Seymour, William J., 30, 31, 34, 35, 39, 96, 157, 159, 161, 225, 226, 227, 230, 232, 238, 265, 298, 342
Sharon Bible School (North Battleford),
Sharon Fellowship, 218
Shelton, James B., 67
Shenk, Wilbert R., 33, 49
Sheppard, Gerald T., xi, 26, 27, 29, 65, 66, 68, 263, 311
Shibley, David, 45
Shinde, Benjamin P., 218
Shriver, Donald, 298–299
Sider, Gerald, 272, 284
Singapore, 184, 189, 190, 196, 198, 201
Singh, G.H., 43

Skinner, Arturo, 239
Smith, Benjamin, 240
Smith, Houston, 384
Smith, Timothy, 250
Sobrino, Jon, 81
Society for Pentecostal Studies (SPS), 11, 26, 28, 58, 237
Sociologist, 363
Sociology, 290, 365
Soelle, Dorothea, 22, 28
Solivan, Samuel, 303
Soneira, Jorge, 146
Sorrow, Watson, 228
South Africa, 128, 134, 151–169, 345
South African Council of Churches, 165
South Asia, 129
South Korea, 189
Southern Asia, 203–221
Southern Asia Bible College, x, 219
Southern Baptist Convention, 241
Southern California College (SCC), viii, 9, 236
Spirit baptism, 13, 14, 15, 16, 19, 21, 36, 54, 159, 160, 161, 164, 166, 171, 175, 196, 197, 238, 301, 316, 318, 319, 320, 321, 324, 327, 328, 353
Spittler, Russell, viii, 8, 9, 10, 14, 26, 27, 28, 65, 111, 147, 220, 356
Spurling, R.G., 265, 341, 357
Stanley, Susie Cunningham, 250
Strathern, Marilyn, 275, 277
Stewart-Gambino, Hannah, 141, 146, 147, 148, 149
Stoll, David, 132, 133, 147
Strang, Stephen, 251
Street children, 345
Stronstad, Roger, 14, 15, 27, 59, 62, 65, 68, 111, 120, 215, 221, 334, 336
Sturgeon, Inez, 202
Sturvedant, Elder, 228
Submodern, 12, 289, 300, 307, 309
Sugden, Christopher, xvi

Sumrall, Lester F., 356
Sundkler, B., 169
Swaggart, Jimmy, 137, 143, 301, 306, 307–308
Switzerland, x, 154
Synan, H. Vinson, 28, 37, 44, 50, 51, 64, 96, 113, 218, 220, 228, 249, 250
Synan, J.A., 95, 358
Systematic theology, 116, 151, 158, 378

Taiwan, 184, 189
Takaki, Ronald, 249
Talvera, Arturo Fontaine, 148
Tamil Nadu, 205
Tate, Magdelena, 225, 235, 251
Taylor, Michael, 66
Teen Challenge, 23, 198, 303
Terry, Neely, 159
Thailand, 184, 189, 191, 192, 301
The Apostolic Faith, 37, 38, 39, 48, 49, 51, 56
The Pentecost, 36
Theological education, 34
Theology, black, 155–157
Theoria, 71
Third Wave, 141, 364
Third Wave Movement, xiii, 96
Tibet, 129, 184, 191, 201
Tienanmen Square, 191
Tillich, Paul, 266, 298, 387, 388
Timberlakes, 237
Tinney, James, 96, 113
Tippet, Alan R., 31, 33, 35, 49
Tirunelveli, 205
Tokyo, 188, 192
Tomlinson, A.J., 225
Tomlinson, Milton A., 56
Topeka, Kansas, 112, 161, 226
Toronto Airport Christian Fellowship, 266, 363, 365
Toronto Blessing, 64, 121, 173, 181, 266, 363–385
Toronto Star, 364, 365
Torrey, R.A., 356
Tranquebar Mission, 204

Tribal people, 188–189
Tribalism, 272
Trinitarian, 15, 25, 122, 213, 239, 256, 348
Trinity Bible College, 236, 246
Trinity Broadcasting Network, 237
Tucker, David M., 250
Tugwell, Simon, 13, 27
Turner, Victor, 279, 280–282, 286, 287, 381, 385
Two-thirds world, 10, 26, 47, 53
Tylor, Edward, 279, 286
Tyson, James L., 249, 355

Union Theological Seminary (New York), 298–301, 302, 303, 307
United Holy Church, 235
United Methodist Church, 241
United Pentecostal Church, 206, 234, 239
Universal Church of the Kingdom of God, 140
University of Halle, 34
Urbanization, 183, 188
Urshan, Andrew D., 226

Valdez, A.C., 249
Van Dusen, Henry P., 43, 49, 50
Vanderbout, Elva, 195
Vanguard University of Southern California, viii, xi, xv, xvi, 236
Vatican, 349, 350, 351
Vatican II, 349
Venezuela, 136, 141
Verwoerd, Hendrik, 159
Vietnam, 129, 184, 191, 198, 201
Vietnam War, 185, 191, 296
Villafane, Eldin, 12, 310, 312
Vineyard Christian Fellowship, 367, 373, 378, 383
Volf, Miroslav, 12, 27
Voodoo, 131

Wacker, Grant, 90, 96, 97,

Wacker, Grant, *contd.*, 104, 111, 112, 113, 146, 223
Wagner, Peter C., 41, 44, 138
Wales, 134
Walker, Nigel, 181
Walker, Paul H., 56
Walters, Alexander, 242
Warfield, Benjamin, 356
Warford, Malcolm, 302
Warneck, Gustav, 34
Warner, Daniel Sidney, 242
Warner, W.E., 251
Warnshuis, A.L., 43
Warrington, Keith, 181
Washburn, Josephine M., 355
Washington, James, 307
Weber, Max, 278, 388
Wenk, Matthias, 174, 175, 180, 181, 182
Wesleyan Holiness Pentecostal, 15, 238, 317
Wesleyan perfectionism, 95, 108, 238
Wesleyan/Holiness, 15, 16, 238, 318, 342
White, Alma, 235
White, Geoffrey, 279, 287
White, John, 377, 379, 385
Wiarda, Howard, 147

Wigglesworth, Smith, 92
Wiley, Ophelia, 227
Wilkerson, Ralph, 241
Willems, Emilio, 133, 139, 144, 146, 148, 149
Williams, Cyril G., 146
Williams, Ernest S., 26, 65
Williams, J. Rodman, 65
Williams, Raymond, 277, 282, 286
Williams, Smallwood, 243, 251
Wilson, Aaron A., 37
Wilson, Everett A., x, xv, 6, 7, 132, 141, 143, 144–145, 148, 150
Wilson, L.F., 26, 251
Wimber, John, 45, 373, 377, 383
Wings of Healing Temple, 240
Winley, Jesse, 301, 302, 312
Winnepeg, 226
Witt, Marcos, 271, 285
Witvliet, Theo, 156–157, 168
Womack, David A., 44
Women in ministry, 148, 224, 264, 313–337
Women ministers, 148, 235, 264, 313–337

Women preachers, 313
Women's authority, 235
Word of Faith movement, 240
World Council of Churches (WCC), 21, 165, 244, 245, 265, 343, 346–349, 350, 351, 353, 354
World Evangelical Fellowship, 165
Wyatt, Thomas, 240

Xenolalia, 56, 121

Yeats, William Butler, 46, 48
Yinger, J. Milton, 114
Yoida Full Gospel Church, 54, 184, 199, 200
Yonggi Cho, David, 184

Zaffato, Ferdinand, 226
Zaretsky Irving I., 111, 114
Zegwaart, Huib, 176, 180, 182
Zikmund, Barbara Brown, 333, 336
Zimmerman, Thomas, 244
Zionist movement, 165
Zopfi, Jakob, 181